SB   Brockman, Christian
481   Frank, 1902-
B66
1973   Recreational use of
              wild lands

DATE			
JUN 9 '78			
NOV 3 '78			
NOV 18'81			
DEC 1 6 '95			
ILL 5489666			
COS 1-4-00			

18646 -2

RECREATIONAL USE
OF WILD LANDS

McGRAW-HILL SERIES IN FOREST RESOURCES

Henry J. Vaux, Consulting Editor

ALLEN and SHARPE   An Introduction to American Forestry
AVERY   Forest Measurements
BAKER   Principles of Silviculture
BOYCE   Forest Pathology
BROCKMAN and MERRIAM   Recreational Use of Wild Lands
BROWN and DAVIS   Forest Fire: Control and Use
BROWN, PANSHIN, and FORSAITH   Textbook of Wood Technology
Volume II—The Physical, Mechanical, and Chemical Properties of the
Commercial Woods of the United States
CHAPMAN and MEYER   Forest Mensuration
DANA   Forest and Range Policy
DAVIS   Forest Management: Regulation and Evaluation
DUERR   Fundamentals of Forestry Economics
GRAHAM and KNIGHT   Principles of Forest Entomology
GUISE   The Management of Farm Woodlands
HARLOW and HARRAR   Textbook of Dendrology
HUNT and GARRATT   Wood Preservation
PANSHIN and DE ZEEUW   Textbook of Wood Technology
Volume I—Structure, Identification, Uses, and Properties of the Commercial
Woods of the United States
PANSHIN, HARRAR, BETHEL, and BAKER   Forest Products
RICH   Marketing of Forest Products: Text and Cases
SHIRLEY   Forestry and Its Career Opportunities
STODDART and SMITH   Range Management
TRIPPENSEE   Wildlife Management
Volume I—Upland Game and General Principles
Volume II—Fur Bearers, Waterfowl, and Fish
WACKERMAN, HAGENSTEIN, and MICHELL   Harvesting Timber Crops
WORRELL   Principles of Forest Policy

Walter Mulford was Consulting Editor of this Series from its inception in 1931 until
January 1, 1952.

RECREATIONAL USE OF WILD LANDS

C. FRANK BROCKMAN
Professor of Forestry, Emeritus
College of Forest Resources
University of Washington

LAWRENCE C. MERRIAM, JR.
Professor of Forestry
College of Forestry
University of Minnesota

with two specially prepared chapters by

WILLIAM R. CATTON, JR.
Professor of Sociology
University of Canterbury
Christchurch, New Zealand

BARNEY DOWDLE
Associate Professor of Economics
and Forest Resources
University of Washington

Second Edition

McGraw-Hill Book Company
New York St. Louis San Francisco Düsseldorf Johannesburg
Kuala Lumpur London Mexico Montreal New Delhi
Panama Rio de Janeiro Singapore Sydney Toronto

Library of Congress Cataloging in Publication Data

Brockman, Christian Frank, 1902-
   Recreational use of wild lands.

   (McGraw-Hill series in forest resources)
   Bibliography: p.
   1. National parks and reserves. 2. Forest
reserves—Recreational use. 3. Wilderness areas.
4. Outdoor recreation. I. Merriam, Lawrence C.,
joint author. II. Title.
SB481.B66 1973   333.7'8   72-6449
ISBN 0-07-007981-1

RECREATIONAL USE OF WILD LANDS

   2 3 4 5 6 7 8 9 0 K P K P 7 9 8 7 6 5 4 3

This book was set in Journal Roman by Creative Book Services,
division of McGregor & Werner, Incorporated.
The editors were William P. Orr and Claudia A. Hepburn;
the designer was Paula Tuerk; the cover
was designed by Edward A. Butler;
and the production supervisor was Thomas J. Lo Pinto.
The printer and binder was Kingsport Press, Inc.

CONTENTS

v

tional policy of the Forest Service; recreation planning and administration of the national forests; distinction between national forests and national parks; recreational resources of national forests; coordination of use of national forest lands; public recreational use of national forests

PREFACE

Since 1959, when the first edition of *Recreational Use of Wild Lands* was published, many noteworthy and exciting events concerned with this form of land use have happened. The report of the Outdoor Recreation Resources Review Commission, issued in 1962, prompted public and official awareness of recreation as a wild-land resource and of the values inherent in the perpetuation of environmental quality. One particular result was that the Bureau of Outdoor Recreation was established. The National Park Service, Forest Service, many state park organizations, and industrial timberland owners, long associated with wild-land recreation, expanded their activities; and other public and private agencies, previously little concerned with recreation, became greatly involved. Such increased emphasis on wild-land recreation was favored by new legislation, particularly the Land and Water Conservation Fund Act, the bill establishing the National Wilderness Preservation System, bills establishing several new national parks, the Wild Rivers Act, and the National Scenic Trails Act. Concurrently with these events great interest in the career possibilities of outdoor recreation developed. In turn, this interest prompted improvement and formulation of relevant curricula at numerous colleges and universities designed to prepare a larger number of qualified workers for many necessary and complicated tasks related to the recreational management of wild lands.

Thus, a revision of this basic text has long been in order. However, the rapidity and often unexpected nature of developments during the past decade created an extremely fluid condition. Any attempted revision during that period would have been doomed to obsolescence before publication. Though additional changes and refinements can be expected in the future, the situation today seems sufficiently established to make a revision practical.

The second edition of *Recreational Use of Wild Lands,* although a complete overhaul of the initial volume, retains the basic purposes, objectives, and philosophy of the first edition. It is intended as a *basic introduction* to this important subject. Each of the various chapters in this revision represents but a skeletonized treatment of a particular aspect of the recreational use of wild lands. Treatment of specific details is the province of specialized publications or the responsibility of various instructors. The latter can expand upon the generalized material in the light of their own experience and research.

A generalized introductory text is even more necessary today. Students planning a career in wild-land recreation should profit from a broad overview of their chosen profession before concentrating upon specific aspects and particular interests. Also, those students majoring in related fields of land management should benefit from an understanding of recreation as one form of wild-land use so that they may better relate recreational requirements to those of their major activities. Such understanding is particularly important for students majoring in forestry, wildlife management, and water-resource management, since lands with which they will deal have high outdoor recreational values. Further, a generalized treatment of the recreational use of wild lands should be valuable to interested laymen. Public understanding of the background in this form of wild-land use, as well as recognition of the complicated ecological, social, economic, and political problems involved, develops public responsibility for the care and perpetuation of the wild land environment and its beauty.

The contents of this edition have been expanded to include new chapters—"The Recreation Visitor: Motivation, Behavior, Impact" (Chapter 5) and "Economics of Outdoor Recreation" (Chapter 13). In addition new material has been presented on the functions of organizations and groups in wild-land recreation, as well as management and planning.

Chapter 5 was prepared by Dr. William R. Catton. Until February 1970, when he accepted a position on the faculty of the University of Canterbury, Christchurch, New Zealand, Dr. Catton was Professor of Sociology, University of Washington. Chapter 13, prepared by Dr. Barney Dowdle, relates economics to the recreational management of wild lands in a manner quite different from that of the first edition. It emphasizes the importance of economics as a means of aiding in providing data useful in making decisions about recreational land planning.

Acknowledgments

To list all who have had a part in the preparation of both the first and the second editions of *Recreational Use of Wild Lands* would be impossible. Many people, directly and indirectly, have made vital contributions, and these are gratefully acknowledged by the authors.

Numerous opportunities to exchange views with others engaged in all forms of wild-land management have been of value, particularly discussions with some whose views are quite different from those of the two authors'. Thus, it was possible to relate better recreational use of wild lands to various other public needs.

Preparation of the second edition of *Recreational Use of Wild Lands* was made easier through cooperation with the National Park Service, the Forest Service, various state park agencies, and a number of private organizations. Similarly, cooperation of other federal, state, and private agencies was an invaluable aid. Particular mention should be made of the help provided by the Bureau of Outdoor Recreation, the Bureau of Land Management, the Bureau of Sport Fisheries and Wildlife, the Bureau of Reclamation, the Corps of Engineers, the Tennessee Valley Authority, the National Recreation and Park Association, and the American Forest Institute.

Individuals deserving special thanks for their assistance in preparing the first edition include John Sieker, Frank Folsom, Richard Bowe, Lawrence O. Barrett, Stanley Olson, William Meyer, Hillary Tolson, Herbert Evison, Ralph Anderson, Harry Parker, Robert McIntyre, Preston Macy, Charles DeTurk, Albert Culverwell, Ruth Pike, Kramer Adams, Frederick Billings, and Robert Hitchman.

Many of the foregoing individuals aided also in the preparation of the second edition. Their help was augmented by assistance from John Bosburgh, Neil Newton, Franklin Mullaly, Edwin Winge, Aubrey Haines, Charles J. Gebler, D. L. Biddison, Donald Winslow, Frederick Weber, Lewis A. Peck, Jr., Gilbert Stewart, Jr., Daniel Saults, Keith G. Hay, Maria Buchinger, Barry S. Tindall, and G. G. Staum.

Mention should also be made of the interest of a number of instructors in wild-land recreational management on faculties of several Western universities, especially Howard R. Alden, Richard Bury, John D. Hunt, David A. King, and Dudley Mattson. This group aided in development of the plan for the present revision, and many of their suggestions are incorporated in this text.

The authors also gratefully acknowledge the counsel of Grant W. Sharpe, College of Forest Resources, University of Washington, who now directs the program of instruction in recreational use of wild lands at that institution; Alan Wagar, leader of the Cooperative Recreation Research Project maintained by the Forest Service in cooperation with the College of Forest Resources, University of Washington; and John C. Hendee, project leader, Wildland Recreation Research, Pacific Northwest Forest and Range Experiment Station, Forest Service. These men read portions of the manuscript at various stages during its preparation and made a number of helpful suggestions about content and arrangement. In addition, the assistance of James A. Crutchfield, Professor of Economics, University of Washington, who aided in obtaining certain economic data for Chapter 1, is appreciated.

Credit should also be given for help and encouragement given by the faculty and staff of the College of Forest Resources, University of Washington. Particular thanks go to Gordon D. Marckworth and James S. Bethel, respectively Dean Emeritus and Dean of the College; Walter H. Shaeffer; David R. M. Scott and his wife, Carolyn; Bernice Smith, librarian of the College, and her predecessor, Barbara Russo. Much of the typing of the manuscript, particularly in its preliminary stages, was done cooperatively by various members of the secretarial staff, including Betty Sears, Colleen Erbland, Donna Paul, Mary Pearlman, Beverly Hill, Lillian Nelson, Ann Tufts, Cheryl Hancuss, and Sallyann Wilson. Dean Frank H. Kaufert of the College of Forestry, University of Minnesota, materially aided our efforts to complete this work.

Finally, an expression of sincere appreciation is accorded our wives, Evelyn G. Brockman and Katherine W. Merriam. Their patience, cooperative support, and help in manuscript preparation made this edition of *Recreational Use of Wild Lands* possible.

C. Frank Brockman

Lawrence C. Merriam, Jr.

RECREATIONAL USE
OF WILD LANDS

INTRODUCTION

THE IMPORTANCE OF RECREATION

Recreation may be defined as the pleasurable and constructive use of spare time. Formulation of an all-inclusive, concise definition of this apparently simple term is not as easy as it might appear, for a multitude of personal, as well as social and philosophical, concepts and interpretations must be considered.

Concepts and Interpretations of Recreation

Many people feel that recreation is merely fun or some activity which varies from the routine of their daily lives. Dictionaries define the term in some such manner as "the act of recreating, or state of being recreated; refreshment of the strength and spirits after toil; diversion, play."[1] Similarly, recreation is defined as "activity that rests men from work, often giving them a change (distraction, diversion), and restores (re-creates) them for work" [6].

Recreation is many things. It involves any activity which is participated in, anytime and anywhere, merely for the enjoyment it affords. Recreation may be purely physical; it may provide intellectual, aesthetic, or emotional outlets; or it may include combinations of these. In its broadest sense, it encompasses much more than simple amusement or play. Moreover, the way free time is used is very definitely individual and personal. An activity which serves as recreation for one person may be work, or a bore, for another. Further, recreational needs of specific individuals vary at different times. They not only change during periods of life, in accordance with physical ability and intellectual capacity, but often at

---

[1] "Webster's Third New International Dictionary," unabridged, G. & C. Merriam Company, Springfield, Mass., 1968.

different periods in one day, depending upon personal needs, preferences, and options.

In our definition of recreation the word "pleasurable" signifies that recreation is fun. Benefit will accrue to the individual only if he voluntarily selects some spare-time recreational activity because of the pleasure it affords. But recreation can do more than merely enable an individual to occupy idle time, to loaf. For this reason the word "constructive" is included in our definition. In this sense recreation has a purpose beneficial to the individual and society, whether consciously recognized or not, and is necessarily related to leisure.

Relation of Leisure and Spare Time

Leisure and spare time, periods not directly involved with work or personal care, are synonymous to many people. But there is a difference [6,16]. Leisure is positive and, in a broad sense, productive. It does not denote aimless indolence; sterile or mismanaged free time may have negative implications. While some uses of spare time may be beneficial, other spare-time activities may be detrimental; in either case the effects may be temporary or lifelong. Leisure implies freedom from the necessity of labor; it is time during which one is free to choose what one wishes to do. Thus, it involves responsibility in proper choice from the entire range of both passive and energetic interests and activities made possible by modern technological advances. Leisure interests and activities may often require expenditure of more time and energy than are demanded by earning a living.

Recreational Benefits

The rewards of recreational activities, whatever their nature, depend upon the degree to which they provide outlets for personal needs and interests not attainable in daily routine. In addition to involving rest and relaxation they provide a change of pace from normal workday activities, important to individual physical and mental well-being and productive capacity. Recreation may also operate as a potent teaching force—it may be creative as well as re-creative. It may improve individual personality and social relationships. By supplementing routine often imposed by modern, highly specialized tasks, it can give balance to life by enhancing personal accomplishment and importance. Recreation can also challenge and stimulate by enriching and broadening individual outlook and horizons, developing individual capabilities, and gratifying man's natural desire for new and more satisfying objectives and ambitions. Indeed, more than a few individuals can credit their interest in a particular vocation to the germ of an idea planted during their early years by inspired direction in some sort of recreational program.

Expanding Opportunities for Recreation and Leisure

Early social systems provided leisure for only a small percentage of the population [6,16]. Many people lived close to a subsistence level, in certain cases as slaves. Modern technological society with its varied mechanical devices for saving time and accomplishing difficult or disagreeable tasks provides increasing opportunities for recreation and leisure for far greater numbers of people.

That each individual needs some form of recreation requires little elaboration; it is axiomatic. If maximum efficiency in the business of living is to be achieved, the stresses and strains of modern life must be relieved by periods of physical and mental relaxation properly coordinated with routine tasks. However, it should be recognized that certain aspects of some jobs may be basically classed as leisure or recreation, particularly if a high degree of personal selection were involved in such employment.

The greatly increased amount of free time now available as a result of technological progress will be used in some way, beneficially or otherwise. The way it will be used and the kind of recreational outlets chosen by various people will depend upon numerous factors: (1) cultural background, (2) physical and intellectual capability, (3) education, training, and experience, (4) age and sex, (5) marital status and family relationships, (6) occupation, (7) economic status, (8) free time, (9) residence, whether urban or rural, (10) varying moods and emotional needs, (11) available opportunities, and (12) the manner in which recreational interests and opportunities are presented.

Responsibility of Society for Public Recreational Needs

The public sector of society has properly assumed an increasing share of responsibility for providing opportunities for constructive spare-time activities. The acreage of various types of both public and private lands available for recreation has greatly increased during the past several decades. Museums, art galleries, zoological gardens, arboretums, and similarly specialized institutions are important adjuncts of recreation. Schools, churches, and a variety of other organizations sponsor a wide assortment of recreational programs for different age groups and promote spare-time activities of almost every conceivable type. The cost of these publicly and privately sponsored recreation opportunities has been great; however, the cost of *not* providing meaningful outlets for the energies, interests, and abilities of all segments of the population could be much greater.

As outlined more fully later, many factors contribute to the expanding need for adequate recreational opportunities, facilities, and services. More people have more spare time and greater opportunity for leisure as a result of modern technological advances. Our population has increased greatly; it is now primarily urban rather than rural, and consequently the general nature of occupations has changed from largely active to primarily sedentary. There are also more old and more young people, and both of these groups, largely unproductive, require outlets for their energies and interests. Further, our standard of living is higher so that more people can afford necessary costs. We also have faster, more dependable, and more diversified means of transportation, making it possible for us to reach places far beyond the dreams of our parents, and to do so easily, in comparative comfort, and within a shorter span of time. In addition, public attitude toward work and recreation has changed significantly over the years.

These changes, which began to develop slowly almost from the time the first colonists established themselves on the Atlantic seaboard, have continued at an accelerated pace in recent years and will undoubtedly be even more rapid in the future [20]. By way of prediction, consider this statement by David Sarnoff, former chairman of Radio Corporation of America, in the January 1955, issue of *Fortune* [14] :

Leisure, of course, will be greatly extended. A much shorter work week will no doubt prevail in 1980, and another ten or fifteen years will have been added to the average life span. . . .
Not labor but leisure will be the great problem in the decades ahead. That prospect should be accepted as a God-given opportunity to add dimensions of enjoyment and grace to life.

This concern for the future of our society has been increasingly noted by other responsible, informed writers [2-9,11-13,16,21-23]. Thus the growing importance of recreation in connection with leisure, together with the requisite maintenance of environmental quality, is not lost on growing numbers of citizens. Public interest is reflected in attitudes and activities of legislators. This is indicated by the growth in number of recreational areas and increasing restrictions relative to improper utilization of natural resources, dangers of air and water pollution, needless environmental destruction in expansion of highways and industrial and urban developments, and related matters affecting the natural interest and beauty of the countryside.

Major Influences on Public Recreational Requirements

Factors which have contributed to our growing recreational needs in the past, and which will exert great influence in the future, include the nature, density, and distribution of our population, as well as the relation between different groups and age classes; the amount of leisure time available to the individual; and the amount of a person's income, the nature of his occupation, and his means of transportation. Change in public attitude toward work and recreation has been another important influence.

Population Changes and Their Effects upon Recreational Patterns

Our expanding population has brought about a phenomenal increase in the number of potential users of recreational lands. Within a few years after the American Revolution the population of the United States was nearly 4 million, largely confined to the Atlantic seaboard. Since that time, with the western boundary of our country extended to the Pacific, our population has increased manyfold. In 1960 it was over 179 million; by 1967, as indicated by later census data [17], it had increased to nearly 200 million. It has been predicted that by the year 2010 the population of the United States will be between 400 and 438 million [20].

The population of the United States has increased tremendously over the years, but it is not uniformly distributed. In 1960 nearly half our people lived in the New England, Middle Atlantic, and East North Central divisions of our country, a region which embraced less than 12 percent of our land. By way of contrast, the Mountain division had slightly more than 24 percent of the land area of the United States but less than 4 percent of our population.

By 1967 population density within the various states ranged from a low of 0.5 people per square mile in Alaska to a high of 928 people per square mile in New Jersey. Other examples of extreme variations in population were high densities per square mile in Rhode Island, 858.0; Massachusetts, 692.1; Connecticut, 600.6; New York 383.0; Maryland, 372.3; Delaware, 263.9; Pennsylvania, 258.3; and Ohio, 255.0. The high densities were in sharp contrast to extremely low densities per square mile in such states as Wyoming, 3.2; Nevada, 4.0; Montana, 4.8; New Mexico, 8.3; Idaho, 8.5; South Dakota, 8.9; and North Dakota, 9.2. Of the Eastern states Maine had the lowest population density per square mile, 31.5; greatest concentration of people per square mile in the West occurred in California, 122.4 [17].

The change in the population pattern in the United States from primarily rural to primarily urban, at about the time of World War I, has profoundly affected the living habits and occupational pursuits of our people. Today most Americans are crowded onto relatively limited areas of land where natural conditions are largely nonexistent; employment is primarily in industrial, commercial, clerical, or professional activities which are essentially sedentary. Thus, many Americans are removed from regular contact with open spaces and to a considerable degree have lost the ability of their forefathers to conduct themselves properly and safely in a truly natural environment. Modern, largely urbanized civilization divorces many people from intimate contact with nature, from recognition of the inherent difficulties and hazards as well as interests involved. Uncomfortable, unpleasant and, on occasion, disastrous experiences result from lack of understanding.

The rapid growth and irregular distribution of our population, together with their effects upon the habits and occupations of the people, have greatly influenced our need for diverse recreational opportunities. It is obvious that we require a greater number of properly distributed recreational areas of widely varying types suited to different spare-time interests and activities. Recreational lands readily accessible to people in more densely populated areas are most important. Overcrowded conditions typical of most recreational lands, particularly those in and near major centers of population, emphasize this need. The growth of metropolitan, county, and state park systems in many sections of the country is a direct result of this demand. Changes in population patterns and living habits also indicate why there is a constantly increasing pressure for the reservation of large unspoiled tracts, such as wilderness areas, where people can completely escape the confines of the city and obtain the benefits of recreation in truly natural surroundings. We cannot afford to overlook the damage done to recreational lands of unique quality, such as national parks, through pressure of increased use together with unenlightened public demand for facilities and services which are inappropriate to such areas.

Effects of Variations in Age Classes

Since people of different ages have varying interests and physical abilities, the relation between various age classes comprised in our population is another factor which bears upon their recreational preferences and, consequently, the nature of recreational facilities required. Of particular importance is the recent increase in number of young people and old people. These two groups, largely unproductive economically and at opposite extremes of physical ability, experience, and maturity, obviously have widely divergent recreational interests.

Young people prefer, and need, facilities for active recreation; the emphasis here is on sports, team play, and active group programs. Declining vigor of more mature years prompts increasingly greater emphasis upon physical moderation and more passive interests and activities; further, areas of our country typified by less rigorous climates have greater appeal to older people.

Improvement of Living Standards and Increase in Leisure Time

Activities of modern people are highly specialized. In our work today most of us contribute to the welfare of society largely through detailed tasks which are but parts of a broad, overall project. Creative elements are largely lacking in our daily routine; many individual workers have little or no idea of how their efforts are related to the finished product. In short, modern man's existence is considerably regimented by an industrialized civilization in which personal satisfaction is often sacrificed for greater productive capacity.

Such a system, however, has many compensations. Together with various technical innovations, modern techniques have materially improved our living standards so that we are better able to afford the costs of spare-time activities of our own choosing. Over the years there has been a noticeable change in the affluence of the American people. Disposable personal income (that portion of the national product left to individuals, after taxes, for spending or saving) has, except for the Depression years in the early 1930s, been rising sharply since 1929 (Table 1-1).

Table 1-1
Disposable personal income and personal consumption expenditures

Year	Current prices, billions of dollars	1958 prices, billions of dollars	Per Capita Current prices, dollars	1958 prices, dollars
1929	83.3	150.6	683.0	1,236.0
1933	45.5	112.2	362.0	893.0
1940	75.7	166.3	573.0	1,259.0
1945	150.2	229.7	1,074.0	1,642.0
1950	206.9	249.6	1,364.0	1,646.0
1955	275.3	296.7	1,666.0	1,795.0
1960	350.0	340.2	1,937.0	1,883.0
1965	472.2	434.4	2,227.0	2,232.0
1967	544.7	466.5	2,736.0	2,393.0

Source: "*Statistical Abstracts of the United States, 1968*" *(table 466), U.S. Bureau of the Census, Washington, 1968 (Alaska and Hawaii excluded prior to 1960).*

Modern technology also makes it possible for us to produce more goods with far less effort and in much less time than formerly. As a result, the amount of spare time available to the individual has been greatly increased.

During the early days of America, when the population was essentially rural in character, people had to labor long hours each day in order to provide the necessities of life for themselves and their families. About 125 years ago the average workweek was seventy-four hours [19]; of the remaining ninety-four hours in each week, eighty-four were required for personal care (eating, sleeping, etc.). Opportunities for those activities now termed "recreation" were severely limited in a schedule which permitted only about ten hours of free time weekly.

It should be stated, however, that the long hours of work characteristic of early America were not without their compensations. A new home, a new community, a new nation was literally being carved from the wilderness. To a degree, such work represented personal achievement, and the long hours may not have had the debilitating effect upon the worker that many routine tasks have today.

Nevertheless, although time for personal care has remained fairly constant over the years, developing technological progress has brought a gradual reduction in the effort required to supply man's basic needs. The average workweek at the time of the Civil War was sixty-eight hours; by the turn of the century, it had been reduced to sixty hours; the ten-hour day and the six-day workweek typical of about three-quarters of a century ago have today been generally replaced by the standard eight-hour day, five days weekly. Thus, within the past hundred years, the average person gained nearly thirty additional hours of free time weekly for use in activities of his own choosing. Indications are that the workweek will be further reduced in the future [1,15,19]. Both young and elderly people have even greater amounts of spare time. Technological advances foster the possibility of earlier retirement for older people and prolong the

economic immaturity of the young. Along with the advantages in such developments are hazards resulting from enforced idleness.

In addition to shortening the workweek, technological progress has broadened opportunities for extended vacation periods. This has a strong bearing upon
recreation, for more people are increasingly able to develop interests of their
own choosing to greater depth, and to travel greater distances to places which
have particular appeal.

Those adequately prepared for proper use of increased spare time in the
future will benefit greatly in satisfying their creative needs. Many benefits will
accrue from various forms of recreational interests and activities. Educational
philosophy, of both an informal and a formal nature, and at all academic levels,
is responding to this challenge in preparing increasing numbers of individuals for
such opportunities.

Improvement in Travel Facilities

Improvement in methods and facilities for travel has developed greatly. As a
result, patterns of both work and play have changed materially. Our horizons, as
well as our activities, are much broader than they once were.

The automobile has been the most vital factor in this development.
Automobile registrations rose from ,4 in 1895 to 2,332,426 in 1915, accelerated
to 77,981,373 in 1966, and continue to rise.

The travel radius of the average American family was phenomenally
increased by the development of the automobile. Practically overnight, recreational journeys consisting of one-day trips to a picnic ground near the end of a
streetcar line were lengthened to weekends spent at points of interest many
miles distant. The automobile also made possible extended trips to places which,
because of the necessity of expensive, time-consuming rail journeys, had been
previously inaccessible to the average citizen.

Development and wider use of motor vehicles by the public and the
consequent interest in extended travel were soon followed by improved and
additional highways. Today, good roads span the length and breadth of our land.
They penetrate to remote nooks and crannies and, except in rare instances, are
usable throughout the year.

The development and improvement of various types of aircraft and the
increasing diversity of sophisticated recreation equipment promise even greater
impact on future recreational travel habits [15]. Such developments have
positive as well as negative implications, but those that provide easier access to
remote backcountry and other relatively inaccessible locations threaten the
overuse of such areas and the destruction of their environmental and related
values.

Change in Attitude toward Recreation

General public attitude toward work and recreation also has undergone a change.
Work simply for work's sake is no longer a primary criterion of the full life for
increasing numbers of people. But during the formative years of our country the

philosophy of the times regarded recreation, per se, as wasteful of time and effort—in effect, not respectable. In New England, particularly, recreation simply for personal enjoyment was severely frowned upon.

As an indication of the early American attitude toward recreation, witness the policy of Cokesbury College, as noted in the "Methodist Discipline" in 1792: "The students shall be indulged with nothing which the world calls play. Let this rule be observed with the strictest nicety; for those who play when they are young, will play when they are old."[2]

Scope and Organization of Book

Recognizing the varied factors which contribute to the importance of recreation, the reader will be better able to relate material presented in this and following chapters if provided with an outline of their scope and organization.

This book seeks to give the reader an understanding of the development of recreational interest in wild nonurban lands; to present and explain differences in land-use philosophies of public agencies and private landowners; to discuss the visitor's concept of recreation land use; to present basic concepts of recreation land use for consideration; and to consider planning, development, administration, and management of United States lands with some related inputs from foreign lands. More questions may be raised than answered for the reader. Many of the opinions expressed in the book are just that—opinion. The extended reference lists at the end of each chapter provide titles for the reader who wishes to go more deeply into topics presented.

To further guide the reader through the material of the text, an organization framework (Figure 1-1) is presented. The introductory chapters discuss the role of recreation in America and its relation to the outdoors. We have a given base of land and water area to work with. Unlike our forefathers we cannot expand to new lands. The system is essentially closed.

Man as manager is working in the given environment to provide goods and services including recreation in perpetuity while maintaining environmental quality. Service agencies and owner types that will be discussed in this book are listed. Officially the manager usually views the land and water resources differently from the vistor-user whose orientation is nonwork and recreational.

Yet, this is the ideal situation. To develop a basis for adequate communication, optimum resource use, and environmental maintenance, there are several procedural steps to pass through. Even then the understanding of these steps may do more to explain inadequacies than ideal situations.

After the introduction, there is historical background and development of policy and programs; the lands, their owners and managers; the visitor's point of view; concepts, possible classifications of the lands. Chapters 1 to 13 cover these

---

[2] Methodist Episcopal Church, "The Doctrines and Discipline of the Methodist Episcopal Church in America," Parry Hall, Philadelphia, 1792, p. 68.

points and lay a foundation for today's conditions. Planning for recreation, from comprehensive national and regional concerns to specific sites is considered in Chapter 14. Tools for recreation management stem from adequate planning and include zoning, development, environmental manipulation, rules, public relations, interpretation, and research. These are covered in Chapter 15. Management operations, including area protection, visitor health and safety, commercial services, budgets, and personnel, are covered in Chapter 16. Implications from the experiences of foreign countries are provided in Chapter 17.

Summary

Although recreation means many things to many people, it involves spare-time interests and activities which embody personal choice and enjoyment. Constructive use of spare time is important to the well-being of the individual, the community, and the nation, since the growth of an individual is determined as much by how he occupies his spare time as by how he performs required workday tasks.

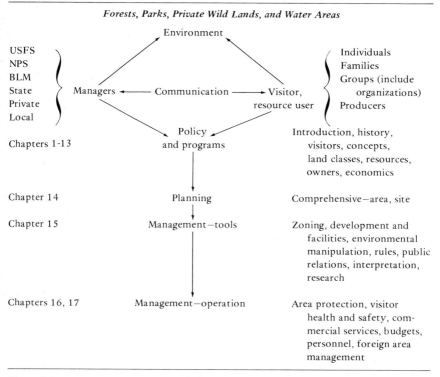

Forests, Parks, Private Wild Lands, and Water Areas

Figure 1-1

Organization framework for "Recreational Use of Wild Lands" (2d edition).

Spare time and leisure are not necessarily synonymous. Leisure, which results in maximum benefit to the individual through free choice of interests and activities, demands the exercise of responsibility in that choice, in positive use of spare time.

Technological progress has developed an essentially urban pattern of life in the United States, raised our general standard of living, increased our spare time, and expanded and improved our transportation facilities. Public attitude toward the relation of work and leisure also has been greatly modified. These facts, together with the growth and changing composition of our population, indicate that the future will witness a growing importance of recreation as a form of leisure. This, in turn, will prompt greater recognition of the fact that abilities necessary to realization of the benefits of recreational opportunities should be developed in the maximum number of people. In addition, there will be increasing pressure to maintain environmental quality basic to many interests and activities; and there will be increasing use of existing recreational lands and facilities and continued demand for additions to such resources, properly distributed in accordance with need, in quantity, quality, and variety.

Chapter 1 concludes with a brief outline of the scope and organization of this book. This is designed as a framework to aid the reader in relating material included in this and following chapters.

Selected References

1. Boyce, Carroll W.: The Four Day Week? *Factory Management and Maintenance,* vol. 114, no. 11, pp. 84-94, November, 1956.
2. Brightbill, Charles K.: "The Challenge of Leisure," Prentice-Hall, Englewood Cliffs, N.J., 1960.
3. Burns, C. D.: "Leisure in the Modern World," Appleton-Century-Crofts, New York, 1932.
4. Clawson, Marion: How Much Leisure, Now and in the Future? in James C. Charlesworth (ed.), "Leisure in America: Blessing or Curse?" Monograph 4, American Academy of Political and Social Science, Philadelphia, 1964.
5. Clawson, Marion, and Jack L. Knetsch: "Economics of Outdoor Recreation," Resources for the Future, Johns Hopkins, Baltimore, 1966.
6. de Grazia, Sebastian: "Of Time, Work and Leisure," Doubleday, Garden City, N.Y., 1962.
7. Harden, Garrett: The Tragedy of the Commons, *Science,* vol. 162, no. 3859, pp. 1243-1248, Dec. 13, 1968.
8. Huizinga, Johann: "Homo Ludens: A Study of the Play Element in Culture," trans. by R. F. C. Hull, Beacon Press, Boston, 1955.
9. Menninger, W. D.: Recreation and Mental Health, *Recreation,* vol. 42, no. 8, pp. 340-346, November, 1948.
10. National Resources Committee: "The Problems of a Changing Population," Report of the Committee on Population Problems to the National Resources Committee, Washington, 1938.

11.   Neumeyer, M. H., and E. S. Neumeyer: "Leisure and Recreation: A Study of Leisure and Recreation in Their Sociological Aspects," Barnes, New York, 1936.

12.   Pack, Arthur N.: "The Challenge of Leisure," Macmillan, New York, 1936.

13.   Prendergast, Joseph: The Evolving Recreation Pattern, *Planning and Civic Comment*, vol. 22, no. 4, pp. 1-6, December, 1956.

14.   Sarnoff, David: The Fabulous Future, *Fortune*, vol. 51, no. 1, pp. 82-83, January, 1955.

15.   Sharpe, Grant W.: Forest Recreation: A Look at the Year 2000 A.D., *Proceedings of the Society of American Foresters Meeting*, Detroit, Mich., Oct. 24-28, 1965, Washington, 1966.

16.   Tolley, William P.: The American Heritage of Leisure, *Proceedings of the National Conference on Professional Education for Outdoor Recreation*, Syracuse, N.Y., 1964, pp. 146-151.

17.   U.S. Department of Commerce, Bureau of the Census: "Statistical Abstracts of the United States, 1968," U.S. Government Printing Office, Washington, 1968.

18.   U.S. Department of the Interior, National Park Service: Recreational Use of Land in the United States, part XI of "Report on Land Planning," prepared for the Land Planning Committee of the National Resources Board, Washington, 1938.

19.   U.S. Department of the Interior, National Park Service: "A Study of the Park and Recreation Problems of the United States," U.S. Government Printing Office, Washington, 1941.

20.   U.S. Department of the Interior: "The Population Challenge," Conservation Yearbook No. 2, U.S. Government Printing Office, Washington, 1966.

21.   Vogt, William: "People! Challenge to Survival," Sloane, New York, 1960.

22.   Wirth, Conrad L.: Is There a Need for a Comprehensive Recreation Program in the United States? *Planning and Civic Comment*, vol. 21, no. 2, June, 1955.

23.   Wrenn, C. G., and D. L. Harley: "Time on Their Hands: A Report on Leisure, Recreation, and Young People," prepared for the American Youth Commission, American Council on Education, Washington, 1941.

chapter two

THE OUTDOORS AND RECREATION

R ecreation may be broadly classified on the basis of the relation of individuals to specific interests and activities, or the nature of the locale involved in the pursuit of those interests and activities. Those engaged may be spectators or active participants. The locale may be indoors or outdoors. Outdoor recreation can be subdivided on the basis of the character of the land area involved, as "wild" or "developed."

The primary concern here is outdoor recreation on wild lands. Outdoor recreation on developed lands, such as municipal and county parks and playgrounds and related high-density areas, has a different basis and is a specialized field of recreation in its own right. Except where specifically related to broad outdoor recreation problems or to recreation on wild lands, recreation on developed areas is not within the sphere of this book.

Relation of Wild and Developed Recreational Areas

Basically, the focus of recreation on wild lands is on environment, whereas that of developed lands is on activities.

Wild lands are natural or largely unmodified; physical development is minimized, limited to small sites or completely lacking, and pursuit and enjoyment of recreational interests and activities are dependent upon protection of basic environmental conditions. Such lands are usually located at some distance from population centers, and some are rather inaccessible. They may or may not be specifically designated for recreation; thus, privately owned lands used primarily for production of agricultural or forest crops are included with lands of a more truly wild or natural character.

Though few outdoor recreational interests and activities are unique to wild lands, such areas are frequently selected for interests and activities that could be conducted elsewhere. Satisfactions and enjoyment of many recreational interests and activities are greatly enhanced by a wild-land setting. For instance, a picnic in a city park is largely conducive to social satisfactions; satisfactions derived from the same type of activity in a wild-land setting are augmented by the varied interests of the more natural environment.[1]

On developed recreational lands the major emphasis is on providing physical conditions and facilities necessary to featured activities (sports, group interests, engineered, or "manicured," surroundings). While care is exercised in maintaining an attractive setting, retention of natural conditions is a minor concern. Some developed recreational areas have resulted from rehabilitation of land on which natural conditions had been completely destroyed; in other cases natural conditions may not be sufficiently distinctive to warrant preservation.

Developed recreational areas are usually within or in proximity to population centers. Being readily accessible, they provide opportunity for a wide variety of beneficial interests and activities for large numbers of people. They can be easily utilized for short periods by individuals with limited free time, and in most cases they are well adapted to types of recreational interests and activities and physical development which are often inappropriate on wild lands. Thus, they are important to perpetuation of wild-land recreational interests, particularly those of unique or fragile lands (national parks, wilderness), for a large part of demand for activities and related necessary physical development often inappropriate to wild lands can be satisfied on developed areas having less-important natural interests.

Values of Outdoor Recreation on Wild Lands

Wild lands offer excellent opportunities for health-giving, outdoor leisure-time pursuits. Enjoyment of natural surroundings in the company of people with

---

[1] Admittedly, the distinction between developed and wild recreational lands is not as sharply defined as indicated here. There are many gradations. Some developed recreational areas include somewhat wild natural sections. Conversely, various sites within larger wild recreational areas (national parks and forests, many state parks) absorb heavy public use and are often highly developed; however, such sites include only a small percentage of the essentially undeveloped areas of which they are a part. Though agricultural and managed forest lands are not literally wild in a truly natural sense, they are essentially undeveloped; in addition, most recreational activities typical of such lands (hunting, fishing) are more closely related to wild than developed lands. Historical and archaeological areas developed by early activities of man normally lack important natural interests. However, they are considered here with wild lands, largely because of their unique character and because they are often under the same administrative authority as certain wild lands. Examples are certain areas under National Park Service administration.

similar interests contributes to social pleasures. Of even greater importance, wild lands provide opportunity for development of physical skills as well as cultural and intellectual interests.

To a large extent the individual engaged in recreational activity on wild land is on his own; his enjoyment is largely dependent upon his own resources. In a limited sense he must meet the physical demands of the outdoors as did his forefathers, and the degree of success he attains is an indication of his self-reliance. Intellectually, too, his enjoyment of such areas depends upon his perception; in some cases major recreational benefits can be achieved only from a combination of physical and intellectual capabilities.

Physical values of recreation on wild land are derived primarily from such activities as fishing, hunting, hiking, riding, picnicking, camping, mountain climbing, skiing, boating, and swimming. Not only purely physical benefits are involved in such activities. To many fishermen, for instance, a full creel is but one of the rewards of a fishing trip; benefits other than exercise are derived from the ascent of a mountain; more than fresh air rewards those who camp in natural surroundings. Their activities can be enjoyed simply in their own right; physical pleasure may be sufficient recreational reward for the effort involved.

Cultural or intellectual values are derived from such interests as photography, painting, handicrafts, nature study, scientific research, understanding of archaeological or historical interests, and even meditation. However, these activities, in addition to being enjoyed for themselves, are often rewarding physically. The photographer or artist who climbs a mountain or journeys to points off the beaten track to obtain a particular picture, or the amateur or professional naturalist who exerts great effort in seeking a particular specimen, frequently develops a high degree of physical skill. In such cases, however, necessary physical activity is a means to an end rather than an end in itself.

Distribution of Wild-land Recreational Areas

Wild lands have long been important in outdoor recreation. Informally, their use for a wide variety of interests and activities (hunting and fishing) has been traditional, and for over 100 years formally designated recreational wild lands (national and state parks, forests, and related areas) have been part of the American scene.

Initially, however, these formally designated areas were not well integrated. They were not established as a result of a carefully conceived plan. Further, there was little recognition of the complementary functions of developed recreational lands and recreation on wild land.

Just as early municipal parks came into being as a result of readily recognizable local requirements, most early wild-land recreational areas were established largely because of the energy, enthusiasm, and perseverance of perceptive individuals who recognized the value of protecting bits of the significant American scene, as a result of pressures from similarly interested groups, or because of a happy coincidence of conditions at the time of their establishment. For instance, it is doubtful if some of our national parks, national monuments, state parks, or wilderness areas would exist today had they not been set aside at a time when they were relatively more remote and consequently less important as a source of raw materials for industry than they are today; or had they not been championed by farsighted employees of land-managing agencies, public-spirited citizens, or organized groups concerned with preserving outdoor interests [8,13].

Initially, satisfying growing public demand for all types of outdoor recreation was characterized by expediency. Insufficient attention was given to provision, adequate dispersal, and proper coordination of both wild and developed recreational areas required to meet demand. The nature and extent of varied outdoor recreational demands were also incompletely understood. Further, little thought was given to the allocation of different types of areas for recreational interests and activities most appropriate to perpetuation of environmental conditions basic to outdoor recreational values. In some sections of the country recreational areas were extensive and diverse; other regions not only lacked some types of recreational lands but, as a result of earlier extensive exploitation, possessed too little space which could be readily designated for such purposes [13]. For instance, most of the larger and better-known, strongly resource-oriented national parks and forests were established in the West. Of even greater significance, only a fraction of our seacoast was retained in public ownership, developed, or capable of being developed, for public recreation [18-20].

This unbalanced state of recreational opportunity often resulted in public pressure which forced the use of certain areas for inappropriate recreational interests and activities; the distressing situation typical of certain national parks is a case in point. Further, recreation was not generally regarded as an important resource of wild lands utilized for production of raw materials for industry. As a result, environmental quality and dependent recreational values of wild lands have suffered severely because of overcrowding, excessive and inappropriate development of related recreational activities, or damaging exploitation of natural resources.

These conditions showed the need for careful planning of both current and future recreational uses of wild lands. It became evident that wild and developed recreational lands had many complementary functions and that both types were required in greater number and variety, properly located in relation to need, to accommodate public demand for diverse recreational interests [13]. It became evident also that recreational and other land uses should be consistent with the nature of environment and that the natural resources on lands where such activities were in the public interest should be utilized in accordance with the perpetuation of all basic land values [9,11,14,21,22]. Certain types of uses, recreational and otherwise, are compatible with one another; others are not. Only enlightened and perceptive planning and management, which adequately consider public recreational demands consistent with perpetuation of environmental quality, foster proper diversity of recreational and other uses important to widest possible public interests and requirements.

Since publication of the findings of the Outdoor Recreation Resources Review Commission in 1962 [13], steps have been taken to alleviate problems relative to public recreational use of wild lands. However, much land primarily valuable for outdoor recreation had already been preempted by other forms of use, and the task of restoring its recreational potential had become herculean in scope, made extremely difficult by tremendous cost, the nature of existing landownership patterns, and technical difficulties.

Competition in Recreational Use of Wild Land

Recreational values of wild land are variously affected by most of man's other activities. Industrial development and the growth of large urban centers have resulted in invasion of open space as well as in the pollution of streams, lakes, and ocean beaches. The erection of dams and the resultant formation of artificial lakes, although occasionally providing certain recreational opportunities, often destroy even more valuable recreational interests through the flooding of distinctive historical, archaeological, biological, geological, or scenic areas, or the serious reduction in numbers of migratory fish. In the latter instance, not only do dams impede periodic upstream movements of certain sport fishes, but resultant development of large artificial lakes may raise water temperatures beyond the limit of tolerance for certain species. Improper methods in harvesting timber adversely affect scenic values; the same may be said of improperly controlled grazing. Further, such ill-advised activities may have far-reaching adverse effects on environmental relationships and natural-resource conservation through the acceleration of upland erosion and silting of streams. Indiscriminate drainage of swamps and marshes greatly affects the numbers of migratory waterfowl, and the settlement and cultivation of marginal farmlands often lead to the disappearance of interesting or valuable birds and mammals. Private acquisition of choice recreational sites, particularly on lakeshores and ocean beaches, has already eliminated a large part of such land from the possibility of general public use; on such high-premium recreational lands the needs of the masses should be given precedence over the desires of the few.

It should be emphasized that these pages hold no brief for recreational management of wild lands at the expense of total exclusion of other uses of land which are vital to modern life. However, it is in the public interest that in each specific case all aspects of human need must be carefully investigated before final decisions are made as to the type and character of most advantageous land use. Lands clearly most valuable for different forms of recreation, especially those typified by fragile or significant values (national parks, wilderness areas), should be so designated. On multipurpose lands utilization of resources, including recreation, should be coordinated wherever possible. No longer can we afford to act hastily or without due consideration for the future and correct mistakes of ill-advised action later. Too often such mistakes are irreparable.

Competitive Recreational Uses of Wild Lands

Many recreational uses of wild lands are themselves incompatible, for people of various recreation interests visualize different possibilities on identical areas. A few examples follow.

Hunters and those who wish merely to observe, study, and photograph wildlife are rarely in agreement on the paramount values of an area. Fishermen are often at loggerheads with water-skiers on the same waters. Skiers who demand elaborate lifts and related facilities and those who champion the natural winter scene as a site for enjoyment of this sport are rarely in accord. Many people regard the expanding use of powerboats, trail bikes, and four-wheeled vehicles, aircraft, and, in winter, snowmobiles for reaching outlying points of interest as a distressing disruption of the quiet and solitude of the outdoors. Campers and picnickers have different objectives; thus, separate sites are desirable for accommodation of these activities. In campgrounds, groups equipped with tents and those with trailers or auto campers have different requirements. And those who desire ready access by road to remote regions, and comfortable, or at least convenient, accommodations when they get there, differ from wilderness enthusiasts in point of view. Such differences of opinion, resulting from absence of uniformity in general recreational objectives, as well as from an incomplete understanding of the overall problems involved, highlight many difficulties pertaining to the acquisition, planning, development, management, and most appropriate use of recreational areas.

Maintenance of Environmental Quality

It is important to recognize that benefits of outdoor recreation depend upon much more than availability of specifically designated lands (parks, forests, wildlife reserves, wilderness areas). Such specifically designated areas are vital to public outdoor recreation, but the maintenance and perpetuation of the quality of our *total* environment is equally important [9,11,14,21,22]. In fact, in the long view, as inevitable urban expansion continues and as remaining wild lands increasingly come under more intensive management, it is likely that maintenance of the interest and beauty of our total environment will be more important than the amount of acreage in specifically designated recreational lands. Man must show greater interest in adjusting to, rather than dominating, his environment.

It is expected that environmental interest and beauty will be maintained in designated areas used for outdoor recreation, but lands beyond the boundaries of such areas also should be utilized in a way to retain their attractiveness. Lands never used or intended for use for any form of outdoor recreation have an important recreational function simply by providing attractive open space or green belts in the vicinity of cities and towns, and bordering highways and related transportation facilities. Thus, well-cared-for farm and forest lands, though managed purely for commercial objectives, are vital to outdoor recreational interests and overall recreational land programs. In short, those engaged in various aspects of recreational management of wild lands, whatever their specific duties, should not gauge the success of their efforts merely by the number of specific recreational areas established, the number of picnic areas or campsites and related facilities provided, or the miles of trails or roads developed. They should also be vitally interested in maintenance of overall environmental quality, both without and within areas they are particularly concerned with.

Need for Qualified Wild-land Recreation Leadership

Professionally educated, enlightened, perceptive, enthusiastic leadership is the key to proper coordination of the many unrelated parts of the recreational picture in the United States. If maximum recreational value is to be provided at minimum cost, varied public recreational services of diverse areas should fit like pieces of a jigsaw puzzle. In that manner recreational interests and activities inappropriate to certain lands and unnecessary duplication of services on contiguous areas within specific regions can be advantageously eliminated. All types of recreational areas, ranging from small municipal neighborhood playgrounds to distant, more extensive national parks and wilderness areas, are interrelated; each provides opportunity for specific kinds of outdoor recreational interests and activities. Both the nature and the environmental associations of such areas differ; understanding these factors is important in allocating to different land uses which are most conducive to the perpetuation of their recreational values. It follows that wild-land recreational workers should be aware of, and interested in, the problems and progress of their contemporaries in municipal, county, and other more highly developed lands, and vice versa.

The sizable investment in lands used solely and specifically for recreation today is, in itself, sufficient reason for qualified professional leadership in recreational land management, without which the recreational values inherent in those lands will not be properly maintained and the investment will be largely nullified. In addition, since the character of public use of recreational areas, as well as the cost of maintenance, is largely determined by the nature and plan of necessary physical facilities (roads, trails, campgrounds), such features must be carefully considered by personnel who not only are qualified in design and construction but are also aware of the relation of such facilities to resultant public use and the impact of such use upon the environment. Also, since recreation is of varying importance on multipurpose lands, those concerned with management of such lands should understand their relation to recreation so that this resource may be properly coordinated with other values. Further, future expansion of recreational opportunities calls for careful advance planning, guided by an understanding of the reasons for recreational demand and the different types of recreational areas suited to prospective users. Thus, public recreational requirements may be anticipated and provision made for them; for instance, before rising costs make it impossible, areas suitable for recreation, and still unused for other purposes, should be acquired.

However, it should be recognized that, regardless of the quality of leadership in recreational management of wild lands, recreational interests and activities of every kind will be subject to an increasing amount of regimentation. Steadily growing demand for such services and conflicting objectives and points of view of various groups of recreationists make this inevitable. Unregulated recreational use of wild lands is no longer possible. We may not like it, but in the future individual preferences will necessarily have to be increasingly subordinated to consideration for the many.

Diverse Capabilities Required

Leadership in the recreational field demands a variety of highly qualified people with a wide range of relevant capabilities. Those concerned with important decision-making problems, as well as with more detailed management and use of recreational areas, include individuals with experience in law and political science, sociology and psychology, economics, land planning and evaluation, geography, architecture and landscape architecture, engineering, forestry, and the greatly varied aspects of biological, geological, and related natural sciences, as well as archaeology and history. To varying degrees, opportunity for meaningful employment exists somewhere in wild-land recreation for people with all the foregoing educational backgrounds. Since wild-land recreation is strongly oriented to perpetuation of environmental interests in the face of increasing, diverse public use, various kinds of environmental specialists with supplementary education in the understanding of public requirements and motivations are needed. Workers whose education is concentrated in highly specialized fields, but who lack knowledge and experience in environmental relationships, play an important but usually supporting role.

Wild-land recreational workers who deal directly with the public in specific areas not only must be well grounded in the fundamentals of their specific fields (administration, protection of area interests and visitor health and safety, interpretation, maintenance) but must also be able to "sell" the interests of the area to visitors through knowledge and understanding of their area and their particular field of interest, their enthusiasm, and their understanding of, and interest in, people. Since recreation bases its appeal primarily on enjoyment, since varied recreational activities are entered into voluntarily, and since human beings are creatures of habit, this freedom of choice may sometimes operate disadvantageously unless guided by inspired recreational leadership.

Individual outlook and interests are often circumscribed by background and environment. Many people will use only those recreational opportunities which are most readily available and demand least personal effort. They not only may ignore opportunity to broaden their perspective through recreational channels but may, on occasion, even resist such opportunities. Only the most experienced, subtle, and perceptive direction can jog such people from a self-imposed routine which, in some cases, may not be a desirable one.

Visitor Understanding of Wild-land Environment

Modern man's leisure-time interests are largely conditioned by his essentially urban environment. Though increase in urban living has accelerated public interest in environmental protection and wild-land recreation, the urban person is often unfamiliar with the outdoors. Consequently he lacks self-reliance and understanding of wild lands, which may cause annoying or even serious difficulties. Today many people must learn how to conduct themselves in the outdoors before they can expect to use and enjoy its opportunities fully without damaging basic values. Assuming that one is physically able, maximum safety and personal enjoyment of varied recreational activities on wild land come only with an understanding of the interests and hazards involved. For instance, competent skiers recognize the signs of potentially dangerous slide areas; good hunters exercise caution in handling their weapons; and a knowledge of native plants and animals, or an understanding of geological processes, enhances the pleasures of a visit to the mountains.

Knowledge and understanding of a natural environment also foster good outdoor manners. Such awareness encourages participation in perpetuating the beauty of unspoiled surroundings; this is extremely important because outdoor recreational values are not inexhaustible and, in many cases, are very fragile. Careless treatment, whether by design or ignorance, reduces the worth of an area. Most people know of formerly attractive places ruined by thoughtless acts or deliberate vandalism.

Residents of large cities are not the only ones who lack an adequate understanding of the outdoors. Frequently the outdoor environment is equally unfamiliar and confusing to inhabitants of smaller towns. Today, by reason of radio, television, and almost universal distribution of newspapers and magazines, modern life tends to follow the pattern of metropolitan centers, even in many rural areas. Moreover, small communities do not usually possess such facilities as museums, zoological gardens, and arboretums, which foster public appreciation of many outdoor interests.

Professional Education in Recreation

Professional education in recreation [1,3,4,6,7,10,12,15-17] has developed along several different lines, owing largely to historical differences in recreational use of various types of land. Three principal concepts are briefly outlined in the following paragraphs. While each of these educational philosophies still retains a high degree of independence, there is a growing tendency toward unification of objectives, at least in fundamental areas which relate to basic needs and problems.

Many educational institutions provide curricula in recreation, incorporated in physical education departments for both men and women. These programs have a long-established history. They are adapted primarily to high-density recreational areas, especially programs in municipal and county parks and playgrounds, where emphasis is on sports and related outdoor activities. Owing to lack of emphasis on subjects related to preservation of environmental interests, such programs, unless modified to provide such emphasis, are not well adapted to recreational use of wild lands.

A second approach, offered in established curricula in a number of institutions of higher learning, deals with park administration and management with strong emphasis on planning and design. This type of education is more relevant to needs of recreational management and use of wild lands, though fundamental concepts relative to basic requirements of different environments, as well as factors responsible for environmental changes, may be minimized for the sake of necessary emphasis on primary objectives of the curricula.

Professional education in recreational management of wild lands, instituted in a meager fashion as early as the 1920s, has been greatly expanded since 1960. Both undergraduate and graduate education in this area are now offered through specialized curricula, often related to colleges of forestry or natural resources.[2] In such cases basic undergraduate forestry curricula are modified to include courses important to wild-land recreational management. Resultant curricula coordinate relevant social science courses with a strong background in biological science.

---

[2] Though forestry is being challenged as a logical base for education in wild-land recreational management, it is natural that forestry and recreational management of wild lands attract young people with similar interests. Both fields of interest are based upon understanding of biological laws pertinent to plants and animals in relation to environment. The basic interests of many wild-land recreational areas are closely related to their forest cover. In addition, basic forestry education emphasizes protection, land survey and planning, trail and road construction, and related activities which are also important in recreational land management. The close affinity of forestry and recreational management of wild lands is further emphasized by the fact that many professional foresters are engaged in various types of recreational work. Many have made notable contributions to the recreational management of wild lands and some, like Aldo Leopold, are recognized as pioneer leaders in this area.

At most institutions offering programs in recreational management of wild lands, the undergraduate curriculum aims at development of a broad educational background, together with exposure to fundamental recreational management techniques. Lower-division years are devoted to basic courses in natural and social sciences. Upper-division courses build upon this foundation. In addition to training in relevant natural and social sciences, students are given a basic introduction to technical skills important to various recreational land management procedures, including land planning, policy determination, and development and operation of facilities and services. Proper use of English, both written and spoken, is necessary for communication of ideas, and mathematics is basic to engineering and statistical analysis in planning and development; both receive considerable attention throughout undergraduate years.

Graduate programs are designed primarily for individuals who demonstrate their potential for upper echelons of management or a career in research or teaching. Such programs are generally related to individual requirements. They may place major emphasis on either the social or the biological approach to wild-land recreational management problems. They may be developed within a formalized recreational land management department or along with other relevant disciplines, such as sociology, economics, geography, landscape architecture, political science, or the biological sciences.

Wild-land Recreational Research

In wild-land recreational management, as in any enterprise, adequate factual information upon which to base effective decisions and to guide development of facilities and services is essential [2,3,5]. Initially, experience gained by trial and error largely served this purpose, but this is no longer adequate. Rapidly expanding and changing patterns of recreational land use, as well as the intangible nature and long-term character of the aesthetic values involved, demand a more scientifically organized approach to decision-making and management problems.

Recreation research is now being directed at basic management problems. With the use of visitor interviews, researchers are learning about the behavior and attitudes of park campers, wilderness hikers, picnickers, family-outing groups, and other recreationists. Also information is being obtained on types of services provided to visitors, such as user outfitting in the Boundary Waters Canoe Area of Minnesota. Ecological studies of vegetation in recreation and park areas and work in plant succession under management or fire protection are in process.

All wild-land recreation research is directed toward understanding man's role in using or manipulating the natural environment. Most studies provide data useful to the land manager in better understanding his role in visitor service. Some studies are more basic, leading to an understanding of natural laws which may have indirect benefits. Economic studies of resource values and costs of alternative uses are particularly helpful in resource planning and area designation.

Research problems in recreational land planning and management may be grouped into such broad categories as (1) site or environmental considerations—ecology, cultural treatments, protection, engineering, and development; (2) human relationships—public motivation, behavior, response to management, measurement and control of numbers; and (3) administration—economics, political relationships, land-allocation problems, personnel.

Summary

In contrast to highly developed recreational areas, wild lands are natural or slightly modified areas, with physical development minimized, localized, or lacking, on which maintenance of basic environmental conditions is a major management concern. Lands managed for agricultural or forest crops are included, even though such areas may not have a specific outdoor recreational function, since they are important in the interest and beauty of our total environment. In addition, historical and archaeological areas are closely related to wild lands because of their unique qualities and similar administrative relationships. Wild lands will be increasingly important as outlets for a wide variety of stimulating physical, cultural, social, and intellectual leisure interests and activities.

In this chapter several major points have been raised that serve as guides to understanding the evolution of wild-land recreation in the United States:

1. Most of the original wild-land park and recreation areas were established because of the energy and persistence of perceptive individuals or groups at a time when lands were less valuable as raw material sources or were relatively more remote.

2. Poor planning characterized early efforts to provide and develop recreational lands. Most of the resource-oriented parks and forests were established on public lands in the West, while the population was, and is, more concentrated in the Eastern United States.

3. Recreation was not generally regarded as an important function of wild lands utilized for raw material production.

4. Diversity of opportunity for wild-land recreation with the avoidance of resource development and recreation use conflicts requires coordinated perceptive planning.

5. As recreation-use pressure increases on limited lands, conflicts often develop between recreationists of different types. There is a need for varied types of recreation areas and differing activity opportunities.

6.   The overall environment is important aesthetically. Well-managed forests and farmlands, though not directly used for recreation, function as green belts for cities, towns, or the rural scene.

7.   In the future the public will have to accept an increasing degree of regimentation of all types of recreational interests and activities on wild land so that the optimum number of people may share in the resultant benefits.

Increasing need for more well-qualified workers in wild-land recreation demands professional status based upon specific academic education on both the undergraduate and the graduate levels in a diversity of fields. The goal of such educational efforts is to provide necessary, qualified leadership in recreational land planning and management.

The growing importance of recreation on wild lands has also focused attention on research as a basis for effective decisions in the allocation and recreational use of such lands. Specialists in a number of fields can make meaningful contributions in this area, by both an individual and an interdisciplinary approach to particular problems.

Selected References

1.   Brightbill, Charles K.: Education for Recreation Leadership, *Proceedings of the National Conference on Professional Education for Outdoor Recreation*, Syracuse, N.Y., 1964.

2.   Clawson, Marion, and Jack L. Knetsch: Recreation Research: Some Basic Analytical Concepts and Suggestions, *Proceedings of the National Conference on Outdoor Recreation Research*, Ann Arbor, Mich., 1963.

3.   Clawson, Marion, and Jack L. Knetsch: "Economics of Outdoor Recreation," Resources for the Future, Johns Hopkins, Baltimore, 1966.

4.   Crane, Lyle E.: Education in Outdoor Recreation, *Proceedings of the National Conference on Outdoor Recreation Research*, Ann Arbor, Mich., 1963.

5.   Dana, Samuel T.: "Problem Analysis: Research in Forest Recreation," U.S. Forest Service, Washington, April, 1957.

6.   Dana, Samuel T., and Everet W. Johnson: "Forestry Education Today and Tomorrow," Society of American Foresters, Washington, 1963.

7.   Floyd, J. Whitney: Forest and Wildlife Education for Outdoor Recreation, *Proceedings of the National Conference on Professional Education for Outdoor Recreation*, Syracuse, N.Y., 1964.

8.   Hendee, John C., Richard P. Gale, and Joseph Harry: Conservationists, Politics, and Democracy, *Journal of Soil and Water Conservation*, vol. 24, no. 6, November-December, 1969.

9.   Jackson, Henry M.: An Appeal for "A Law of Environmental Rights," *Seattle Times* (magazine section), Sunday, May 25, 1969.

10.   LaGasse, Alfred B., and Walter L. Cook: Historical Development of Professional Education Programs for Outdoor Recreation, *Proceedings of the National Conference on Professional Education for Outdoor Recreation*, Syracuse, N.Y., 1964.

11. Lindsay, Alton A.: Our Environment: Exploitation or Renewal, *Concern*, Feb. 1, 1965.

12. Marckworth, Gordon D.: Statistics from Schools of Forestry for 1968: Degrees Granted and Enrollments, *Journal of Forestry*, vol. 67, no. 9, September, 1969.

13. Outdoor Recreation Resources Review Commission: "Outdoor Recreation for America: A Report to the President and to the Congress by the ORRRC," U.S. Government Printing Office, Washington, 1962.

14. President's Council on Recreation and Natural Beauty: "From Sea to Shining Sea," U.S. Government Printing Office, Washington, 1968.

15. Shirley, Hardy L.: "Forestry and Its Career Opportunities," 2d ed., McGraw-Hill, New York, 1964.

16. Smith, Julian W.: Leadership Preparation for Outdoor Recreation, *Proceedings of the National Conference on Professional Education for Outdoor Recreation*, Syracuse, N.Y., 1964.

17. Taylor, Loren E.: Let's Get the Elephants Out of the Volkswagen, *Parks and Recreation*, vol. 2, no. 2, February, 1967.

18. U.S. Department of the Interior, National Park Service: "A Report on Our Vanishing Shoreline," Washington, 1958.

19. U.S. Department of the Interior, National Park Service: "Our Fourth Shore, Great Lakes Shoreline Recreational Survey," Washington, 1959.

20. U.S. Department of the Interior, National Park Service: "Pacific Coast Recreation Area Survey," Washington, 1959.

21. U.S. Department of the Interior: "The Race for Inner Space," U.S. Government Printing Office, Washington, 1964.

22. U.S. Department of the Interior: "The Quest for Quality," Conservation Yearbook No. 1, U.S. Government Printing Office, Washington, 1965.

23. Wagar, J. V. K.: Some Fundamental Characteristics of Outdoor Recreation, *Journal of Forestry*, vol. 64, no. 10, October, 1966.

24. Wirth, Conrad L.: Is There a Need for a Comprehensive Recreation Program in the United States? *Planning and Civic Comment*, vol. 21, no. 2, June, 1955.

25. Wirth, Conrad L.: Basic Need for Land, *Planning and Civic Comment*, vol. 23, no. 4, December, 1957.

HISTORY, THE VISITOR, CONCEPTS

chapter three

INITIAL INTERESTS IN RECREATIONAL LAND VALUES

Recreational values have always been present in the outdoors, but only in recent times have steps been taken to manage, preserve, and utilize them on a continuing basis.

In one guise or another, tracts of land have been reserved for park and recreational purposes since time immemorial. The earliest of these were established by the nobility, primarily for personal pleasure or self-aggrandizement. The concept of establishing such areas for general public use, though existing in early periods of recorded history, did not assume importance until the nineteenth century.

In hunting one finds a close affinity between primitive and modern concepts of outdoor recreation. To early man hunting was a means of sustaining life rather than recreation; various primitive peoples recognized their dependence upon a continuing supply of wild game and developed certain rules by which the taking of that game was guided. The modern science of wildlife management, the keystone of good hunting and fishing and an important aspect of recreation on wild lands, has evolved from practices which date from antiquity [8,14].

Earliest Recorded Recreational Lands

The first parks on record, featuring woodlands, vineyards, and other vegetation, and interspersed with trails and ponds, date from 1000 to earlier than 2500 B.C. in ancient Babylonia and Sumer in western Asia. Similarly, parklands were not uncommon during the heyday of Assyria, Persia, Greece, and Rome [5,7]. Some of these were designated as private hunting preserves, a practice that was continued during medieval times by European nobility.

In particular, wild land for modern recreation has a close relation to areas of this type in Great Britain. In feudal England, where a forest was more important as a source of game than of timber, hunting by the nobility, greatly extended by William the Conqueror and later Norman kings, was not modified until after the adoption of the Magna Charta in 1215 [8,14].

Today most of those medieval English preserves are but historical memories, but two areas exist as modern survivals of that period. Both the Forest of Dean, west of Gloucester [9], and the New Forest, near Southampton [10], can trace their ancestry directly to the Norman period and earlier.[1]

During the Renaissance, lavish private formal gardens became the vogue on the European continent. This fashion, originating in northern Italy, continued to the latter part of the eighteenth century, with Versailles, just outside Paris, and Schönbrunn, near Vienna, being among the more noted examples. Development of English estates, however, though affected by such interest on the Continent, generally followed a natural rather than a highly formal pattern [5,7].

While attention to recreation was largely in the interests of privileged classes during ancient and medieval times, the needs of the general public were not completely ignored. Public parks are known to have existed in the twelfth century B.C. in certain cities of what are now Ceylon and India [5,7]. Ancient Greece and Rome made provision for certain types of public recreational needs, and by the end of the thirteenth century, public squares and, later, areas suited for games and various athletic contests came into existence in many parts of Europe [5,7].

By the nineteenth century, many nations of the world began to adopt more democratic principles, largely as a result of the American and French Revolutions. Thus, restricted private parks and hunting preserves were made increasingly available to the general populace [5,7].

Eventually many such areas which formerly had been the sole property of wealthy or powerful individuals came under state control with provision for general public access and use. For example, the many public parks which are such an attractive feature of modern metropolitan London once were, like the

---

[1] In 1087 the New Forest was decreed by William the Conqueror to be his royal domain, thus giving rise to its name, which has persisted to the present time. Today, by the slow processes of history, this area has become the common heritage of all Englishmen, administered by the British Forestry Commission for grazing, timber production, and public recreation. Its boundaries embrace 144 square miles of forest, meadow, and moor, of which about 100 square miles is publicly owned crown land. The Forestry Commission, principal administrative agency of this and similar areas in England, is a direct descendant of the lord wardens appointed by the medieval kings to preserve their personal domain, and the principal administrative officer of the New Forest is still known by the ancient title of deputy surveyor [10].

more distant and extensive Forest of Dean and the New Forest, the personal property of the Crown [5,7].

Establishment of specific areas of wild land primarily for preservation and public understanding of varied significant interests (geological, biological, archaeological, historical) and enjoyment of scenic and related outdoor recreational values (sight-seeing, hiking, climbing, camping, boating, fishing, hunting) is generally conceded to have followed the initial steps taken in the United States toward the end of the nineteenth century. Today this concept of land use is widely recognized throughout the world. Over 100 nations have established national parks and various types of related reserves for preservation of significant interests and for public enjoyment.

Recreation and the American Conservation Movement

In the United States the current extensive and growing interest in the recreational use of wild land is commonly regarded as having evolved from our general interest in the regulation of forests, wildlife, soils, water, and similar natural resources. However, the record indicates that this is not entirely the case. True, until recent years, progress in the conservation of other more tangible land values has been more obvious; but rather than being incidental to the broad conservation movement, interest in recreational value of wild land was one of several principal motive forces if not the primary one. Evidence of this is the fact that the first extensive areas of wild land to be reserved for public benefit were dedicated to an outdoor recreational objective. The Yosemite Grant (1864), Yellowstone National Park (1872), and the Niagara Falls Reservation (1885) came into being well in advance of our national and state forests, federal and state wildlife reserves and refuges, and similar areas of specifically dedicated public lands important to varied objectives of modern American conservation practices.

There were, of course, earlier manifestations of public interest in the regulation of natural resources in the United States. However, establishment of the Yosemite Grant, Yellowstone National Park, and the Niagara Falls Reservation served largely in preparing public opinion for acceptance of more complete conservation principles involving the perpetuation of scenic, environmental, and recreational resources of wild land.

The American conservation movement was marked by many important early milestones. Among the most noteworthy were restrictive colonial laws relating to game and timber, the passage of the Great Ponds Act by the Massachusetts Bay Colony, the origination and initial development of municipal parks, the reservation of lands surrounding the mineral springs in the Ouachita Mountains of Arkansas, and the birth of the national park concept. The latter involved the first suggestion of a national park and the establishment of the Yosemite Grant, the first area of wild land set aside specifically for public recreational use.

Early Reservation of Wild Land for Public Benefit

The Great Ponds Act, passed by the Massachusetts Bay Colony in 1641, was the first important milestone in the reservation of wild land for the public benefit. As such it has a direct relation with outdoor recreation.

The act decreed that about two thousand bodies of water, each exceeding 10 acres in size and collectively amounting to an area of approximately 90,000 acres, were to remain as a public resource forever open to the public for "fishing and fowling." With the passing of time, the Great Ponds lost much of their earlier utilitarian value and became more important and most generally used for recreational purposes. In 1923, when this trend from the original concept was questioned, the attorney general of Massachusetts ruled that the Great Ponds Act, permitting public access to, and use of, these waters, was still valid even though the character of public use had changed [15].

The second major milestone in the history of American conservation, as it relates to outdoor recreation on wild land, occurred in 1832, when Congress passed an act for reserving four sections of land in the Ouachita Mountains of Arkansas "for the future disposal of the United States" [19,22]. The act stated further that this reservation "shall not be entered, located, or appropriated, for any other purpose whatever" [19]. This area included a number of hot mineral springs whose waters were thus reserved for posterity and removed from the danger of private monopoly and exploitation.

Although the Hot Springs Reservation was not established because of its recreational values, these assumed increasing importance in later years. As a result, the hot springs area was incorporated into the National Park System in 1921 as Hot Springs National Park [21,23].

Early Municipal Parks in the United States

The common, or green, typical of many New England towns has its roots in the American colonial period, and although such areas were established for reasons other than recreation, their recreational values eventually assumed a dominant role as the communities grew. One of the most noteworthy examples of such early municipal public areas is the Boston Common, established in 1634, which has served the citizens of Boston for over 300 years [5,18].

Recognition of the need for open spaces in town planning was expressed in somewhat similar fashion in other sections of the United States during its formative period. In accordance with Spanish custom, a public square, or plaza, was reserved in the development of most early Spanish settlements in America [20]. In 1682 William Penn reserved a number of tracts for public use within the city of Philadelphia [5,12,20]. James Edward Oglethorpe was guided by related ideas in developing the city of Savannah, Georgia, in 1733 [5,20], and open areas were provided for by Major Pierre Charles L'Enfant in planning Washington,

D.C., in 1791 [5] . Other early examples of public open spaces include a bowling green in New Amsterdam, forerunner of New York City, in 1732; the site of old Fort Dearborn in Chicago, in 1839 [5]; and public squares reserved in the initial planning of Salt Lake City by Brigham Young, in 1847 [20] .

Central Park in New York is one of the most significant of municipal parks in the United States. Established in 1853,[2] it was the first large area acquired largely by purchase of land by a municipality exclusively for public recreational use. Its early administration, planning, and development were largely directed by Frederick Law Olmsted, who from 1864 to 1866 played a major role in the establishment and early administration of the Yosemite Grant.[3]

Birth of the National Park Concept

As previously stated, the reservation of wild land for recreational purposes was a potent force in the modern American conservation movement. Since the establishment of national parks figured prominently in such affairs, the birth date of the national park concept is highly important.

First Proposal of a National Park

In 1833, the influential and widely circulated *New York Daily Commercial Advertiser* published a series of letters by George Catlin,[4] explorer and artist, who had visited the Indian country of the upper Missouri in 1832 [12] . Catlin's experiences prompted his interest in the American Indian and caused him to ponder ways and means of preserving segments of native interests for the future. One of his letters included this significant observation:

. . . and what a splendid contemplation too, when one (who has traveled these realms and can duly appreciate them) imagines them as they might in the future be seen (by some protective policy of government) preserved in their pristine beauty and wildness, in a magnificent park, where the world could see for ages to come, the native Indian in his classic attire, galloping his wild horse amid the fleeting herds of elks and buffalos. What a specimen for America to preserve for her refined citizens and the world, in future ages. A nations park, containing man and beast, in all the wild and freshness of their nature's beauty. I would ask

---

[2] Central Park, the outgrowth of numerous earlier suggestions for a large public park on Manhattan Island, was first proposed by a group of prominent citizens in 1850. In 1853 the state Legislature authorized its establishment and the purchase of necessary lands; land acquisition was begun late in the same year [2,5,16] .

[3] Olmsted was appointed superintendent of Central Park in 1857. In 1858 the design for improvement of the area proposed by Olmsted and Calvert Vaux was approved by the park commissioners; in general outline, this plan served as a guide to subsequent development [2,5,16] . Olmsted's connection with the Yosemite Grant occurred during the period when he was manager of General Fremont's Mariposa Estate in California [3,17] .

[4] Catlin's letters, together with his drawings, were later published in book form [4] .

no other monument to my memory, nor any other enrollment of my name amongst the famous dead, than the reputation of having been the founder of such an institution [4].

This statement is highly significant in that it antedates by more than three decades the establishment of the first area of wild land for public benefit primarily because of recreational values (Yosemite Grant, 1864), and by nearly forty years the establishment of the first national park (Yellowstone, 1872). It is a reflection of the change from negative American attitudes toward nature, which began early in the eighteenth century. This change in attitude resulted in large measure from poets, writers, and artists whose works extolled nature's beauties, thus making the interests of the outdoors more meaningful [12]. In Catlin's remarks one observes the dawn of an awareness of the aesthetic and cultural qualities inherent in significant segments of typical, primitive America and the need for their preservation. In a somewhat similar vein Thoreau also expressed the growing interest in protection of wild places about the middle of the past century [12]. Such ideas, firmly linked with the establishment of national parks, were also important in the designation of other types of wild land for various outdoor recreational purposes.

The Yosemite Grant.   The Yosemite Grant, established in 1864, was the first extensive area of wild land to be set aside primarily for public recreation. Although the federal government did not assume administrative authority for the Yosemite Grant at the time of its establishment, and did not recognize its responsibility in that direction, interest in the unique character of the Yosemite Valley and the nearby Mariposa Grove of Big Trees[5] prompted it to entrust these parts of the public domain to the state of California "upon the express conditions that the premises shall be held for public use, resort, and recreation; shall be inalienable for all time. . . ."[17,19][6]

---

[5] Commonly known as giant sequoia (*Sequoia gigantea*); some authorities consider this tree as a single species in a distinct genus—*Sequoiadendron giganteum*.

[6] The first civilized men to see the valley were American trappers, members of the Walker expedition, who viewed it from the north rim in the fall of 1833, while laboriously journeying westward across the Sierra Nevada [6,17]. In March, 1851, the valley was first entered by the Mariposa Battalion, a group of American citizen-soldiers organized to put down an Indian uprising that followed the discovery of gold in California [17]. The recalcitrant Yosemites, for whom the Mariposa Battalion named the valley, were pursued to this point.

    The first "tourist party" visited Yosemite Valley in June, 1855 [17]. This journey was prompted by accounts of the earlier military expeditions which appeared in San Francisco newspapers. One of these accounts mentioned a spectacular waterfall of prodigious height. James M. Hutchings, then publishing the *California Magazine* in San Francisco, became intrigued with the possibility of describing such a spectacle in his publication; with several companions, including an artist and two Indian guides, he made the long horseback

The bill concerning the Yosemite Grant was introduced into Congress on March 28, 1864, by Senator John Conness of California, who stated that its purpose was:

. . . To commit them [Yosemite Valley and the Mariposa Grove of Big Trees] to the care of the authorities of that State for their constant preservation, that they may be exposed to public view, and that they may be used and preserved for the benefit of mankind. . . . The plan [of preservation] comes from gentlemen of fortune, of taste, and of refinement. . . . The bill was prepared by the commissioner of the General Land Office, who takes a great interest in the preservation both of Yosemite Valley and the Big Trees Grove [17]. [7]

It was passed by the Senate on May 17, passed by the House on June 29, and signed by President Abraham Lincoln on July 1, 1864 [17].

This was a memorable event, especially when one considers that it occurred during the Civil War, one of the darkest periods of our history. It is also significant that the language of the bill establishing the Yosemite Grant paralleled the intent of later national parks. Further, Frederick Law Olmsted, one of the planners and an early administrator of Central Park in New York City, as previously noted, was one of those who supported the establishment of the Yosemite Grant; he also served as one of its original commissioners [3,17]. [8]

---

journey into the Sierra and "spent five glorious days in scenic banqueting" in the valley [11,17]. As a result of publicity given Yosemite Valley by Hutchings, interest in the area quickly developed. Soon, various well-known publications of the period began extolling the interests of the area, and prominent writers, artists, photographers, and public figures added their praise.

Coincident with developing interest in Yosemite Valley was the discovery of several groves of giant sequoia on the western slope of the Sierra, including the one located a few miles south of Yosemite Valley. In 1857 and 1858, the *Atlantic Monthly* and *Harper's Weekly* began agitating for the preservation of these groves [12].

Thus the idea of preserving significant areas in their natural state for the enjoyment of present and future generations began to take form. Further, by 1864, there was need for immediate positive action; as part of the public domain Yosemite Valley was subject to entry, and several units of it had already been acquired by private individuals. The establishment of the Yosemite Grant gave priority to public rights in the area and, after considerable litigation, claimants to certain lands in the valley were satisfied with a financial settlement [13,17].

[7] Also see *Congressional Globe,* May 14, 1864, p. 2301.

[8] Olmsted had left New York City a few years earlier to undertake the management of the Mariposa Estate, a large tract of land owned by General Fremont and located in the foothill region near Yosemite [17]. Primarily because of his experience in landscape architecture and park planning, Olmsted assumed the major responsibility of the early administration of the Yosemite Grant; he served as its original custodian [3].

Early Commercial Recreational Facilities

In passing, one should not overlook the significance of early interest in general recreational travel and commercial recreational facilities in the outdoors [12]. This interest was, naturally, first manifested in the East. Accommodations for visitors were available at Franconia Notch in the White Mountains as early as 1820, and a hotel, later considerably enlarged in response to public patronage, was built in the Catskills in 1825. These were among the earliest visitor accommodations in out-of-the-way places, although a number of health resorts and more readily accessible beach locations on the Atlantic had been utilized by the public for some time. Following the opening of the Erie Canal, in 1827, canalboats offering sleeping and eating facilities began making trips through New York State to Lake Ontario. For more than a decade this mode of travel was in high favor. Soon thereafter, travel to outlying areas was extended by early railroads of the Eastern seaboard region. Thus, early public interest in the recreational values of wild land preceded the first official actions concerning the perpetuation of them.

These early recreational facilities were the seeds from which our modern, diversified, and extensive "tourist industry" has grown. Slowly, as communities in various parts of the United States developed and achieved a sense of permanence, and as travel facilities improved, public recreational interest in distant places expanded.

Summary

The recreational use of land dates from antiquity. Origins of such use can be traced to ancient parks and related areas of the Middle East and parts of southern Asia. Later such use was manifested in early Greece and Rome, eventually spreading to other sections of Europe during feudal times and the Renaissance.

Although there were exceptions, such lands were initially established by the nobility for their personal pleasure and prestige. Through different periods of history they assumed different forms, according to the mode of the times, such as sites set aside for games and athletic contests, hunting preserves, and formal gardens.

Eventually, as democratic principles gradually replaced earlier autocratic systems of government, many of these areas were made increasingly available to the general public. Some surviving remnants of these early European areas are now well-known public parks and reserves.

Establishment of wild lands for public recreational use was one of the important aspects of the American conservation movement, which began to take form during the latter part of the nineteenth century, and which also involved protection of forests, wildlife, and related natural resources. Earliest manifestations of public interest in such matters included the reservation of the Great

Ponds by the Massachusetts Bay Colony in 1641, establishment of the Hot Springs Reservation in the Ouachita Mountains of Arkansas in 1832, and the birth of the national park concept—including the first proposal of a national park in 1833 and the establishment of the Yosemite Grant in 1864. The Yosemite Grant, forerunner of Yosemite National Park, was the first area of wild land set aside specifically for public recreational use.

Establishment of public areas by pioneer communities during the American colonial period is closely related to concepts of public recreational use of wild lands. Though recreation was but one of the initial values of such early public areas, recreational uses expanded and eventually became dominant as these communities grew in size. They were the basis of our present municipal park systems. One of the most noteworthy municipal parks is Central Park in New York City, which dates from 1853. Its early administration, planning, and development were largely in the hands of Frederick Law Olmsted, who later supported establishment of the Yosemite Grant, was one of its original commissioners, and served as its original custodian.

Olmsted was a most competent land-use planner. He understood the separation of land uses and natural scenery. Some of his development principles for Yosemite Valley are still in effect today.

However, public interest in the recreational values of wild lands preceded recognition of official responsibility in the protection of these values. The first commercial accommodations necessary for recreational use of wild lands were provided in the Northeast as early as the 1820s. Later expansion of such facilities, together with early development of relatively comfortable means of travel, were the nuclei of our present important "travel industry."

Selected References

1. Allen, Shirley W., and Grant W. Sharpe: "An Introduction to American Forestry," 3d ed., McGraw-Hill, New York, 1960.

2. Anonymous: "An Outline History of Central Park," City of New York, Department of Parks, n.d. (Mimeographed.)

3. Brockman, C. Frank: Principal Administrative Officers of Yosemite: Frederick Law Olmsted, *Yosemite Nature Notes,* vol. 25, no. 9, pp. 106-110, September, 1946.

4. Catlin, George: "The Manners, Customs, and Condition of the North American Indians," London, 1841, vol. 1, pp. 261-262.

5. Doell, Charles E., and Gerald B. Fitzgerald: "A Brief History of Parks and Recreation in the United States," Athletic Institute, Chicago, 1954.

6. Farquahar, Francis W.: Walker's Discovery of Yosemite, *Sierra Club Bulletin,* vol. 27, no. 4, pp. 35-49, August, 1942.

7. Gotheim, Marie Luise: "A History of Garden Art" (Walter P. Wright, ed.; translation by Laura Archer-Hind), 2 vols., Dent, London, Dutton, New York, 1928.

8. Graham, E. H.: "The Land and Wildlife," Oxford, New York, 1947.

9. Great Britain, Forestry Commission: "Forest of Dean: National Forest Park Guides," His Majesty's Stationery Office, London, 1947.

10. Great Britain, Forestry Commission: "New Forest: Forestry Commission Guide," Her Majesty's Stationery Office, London, 1951. (Reprinted 1952.)

11. Hutchings, James M.: "In the Heart of the Sierras," Pacific Press, Oakland, Calif., 1886.

12. Huth, Hans: "Nature and the American," University of California Press, Berkeley, 1957.

13. Ise, John: "Our National Park Policy," Johns Hopkins, Baltimore, 1961.

14. Leopold, Aldo: "Game Management," Scribner, New York, 1947.

15. Nelson, Beatrice: "State Recreation," National Conference on State Parks, Washington, 1928.

16. Reed, Henry Hope, and Sophia Duckworth: "Central Park: A History and a Guide," Potter, New York, 1967.

17. Russell, Carl P.: "100 Years in Yosemite," University of California Press, Berkeley, 1947.

18. State Street Trust Co.: "State Street: A Brief Account of a Boston Way," Boston, 1906.

19. Tolson, Hillary A.: "Laws Relating to the National Park Service, the National Parks and Monuments," U.S. Government Printing Office, Washington, 1933.

20. U.S. Department of the Interior, Bureau of Labor Statistics: "Park Recreation Areas in the United States," Miscellaneous Publication No. 462, U.S. Government Printing Office, Washington, 1928.

21. U.S. Department of the Interior, National Park Service: "Annual Report of the Superintendent of National Parks to the Secretary of the Interior for the Fiscal Year Ended June 30, 1916," U.S. Government Printing Office, Washington, 1916.

22. U.S. Department of the Interior, National Park Service: "Hot Springs National Park, Arkansas," U.S. Government Printing Office, Washington, 1950.

23. U.S. Department of the Interior, National Park Service: "National Parks and Landmarks," U.S. Government Printing Office, Washington, 1966.

chapter four

GROWTH OF INTEREST IN RECREATIONAL USE OF WILD LAND

Public awareness of the need for all aspects of conservation developed greatly between the establishment of the Yosemite Grant, in 1864, and 1900. During that period our first five national parks, as well as initial state parks, were established. In addition, a number of states formed forestry commissions and state forests, the first federal forest reserves (now known as national forests) were formed, and the nucleus of the U.S. Forest Service evolved. Also important during those years was the establishment of two agencies which were later merged to form the U.S. Fish and Wildlife Service, of which the Bureau of Sport Fisheries and Wildlife administers our National Wildlife Refuge System.

The momentum developed during this period continued beyond the turn of the century and, despite resistance and occasional reverses, lent its force to the expansion and refinement of the entire program of natural-resource and environmental conservation in the United States. A significant feature of such developments was the increase in number and type of areas of wild land to serve the growing demand for recreation.

Development of the National Park System

The National Park System had its genesis in the establishment of the early national parks and monuments. The first area officially designated as a national park was Yellowstone. Claims are sometimes made that the National Park System originated with the establishment of the Hot Springs Reservation in 1832 or with the establishment of the Yosemite Grant in 1864 since both were later given national park status. However, the national park concept had not fully matured at the time those earlier reservations were established, and they were not officially designated as national parks.

The First National Park

Yellowstone National Park, established March 1, 1872 [19,33,56], was the first national park in the United States, as well as in the world. Though it was antedated by several reserves—Hot Springs, 1832; Fontainebleau, near Paris, France, 1853; Yosemite Grant, 1864—establishment of Yellowstone National Park introduced the dramatic new term "national park," which gave emphasis to conservation and crystallized interest in later establishment of other national parks in the United States and throughout the world.

The history of events leading to the establishment of Yellowstone National Park began with the first exploration of that region by John Colter, a member of the Lewis and Clark expedition, in 1807 and 1808 [8].[1] Other adventurers followed in Colter's footsteps.[2] All told unbelievable stories of the Yellowstone area when they returned to civilization. These stories eventually aroused official curiosity, resulting in a number of expeditions to the region.[3]

The most significant exploration of the Yellowstone was conducted in 1870 by a group of nine prominent Montana citizens, led by Henry D. Washburn and Nathaniel P. Langford, with a military escort of five cavalrymen under the command of Lieutenant G. C. Doane. Our first national park resulted from the efforts of this group. The suggestion of a national park is credited to Cornelius Hedges, a lawyer from Helena, Montana, during a discussion about their camp-fire at the junction of the Firehole and Gibbons Rivers, their last camp in what is now Yellowstone National Park, concerning what to do with the results of the expedition. The area was in public domain at that time; anyone had the privilege of establishing a claim in accordance with the law governing such action and

---

[1] Colter had become interested in the upper Missouri region during the expedition's westward trek to the Pacific in 1805. In 1806, upon the expedition's return to the Missouri, he was released at his own request in order to explore that area. He discovered the geysers and other evidences of hydrothermal activity in the Yellowstone, but his reports of these phenomena were received by the outside world with derision. As a result, the Yellowstone country was known for many years as "Colter's Hell" [8].

[2] Joseph Meek, one of a number of "mountain men" engaged in the fur trade, visited Yellowstone in 1829; Warren A. Ferris, clerk of the American Fur Company, penetrated the area on several occasions in the 1830s and 1840s; and James Bridger, fur trader and "mountain man," made numerous visits to the Yellowstone previous to 1850. Like Colter, all these early explorers told of the wonders which they had observed, only to be met with public skepticism. Bridger embellished accounts of his observations with the wildest fancies of his imagination, and his tall tales of Yellowstone have earned him a unique place in the folklore of the early American West [8].

[3] In 1859 and 1860, a government expedition under the command of Captain W. F. Raynolds skirted, but unfortunately never entered, the area now included in the park [8,19]. In September 1869, the Folsom-Cook-Peterson expedition spent a month in the Yellowstone area, during which time many of its wonders were seen. Folsom's account of that trip appeared in the *Western Monthly,* a Chicago publication, in July, 1870. The experience of this group greatly influenced later expeditions; in fact, there is evidence that the idea of a national park was first suggested by Folsom [8].

eventually gaining ownership of desired property. Hedges proposed that the group forgo personal claims and favor establishment of a national park forever to be protected and available to all the people. His suggestion met with general favor [20,28].

However, there is some doubt as to the authenticity of this oft-told tale. It is derived from a statement made by Langford some years later. Others also claimed to have made such a suggestion; and there is evidence that the idea of Yellowstone National Park was influenced by the language of the bill establishing the Yosemite Grant in 1864. Nevertheless, the Washburn-Langford-Doane expedition was primarily responsible for the establishment of the first national park.

After returning to Helena, Langford took steps to achieve the establishment of Yellowstone National Park. The aid of William H. Clagett, newly elected delegate to Congress from Montana, was enlisted. Later, in Washington, Clagett and Langford drew up the Yellowstone bill, which was introduced into the House by Clagett on December 18, 1871 [8].

During the summer of 1871, two government parties made additional studies of the Yellowstone region, one under the leadership of Dr. F. V. Hayden, United States geologist, who became an ardent supporter of the proposed park [8]. In the Hayden party was W. H. Jackson, pioneer photographer, who made a remarkably fine series of Yellowstone photographs, samples of which were placed in the hands of all senators and congressmen by Dr. Hayden. Following a favorable opinion by the Secretary of the Interior, in 1872 the Yellowstone bill was adopted by the House on January 30, passed by the Senate on February 27, and signed by President Grant on March 1 [8,19,33].

Other Early National Parks. In 1890, Sequoia, General Grant (incorporated into Kings Canyon National Park in 1940), and Yosemite National Parks[4] were established [19,56].

In the case of Yosemite, federal parklands surrounded the state-controlled

---

[4] Sequoia and General Grant National Parks owe their existence largely to the efforts of George W. Stewart, editor of the *Visalia Delta* [19,28]. Beginning in 1879, in cooperation with a group of public-spirited citizens, Stewart conducted an active campaign for the preservation of those areas which contain extensive representative stands of giant sequoia.

Yosemite National Park is a monument to John Muir. Muir arrived in Yosemite in 1868 [60]. For several years, he lived and worked in Yosemite Valley and the adjacent Sierra Nevada area, studying that region and observing its despoliation. His enthusiasm and knowledge, gained through personal investigation, soon brought him into national prominence as a writer. His first article appeared in the *Sacramento Record-Union* on Feb. 2, 1876 [27]. Later writings, based upon a hiking trip south from Yosemite in 1875, emphasized the need for preserving the magnificent groves of giant sequoia; these articles aided Stewart and his associates in their efforts to establish Sequoia and General Grant National Parks. Muir attracted the interest of Robert Underwood, editor of *Century Magazine,* and in 1889 he became a regular contributor to that publication [28,60]. His work was to influence thousands of people on matters pertaining to the preservation and wise use of our natural resources.

Yosemite Grant, which was not receded to the federal government until 1906 [19,27,56]. Just before the turn of the century, on March 2, 1899, Mt. Rainier National Park,[5] the fifth of these areas, came into being [19,23,56].

The Antiquities Act. June 8, 1906, marked another important milestone in the development of the National Park System. On that date the Act for the Preservation of American Antiquities, introduced into Congress by Representative John F. Lacey, received the signature of President Theodore Roosevelt and became law [19,28,56]. This act empowered the President of the United States to set aside, as national monuments, areas of federally controlled land containing historic landmarks, historic or prehistoric structures, or other objects of historic or scientific interest.

The Antiquities Act is designed to protect and preserve such interests for the benefit of future as well as present generations; it is similar in general purpose to legislation establishing national parks, except that Presidential proclamation rather than congressional action is usually required.[6] It had the support of numerous archaeologists, historians, and scientists who had recognized the need for such action as a result of gross vandalism at many significant unprotected sites. Within one year after passage of the Antiquities Act, five of our present series of more than fourscore national monuments had been established.[7]

A number of national parks[8] were originally national monuments [56]. In those cases, the areas were protected until legislation necessary for their redefinition as national parks could be prepared and passed by Congress.

Although an area receives more secure protection as a national park than as a national monument, considerable time is often required before the support of a majority of the members of Congress can be obtained for the establishment of a national park. In such cases there is danger that efforts may become mired in a morass of legal and political technicalities. Further, forewarned by public interest in an area, those having selfish interest may take

---

[5] The establishment of Mt. Rainier National Park resulted from the combined efforts of the National Geographic Society, the American Association for the Advancement of Science, the Geographical Society of America, the Sierra Club, and the Appalachian Mountain Club [19,23]. Although the original bill, introduced into Congress by Senator Watson Squire of the state of Washington in 1894, did not receive favorable action, a revised bill passed both houses of Congress in 1899 and, on Mar. 2 of that year, was signed by President McKinley.

[6] A number of national monuments have been established by congressional action, representing exceptions to normal procedure.

[7] Devils Tower, Wyoming, Sept. 24, 1906; El Morro, New Mexico, Dec. 8, 1906; Montezuma Castle, Arizona, Dec. 8, 1906; Petrified Forest, Arizona, Dec. 8, 1906; Chaco Canyon, New Mexico, Mar. 11, 1907. Casa Grande National Monument, established Mar. 2, 1889, was administered as a national park until Aug. 3, 1918, when it was changed to national monument status [53].

[8] Carlsbad Caverns, Grand Canyon, Olympic, Zion, Bryce, Petrified Forest.

advantage of the time lag, legally establish themselves, and destroy, or at least greatly modify, the unique character of the area in question. Since establishment of a national monument usually involves action by but one man—the President— it can be accomplished with greater dispatch. Although national monuments can be decreased or increased in area by Presidential proclamation, only congressional action can eliminate them. Thus, although the protection given these areas is not so absolute as that given national parks, it renders them inviolate as long as they retain a satisfactory area or, as has been desirable in several cases, until they are redefined by congressional action as national parks.

National Park Service Formed

The National Park Act, passed by Congress in 1916 and signed by President Woodrow Wilson on August 25 of that year, coordinated the administration of the national parks then in existence, as well as that of certain national monuments, under a central, specialized authority and laid down certain basic tenets for their proper management and use [19,28,30,33,52,53,56].

Early Difficulties in National Park Administration. Establishment of the **National Park Service was prompted by numerous difficulties in national park** administration which developed as the number of parks increased [19,28,30]. The difficulties were manifested almost immediately after the establishment of Yellowstone National Park in 1872, for in the designation of that area Congress made no provision for financial support of an adequate program of administration or protection, or for legal authority to enforce rules and regulations. These important considerations were also largely neglected in the establishment of many later national parks. As a result, there developed a disjointed relation between various national parks, and the lack of a cohesive administrative authority threatened to undermine the concept upon which the parks had been founded and to impair the public services they were intended to render.

During the first five years of the existence of Yellowstone National Park, N. P. Langford served as superintendent without remuneration. The protection of wildlife in Yellowstone National Park was generally ignored during its early years; not until 1894, after a particularly flagrant violation involving hunting in the park, did Congress provide for formal law enforcement or define park offenses and specific penalties. Meanwhile, many applications for leases and concessions of various kinds were received from people who failed to understand national park objectives, and some of the early superintendents who followed Langford not only lacked appreciation of the basic concept of the national park idea but even became unwisely involved in irregular practices in operating facilities for visitors. This untenable situation eventually prompted action. In 1883 a bill was passed by Congress permitting the Secretary of the Interior to request the War Department to assign troops to Yellowstone National Park for the purpose of patrolling the area. Soon thereafter, such a request was made, and from 1886 to 1918, units of cavalry protected Yellowstone National Park; their commanding officers served as acting superintendents. This period also witnessed the construction of the park's basic highway system by the Corps of Engineers [8,15,28,30].

From 1901 to 1914, Sequoia, General Grant, and Yosemite National Parks also were protected by the United States Cavalry [15,19,27,28]. As in the case of Yellowstone, the officers who served as acting superintendents left an outstanding record of achievement.

For a number of years several national parks, such as Mt. Rainier National Park in the state of Washington [19], and many national monuments which were adjacent to, or surrounded by, national forests were administered by the U.S. Forest Service. In such cases the forest supervisor also acted as the principal administrative officer of the national park or national monument.

Such irregular divisions of responsibility in the field had a counterpart in the lack of unified authority in the office of the Department of the Interior in Washington, D.C. There, responsibility for the national parks was assigned to various officials of the Department who handled such matters in addition to their regular duties [19,28].

Early Suggestions of a National Parks Bureau.   A bureau of national parks was first suggested by Dr. Horace McFarland, president of the American Civic Association, and Charles Evans Hughes, governor of New York, during the National Conservation Conference of Governors in 1908 [19,28,30]. Although nothing tangible resulted from the suggestion, McFarland, with the backing of the American Civic Association, continued to work toward that goal. The U.S. Forest Service, which the dynamic Gifford Pinchot had welded into a coordinated whole in 1905, served as his example. In 1910, McFarland found official support in Secretary of the Interior Richard A. Ballinger, who, in his report to the President that same year, advocated a national parks bureau with an adequate qualified staff [28].

In 1911, Walter L. Fisher became Secretary of the Interior. He had a deep interest in the national parks and, backed by the railroads and the American Automobile Association, he called a meeting of national park officials and other interested individuals in Yellowstone National Park [28].

A similar conference was held in Yosemite National Park in 1912. Thus, for the first time, friends and officials of the national parks joined in a discussion of common problems; on both occasions a national parks bureau was advocated. These meetings had the personal blessing of President Taft, who, in a speech before the American Civic Association in 1911, stated that he was keenly aware of the unsatisfactory administrative status of the national parks [28].

During this period, W. B. Aker, an assistant attorney in the Department of the Interior, served as liaison officer for the national parks in addition to other duties [19,28,30]. Although he was required to concern himself with only the fiscal affairs of the national parks, he was sincerely interested in all aspects of national park matters. He rendered a service far greater than could normally have been expected from anyone in a similar position.

By 1912, the need for a national parks bureau was so obvious that on February 2 President Taft sent a special message to Congress in which he stated:

I earnestly recommend the establishment of a Bureau of National Parks. Such legislation is essential to the proper management of these wonderful manifestations of nature. . . . The first step in that direction is the establishment of a responsible bureau, which shall take upon itself the burden of supervising the parks and of making recommendations as to the best method of improving their accessibility and usefulness [28].

Although Congress failed to take action on the President's suggestion, the idea continued to ferment. In 1913, Franklin Lane became Secretary of the Interior, and, in lieu of a national parks bureau, he broadened the responsibilities of the position of assistant to the secretary and gave that post to Adolph C. Miller, professor of economics at the University of California [28]. Miller, to whom specific responsibility for the national parks was delegated, supervised work on appropriate bills relative to the establishment of a national parks bureau; in addition, he set up the framework for better correlation between national parks then in existence by appointing Mark Daniels as superintendent of national parks [28].

Before Miller had completed six months of service, he was "drafted" by President Wilson for a post concerned with the Federal Reserve Act [28]. Daniels continued as superintendent of national parks, but the problem of finding a suitable replacement for Miller was not solved until the following year. At that time Secretary Lane received a letter of complaint about the administration of the national parks, signed by Stephen T. Mather. Lane knew this man well. He was a friend and former classmate at the University of California, a successful Chicago businessman who had been making regular summer pilgrimages into the western mountains for years, and a member of the Sierra Club of California, the Prairie Club of Chicago, and the American Civic Association. Lane asked Mather to assume responsibility for the administration of the national parks and, at a considerable financial sacrifice, Mather accepted. On June 21, 1915 [19,28,30], he was sworn in as assistant to the secretary. Horace Albright, who had come to Washington with Miller the previous year, was assigned to work with Mather [19,28,30]. These two men continued in intimate association from that day until the time of Mather's resignation in 1929.

Passage of the National Park Service Act.   Soon after his appointment as assistant to the secretary, Stephen T. Mather vigorously attacked the problem of establishing a bureau of national parks. With the help of Horace Albright he enlisted the aid of Congressman William Kent and a group of men[9] who were vitally interested in the national parks. This group worked cooperatively to

---

[9] John Raker, Dr. Horace McFarland, Frederick Law Olmsted, Robert S. Yard, Robert B. Marshall, Enos Mills, Henry A. Barker, Richard E. Watrous, and Gilbert Grosvenor.

prepare a park service bill which was finally passed by both the House and the Senate. On August 25, 1916, the act establishing the National Park Service was signed by President Woodrow Wilson [19,28,33]. Stephen T. Mather was named Director of the fledgling bureau.

Mather was a strong, dedicated leader who attracted supporters, and was able to organize a loyal and competent staff to operate the National Park Service. Wealthy in his own right, he invested his own funds for worthy park projects which he personally inspected whenever possible. Though interested in the preservation of parks as natural preserves, he also felt the need for roads and adequate hotel developments in the parks to encourage travel and thus gain support from the automobile and railroad traveler. He was also concerned for the education of the visitor and encouraged the establishment of interpretive services in the National Park system.

Aided by his able assistant, Horace Albright, who followed him as Director from 1929 to 1933, Mather's philosophy and policies persisted for many years in the National Park Service. His influence was crucial in the development of the National Park Service and established a pattern for strong agency growth and personnel loyalty. The orientation of the service has been primarily toward the national seasonal visitor rather than the local community. This is contrary to the Forest Service position, which has been toward the local community and its economic interest.

At the time of its establishment the National Park Service was given jurisdiction over fifteen national parks then in existence,[10] as well as twenty-one national monuments [52]. Since that time the National Park Service has greatly expanded in size, diversity of areas, and responsibilities. The number of national parks and national monuments has increased, and additional legislation has provided for the inclusion of other types of areas within the National Park System.[11] By 1937, growing complexity of the National Park System prompted

---

[10]National parks under the jurisdiction of the National Park Service upon its establishment on Aug. 25, 1916, were Casa Grande Ruin (established 1889), Crater Lake (established 1902), General Grant (established 1890), Glacier (established 1910), Hawaii (established Aug. 1, 1916), Lassen Volcanic (established Aug. 9, 1916), Mesa Verde (established 1906), Mt. Rainier (established 1899), Platt (established 1906), Rocky Mountain (established 1915), Sequoia (established 1890), Sullys Hill (established 1904), Wind Cave (established 1903), Yellowstone (established 1872), and Yosemite (established 1890) [52].

In addition to the aforementioned national parks, the Hot Springs Reservation was also placed under National Park Service administration [52].

Casa Grande Ruin, established Mar. 2, 1889, was reclassified as a national monument on Aug. 3, 1918 [54]. Sullys Hill National Park was abolished and turned over to the Biological Survey, now the U.S. Fish and Wildlife Service, for a game preserve on Mar. 3, 1931 [55]. General Grant National Park was incorporated into Kings Canyon National Park upon the establishment of that area on Mar. 4, 1940 [56].

[11]The act of Feb. 21, 1925, provided for the acquisition of lands, through donations, in the southern Appalachian Mountains and Mammoth Cave regions of Kentucky for national parks. Previously, national parks and national monuments had been set aside from public

establishment of several regional offices for purposes of decentralized administration [56].

Early Interest in Forest Conservation

As early as 1867 the states of Michigan and Wisconsin formed fact-finding committees for the purpose of studying and reporting upon the destruction of their forest resources. Similar action was taken by Maine in 1869 and, within a few years, by a number of other Eastern states. By 1885, the states of New York, California, Colorado, and Ohio had formed forestry commissions.[12]

The first tangible interest in forest conservation by the federal government was manifested in 1876, when Dr. Franklin B. Hough was appointed as a forestry agent in the Department of Agriculture. Hough's appointment, resulting from official interest in an address he gave at the annual meeting of the Amer-

---

lands. Following authorization by Congress in 1926, the act eventually resulted in the establishment of Great Smoky Mountains, Mammoth Cave, and Shenandoah National Parks, supplementing Acadia, first national park in the eastern United States [57].

The act of Mar. 3, 1933, provided for an Executive order consolidating all national parks and national monuments, national military parks, national battlefield parks and sites, certain national cemeteries, national memorials, and the national capital parks under the administration of the National Park Service. Previously, some of the aforementioned areas had been administered by the War Department, U.S. Forest Service, and other federal agencies [56,57].

The Historic Sites Act of Aug. 21, 1935, provided for the establishment and protection of national historic sites, as well as a wide range of relevant historical programs [56,57].

The Park, Parkways and Recreation Area Study Act of June 23, 1936, authorized studies related to development of the National Park System, including areas having primary recreational interests [57].

The act of June 30, 1936, provided for the administration and maintenance of the Blue Ridge Parkway by the National Park Service, thus introducing the concept of the rural parkway into the National Park System [57].

The act of Aug. 17, 1937, established Cape Hatteras National Seashore, first area of its type in the National Park System [57].

The act of Aug. 7, 1946, provided the National Park Service with authority to administer recreation on areas under jurisdiction of other federal agencies. This resulted in cooperative agreements with the Bureau of Reclamation and other federal agencies for administration of recreation on such areas as Lake Mead and Glen Canyon National Recreation Areas [56,57].

The act of Aug. 7, 1961, authorizing the establishment of Cape Cod National Seashore, provided for the use of appropriated funds at the outset for the purchase of lands for park use. Previously such areas had been established by setting aside public lands, or through initial donations of land to the federal government by public or private interests [57].

[12]Initial forestry commissions in California, Colorado, and Ohio soon became inoperative; thus, New York has the distinction of having the oldest record of official state forestry activities [1,18].

ican Association for the Advancement of Science in 1873, was the seed from which the U.S. Forest Service grew [1,18]. Today this agency administers the important recreational resources of the national forests as part of its multiple-use program.

Development of the U.S. Forest Service

By 1881, as a result of the activities of Franklin B. Hough and supporters of his program, federal interest in forestry broadened [1,18]. In that year the Division of Forestry was established in the Department of Agriculture; its purpose was purely advisory. It was not until 1891 that the first federally controlled forest, known as the Yellowstone Timberland Reserve, was established from the public domain. For more than a decade, the administration of this and other early reserves was vested in the General Land Office of the Department of the Interior. The completely separate Division of Forestry, elevated to the status of a bureau in 1901, continued to serve in an advisory capacity in their management. It was 1905 before the federal forest reserves were placed under the control of federal foresters of the Bureau of Forestry; soon thereafter the names Bureau of Forestry and forest reserve were changed, respectively to U.S. Forest Service and national forest—designations by which they are known today.

The amalgamation of federal foresters and federal forest lands under a unified administration and the organization of the U.S. Forest Service in approximately its present form resulted largely from the efforts of Gifford Pinchot, charismatic early forestry leader.

Pinchot, who had become affiliated with the Division of Forestry during the early stages of its development, was placed in charge of its activities in 1898 [1] and immediately instituted a militant campaign to correlate federal forestry activities. When these efforts bore fruit in 1905, he continued as chief of the U.S. Forest Service,[13] greatly strengthening this bureau and surrounding himself with loyal associates. He received the cooperation of President Theodore Roosevelt, whose interest in various phases of natural-resource conservation was manifested in many ways. President Roosevelt called a conference of political, business, and scientific leaders in 1908 to consider broadly interrelated problems concerning the conservation of natural resources. This conference, known as the National Conservation Conference of Governors [1,18], had far-reaching effects. It was responsible for extensive additions to the national forests, the establishment of many state conservation commissions, and a National Conservation Commission, appointed by the President with Pinchot as chairman [1,18]. This

---

[13]Although Pinchot resigned as chief of the U.S. Forest Service during the administration of President William Howard Taft as a result of a controversy with Secretary of the Interior Ballinger over public-land-management questions, he organized the U.S. Forest Service along fundamental lines which continued to guide the programs of his successors [1,18].

commission developed an inventory of the nation's natural resources and suggested plans for their proper use. However, recreational land values were ignored.

Early proponents of forest conservation did not consider recreation as an important natural resource of forest land. The establishment of forest reserves and, later, the organization of the U.S. Forest Service were motivated by interest in the sustained yield of other values such as timber, forage, and water. Orientation was toward local economies and needs for forest products.

For many years the two major aspects of natural-resource conservation, one concerned with the preservation of significant or scenically beautiful areas in parks and the other with the proper use of more tangible assets in forest reserves, were considered as separate entities with little in common and largely incompatible. Nevertheless, as will be noted later, legislation, by which the original forest reserves were established, provided for eventual broadening of the program of multiple use of national forest resources to include recreation.

Development of Recreational Use of National Forests

In addition to being an important source of timber, forage, and other tangible natural resources, national forests today are vital units in our outdoor recreational program. The U.S. Forest Service has developed the recreational potential of areas in its charge as one of several important values of the national forests, and it has coordinated such recreational uses with those of other important recreational lands. But the current extensive recreational use of national forests was not typical of the first years of the forest conservation movement in the United States. Early foresters could not envisage today's great public interest in the recreational values of the national forests; at that time, few people did. There was little to indicate the eventual need for our present extensive system of varied outdoor recreational areas. Consequently, although a few forestry leaders began calling attention to growing public interest in, and use of, national forests for outdoor recreation about 1910, official U.S. Forest Service recognition of recreation as a valid national forest resource did not develop for more than a decade. Further, for many years many foresters exhibited a negative attitude toward such use.

The reasons for this early negative attitude are not difficult to understand. In their formative period the national forests were largely undeveloped: their boundaries were not clearly defined; the nature and abundance of their varied natural resources were not fully inventoried or understood; road and trail development was meager; and, when it existed, the technical training of limited personnel was largely based upon European standards which had to be reevaluated to meet American conditions. These and related difficulties were slowly corrected as appropriations increased and as experience developed.

In addition, early American forestry education emphasized technical matters pertaining to the production, harvesting, and utilization of tangible forest products. Recreation, which it neglected, posed problems of a very different and more intangible kind.

The early negative attitude of foresters toward recreation was further influenced by unfortunate personality clashes between forestry leaders and exponents of complete preservation, mostly relative to controversies over jurisdiction of certain lands.[14]

Although interest in other values of forest land prompted the establishment of the first federal forest reserves, early legislation relative to these areas can be interpreted as providing for public recreational use. The act of June 4, 1897,[15] which outlined the broad policy of management for the forest reserves, included the following provisions [34] :

He [the Secretary] may make such rules and regulations and establish such service as will insure the objects of such reservations, namely, to regulate their occupancy and use and to preserve the forests theron from destruction. . . .
Nor shall anything herein prohibit any person from entering upon such forest reservations for all proper and lawful purposes. . . . Provided, that such persons comply with the rules and regulations covering such forest reservations.

The act of February 28, 1899,[16] opened the door still wider for the public utilization of recreational values in the national forests, as indicated in this passage [34] .

The Secretary of the Interior . . . hereby is authorized, under such rules and regulations as he from time to time may make, to enter or lease to responsible persons or corporations applying therefore suitable spaces and portions of ground near, or adjacent to, mineral, medicinal, or other springs, within any forest reserves established within the United States, or hereafter to be established, and where the public is accustomed or desires to frequent, for health or

---

[14]One of the earliest of the controversies involved the damming and subsequent flooding of Hetch Hetchy Valley in Yosemite National Park, a struggle which began about the turn of the century, when the city of San Francisco became interested in reservoir sites in the Sierra Nevada as a source of water for her expanding population [28,30,60]. Gifford Pinchot, chief of the U.S. Forest Service, favored the development of the Hetch Hetchy project. He was opposed by a group led by John Muir, famous writer, naturalist, and founder of the Sierra Club. The issue was not resolved until 1908, when access to the Hetch Hetchy Valley was granted to the city of San Francisco [27] . Construction of the dam and development of the reservoir resulted.

Later, a number of areas which qualified for national park status were withdrawn from the national forests and placed under a separate administration as national parks [28]. Several of these transfers evoked bitter debate over the priority of land use; these disagreements further embittered foresters, delaying their recognition of recreation as a valid forest resource.

[15]30 Stat. 35; 16 U.S.C. 551; and 30 Stat. 36; 16 U.S.C. 482.
[16]30 Stat. 908; 16 U.S.C. 495.

pleasure, for the purpose of erecting upon such leased ground sanitoriums or hotels, to be opened for the reception of the public.

It should be pointed out that the early negative attitude toward recreation on national forest lands was not shared by all Forest Service employees and members of the forestry profession. Many, notably Aldo Leopold, Robert Marshall, and Arthur Carhart, were responsible for many advances in recreational use of national forest lands which are of primary importance today. In particular, both Leopold[17] and Marshall[18] were exponents of wilderness. The nuclei of our National Wilderness Preservation System were the primitive, wilderness, and wild areas of the national forests,[19] administratively designated by the U.S. Forest Service [44].

One of the first employees of the U.S. Forest Service to publicly recognize the recreational values of the national forests, and the trends of public interest in them, was Treadwell Cleveland, Jr. In an article "National Forests as Recreation Grounds," published in 1910 by the American Academy of Political and Social Science, Philadelphia, Cleveland made this statement [10,22] :

Fortunately, the objects for which the National Forests were created and are maintained, will guarantee the permanence of their resources and will bring about their fullest development for every use. . . .

So great is the value of national forest area for recreation, and so certain is this value to increase with the growth of the country, and the shrinkage of the wilderness, that even if the forest resources of wood and water were not to be required by the civilization of the future, many of the forests ought certainly to be preserved, in the interest of national health and well-being, for recreation use alone.

Recognition of the recreational values of the national forests at the highest level is noted for the first time in this excerpt from the annual report of Henry Solon Graves, chief of the U.S. Forest Service, for the fiscal year ending June 30, 1912 [37] :

With the construction of new roads and trails the forests are visited more and more for recreation purposes, and in consequence the demand is growing rapidly for sites on which summer camps, cottages, and hotels may be located. In some

---

[17]See *Journal of Forestry,* vol. 46, no. 8, pp. 605-606, August, 1948.

[18]See *Journal of Forestry,* vol. 38, no. 1, pp. 61-62, January, 1940; also *The Living Wilderness,* vol. 16, no. 38, pp. 10-23, Autumn, 1951.

[19]First of these areas was the Gila Primitive Area in the Gila National Forest of New Mexico, designated in 1924 largely through Leopold's efforts; a portion was reclassified as a wilderness area in 1953. The Bob Marshall Wilderness Area in the Flathead and Lewis and Clark National Forests of Montana memorializes Marshall's efforts.

of the most accessible and desirable locations the land has been divided into suitable lots of from 1 to 5 acres to accommodate as many visitors as possible. The regulations of this department for handling this class of business seem to be entirely satisfactory. Permits are issued promptly and on conditions with which permittees willingly comply.

Some objection is heard to the fact that the permit is revocable in the discretion of the department. If occupancy of lots wanted for summer camps, cottages, and hotels for a period of years could be authorized, more substantial buildings than are now being erected would probably be put up.

Less than three years later, the act of March 4, 1915, authorized the Secretary of Agriculture to issue, for periods not exceeding thirty years, permits to responsible citizens for sites, not to exceed 5 acres, needed for recreation and public convenience [34].

Increasing use of national forests for recreation prompted this statement from Chief Forester Graves in his report for the fiscal year ending June 30, 1917 [38]:

The use of some of the National Forests for recreation purposes is growing to such importance as to be one of the major activities. Upon the Angeles National Forest permits for 814 residences, 26 hotels, and 28 summer resorts were in force at the end of the fiscal year.

It is believed that the use of National Forests along this line, as shown by the foregoing figures, represents only a promising beginning of the development which is to follow.

In 1918, the U.S. Forest Service employed F. A. Waugh to make a five months' field investigation of the recreational values of national forest lands [22]. Waugh's recommendations were outlined in a small booklet, "Recreation Uses on the National Forests," published by the U.S. Government Printing Office in 1918 [59]. This was the first official Forest Service study of recreation; it is important in that it recognized recreation as one of the major uses of the national forests. Recreation, however, was not given specific financial support by the U.S. Forest Service until 1922. Previous to that year limited recreational facilities had been provided without special allotments for that purpose, largely as a matter of expediency and primarily as a means of protecting public health and property. Since the number of people using the national forests for recreation was constantly increasing, such procedure could not continue indefinitely; as a result, annual reports of the Chief Forester began urging official recognition of recreation as a valid resource of the national forests. An excerpt from the report for the fiscal year ending June 30, 1920, follows:

As an important use, it [recreation] bids fair to rank third among the major services performed by the National Forests, with only timber production and stream flow regulation taking precedence of it [39].

The act of May 11, 1922 (Agricultural Appropriation bill), provided $10,000 for recreational development in the national forests [22,44], a sum largely earmarked for improvement of existing campgrounds. That meager appropriation, infinitesimal by present-day standards, is significant in that it was the first tangible support given to recreational use of the national forests. It initiated a trend which soon established recreation as a recognized national forest resource, along with timber, forage, water, and related values. Today, recreation is regarded as of dominant importance on many national forests.

Even in its early stages, development of an active recreational program on national forest lands was recognized as advantageous to forestry as well as to the general public. In an article published in the *Ames Forester* in 1922, Robert G. Schreck of the U.S. Forest Service made this statement regarding recreational development in the national forests [22]:

The recreational movement in the National Forests has done what years of propaganda could never have accomplished. For years the Forest Officers have tried to interest the public in their work and the great necessity for adequate fire protection.

The insertion of recreation into our Forests has [accomplished] and is accomplishing more for the interest of conservation than any other method resorted to. It has not only converted the local people to fire protection, game preservation, and reforestation, but it is acting as a stimulant to increase and arouse interest in the good things that the U.S. Forest Service stands for.

Col. William B. Greeley, chief forester of the U.S. Forest Service from 1920 to 1928, included these paragraphs in his reports for the fiscal years ending June 30, 1924 and 1925:

The coordination of outdoor recreation with timber production is wholly germane to the practice of forestry, and is an essential part of any sound plan of national forest administration [42].

Recreation use, under proper safeguards and supervision, is wholly compatible with timber production and watershed protection and may properly be planned for in systematic forest management [43].

Thus, as implied by Colonel Greeley's words, increasing recreational use of the national forests prompted the U.S. Forest Service to prepare, for the first time, a formal policy to guide the development of such activities. Formulated in 1925 by E. A. Sherman, associate forester, this policy [29] has since been greatly expanded.

Today the importance of recreation as a national forest resource is indicated by the fact that all levels of the U.S. Forest Service organization include recreation specialists with varying degrees of authority and responsibility. Further, though the act of June 4, 1897, which outlined the initial broad management policy of the forest reserves, failed to mention recreation specifically, it was supplemented by the Multiple Use Act of 1960 (P.L. 86-517), which stated that "the national forests are established and shall be administered for outdoor recreation, range, timber, watershed, and wildlife and fish purposes" [44]. Thus recreation was finally recognized, officially, as having importance comparable to that of other national forest resources.

Growth in Recreational Importance of the Public Domain

Over 452 million acres of land, the remaining portion of the original public domain, which at one time exceeded 1.8 billion acres, is administered by the Bureau of Land Management of the Department of the Interior. This agency was formed in 1946 through consolidation of the General Land Office and the Grazing Service. The General Land Office was established in 1812 to survey and, as authorized by various land laws, to dispose of the public domain in various ways conducive to the development of the country;[20] it was also charged with maintaining records of public-land transfers and subsequent ownership and use of such lands. The Grazing Service was established in 1934 to facilitate more orderly management of livestock grazing on about 176 million acres of public rangeland, as directed by the Taylor Grazing Act of the same year. In addition, the Bureau of Land Management inherited responsibility for the multipurpose management of about 2.6 million acres of forest land in western Oregon known as O & C lands,[21] as stated in the O & C Sustained Yield Forestry Act of 1937.

Lands administered by the Bureau of Land Management have long been indirectly related to recreation. Historically they have been used for various unorganized forms of outdoor recreation (hunting and fishing, subject to state laws, as well as hiking, camping, picnicking, and related activities). In addition, large areas of the original public domain were transferred to other public agencies which directly provide for many types of recreational opportunity (national parks and forests, wildlife refuges).

In 1926, as a result of the passage of the Recreation and Public Purposes Act (P.L. 69-386), later amended in 1954 (P.L. 83-287), recreation was officially recognized as a resource along with forage, timber, minerals, and re-

---

[20] Over 1 billion acres of the original public domain have been disposed of since 1786. This includes approximately 301 million acres by cash sale and miscellaneous methods; 287 million acres granted or sold to homesteaders; 229 million acres granted to states for support or schools, colleges and universities, and public projects; 94 million acres granted to certain railroads; 61 million acres given as military bounties; 34 million acres in settlement of private claims; and 34 million acres granted or sold under the Timber Culture Act and related legislation [9,47].

[21] These included public-land grants to the Oregon and California Railroad Co. to aid in construction of a railroad, and to the state of Oregon to aid in construction of the Coos Bay Military Wagon Road. Terms of these grants were not fulfilled, and lands involved were reconveyed to the federal government.

lated values. Many states, counties, municipalities, and nonprofit organizations have obtained lands for recreation under provisions of this act and related land laws. Subsequently, provisions of the Taylor Grazing Act of 1934 (P.L. 73-482), as amended, the O & C Sustained Yield Forestry Act of 1937 (P.L. 75-405), and the Small Tract Act of 1938 (P.L. 75-577), as amended, gave further emphasis to recreational values and use of such lands [46,47,51].

As the pressure of constantly growing demand for additional recreational areas developed, these lands became more directly involved with recreation. By 1958 the first official, specific recreational land-use policy was formulated by the Bureau of Land Management for lands under its jurisdiction [45]. This policy emphasized cooperative activities in the provision of lands for sale, lease, or transfer for recreational purposes; actual development of areas so acquired for recreational use was considered the responsibility of various cooperative agencies. This policy was modified in 1960, when recreational facilities were first constructed by the Bureau of Land Management on O & C lands in western Oregon [47]. By 1963 a separate recreational staff was established to undertake necessary planning and development of recreational resources, together with supervision of related details, on BLM lands. A further significant departure from earlier policies was the designation of certain areas for permanent management, including recreational management, by this agency. Thus, uses of lands administered by the Bureau of Land Management, initially considered of little importance for general public recreational purposes, are now being closely coordinated with recreational uses of other public and private lands to give force and effect to national policies concerned with the provision of varied outdoor recreational opportunities and the perpetuation of environmental interest and beauty.

Wildlife Conservation Developments Pertinent to Recreation

Federal wildlife conservation programs, gradually expanded and improved over many years, make significant contributions to public outdoor recreation. Though hunters and fishermen are the major beneficiaries of such programs, the benefits are by no means limited to those groups. Recreationists interested primarily in observing or photographing wildlife also are favored.

Bureau of Sport Fisheries and Wildlife, U.S. Fish and Wildlife Service

The history of tangible steps toward the conservation of native wildlife species in the United States by the federal government covers approximately 100 years, dating from 1871, when Congress passed the act establishing the Commission of Fish and Fisheries [6], predecessor of the Bureau of Fisheries of the Department of Commerce. In 1886 Congress passed another act, establishing the Division of Economic Ornithology and Mammalogy, later the Bureau of Biological Survey of the Department of Agriculture [6]. Although these two federal agencies were originally concerned only with research and investigation, their scope in later years was gradually broadened to encompass the protection and management of native fishes and wildlife. In 1939 the Bureau of Fisheries of the Department of Commerce and the Bureau of Biological Survey of the Department of Agriculture were, by authority of the Reorganization Act of 1933, amalgamated into one organization known as the U.S. Fish and Wildlife Service[22] and placed in the Department of the Interior [6]. Since 1953 the U.S. Fish and Wildlife Service has comprised two separate bureaus, the Bureau of Sport Fisheries and Wildlife and the Bureau of Commercial Fisheries. The diversified program of the Bureau of Sport Fisheries and Wildlife is highly important to recreational use of wild land. In particular, this bureau manages our extensive National Wildlife Refuge System.

National Wildlife Refuge System

The federal program of wildlife refuge acquisition and development originated in 1903, when the Pelican Island National Wildlife Refuge, a 5-acre area on the east coast of Florida, was established by Executive order of President Theodore Roosevelt. It protects a favorite nesting site of the brown pelican [6]. However, the federal program of wildlife refuge acquisition and development first assumed major importance in 1929 when the Migratory Bird Conservation Act was passed [6]. This act was the cornerstone of the National Wildlife Refuge System, which includes over 300 units of land with an aggregate area of over 28 million acres [6,50].

National wildlife refuges, game ranges, and fish hatcheries, though established for conservation of wildlife and their environments, are increasingly utilized by the general public for outdoor recreation. Such use, provided that it is compatible with the primary wildlife purposes of such areas, was authorized in 1962. In addition, acquisition of limited areas of adjacent lands for necessary recreational development, where such development on refuges may have adverse effects on fish and wildlife populations, or on management operations, was also authorized.[23]

---

[22]Between 1871 and 1939 a number of other important steps were taken by the federal government in the interest of wildlife protection and management. The Lacey Act, passed in 1900 [6,14], was designed to halt indiscriminate slaughter of native birds and mammals. In 1918, following the ratification in 1916 of a treaty between the United States and Great Britain relative to the protection of birds migrating between the United States and Canada, the Migratory Bird Treaty Act was passed. This act was later amended to fulfill requirements of a migratory-bird treaty with Mexico, ratified in 1937 [6,7,13,14].

Other legislation includes the Migratory Bird Hunting Stamp Act of 1934, amended in 1939, and the Federal Aid in Wildlife Restoration Act of 1937 [6,12]. The former provided for the annual purchase of a duck stamp by all migratory-bird hunters for the purpose of financing research in waterfowl management, as well as for the acquisition of waterfowl sanctuaries; the latter levied an excise tax on hunting arms and ammunition for the purpose of developing a special fund to be used in aiding the state in various wildlife projects.

[23]Act of Sept. 29, 1962 (P.L. 87-714), as amended (16 U.S.C. 460 (b)-460 (k) (4).

Recreational Use of Federal Reclamation Projects

Projects developed by the Tennessee Valley Authority, the Bureau of Reclamation, and the Corps of Engineers, primarily for irrigation, hydroelectric power, flood control, improvement of navigation, and related purposes, began to assume major importance for recreation in the 1930s. Today recreation is officially recognized as one of many benefits of these multipurpose projects.

However, only in the case of the Tennessee Valley Authority, established in 1933 [13], was legal provision made for development of recreational resources at its inception. For the Bureau of Reclamation and the Corps of Engineers, both established at a much earlier date.[24] recreation was largely an afterthought. Legal authority for recreational development was provided only after problems developed from increasing public recreational use of their reservoirs despite lack of adequate facilities. Thus, these agencies "backed into" recreation because of public demand rather than initial official recognition of the inherent recreational values of waters and lands under their jurisdiction.

All three of these agencies have since developed recreational policies in response to expanding public interest in recreational opportunities available on these reclamation projects. These policies, founded upon various legislative acts, are basically similar. They lean strongly toward indirect rather than direct development and management of recreational potential, usually involving provision of recreational land by various means to other public and, in some instances, private interests, or transfer of recreational responsibilities to other public agencies more directly concerned with, or having longer experience in, management.

Tennessee Valley Authority [12,13,31,32,51]

Authorization for development of the recreational potential of TVA projects is contained in the Tennessee Valley Authority Act of 1933 (P.L. 73-17) and Executive Order No. 616, June 8, 1933. This act provided for transfer, lease, or sale of lands having recognized recreational potential to other federal as well as state and local agencies and, under certain conditions, to private organizations and individuals. Between 1933 and 1937 TVA also developed several recreation demonstration areas in cooperation with the National Park Service and the Civilian Conservation Corps to stimulate the interest of public and private agencies in the recreational potential of TVA developments. Later broadening of TVA recreational policy involved direct development and management of recreational potential on a 170,000-acre national recreation area known as the Land Between the Lakes. This long-term project, initiated by TVA in 1959, received Executive approval in 1963, and the Public Works Appropriation Act of 1964 provided 4 million dollars for initial planning, development, and land acquisition; first facilities were available to the public in June of the same year.

---

[24] The Bureau of Reclamation was established in 1902; the Corps of Engineers, established in 1802, was engaged in nonmilitary engineering and construction before enactment of the first Rivers and Harbors Act in 1924 [13].

Bureau of Reclamation [12,13,21,51]

Since 1934 matters relevant to the protection and management of fish and wildlife resources of Bureau of Reclamation reservoirs and contiguous lands have been handled by the Bureau of Sport Fisheries and Wildlife of the U.S. Fish and Wildlife Service, or comparable state agencies, by authority of the Fish and Wildlife Coordination Act of 1934, as amended in 1946 and 1958 (P.L. 85-624). Further, the act of August 7, 1946 (P.L. 79-639), authorized transfer of responsibilities for recreational development and management of Bureau of Reclamation projects to other federal agencies, or comparable state or local interests, largely through cooperative agreement pursuant to this bureau's authority for appropriate utilization of project resources. Prior to 1965, recreation development on new projects was included in project plans only as specifically provided for by Congress in individual project-authorizing acts. However, the Federal Water Project Recreation Act of 1965 (P.L. 89-720) provided general authority for recreation on new developments and limited authority to develop and expand recreational opportunities on existing projects.

Corps of Engineers [12,13,51]

Authority for recreational development and public use of recreational opportunities on projects developed by this agency is contained primarily in the Flood Control Act of 1944, as amended in 1946, 1954, and 1962 (P.L. 87-874). In addition, protection and management of fish and wildlife resources of Corps of Engineers' projects, like those of the Bureau of Reclamation, are handled by the Bureau of Sport Fisheries and Wildlife of the U.S. Fish and Wildlife Service, or comparable state agencies, by authority of the Fish and Wildlife Coordination Act of 1934.

Development of State Park Systems

Establishment of the Yosemite Grant in 1864 initiated the concept of the reservation of wild land for recreational use. Since the federal government entrusted this area to the care of the state of California, and since it was so administered for about forty years, it was also the first state park. Thus, the state parks have a longer history than any other type of wild-land recreational area.

Though the Yosemite Grant was receded to the federal government and incorporated into Yosemite National Park (established 1890) in 1906, a number of early state parks were established before the turn of the century. The movement to preserve an area surrounding Niagara Falls, initiated in 1867, achieved success in 1885, when the Niagara Falls Reservation was dedicated [17,25]. The year 1885 also witnessed the transfer of an obsolete military reservation on Mackinac Island from the federal government to the state of

Michigan; previously this area had had a brief existence as a national military park [19,25,28]. Minnesota established the first portion of Itasca State Park in 1891; two historical areas were also established by that state about the same time—Birch Coulee in 1889 and Camp Release in 1895 [25].

Also, in 1885 the state Legislature of New York established the Adirondack Forest Preserve. Since cutting of timber was forbidden in that area in 1897 and on state lands in the Catskills in 1899, both the Adirondack and Catskill areas assumed the essential character of state parks. The famous Palisades Interstate Park of New York and New Jersey had its origin in 1895, when the first lands of the area were acquired [25].

However, despite its early beginning the state park movement did not begin to attract significant attention until 1921, several years after establishment of the National Park Service. Establishment of the National Park Service and resultant development and improvement of areas in its charge soon drew public interest and attention to these areas, resulting in constantly increasing numbers of visitors. It became evident that the term "national park" embodied commercial magic, which was reflected in the economy of adjacent communities. A veritable flood of proposals for the establishment of additional national parks developed; many of these proposed areas, largely sponsored by biased interests, were unworthy of national park status. In 1916 alone, sixteen areas were proposed for inclusion in the National Park System [28,52].

Stephen T. Mather, director of the National Park Service, was aware of the danger of diluting national park standards through the addition of areas lacking in outstanding, nationally significant features, and he recognized that many areas other than national parks possessed recreational values which were needed and would be increasingly valuable in later years. He diverted the pressure for additional national parks into proper channels by calling a conference of interested parties for the purpose of planning the extension and development of state park systems [28].

Des Moines, Iowa, was selected as the convention site and about two hundred delegates from twenty-five states gathered there in January 1921. As a result, a permanent organization known as the National Conference on State Parks was formed [25,28]. Since that time this body has met annually to discuss common state park problems and to further common interests. Much of the progress in the development of state parks stems from activities of this organization. Today, each of the fifty states has a state park system, the number of individual state parks has greatly increased, they are more adequately financed, and they are better administered. By 1962 there were more than 2,500 state parks, with an aggregate area of between 5 and 6 million acres [48]. Varying widely in size and character, they are among the most heavily used of specifically designated recreational lands.

In addition, state forests, fish and wildlife areas, reservoirs, areas contiguous to state highways, and related state lands have been increasingly used for recreation. In 1962 there were more than 28,000 such state recreational areas, aggregating more than 48 million acres; thus, including state parks, the number of state recreational lands exceeded 30,000, with a total of nearly 54 million acres [48].

Local Recreational Areas

Though establishment of Central Park in New York City, as outlined in Chapter 3, was followed by increased interest in municipal parks elsewhere, such interest developed slowly. By 1877 only twenty of our larger cities had municipal parks, and by 1892 only a hundred cities had made provision for them. Expansion of municipal parks was more rapid after the turn of the century, paralleling early growth of public interest in natural-resource conservation and provisions for recreational use of wild lands. Between 1902 and 1926 the number of cities with municipal parks more than doubled, from nearly 800 to almost 1,700. The aggregate area of municipal parks and related recreation areas in 1926 was about 250,000 acres [58]. In 1965 nearly 2,400 municipal park agencies reported a total park acreage slightly exceeding 805,000 acres [24].

Expansion of municipal park systems, in turn, led to development of parkways, as well as the acquisition of municipally owned and administered park areas outside city limits, often at some distance. Cities with such areas are Phoenix, Arizona, and Denver, Colorado [58].

The nature and philosophy of municipal park use have changed over the years. Initially conceived as sylvan open spaces primarily for more passive recreation, municipal park systems have become increasingly important as centers of active outdoor recreation. Thus, modern city park systems provide a variety of areas for diverse recreational interests and activities [11].

County and regional or district park systems, of increasing importance in more densely populated sections of the country, also have a long history. The county park movement originated in Essex County, New Jersey, in 1895 [58]; however, only a few areas of this kind were established prior to 1920. By 1965 there were over 325 county and regional or district park agencies throughout the United States, administering over 4,000 county and regional or district parks with an aggregate area of approximately 691,000 acres [24].[25]

Public Recreational Use of Private Lands

Private enterprise, particularly the resort industry, has long been associated with public recreation through the provision of necessary commercial services within

---

[25] Excluding school recreation areas: about 14,400 areas totaling approximately 97,000 acres administered by municipal agencies, and about 2,100 acres aggregating nearly 20,000 acres administered by county school agencies [24].

or en route to various recreational areas on wild land. In addition, private enterprise has been increasingly involved with the development and sale of specialized types of recreation equipment. But today the recreational functions of private lands are very different from those of early-day mountain and beach resorts mentioned in Chapter 3. And the baroque hostelries typical of the early part of this century, where people customarily spent an entire vacation period, have been replaced by operations of greater variety geared to rapid visitor turnover.

The profit motive, though a dominant factor in public recreational use of private lands, is not always a primary objective. Increasingly, many areas serving varied outdoor recreational purposes are owned or otherwise controlled by public-spirited individuals and different types of nonprofit organizations,[26] including youth, religious, and civic groups; educational, scientific, or historical institutions; and outdoor and conservation clubs [36]. In some cases, initiation of such activities antedates the turn of the century. Commercial aspects of such operations are usually confined to minimum charges designed to defray costs of operation and maintenance. In some cases recreational use of lands requires an organization membership, but membership requirements are so liberal that, in effect these areas are essentially public in character.

Public Recreation on Agricultural Lands [35,36]

Privately owned farms and ranches offer increasing opportunity for a variety of commercial recreational services and facilities. Charging for hunting privileges on farms and ranches, as well as for fishing in ponds and lakes on private land, is now a common practice. In some parts of the country, management of agricultural land primarily for revenue derived from hunting leases to specific groups or organizations is rapidly expanding. Maintenance of suitable environmental conditions and adequate stocking of game and fish are often based on scientific wildlife management techniques carried on by landowners with assistance of various government experts. Where there is sufficient demand, other recreational

---

[26]Noteworthy examples include the Sierra Club, organized 1892; Mazama Club, organized 1894; Mountaineers, organized 1906; Appalachian Mountain Club, organized 1876; and Audubon Society, established 1886.

The Mount Vernon Ladies Association, organized in 1858, owns the plantation home of George and Martha Washington. The first 200 acres (later increased to 481 acres) were purchased in 1858; originally run-down, it was subsequently restored by the association, which maintains this beautiful historic shrine by means of visitor fees.

Restoration of the colonial city of Williamsburg was begun in 1926 with funds provided by John D. Rockefeller, Jr. It includes a 130-acre restored area with more than 500 buildings and 84 acres of gardens and greens representative of this city during the eighteenth century, when it was the capital of Virginia, at the time of Washington, Jefferson, Patrick Henry, and other American patriots.

The Nature Conservancy, initiated in 1917 by a group of scientists within the Ecological Society of America, was incorporated in 1951 as a nonprofit corporation under the laws of the District of Columbia.

opportunities also are being offered to the public on a commercial basis. The potential of such activity is considerable, considering that farm and ranch acreage, including private woodlands, is greatly varied and constitutes nearly 70 percent of all land.

Dude ranching in the West dates from the turn of the century. Vacation farms, a more recent variation of this activity, are of increasing importance in more densely populated regions, particularly in the East. Commercial picnic and various types of sports areas; campgrounds and vacation trailer parks; areas of rented, leased, or privately owned vacation cottages; and even scenic or nature recreation areas are increasing on agricultural land that has attractive terrain, vegetation, lakes, streams, suitable winter conditions, and related features.

Expansion in recreational use of agricultural land created the need for technical and financial assistance to landowners desirous of entering this field of activity. An early step in this direction was the Food and Agriculture Act of 1962 (P.L. 87-703) and the subsequent Food and Agriculture Act of 1965 (P.L. 89-321), provisions of which enabled various agencies of the U.S. Department of Agriculture, in its Rural Areas Development Program, to offer the technical and financial assistance needed.[27]

Public Recreation on Private Industrial Lands

Since the 1920s the number of large land-owning industrial firms permitting certain types of public recreation on lands under their control has been slowly but steadily growing [36]. Though initially, such activities were considered merely a public relations gesture, they are becoming more firmly established as part of general company policy. The growth of such activities on private industrial forest lands is most noteworthy.

Since the primary interest of industrial forest land owners is the production of successive crops of timber, anything that might interfere with this objective was initially viewed with disfavor. Hunting and fishing were condoned on such areas for many years, but even these informal activities were not encouraged until recently. In fact, insofar as it was possible, some owners attempted to prohibit such use largely because of possible vandalism, owner liability responsibilities in case of accidents, and cost. However, with time, this attitude was gradually tempered by broader recognition of owner-land-stewardship responsibility. All forms of long-term multiple-use benefits now receive more adequate consideration than formerly, including watershed protection, soil stabilization, wildlife management, and, most recently, maintenance of environmental interests and provision for varied public outdoor recreational

---

[27]These agencies include the Agricultural Stabilization and Conservation Service, Economic Research Service, Farmer Cooperative Service, Farmers Home Administration, Federal Extension Service, U.S. Forest Service, Rural Community Development Service, Rural Electrification Administration, Soil Conservation Service, and state agricultural experiment stations. Other agencies of the federal government also may be of assistance [49].

activities. This attitude of the forest industry was prompted largely by growing public interest in the recreational potential of such lands and the concomitant opportunity for improving the industry's public image, which had suffered as a result of earlier destructive logging practices. This resulted in gradual relaxation of former restrictions on trespassing on industrial land and in increasing the facilities necessary for many forms of outdoor recreation for the general public. By the 1930s a number of the larger industrial forest land owners had begun to develop cooperative programs, whereby company personnel aided in the controlled use of their lands for hunting, fishing, berry picking, and similar activities that did not require specially developed facilities. Many company logging roads were opened to public use at specified times and under specified conditions, area maps were provided to help travelers find recreational objectives and, in some cases, regularly manned information stations were maintained at strategic points to aid visitors. Eventually, these informal cooperative ventures were further expanded to include development of specifically designated tree-farm parks with varied developed public facilities for camping, picnicking, and related activities and, in some instances, fairly sophisticated forest recreational use policies administered by special forest recreational personnel.

The tree-farm park movement was originated by the Weyerhaeuser Company in 1941 in the state of Washington [5]. After World War II, the company revitalized and expanded its recreational program, and the idea was adopted by other industrial forest land owners in the Pacific Northwest as well as in other parts of the country.

Expansion of public recreational use of industrial forest lands prompted the American Forest Institute[28] to undertake the first survey of the nature and extent of that use in 1956. Additional surveys in 1960, 1962, and 1968 [2,3,4] indicate the expanding and changing character of public recreational use of these lands as well as continuing cooperation of industrial forest land owners. The future of this voluntary program depends on the responsibility of recreationists who use these lands as guests, as well as on the solution of some still-unsolved problems relative to the cost of providing and maintaining recreational opportunities and facilities.

Summary

The decades following the establishment of the Yosemite Grant in 1864 and extending well into the twentieth century were characterized by many significant developments in recreational land use. Yellowstone National Park, established in 1872, was followed by the designation of other early national parks, as well as other types of areas now included in the National Park System. Difficul-

---

[28]Name changed from American Forest Products Industries in 1968.

ties in independent administration of early national parks eventually resulted in the establishment of the National Park Service in 1916.

Other important developments led to the establishment of the U.S. Forest Service. In the case of both the National Park Service and the Forest Service, we see the role of strong dominant leaders initiating programs and long-range policy directions. Mather, of the Park Service, was concerned for the preservation and public use of parks; Pinchot, of the Forest Service, established a pattern of forest use for production with recreational values in a secondary role. Broadening of the recreational policy of the U.S. Forest Service, officially initiated in 1925, eventually resulted in recreation being legally recognized as one of the major resources of the national forests. Still, there was, and is, a basic difference in the way resource managers in the Park Service and the Forest Service define the land resources for which they are responsible. Consequently the management approaches are different, as will be pointed out later. Herein lies the basis for many of today's land-use conflicts.

By the 1930s recreational use of federal reclamation projects was becoming increasingly apparent. As a result, the Tennessee Valley Authority, the Bureau of Reclamation, and the Corps of Engineers formulated policies to develop adequate recreational opportunities on areas under their respective jurisdictions. Today recreation is recognized as one of several important resources on these multipurpose projects.

The period since 1945 has been characterized by the growing recreational importance of lands administered by the Bureau of Land Management, as well as lands of the Bureau of Sport Fisheries and Wildlife of the U.S. Fish and Wildlife Service. The National Wildlife Refuge system dates from the establishment of the Pelican Island National Wildlife Refuge in 1903.

State park establishment, begun before the turn of the century, received a strong assist from the National Park Service, resulting in the establishment of the National Conference on State Parks in 1921. Here again we see the role of the great park leader Mather in setting policy. Was his insight correct? In time, as public demand developed, state parks systems were formed in each of the fifty states. In addition, other types of state lands were increasingly used for recreation. Further development of municipal park systems, dating from the establishment of Central Park in New York City in 1853, as well as county and regional or district parks, dating from 1895, paralleled expanding interest in recreational value of federal and state lands.

Increasing public demand for recreational opportunity also emphasized the importance of private lands for public recreation. Many individual private landowners began developing their lands for public use, often on a commercial basis, and by 1962 legal authorization was provided whereby federal agencies could offer technical and financial assistance in such development. Of particular importance was the increasing willingness of industrial landowners to permit public recreational use of their lands, culminating in tree-farm parks, the first of which was established in 1941. What role will private forest lands play in future American wildland recreation use?

Selected References

1. Allen, Shirley W., and Grant W. Sharpe: "An Introduction to American Forestry," 3d ed., McGraw-Hill, New York, 1960.

2. American Forest Products Industries: "Recreation on Forest Industry Lands," Washington, 1960.

3. American Forest Products Industries: "Comparison of 1960 and 1962 Survey Results of 87 Selected Companies: Recreation," Washington, n.d. (Dittoed.)

4. American Forest Institute: "1968 Forest Industry Recreation Survey," Washington, 1968. (Mimeographed.)

5. Billings, Frederick: Public Parks on Private Property, *Planning and Civic Comment,* vol. 22, no. 4, pp. 51-60, December, 1956.

6. Butcher, Devereux: "Seeing America's Wildlife in Our National Refuges," Devin-Adair, New York, 1955.

7. Carson, Rachel: "Guarding Our Wildlife Recources" (Conservation in Action No. 5), Fish and Wildlife Service, U.S. Department of Interior, Washington, 1948.

8. Chittenden, J. M.: "Yellowstone National Park" (Rev. by Eleanor Chittenden Cress and Isabelle Story), Stanford University Press, Stanford, Calif., 1954.

9. Clawson, Marion: "Man and Land in the United States," University of Nebraska Press, Lincoln, 1964.

10. Cleveland, Treadwell: National Forests as Recreation Grounds, *Annals of the American Academy of Political and Social Science,* vol. 35, no. 2, pp. 241-247, March, 1910.

11. Doell, Charles E., and Gerald B. Fitzgerald: "A Brief History of Parks and Recreation in the United States," Athletic Institute, Chicago, 1954.

12. Federal Interagency Committee on Recreation: "Role of the Federal Government in the Field of Recreation," No. 3, U.S. Government Printing Office, Washington, 1961.

13. Frederick Burke Foundation: "Federal Agencies and Outdoor Recreation," ORRRC Study Report no. 13, U.S. Government Printing Office, Washington, 1962.

14. Gabrielson, Ira N.: "Wildlife Management," Macmillan, New York, 1951.

15. Hampton, H. Duane: The Army in the National Parks, *Forest History,* vol. 10, no. 3, October, 1966.

16. Hartesvelt, Richard John: "The Effects of Human Impact upon *Sequoia gigantea* and Its Environment in the Mariposa Grove, Yosemite National Park, California," Ph.D. dissertation, University of Michigan, 1962. (Microfilmed, University Microfilms, Inc., Ann Arbor, Mich.)

17. Huth, Hans: "Nature and the American," University of California Press, Berkeley, 1957.

18. Ise, John: "The United States Forest Policy," Yale University Press, New Haven, Conn., 1920.

19. Ise, John: "Our National Park Policy," Johns Hopkins, Baltimore, 1961.

20. Langford, N. P.: "The Discovery of Yellowstone National Park, 1870," J. E. Haynes, St. Paul, Minn., 1923.

21. Library of Congress, Legislative Reference Service: "Reclamation: Accomplishments and Contributions," 86th Cong. 1st Sess. Committee on Interior and Insular Affairs, House of Representatives, Committee Print No. 1, U.S. Government Printing Office, Washington, 1959.

22. Maughan, Kenneth O.: "Recreation Development in the National Forests," Technical Publication No. 45, New York State College of Forestry, Syracuse University, Syracuse, N.Y., 1934.

23. Meany, E. S.: "Mount Rainier: A Record of Exploration," Macmillan, New York, 1916.

24. National Recreation and Park Association: "Recreation and Park Yearbook, 1966," Washington, 1967.

25. Nelson, Beatrice: "State Recreation," National Conference on State Parks, Washington, 1928.

26. Pinchot, Gifford: "The Fight for Conservation" (intro. by Gerald D. Nash), University of Washington Press, Seattle, 1967. (Original published by Doubleday, Page and Co., 1910.)

27. Russell, Carl P.: "100 Years in Yosemite," University of California Press, Berkeley, 1947.

28. Shankland, Robert: "Steve Mather of the National Parks," Knopf, New York, 1951.

29. Sherman, E. A.: "Outdoor Recreation on the National Forests," U.S. Forest Service, Washington, May, 1925. (Mimeographed.)

30. Swain, Donald C.: The Passage of the National Park Service Act of 1916, *Wisconsin Magazine of History,* vol. 50, no. 1, Autumn, 1966.

31. Tennessee Valley Authority: "Outdoor Recreation for a Growing Nation," Knoxville, Tenn., 1961.

32. Tennessee Valley Authority: "Land Between the Lakes, Annual Report, 1966," Knoxville, Tenn., n.d.

33. Tolson, Hillary A.: "Laws Relating to the National Park Service, the National Parks and Monuments," U.S. Government Printing Office, Washington, 1933.

34. U.S. Department of Agriculture: "The Principal Laws Relating to the Establishment and Administration of the National Forests and to Other Forest Service Activities," Miscellaneous Publication No. 135, Washington, 1939.

35. U.S. Department of Agriculture: "Rural Recreation: A New Family-Farm Business," U.S. Government Printing Office, Washington, 1962.

36. U.S. Department of Agriculture, Economic Research Service: "Private Outdoor Recreation Facilities," ORRRC Study Report No. 11, U.S. Government Printing Office, Washington, 1962.

37. U.S. Department of Agriculture, Forest Service: "Report of the Forester for 1912," Washington, 1912.

38. U.S. Department of Agriculture, Forest Service: "Report of the Forester," Washington, 1917.

39. U.S. Department of Agriculture, Forest Service: "Report of the Forester," Washington, 1920.

40. U.S. Department of Agriculture, Forest Service: "Report of the Forester," Washington, 1921.

41. U.S. Department of Agriculture, Forest Service: "Report of the Forester," Washington, 1922.

42. U.S. Department of Agriculture, Forest Service: "Report of the Forester," Washington, 1924.

43. U.S. Department of Agriculture, Forest Service: "Report of the Forester," Washington, 1925.

44. U.S. Department of Agriculture, Forest Service: "Outdoor Recreation in the National Forests," Agriculture Information Bulletin No. 30, U.S. Government Printing Office, Washington, 1965.

45. U.S. Department of the Interior: "Secretary Seaton Approves Policy Statement of Bureau of Land Management on Recreational Land Use," Apr. 16, 1958. (Mimeographed.)

46. U.S. Department of the Interior, Bureau of Land Management: "Community Recreation and the Public Domain," U.S. Government Printing Office, Washington, 1963.

47. U.S. Department of the Interior, Bureau of Land Management: "Public Land Statistics—1966, 1967," U.S. Government Printing Office, Washington, 1967, 1968.

48. U.S. Department of the Interior, Bureau of Outdoor Recreation: "State Outdoor Recreation Statistics, 1962," Report No. 1, Statistical Series, Department of Research and Education, U.S. Government Printing Office, Washington, 1963.

49. U.S. Department of the Interior, Bureau of Outdoor Recreation: "Federal Assistance in Outdoor Recreation." U.S. Government Printing Office, Washington, 1966.

50. U.S. Department of the Interior, Fish and Wildlife Service, Bureau of Sport Fisheries and Wildlife: "National Wildlife Refuges," U.S. Government Printing Office, Washington, 1968.

51. U.S. Department of the Interior, Bureau of Outdoor Recreation: "Federal Outdoor Recreation Programs," U.S. Government Printing Office, Washington, 1968.

52. U.S. Department of the Interior, National Park Service: "Annual Report of the Superintendent of National Parks to the Secretary of the Interior for the Fiscal Year Ended June 30, 1916," Washington, 1916.

53. U.S. Department of the Interior, National Park Service: "Annual Report of the Director of the National Park Service to the Secretary of the Interior for the Fiscal Year Ended June 30, 1917," Washington, 1917.

54. U.S. Department of the Interior, National Park Service: "Annual Report of the Director of the National Park Service to the Secretary of the Interior for the Fiscal Year Ended June 30, 1918," Washington, 1918.

55. U.S. Department of the Interior, National Park Service: "Annual Report of the Director of the National Park Service to the Secretary of the Interior for the Fiscal Year Ended June 30, 1931," Washington, 1931.

56. U.S. Department of the Interior, National Park Service: "National Parks and Landmarks, Areas Administered by the National Park Service and Related Properties," U.S. Government Printing Office, Washington, 1968.

57. U.S. Department of the Interior, National Park Service: "Road to the Future," n.p., 1964.

58. U.S. Department of Labor, Bureau of Labor Statistics: "Park Recreation Areas in the United States," Miscellaneous Publication No. 462, Washington, 1928.

59. Waugh, F. A.: "Recreation Uses on the National Forests," U.S. Government Printing Office, Washington, 1918.

60. Wolfe, Linnie M.: "Son of the Wilderness: The Life of John Muir," Knopf, New York, 1947.

chapter five

THE RECREATION VISITOR: MOTIVATION, BEHAVIOR, IMPACT[1]

This chapter is intended as an *introduction* to the array of basic insights available from the fields of knowledge mentioned in following paragraphs, and as an indication of their utility to people in the profession of wild-land management. No one chapter can be a substitute for thorough training in university courses in the several disciplines which provide these insights. The principal emphasis here is sociological and social-psychological, but the comparable importance of other social sciences is acknowledged and should be kept in mind.

Importance of Insights from Social Science

Wild-land recreation means many forms of *interaction* between people and wild-land environments. People have an impact on environments, and vice versa. Adequate management therefore requires more than the direct protection, renewal, or development of wild-land recreational resources. It requires also that human behavior be influenced, channeled, or regulated. Its proper goals cannot be attained without some guidance from those disciplines which contribute to our knowledge of human behavior.

There are economic and political aspects of wild-land recreation, e.g., allocation of resources, material and financial, to this use in competition with other uses, and allocation of regulative authority to one agency or another. These issues call for insights from economics and political science. Adequate under-

[1] Prepared by Dr. William R. Catton, Jr., formerly Professor of Sociology, University of Washington; now Professor of Sociology, University of Canterbury, Christchurch, New Zealand.

standing of people's desires, interests, motivations, habits, and any potential there may be for modifying any of these, calls for insights from psychology, especially social psychology. Sociology, too, can contribute knowledge on such matters, as well as some understanding of probable trends in the composition of the wild-land recreation clientele, tendencies among wild-land recreationists toward depreciative or deviant uses of recreation resources, and knowledge of the social factors influencing public preferences among alternative management policies.

Sociological knowledge is needed also regarding pertinent organizational processes, both in the bureaucratic agencies responsible for recreational wild lands and in the numerous voluntary associations which exert pressure upon them from time to time.

Self-fulfilling Expectations

Normally, it might seem inappropriate to look to a smog-ridden and automobile-glutted metropolis for clues on how to preserve primeval environments for recreational enjoyment. Nevertheless, in these changing times, a remark by a member of the Los Angeles Fire Department epitomizes the *interrelated* deterioration of cities and a growing threat to recreational wild lands. City firemen have sometimes been stoned, shot at, and verbally abused while battling flames in American urban ghettos. "It's frustrating," said one of them, "to be despised by the very people you're trying so hard to help."

As man's habitat fills up with people, more people become frustrated in more ways and on more occasions. Their wrath seeks *available* targets, often without sufficient concern, as social psychologists have noted, as to whether availability reflects culpability [11,20,25,38].

Under modern conditions, wild-land protection could become a thankless task. If the devoted efforts of management personnel go unacknowledged and the best-intentioned decisions of officials in protective agencies are consistently depreciated for falling short of the ideal, eventually the result could be serious demoralization rather than the reinforcement required if the achievements of such agencies are ever to approach perfection.

There is a social-psychological tendency that is taken into account in the common practice of campground managers who try to reduce the amount of littering by frequent and thorough collection of trash. It is understood that litter on the ground invites more litter; people who experience (and thus expect) a messy environment tend to behave in ways which keep it messy, but people who experience (and thus expect) neat surroundings tend to behave in ways that preserve neatness. The prominent placement of a visitor register book, where visitors may leave their mark, is likewise commonly used as a deterrent to defacement of public facilities and natural features.

If the nature and source of the threat to wild-land recreation areas are misperceived, interested parties may try to "defend" these areas by actions which actually endanger them. Unjustly abusing their humanly imperfect guardians would be one example of an action that could have this unintended effect. The classic illustration of such "self-fulfilling expectations" was offered by Robert K. Merton, Columbia University sociologist. He cited the example of a bank's failing because of panic efforts of depositors to withdraw funds in response to unfounded (but believed) rumors of the bank's insolvency [27].

In much the same manner, those who wish to ensure the preservation of wild areas for the enjoyment of future generations probably contribute inadvertently to their erosion and desecration. Now that large numbers of people have the time and the affluence and the desire to seek their recreation in such environments, these areas *need* protection more than ever before. To provide this protection is the task of various governmental agencies having jurisdiction over these lands. They can succeed in this task only if the vast majority of their personnel at all levels are truly dedicated to it. Essential as such dedication is, it can be undermined by excessive, uninformed, or unsympathetic criticism from a public which misunderstands the causes of previous deterioration.

This unwanted outcome might result not only from abrading the spirit of the individuals whose patient and earnest guardianship is required to keep the visions of wild-land integrity real. It might result also from a kind of organizational attrition. Any such management agency as, for example, the National Park Service, is more than a group of high-minded individuals. Of necessity it is also a government bureau with a formal structure. It is dependent for funds and authority on a politically oriented Congress that is beholden to a constituency it more often conceives as reluctant taxpayers than as devotees of nature. Organizational constraints can sometimes run counter to the values of the organization's own personnel [1,14]. When this happens, the relationship between the organization and its clients may help determine whether noble values or more mundane influences will prevail. Many men in the Park Service are alert to and would welcome any concrete indications of public support for the ideals of wild-land preservation. Their performance of organizational duties can benefit from a "watchdog" function carried on by various voluntary associations like the Sierra Club, the Wilderness Society, or the National Parks Association. But if *excessive, carping* criticism seemed to be all they got from the conservation-minded citizens from whom they would tend to expect gratitude and moral support, the result could be that the most conscientious members of the service would become demoralized and would resign. Their places would then tend to be filled by less devoted, more bureaucratic-minded mercenaries, for whom park protection tasks would increasingly be seen as a job, not as a calling. The self-fulfilling expectation would thus have operated at the organizational level, changing the composition of an agency's personnel in the direction of an initially inaccurate image.

To ensure the continued integrity of wild-land environments, management agencies must continue to recruit men as able and dedicated as those who have served them in their most mission-oriented periods. But unless they can ensure that the men who rise to the top echelons of each government bureau, where policies are formulated, will always be the most idealistic men in the service (not merely the ones with the greatest efficiency at upward mobility), the nature of the bureau's stewardship will change. Such change is likely if the recreating public blames the management agency for circumstances over which it has had no control.

Basic Sociological Principles

Sociological Perspective

Modern sociology starts from the premise that human beings get to be what they are from their experiences in groups, and can do things collectively and as socially nurtured beings which they could not do otherwise. The seemingly infinite variety of social encounters and social situations can actually be reduced to a finite set of categories. The probable behavior in any given class of encounters is predictable, in principle, partly by taking into account the web of group memberships in which people are involved [15,24].

Norms, Ethnocentrism, Culture

In ongoing groups, norms develop. Groups impose sanctions to minimize the deviation of their members' behavior from the norms. Members also comply with group norms as a result of internalizing them in a socialization process. "Socialization" is a term sociologists use to refer to the process whereby attitudes, habits, skills, and social standards of judgment are transmitted to people through their group involvements and their interactions with other human beings.

Each human being born into a social environment undergoes a socialization process which links him to groups and to society. In this process he acquires his personality, including his ability to speak and think, his many other skills, his unique personal constellation of attitudes, and even his conception of himself. Socialization is a lifelong process, and each person is both a product of it and an agent engaged in socializing others whenever he interacts.

In most societies, the principal context for early socialization is the family. The family not only links generation to generation by providing for care and training of children; it also regulates sexual behavior and reproduction, provides role models, and affords the satisfactions of intimate group life which tend to ensure its continuation. But family functions and family structure change as society changes. Family systems vary markedly from one society to another, and each people tends to regard its accustomed forms as normal and natural. "Ethnocentrism" refers to the universal human tendency to evaluate the behavior of other groups not by their standards but by the standards of one's own group. Ethnocentrism is a fact of life that can be important to anyone whose profession requires him to try to redirect any aspect of human behavior. It is a natural result of the fact that human personalities are social products.

Patterns of action which become valued, however they may have originated, tend to give rise to norms. Once established, a norm will tend to perpetuate the behavior it prescribes. That norm will seem "real" or "natural" to those who embrace it, and it may be thought by them to have "existed" always. Thus people have ethnocentric tendencies in regard to all sectors of life.

Norms themselves may be interrelated. Some norms apply to all members of a group. Others, called "role expectations", are specific to certain positions. The kind of norms which will prevail in any given group, community, or society will depend in part on its relation to a physical, biological, and social environment. Through such processes as concentration, centralization, decentralization, segregation, invasion, and succession, human beings adapt themselves to the conditions of life set by these environments. Not all norms arise out of this kind of ecological patterning, but norms which require ecologically probable behavior can be more readily enforced than those which require ecologically improbable behavior. For example, in a campground where parking stalls are physically too small to accommodate two cars, or are laid out a foot or so below the grade level, or are bounded by a neat row of logs, the environment-protecting rule of "one party per campsite" will require little overt enforcement. If the rule is instead communicated only verbally, by leaflet, or by sign, not by physical circumstance, its enforcement may be difficult or impossible in periods of peak use. Much environmental damage may then ensue.

Despite apparent ecological constraints on human behavior, man does differ from other species in that his behavior *can be* extensively shaped by normative considerations as well as by nonnormative circumstance. One of the key concepts of sociology and anthropology is "culture." This term refers to a system of socially acquired and socially transmitted standards of judgment, belief, and conduct. It may refer also to the material and symbolic products of the resulting conventional patterns of behavior. Differences among cultures have much to do with bringing about differences in the actions and expectations of people in different nations or regions. Cultures change, but usually with some resistance and in response to significant pressures of various kinds.

Communication and Organization

Human society and culture are possible because of man's unparalleled capacity for communication as a language-using animal. But language shapes as well as permits perception and thought. It links person to person and gives man an extensive social heritage in addition to his biological heritage. Social heritage is, of course, much less fixed than biological heritage, and it provides man with many niches (rather than just one) in the ecosystems in which he is involved.

Organization extends human capabilities. Large-scale pursuit of complex technical goals tends to foster the establishment of a type of formal organization approximating what is called bureaucracy. Sociologists use the term "bureaucracy" in a descriptive, not a derogatory, sense. In this objective sense, bureaucracy involves a clear-cut division of labor, a clear hierarchy of administrative authority, explicit rules and circumscribed role expectations, a detached and impersonal approach to all tasks, and assignment of personnel to positions according to technical qualifications. Real organizations fall short of the bureaucratic model because people holding positions in them (who have experienced socialization in more intimate group contexts) tend to resist depersonalization of themselves and their interactions. People in organizations which are structurally similar tend to show similar attitudes and behaviors in spite of differences in organizational goals or in their individual personalities.

Production, distribution, and consumption of goods influence and are influenced by norms, social structure, and many facets of the social process that would not usually be regarded as strictly economic. Economic goals and means are subject to change, but they cannot be changed without affecting other aspects of social life.

Society is a self-perpetuating system. Social organization is inherently resistant to change. But social changes do occur. Rates of social change vary in different times and different social settings. Innovative behavior, not easily distinguished immediately from deviant behavior, results from imperfect socialization which was adequate to bestow skills but inadequate to preclude unconventional applications thereof. Rates of innovation depend on the richness of the accumulated cultural base, and also upon opportunities for emancipation from cultural preconceptions. Rates of acceptance of innovations depend on their perceived utility. How useful an innovation will be thought to be may in turn depend on such factors as the prestige of the source, the prestige of previous adopters, generalized social resistance or receptivity to novelty, perceived compatibility of the innovation with (or adaptability to) preexisting culture patterns, and past experience with change. Change in one sector of culture or social organization tends to produce change in other sectors, often after some delay during which there is social stress.

Disorganization

A social system may be more or less disorganized. Social disorganization consists of discrepancies between any two of the following: the behavior that is prescribed by norms, the behavior that is anticipated, and the behavior that actually occurs. Disorganization of a society can cause deviant acts by its members. Deviance is facilitated by changes in a society's scale of values, inconsistencies in its normative prescriptions and expectations, impediments to the application of sanctions, and prevalent anticipations of nonconformity. Societal tolerance limits are subject to change. Behavior regarded as deviant at one time may subsequently become the accepted standard of the group, and vice versa. The incidence of deviant acts depends in part on the availability of opportunities. Insofar as wild-land recreation tends to isolate people from surveillance by others, it affords such opportunities. Activities considered deviant by the larger society may be fostered by deviant normative subsystems and by illicit organization. The population categories most involved in wild-land recreation tend to be the ones least involved in such deviant subcultures or illicit organizations.

Voluntary Associations

In urbanized society, most people interact in a segmental (only partially involved) way with others—except within families or intimate groups of friends, which sociologists call "primary groups." This segmentalism of urban life has fostered the development of assorted voluntary associations which engage in activities that vary from highly consummatory to highly instrumental. Many of these organizations serve their members as partial and occasional substitutes for the decreasingly common primary group experience. Some provide certification of status and rank of their members in an occupational specialty or some other significant category in the larger community. This function stands out in societies with large populations and extensive occupational specialization. Some voluntary associations, called "social movements," engage in concerted efforts to change attitudes, behavior, or social relationships in a larger society.

Various outdoor activity clubs, organized to facilitate their members' interest in skiing, hiking, camping, boating, etc., constitute clear examples of *consummatory* voluntary associations. Conservationist organizations, on the other hand, tend to be more *instrumental* and may be regarded as social movements since they expressly seek to influence public policies. Such groups as the Society of American Foresters and other professional organizations perform —among numerous other functions—the public certification of status and rank.

Human Differences

Human beings differ. Many human differences are socially produced; other differences are socially endowed with meanings that are not inherent in their biological origins. Age and sex are universal dimensions of social differentiation, but they are differently used in different societies. Other readily visible differences (such as race) are often but not uniformly taken into account in the patterning of human interactions. Social differentiation provides the basis for elaborating organization. If all men were alike, there could hardly be any of the complex organizations by which men accomplish complex tasks. Variation is thus a useful fact of human life, but it is also a source of many problems. In both respects awareness of it is important in wild-land recreation planning and management.

Social Stratification and Recreation

The world of recreation, as truly as the world of work, provides an arena for study of both the causes and the consequences, as well as the processes, of stratification and differentiation [3,33]. Recreation and stratification bear a dynamic relation to each other. Each may be fruitfully examined both as cause and as effect. Existing patterns of social differentiation, both vertical and horizontal, as well as changes in these patterns through time, may be a partial cause of some variations in recreational activity. In other contexts, however, recreational behavior may be seen as the independent variable, making its own contribution to an ever-evolving system of social differentiation and stratification. And in some situations, stratification may be more appropriately viewed as a *control* variable, rather than as either cause or effect.

Stratification as Cause

Social classes still differ in their relative access to recreational opportunities despite the undeniable changes of the past century. In many American cities, for example, the share of recreational land located in the lowest-income parts of the city is even less than the share of personal income received by the residents of those areas. Conversely, the share of recreational land located in the higher-income sections is even more generous than the share of monetary wealth. Consequently, urban Negroes lack proportionate access to public parks, owing indirectly to discriminatory employment and residential segregation [10, p. 151].

Free admission to public parks in the United States does not much offset the disadvantage of the poor. In crowded cities where poor people are concentrated there are proportionately fewer public parks than in wealthier and suburban areas. Moreover, access to most state parks, or national parks and national forests, depends on automobile ownership and ability to afford travel costs. Admission fees, if any, are a negligible fraction of the total cost of access to such places [10, pp. 270-271].

It is not only in differential access to recreation sites that stratification affects leisure behavior. Tastes, desires, and interests are also stratified, presumably as a result of unlike socialization experiences [8, p. 304; 30, p. 83]. As the occupational structure of a nation's economy changes, the way that nation's people will perceive the natural environment may change as a consequence. From Figure 5-1 it is apparent that a sharply declining proportion of Americans are employed in occupations which would tend to define the land chiefly as a source of *materials*. Conversely, there has been a marked increase in the proportion who can earn their living by rendering some service (rather than by growing things or making things). It is probably easier for people in such nonextractive and nonfabricating roles to regard land as a locale for having experiences. In short, American labor-force trends are consistent with the trend toward redefin-

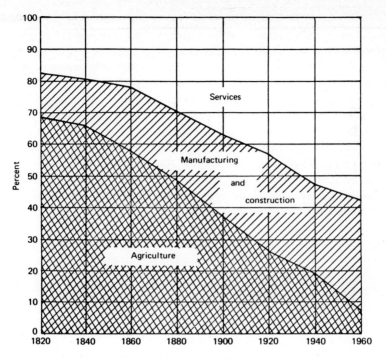

Figure 5-1 Changing pattern of work among U.S. working population

ing the natural environment as a source of desired experiences rather than a source of desired things.

There are evident links between occupational milieu and behavior outside the occupational role. Both the work situation and the nature of the work, together with influences from occupational categories [16]. The extent to which recreation is commercialized varies for different social strata. One study found that the percentage of respondents who reported that they devoted most of their leisure time to commercial-type activities was highest in the lowest occupational prestige level [8, p. 305].

There are occupational differences in the probability of moonlighting, or holding a second job. In 1963, one worker in twenty in the United States held a second job more or less regularly. Almost half of these moonlighters were self-employed in one of their jobs—farming, a profession, a small business. Men are more likely than employed women to hold two jobs, especially in the 25 to 54 age bracket. In some occupations, moonlighting is especially prevalent. For example, 60 to 70 percent of New York policemen and 50 to 60 percent of New York firemen hold other jobs [10, pp. 16-17].

One survey technique that has been used to investigate leisure-time *interests* (as distinct from situationally conditioned leisure-time *activities*) has been to ask people what they would do with one or two hypothetical extra hours per day. Response patterns commonly reflect occupational differences or other types of stratification. In one such study, the modal response of the highest occupational prestige level was that the extra hours would be devoted to reading or studying. These people, mostly in the professions, were less inclined than any other level to sleep, rest, relax, or loaf in the extra time. None of them said they would use it for television viewing. More people on this level than on any other said they would devote the extra time to working at their jobs. In contrast, for the lowest occupational prestige level, the most common response was that the hours would be used to sleep, relax, rest, or loaf. This lowest level was also more inclined than any other to use the extra time for watching TV.

It has been suggested that leisure time can be best used only if some of it is *invested* in preparation for subsequent leisure activities [36, p. 25]. More gratifying experiences can be had later if some present leisure is used to cultivate interests and skills. But social strata apparently differ in their recognition of this relationship between present and future. Ability and willingness to defer gratification are learned traits [2, pp. 108-109] and are unequally acquired by members of different social classes.

Differential receptivity to educational recreation may partly explain the existence of a socioeconomic gradient in certain forms of outdoor recreation. The more or less steady increase in recreational use of wild lands may be partly due to the parallel rise in educational attainment of the general population. Various studies have found that some 60 percent or more of the visitors to wilderness areas are drawn from the top 10 percent of the population (in terms of educational attainment). Wilderness recreation has grown at conspicuously faster rates than other types of outdoor recreation. There is some evidence to suggest that the educational upgrading of the population has contributed to this growth [18, pp. 12-13]. Educated people are mentally equipped to derive aesthetic and intellectual satisfactions from contacts with primeval nature to a greater extent than are the less educated.

Some leisure activities have had elite origins and have later become comparably widespread among lower strata, too. Such downward diffusion often depends on technological progress, which can reduce the expense involved in the activity. It is not always possible, however, to disentangle the effects of such progress from whatever universal tendency there may be for lower strata to emulate the behavior of higher strata as much as circumstances allow.

By the middle of the nineteenth century, travel was becoming quite feasible for the wealthy as a form of recreation. Turnpikes, canals, and railroads had been built, the steamboat had developed, and all these afforded geographic mobility to those with money. Construction of summer resorts was one result. At first Easterners constituted the principal clientele. Westerners with social aspirations soon joined their Eastern countrymen, and every summer Southern plantation owners too, came north to the resorts of New England and the mid-Atlantic coast. By 1890, there were numerous middle-class summer hotels, and the downward diffusion was well under way [12].

Automobiles, in the first few years after their introduction, cost almost as much to maintain and operate for a year as to buy. In 1907, the president of Princeton University, Woodrow Wilson, warned that automobiles were giving workers and farmers direct glimpses of the "arrogance of wealth" and thus spreading socialistic feelings. But even before World War I, owning and operating automobiles ceased to be such an exclusive avocation. Their diffusion downward through the social hierarchy continued through and beyond the war. As cars became cheaper to buy and to use, and as highways improved and became more abundant, country people gained increased access to urban leisure-time opportunities, and city people regained access to the country. This new mobility was so significant for both groups that gasoline sales remained remarkably steady right through the Great Depression when renewed poverty exacted many sacrifices.

Stratification as Effect

Provision of facilities and conditions required by various recreational activities becomes organized into an assortment of ranked and coordinated occupations. When hundreds of thousands took up skiing, for example, the manufacturing and selling of skiing equipment and clothing became substantial businesses. Jobs arose for builders and operators of ski resorts. Early entrants in such a boom have unusual opportunities for upward social mobility. As such a new industry expands, it exerts growing pressure for reallocation of public lands for a new recreational use.

Patterns of recreational behavior can thus be the independent variable, and labor-force structure can be, to some extent, a dependent variable. It has been suggested that "the way leisure is used affects a culture as much as or more than the 'productive' work of that culture" [9, p. 1]. In many instances a large industry has provided the means for pursuit of fun, and society has never again been the same [32]. Widespread diffusion of automobile ownership through the population of the United States, for example, led to patterns of vacation travel which fostered construction of new forms of tourist accommodation. In the 1930s, in the Western states, the forerunner of the motel came into being— clusters of overnight frame cabins, usually without private plumbing at first, and sometimes even requiring the tourist to provide his own bedding. Before long, the signs at the side of the road began using the word "modern" as a euphemistic intimation that a group of these cabins had inside plumbing. By the 1960s the erstwhile "cabin camp" had evolved into more or less luxurious motels in which tiled bathrooms and carpeting were ubiquitous and television and swimming pools nearly so. Attractive restaurants were often part of the premises, too [12, pp. 323-324].

In 1900 the summer-resort business was small. It catered mostly to the wealthy. Half a century later there was a massive "vacation industry" catering in many ways to a much broader clientele. There are many communities whose economic base consists mainly of the expenditures of tourists and vacationists. Such business is actively sought by some communities as the answer to local economic problems.

In the future, some leisure-dependent occupations or communities or industries will expand and some will contract. Others will merely hold steady. Which will do which may depend upon, among other things, the form in which additional increments of leisure are attained. If the working *day* is shortened, city parks may be affected, but this increase in leisure would have little direct impact on most state parks, or national parks and forests. It would thus have little impact on the tourist industry. If the working *week* is shortened, gasoline sales are likely to rise, and campground construction within a hundred-mile radius of each large city is likely to boom. If *annual* vacations are lengthened or made more numerous, overseas airlines will do increased business, but so will winter resorts and the builders of summer homes. Campgrounds hundreds of miles from major urban agglomerations will be inundated. Already a large fraction of the labor force is in occupations directly or indirectly dependent upon the outdoor recreational expenditures of others, e.g., the automobile complex, producers and distributors of camping, skiing, fishing, hunting, and mountaineering equipment.

Stratification as Control Variable

The amount of leisure time per capita in a society and the way it is distributed among various activities depend partly on the way the population is distributed among different phases of the life cycle and among different occupations. In America, agricultural employment has declined markedly, and this has contributed to the increase in per capita leisure. Increased longevity—making for more years spent in retirement—has also been important. Increased participation of women in the labor force has partially offset these trends by reducing the average per capita leisure. But married female employment has augmented the financial ability of families to make choices regarding the use of whatever nonworking time their members do have [9, pp. 3, 5-8]. Projection of probable future trends in such matters has become a fairly routine task for demographers, and it will be of increasing importance to agencies and persons managing recreational wild lands.

The actual growth of leisure cannot be accurately seen without considering changes in the social structure. Some major changes have confused the picture. Since 1850, leisure has increased more in the manufacturing and mining industries than elsewhere. Agricultural leisure did not increase appreciably until the twentieth century. Most of its increase came after 1940. But millions of people left agriculture in the meantime, and went into urban occupations. So the mean leisure per capita in the whole population was more conspicuously changed than in most occupations considered alone. Self-employed persons, civil servants, professionals, and executives have experienced little or no increase in leisure.

The fastest recent drop in hours of work per week has been in low-ranked jobs. Here there is also often a period of some weeks of unwanted leisure (unemployment) each year [37, pp. 35-36]. For lower-ranked occupations, leisure is often unstable, unpredictable, and intermittent. For elite occupations, it tends to be bunched and predictable. Its use varies accordingly.

Motivations and Wild-land Recreation Norms

People are likely to acquire appetites for the recreational activities in which they had the most abundant and gratifying experience as they were growing up. There are intergenerational continuities in recreation preferences. Any recreational activity that is typically engaged in together by the members of a family may be expected to persist into the next generation—if its enjoyment has been shared in common. Recreational values may be learned in childhood. According to the psychological "law of effect," the probability of any behavior in a given situation depends on the consequences which have followed similar acts in the past in similar situations [21, pp. 318-319]. Human beings, however, more than other creatures, can learn by observation and "vicarious reinforcement." We can learn to value recreational activities which have been *rewarding to others*, even if we ourselves have rarely experienced them, provided the others are persons with whom we identify.

One can observe a man taking his family up a wilderness trail on a summer weekend, but one cannot directly observe the values that cause him to do it. It is possible to *infer* his motivation in various ways. One might go to his destination, see what the place is like, and infer that he went there in order to be in that kind of place. Or one might watch what he does (or ask what he does) when he gets there and infer that he went there for the opportunity to do those things. Or one might go and look at the place he came from and infer that he went into the wilderness to get away from that place. Or one might watch (or ask) what he does in the place he comes from and infer that he goes into the wilderness to get away from doing those things.

Motivations are inferential constructs; they cannot be directly observed. One might ask the trail user some questions, and he might answer that he likes to hike up this trail because . . . , and his words might be *assumed* to have some causal connection with his nonverbal behavior [23]. But it would be important to realize that without further evidence one couldn't really be sure whether the visitor's verbalized reasons motivated his hiking behavior or whether his hiking behavior motivated his verbalized *rationalization* [29].

Thus, there is a need to be tentative in what is said about the motivations of recreational users of wild lands. It is important to be as meticulous and precise as possible in stating the observational facts upon which motivational inferences are to be based [7, pp. 124-154].

To draw some boundaries around this inferential process, consider two extremes: first, the ardent mountain climber and, second, the sedentary camper who spends the weekend with his family, his dog, his transistor radio, his ice chest filled with beer or soft drinks, and his trailer, relaxing in a forest recreation facility within 50 or 100 miles of the city in which he lives and works.

The Quest for Uncertainty

Mountaineering has been studied as a way of gaining insight into recreational motivations [13]. Mountain climbing can hardly be attributed to the ordinary *instrumental* motivation that presumably characterizes the rational activities of the world of work; there are rather obvious reasons for *not* climbing a mountain, such as fatigue and danger. People do it in increasing numbers, even so.

The American expedition which Emerson studied as a climbing member was attempting to climb Mt. Everest from two different approaches—the Southeast Ridge, which had been climbed before, and the West Ridge, by which the summit had never been reached. At the end of each day, Emerson had each member of the expedition write in his diary a subjective estimate of the likelihood of success by each route. Each climber also wrote each evening what activities he wanted to perform next day. From these activity statements Emerson derived a measure of task motivation strength.

He compared day-to-day variations of an individual's responses, and he compared the responses of the West Ridge party with the responses of the party climbing the conventional Southeast Ridge. Both comparisons showed that if success seemed highly probable, *or* if failure seemed highly probable, then motivation was reduced! When there was genuine uncertainty as to whether the party would succeed or fail, then motivation was high. Communications between climbers tended to fall into a pattern which had the effect of *fostering* uncertainty about end results. If success began to seem assured to one climber, his companions would begin to point out ominous signs. If failure began to seem inevitable, a climber's partners began asserting grounds for optimism.

The *fun* obtained from mountain climbing is in carrying on the task in the face of doubt as to whether the summit will be reached or will prove unattainable. The summit of a mountain defines a problem. A problem which has never yet been solved may not be soluble; but it may not be known to be insoluble. First ascents are especially valued because a summit which has never been reached may not be reachable; but it is not known to be unreachable. However, a mountain which *has* been previously climbed, or a puzzle which has been solved many times, does not thereby lose all its value. For any given individual it may remain uncertain whether *he* can climb that mountain or solve that puzzle.

Group norms emerge even in recreation. In other realms of behavior, norms may have other functions, but in recreation they perform the function of preserving uncertainty. In mountaineering, for example, climbers shun equipment which makes the climb too easy. The legitimacy of carrying oxygen in climbing Everest has come to be questioned. The former uncertainty as to whether Everest could be climbed by man has thus been escalated (in response to its affirmative resolution) into the next higher uncertainty: can man climb it without oxygen?

Generalizing, it may be suggested that one important type of value underlying the recreational use of wilderness by its *average* devotee appears sometimes to be the mystery it holds for him. It presents puzzles to be solved. The visitor implicitly asks by entering the wilderness, "How well can I do with limited resources?" The challenge lies not merely in coping *physically* with the uncertainties posed by the environment, but also in coping with its intellectual problems. Norms arise which prescribe patterns of behavior perceived by the recreationist as germane to this value. Some of these norms may incidentally help protect the environment, but there is no guarantee that protection of fragile environments and enhancement of user fun can always be fostered by the *same* norms. The user's quest for uncertainty may sometimes but not always be a force for ecological balance. Moreover, it is not the only source of user norms.

The Quest for Freedom from Responsibility

Another sociologist has provided some clues to the motivations implicit in wild-land recreation by studying depreciative behavior in forest campgrounds [4]. It seems to be commonly believed both by recreationists and by campground managers that there are no thieves among campers. Accordingly, expensive equipment is left unguarded, often out in the open, and cars and trailers are often left unlocked and unattended. Implicit norms arise prescribing this casual style of campground living. Both the expectation that theft is unlikely and the tendency not to report it when it does occur probably are indicative of major motivations for camping. Camping may be motivated to a considerable extent by the desire to participate in a way of life that is thought to be free from such urban irritations.

Campbell and his associates noted instances of theft ranging from the teen-age pilfering of beer and carbonated beverages from campers' ice chests to the systematic looting of locked automobiles. It was found that campers who had been victims of campground theft were stubbornly reluctant to redefine the campground as anything but a crime-free environment. Not all campground damage is done, as imagined, by noncamping vandals who invade the campground for malicious purposes. Children of camping families, representing a broad segment of the camping public, it was found, also are involved, partly because camping parents seem to define the campground naïvely as a hazard-free and invulnerable environment.

As Figure 5-2 clearly shows, the composition of the population by which children are socialized underwent marked change between 1940 and 1960. For each child under fifteen years of age in the United States in 1960 there was about 0.65 person in his parents' age bracket (over twenty-five but under forty). In 1940 this ratio had been 0.95. Thus the children of 1960 were being socialized proportionately more by interaction with age-mates and proportion-

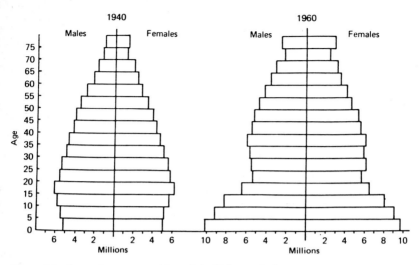

Figure 5-2   Age and sex composition of the U.S. population

ately less by parents, other things being equal. Even without the further effects of urbanization, affluence, and television, this change alone should have been expected to produce a rise in deviant behavior among the youths and young adults of the late 1960s and early 1970s.

Upon arriving in a campground, many parents readily cast off the burden of supervising their children. The chance to attain temporary freedom appears to be one motive for camping. Many problems arise under such circumstances from the activities of people who are often ill-informed as to the consequences of their actions in the campground. It is an environment whose requirements they do not fully understand. They thus become temporarily and inadvertently inconsiderate. When firewood is scarce, for example, they may simply obtain it from an adjacent campsite (which amounts to unwitting theft from another camper) or by chopping down an available tree with little or no recognition of the number of growing years required for its replacement. Campers unaware of the danger to tinder-dry forests often build fires outside designated fireplaces, without meaning to be arsonists. The fun value of fire play underlies a whole series of ecologically inappropriate norms insofar as it leads the pleasure-seeking visitor to regard a campfire as his rightful prerogative be be enjoyed by whatever means.

To understand the behavior of campers, it must be remembered that the campground is an environment whose requirements are not fully comprehended by many of its users. The naïve quest for short-run solutions to one's own immediate problems, in simple pursuit of fun and ignorance of the long-run ramifications for others or for the environment, apparently underlies much depreciative behavior in campgrounds. One important motivation for camping seems to be the desire to escape the usual necessity for considering the consequence of one's actions. Campgrounds are thought to be environments which permit such abrogation of responsibility.

In cities, privacy is created in public places by walls of indifference toward the strangers one encounters so constantly. The anonymity which creates privacy also frees the individual from responsibility for controlling others' behavior. This releases time and energy for performing other tasks. The norm of noninvolvement has been transferred from cities to the public campground. Campers may be observed passively standing by as their neighbor or their neighbor's child violates campground law, damages facilities, or creates a public nuisance. It may be tentatively inferred from this that part of the camper's motivation in coming to the campground was to be among strangers in a live-and-let-live atmosphere. Moreover, the campground is thought by such visitors to be a setting in which the privacy thus gained entails minimal risks. Accordingly, some of the innocently antisocial behavior of children might be curbed by locating campgrounds in places where there is just enough of an obvious physical hazard (such as a small gorge with a rushing stream in its bottom) to prevent the camper from discontinuing his parental surveillance the moment he and his children arrive.

Increased volume of recreational use of wild lands makes formal and explicit rules increasingly necessary. These often conflict with behavior patterns that were established in the days of low-density camping. This is a cogent example of what sociologists have come to call "cultural lag"—stress that occurs when interconnected parts of a culture change at different rates of speed [28]. Campground rules which interfere with what campers apparently regard as an inherent right to have an enjoyable time are likely to be violated. These people are at play, and, in play, rules are made to keep the fun going. So a rule which interferes with fun tends to be seen as no rule at all. This is why users of various kinds of motorized equipment that are taboo in a wilderness setting (because they not only destroy tranquility but can seriously damage fragile ecosystems) simply do not accept their exclusion from such areas.

Some Dimensions of Variation

Two polar opposites of motivation have thus been delineated and yet shown to be related—the mountaineer's quest for uncertainty and the urbanized camper's quest for privacy, freedom of association, and freedom from responsibility for the consequences of his actions. Several ways in which motivations for recreational *travel* vary may next be considered [6].

First, in response to the question, "What was the chief purpose of your trip?" tourists' answers may vary between specificity and diffuseness. Some people who received a questionnaire after visiting Mt. Rainier National Park indicated a very *specific* wish to camp in a particular spot in the park. On the other hand, one family from Illinois wrote, "To see the West and visit relatives." Their motivation was *diffuse*, and their visit to Mt. Rainier was hardly attributable to the specific features of the natural environment in that park. In addition to Mt. Rainier, their trip had included six other national parks. Such visitors appear to be truly motivated at least in part by *environmental* attractions but in a very general way rather than by the precise attributes of a particular locale.

Second, some people visit national or state parks or forests quite incidentally to their travels to visit relatives, urban centers, world's fairs, etc. Variation in this regard can be attributed to a motivational dimension of qualitative *similarity* or *diversity* of goals. A family from a suburb of Portland, Oregon, said after visiting Mt. Rainier during the summer of 1962, "We have never visited any other national park because of a habit over past years of spending our brief vacation times visiting relatives and friends. There are several national parks that we would very much like to see and we plan to make up for lost time in future years by visiting them. Especially interested in Grand Canyon, Crater Lake, Yosemite, Bryce Canyon, Glacier, Rocky Mountain, and Zion." These people already had formed latent preferences among national parks, even though they had never visited any, having been deterred by qualitatively different vacation destinations—friends' and relatives' homes. An incidental visit to one national park *with relatives* had evidently broken a barrier for them.

Third, people who do deliberately go into wild-land recreation areas as destinations vary along a continuum of *social* versus *environmental* interests. For many campers, camping appears to be more motivated by social than environmental concerns. Their activities are primarily oriented to other campers rather than to attributes of the natural environment [19]. Rules designed to protect the environment or even to protect its visitors from its hazards are often not comprehended and are ignored if they interfere with social pleasures. Interpretive facilities and activities are similarly ignored and remain ineffective, unless perceived as an arena for pleasurable social encounters. People can change, however, given time. Outdoor recreationists whose interests are initially more social than environmental may acquire an increasing orientation to the environment through repeated exposure to it, particularly if reinforced by stimulating interpretive experiences. The latter may be derived not only from resource management agencies like the National Park Service and the U.S. Forest Service, but also from oil company promotion efforts, or from entertainment media (e.g., National Geographic television specials or Walt Disney "True Life Adventure" films). Perhaps even more important, a socially oriented visitor may occasionally come under the primary group influence of another visitor who is more environment-oriented. The latter may pass on to him a personalized version of the lessons he has learned from the more formal interpretive sources. Interpretive programs may thus have second-stage effects.

A fourth type of variation in travel motivation pertains to spatial locations of travel destinations relative to the traveler's point of origin. He is more likely to visit two destinations on the same trip if the two lie roughly in the same compass direction from his home, so that one can serve as a stepping-stone en route to the other [6]. The typical itinerary of the national park visitor appears to be an elongated oval or crescent. Such itineraries generally include one or more other parks en route to or from the most remote park visited. This proclivity for multidestination itineraries results in the fact that a wild-land recreation site is likely to be more often visited if it is near another such site, and also that visits are in proportion to its proximity to a population center.

Attitude Differences by Urban versus Rural Upbringing

Urban living implies a life-style in which there is a diversity of both things and activities. Sociologists have developed two opposite views of the value orientations likely to be fostered by urbanization. One view holds that persons brought up in cities have their sensitivity to environmental diversity dulled and degraded and thus should be more likely than those not socialized in cities to carry over into their wild-land recreation activities an expectation of doing urban things. The other view implies just the opposite, that *wilderness purist* value orientations would be more common among city-raised people because they are more sensitive and discriminating than those socialized in nonurban surroundings.

In a study designed to test whether urban upbringing increases or decreases sensitivity to wilderness values, a psychometric scale was devised to measure attitudes ranging between *wilderness purism* (a desire to adapt one's habits to the environment rather than adapting the environment to one's habits) and *urbanism* (imposing urban apparatus and activities upon wild-land recreation environments). Over 1,300 wilderness area users who responded to a questionnaire containing this scale were categorized by their responses as "urbanists," "neutralists," "weak wildernists," "moderate wildernists," or "strong wildernists." Most persons in the sample tended to have wildernist attitudes, of course, but even these users of wilderness areas varied appreciably in the intensity of this value orientation [18].

The questionnaire asked respondents whether they had been brought up mainly in a city, a small town, or a rural area. Only 6.3 percent of the city-bred respondents had urbanist or neutralist attitudes, compared with 8.3 percent of those raised in small towns, and 11.4 percent of those who grew up in the country. Of those brought up in a city, 67 percent were moderate or strong wildernists, compared with 59.6 percent of those raised in small towns, and 53.1 percent of those from rural backgrounds.

Holding an urbanist value orientation and applying it in wilderness environments apparently goes with a lower level of attained education than does adherence to wildernist value orientations. Strong wildernists constituted 13.3 percent of those respondents who had not completed high school, 15.9 percent of those who were high school graduates, 19.6 percent of those with some college education, 27.2 percent of those who were college graduates, and 28.7 percent of those with post college education.

Another questionnaire study [4] obtained data from 4,600 persons who had camped in national forest or national park car campgrounds and backcountry in the state of Washington. In addition to a slightly revised wildernism scale, this questionnaire included (1) a scale measuring attitudes toward utilization versus preservation of natural resources, (2) a scale to measure respondents' tendencies to distinguish between and expect to behave differently in different environments, and (3) questions designed to elicit respondents' preferences for various types of recreation area.

Utilizationist attitudes were found to be more common among campers with rural backgrounds, while preservationist attitudes were more often expressed by city-bred campers. A respondent was more likely to be a strong differentiator of environments if he had been brought up in a city than if he was raised in a small town, and least likely if he had grown up in the country. Having an urban background made the wilderness-using respondent more likely to favor Park Service backcountry rather than Forest Service backcountry.

The city-bred user was more likely than his country cousin to experience wilderness with companions, but his companions were more likely to be wildernists, preservationists, natural-environment differentiators, and people who prefer backpacking to car camping. The person brought up in a rural area is less likely to associate with that kind of companion. Thus, through interpersonal contacts as well as through formal educational channels, the intellectualizing and sacralizing influences of urban socialization are enabled to outweigh the alleged urban degradation of sensitivity.

If, at present, the greatest threat to recreational wild lands stems from overuse, it is important to recognize the concentration of wild-land recreation interest among the urban-bred, the highly educated, and the professional stratum of the occupational hierarchy. Present and foreseeable demographic trends are toward more urbanization of the population, further impressive increases in median educational attainment, and increased professionalization of the labor force. In spite of continued increases in longevity, the proportion of our population in the age brackets most inclined toward backcountry recreation has been going up and will go up farther. There seems, therefore, to be no prospect of an imminent reduction in the size of the wild-land recreation clientele, and management problems seem destined to continue increasing unless some overt form of rationed admission is devised and put into effect. Even that sort of protective policy would be fraught with organizational problems.

Organizational Development Processes

Sociological principles can also shed light on the present capacity and probable future capacity of existing land management agencies to anticipate, diagnose, and cope with such problems. For one thing, it is useful to acknowledge that these agencies, like other social institutions, have evolved in an often piecemeal fashion. This is evident in the brief accounts of their histories presented elsewhere in this book. There have been noble visions, and both the National Park

Service and the U.S. Forest Service, as examples, can claim heroic ancestry. But it could not be claimed with accuracy that clearly articulated values came into being first and gave rise to logically consistent statements of land management policy which were then used as guides in rationally constructing organizations to implement such values. Organizational development is seldom if ever such a deliberate process.

If organizational growth and policy development are at least partly unplanned processes, there are nevertheless some models by which we can begin to understand them. For example, biological models have shed some light on problems of this type by directing sociologists' attention to growth factors indigenous to the growing organization and to forces that reshape it as it grows [17]. Relations between size, form, and function apparently must undergo change as an organization develops, just as they do when an organism grows. It is easy to see that an organism cannot retain the same relation between weight or volume and surface area as it grows. If it were to double its length, breadth, and height, its weight would increase as the cube of 2 while its surface area would increase only as the square of 2. A man ten times as tall as the reader could not have the same shape, for if he did he would weigh 1,000 times what the reader weighs and would have to support such weight with bones having only 100 times the cross section of the reader's bones. This "square-cube law" explains also why we must have lungs to take in oxygen sufficient for our bodily needs, whereas one-celled protozoa have sufficient surface membrane in proportion to their volume to breathe without such apparatus.

Sociologists do not assume that this square-cube principle can be applied directly and simply to organizational growth; the life space inhabited by organizations is not necessarily a three-dimensional Euclidean space [26]. Some tentative efforts to apply the principle have been made, however, and it does turn out that as an organization grows, its functional parts are compelled to grow at different rates. In one study of four business firms, each firm began with all (or nearly all) its people occupying "line" positions, but as each grew, the proportion of its people holding "staff" positions increased until an equilibrium was reached [17, pp. 365ff.]. Perhaps in any modern organization—including agencies responsible for wild-land recreation environments—it could be said that the personnel who are mainly handlers of paper will increase disproportionately as the system matures. The general function of communication and coordination increases more rapidly than overall organizational size. Such a principle helps account for the possibility that some people employed by resource management agencies find the work they do unlike what they imagined it would be, and why some people both inside and outside these agencies may regard the agencies' current activities inimical to the original missions.

Other biological models have also been sociologically useful. An organization, like an organism, may go through a more or less predictable life cycle. Only within such a developmental framework is it possible to understand some of the changes in structure and rules of procedure that have taken place in certain land management agencies. In the beginning, the U.S. Forest Service and the National Park Service each had a somewhat charismatic leader who inspired his men with a certain degree of missionary zeal [31,34]. But charismatic authority is foreign to routine organizational structures. If the relations arising from it are to be more than transitory, authority must cease to be merely personal and must be either traditionalized or given a basis in legal rules. A charismatically recruited and united administrative staff must somehow be adapted to everyday conditions [35, pp. 358-373]. Subsequent Forest Service chiefs and Park Service directors were not necessarily lesser men than Pinchot and Mather, but the task of administering a going bureau differs fundamentally from the task of creating a new organization out of chaos or controversy. The same people, even, may be expected to perform their roles differently in different phases of the life cycle of an organization.

Without the insights provided by the inquiries of social scientists, as sampled in this chapter, such differences could easily be misunderstood. Such misunderstanding—either by members of management agencies or by members of their publics—would almost always reduce the effectiveness of earnest efforts toward professional management of the recreational uses of wild lands.

Selected References

1. Blau, Peter M.: "Bureaucracy in Modern Society" Random House, New York, 1956.

2. Bredemeier, Harry C., and Richard M. Stephenson: "The Analysis of Social Systems," Holt, New York, 1962.

3. Burch, William R., Jr.: The Play World of Camping: Research into the Social Meaning of Outdoor Recreation, *American Journal of Sociology*, vol. 70, pp. 604-612, November, 1965.

4. Campbell, Frederick L., John C. Hendee, and Roger Clark: Law and Order in Public Parks, *Parks and Recreations*, vol. 3, pp. 28-31, 51-55, October, 1968.

5. Catton, William R., Jr.: Letting George Do It Won't Do It, *National Parks Magazine*, vol. 38, pp. 4-7, March, 1964.

6. Catton, William R., Jr.: Intervening Opportunities: Barriers or Stepping Stones?" *Pacific Sociological Review*, vol. 8, pp. 75-81, Fall, 1965.

7. Catton, William R., Jr.: "From Animistic to Naturalistic Sociology," McGraw-Hill, New York, 1966.

8. Clarke, Alfred C.: The Use of Leisure and Its Relation to Levels of Occupational Prestige, *American Sociological Review*, vol. 21, pp. 301-307, June, 1956.

9. How Much Leisure, Now and in the Future? in James C. Charlesworth (ed.), "Leisure in America: Blessing or Curse?" American Academy of Political and Social Science, Philadelphia, 1964.

10. Clawson, Marion, and Jack L. Knetsch: "Economics of Outdoor Recreation," Johns Hopkins, Baltimore, 1966.

11. Dollard, John, Neal Miller, Leonard Doob, O. H. Mowrer, and R. R. Sears: "Frustration and Aggression," Yale University Press, New Haven, Conn., 1939.

12. Dulles, Foster Rhea: "A History of Recreation: America Learns to Play," 2d ed., Appleton-Century-Crofts, New York, 1965.

13. Emerson, Richard M.: "Games: Rules, Outcomes and Motivation," paper presented to AAAS Symposium: Psychology and Sociology of Sport, Dallas, Tex., December, 1968.

14. Etzioni, Amitai: "Modern Organizations," Prentice-Hall, Englewood Cliffs, N.J., 1964.

15. Faris, Robert E. L. (ed.): "Handbook of Modern Sociology," Rand McNally, Chicago, 1964.

16. Gerstl, Joel E.: Leisure, Taste and Occupational Milieu, *Social Problems*, vol. 9, pp. 56-68, Summer, 1961.

17. Haire, Mason: Biological Models and Empirical Histories of the Growth of Organizations, chap. 39 in Amitai Etzioni and Eva Etzioni (eds.), "Social Change," Basic Books, New York, 1964.

18. Hendee, John C., William R. Catton, Jr., Larry D. Marlow, and C. Frank Brockman: "Wilderness Users in the Pacific Northwest: Their Characteristics, Values, and Management Preferences," U.S. Forest Service, Pacific Northwest Forest and Range Experiment Station, Research Paper PNW-61, Portland, Ore., 1968.

19. Hendee, John C., and Frederick L. Campbell: Social Aspects of Outdoor Recreation: The Developed Campground, *Trends in Parks and Recreation*, vol. 6, pp. 13-16, October, 1969.

20. Henry, Andrew F., and James F. Short: "Suicide and Homicide: Some Economic, Sociological, and Psychological Aspects of Aggression," Free Press, New York, 1954.

21. Hill, Winfred F.: Learning Theory and the Acquisition of Values, *Psychological Review*, vol. 67, pp. 317-331, October, 1960.

22. Keller, Albert Galloway (ed.): "Earth Hunger and Other Essays [of William Graham Sumner]," Yale University Press, New Haven, Conn., 1913.

23. Lundberg, George A.: The Natural Science Trend in Sociology, *American Journal of Sociology*, vol. 61, pp. 191-202, November, 1955.

24. Lundberg, George A., Clarence C. Schrag, Otto N. Larsen, and William R. Catton, Jr.: "Sociology," 4th ed., Harper & Row, New York, 1968.

25. Maier, Norman R. F.: "Frustration: A Study of Behavior without a Goal," McGraw-Hill, New York, 1949.

26. McWhinney, W. H.: On the Geometry of Organizations, *Administrative Science Quarterly*, vol. 10, pp. 347-363, December, 1965.

27. Merton, Robert K.: "Social Theory and Social Structure," enlarged ed., Free Press, New York, 1968.

28. Ogburn, William F.: Cultural Lag as Theory, *Sociology and Social Research*, vol. 41, pp. 167-174, January-February, 1951.

29. Pareto, Vilfredo: "The Mind and Society," Harcourt, Brace & World, New York, 1935.

30. Riessman, Leonard: "Class, Leisure and Social Participation, *American Sociological Review*, vol. 19, pp. 76-84, February, 1954.

31. Shankland, Robert: "Steve Mather of the National Parks," Knopf, New York, 1951.

32. Soule, George: The Economics of Leisure, *Annals of the American Academy of Political and Social Science*, vol. 313, pp. 16-24, September, 1956.

33. Thompson, Richard: "Race and Sport," Oxford, London, 1964.

34. Udall, Stewart L.: "The Quiet Crisis," Holt, New York, 1963.

35. Weber, Max: "The Theory of Social and Economic Organization," by Talcott Parsons, Oxford, New York, 1947.

36. Weiss, Paul: A Philosophical Definition of Leisure, in James C. Charlesworth (ed.), "Leisure in America: Blessing or Curse?" American Academy of Political and Social Science, Philadelphia, 1964.

37. Wilensky, Harold L.: The Uneven Distribution of Leisure: The Impact of Economic Growth on "Free Time," *Social Problems*, vol. 9, pp. 32-56, Summer, 1961.

38. Zawadski, Bohdan: Limitations of the Scapegoat Theory of Prejudice, *Journal of Abnormal and Social Psychology*, vol. 43, pp. 127-141, April, 1948.

chapter six

EVOLVING PROGRAMS AND CONCEPTS OF WILD-LAND RECREATION

Many current concepts of wild-land recreation and perpetuation of environmental quality originated in earlier years. The conditions which brought them about were recognized, in incipient stages of their development, by numerous persons who tried to stir interest in prompt, timely action; though minor successes were occasionally scored, their efforts were generally abortive. A "climate" necessary for general wide-scale acceptance and implementation of their proposals had not yet developed. But by the mid-fifties conditions had changed noticeably, and within a decade values inherent in wild-land recreation and perpetuation of environmental quality were recognized and became "fashionable." As a result, many early recommendations were eventually accepted and activated; in some instances resultant programs exceeded initial expectations.

One of the earliest indications of these changes was the recognition of the need for national recreational land planning. In turn, this was followed by important developments that made recreational use of wild lands and environmental protection become important national issues.

Significant Events in National Recreational Land Planning

The Outdoor Recreation Resources Review Commission, which functioned from 1958 until shortly after the publication of its report in 1962, was a catalyst in the development of public interest in comprehensive national recreational land planning and a major factor in implementing positive action toward that goal. Recommendations of this commission also prompted broader actions concerning perpetuation of environmental interest and quality.

However, national recreational land planning did not develop suddenly.

Interest in coordinated recreational land planning on a national level began in 1924, when the President appointed a Committee on Outdoor Recreation[1] to coordinate widely separated viewpoints and interests of various federal, state, and local agencies in formulating a national recreational policy to serve as a guide for future action. To assist the committee in considering all aspects of this problem, the first National Conference on Outdoor Recreation was held in Washington May 22-24, 1924. Numerous public and private recreational leaders attended, and an executive committee and various advisory councils were appointed to undertake aspects of the task. An emerging national recreational plan, resulting from work during intervening years, was reviewed at the second National Conference on Outdoor Recreation, held in Washington January 20-21, 1926. One result of these meetings was a report on Recreational Resources of Federal Lands, by a Joint Committee of the American Forestry Association and the National Parks Association under auspices of the National Conference on Outdoor Recreation, issued in 1928. This effort, ahead of the times, unfortunately was not productive of anything permanent [1,2,3].

Planning for proper development and use of natural resources, including recreation, was implemented during the Depression by various emergency agencies. In particular, the National Planning Board was established to advise and assist the Public Works Administration in coordination of efforts between federal, state, and local governments. Its report, submitted to the President in 1934, led to its reorganization as the National Resources Board with broader responsibilities, including development of a "program and plan of procedure dealing with physical, social, governmental, and economic aspects of public policy for the development and use of land, water, and other national resources and such related subjects as may from time to time be referred to the Board by the President." Various reports of the National Resources Board led to the creation of the National Resources committee on June 14, 1935, which was expected to have more permanent status. It developed considerable information on natural resources but ceased to function when the United States entered World War II [10,28].

Recreation Gains during Depression Years

Recreation, historically regarded in America as incidental to the business of living, did not begin to evolve as a modern concept until the Depression of the

---

[1] The committee consisted of John Wingate Weeks, Secretary of War and author of the Weeks Act for the conservation of Eastern forests; Hubert Work, Secretary of the Interior, in charge of the National Parks System, reclamation projects, Indian reservations, and public lands; Henry Cantwell Wallace, Secretary of Agriculture, in charge of the national forests and wild life sanctuaries; Herbert Hoover, Secretary of Commerce, in charge of the Bureau of Fisheries; James J. Davis, Secretary of Labor; and Franklin Roosevelt, Assistant Secretary of the Navy, Executive Chairman.

1930s. Before then the meager financial support of recreation areas and programs seriously limited the number of competent employees attracted to this line of work. Many who chose recreation as a career did so out of dedication to an idea, rather than because of opportunity for personal recognition or financial gain. In particular, appropriations for early national and state parks and national forest recreation areas were so limited that maintenance of even basic standards was difficult; achievement of that goal often demanded some measure of personal sacrifice.

Although the Depression materially affected the economic and social climate of the nation, it was a boon to recreation [5]. Faced with the possibility of serious problems resulting from widespread unemployment, Congress passed various laws to initiate a number of emergency works programs [10,28]. Agencies such as the Public Works Administration (PWA), Civilian Conservation Corps (CCC), Works Progress Administration (WPA), and National Youth Administration (NYA),[2] though sometimes ridiculed for worker inefficiency, nevertheless contributed greatly in many ways to the expansion and improvement of recreational facilities and opportunities. Activities in which these agencies were involved included reforestation; prevention and suppression of forest fires and outbreaks of destructive forest insects and diseases; research and publication of research results; improvement of interpretive exhibits; construction of equipment for proper housing of scientific collections; erosion and flood control; improvement and expansion of trails, campgrounds and picnic areas, water systems, sanitary facilities, and related needs often inadequately dealt with in recreational areas of that time. Many employees of these emergency agencies were highly qualified specialists who normally might not have been attracted to this field of activity. Though lacking in specialized abilities, the great majority, usually young people, benefited from trained leadership in development of particular skills or interests, as well as from the opportunity to engage in productive work. Some continued their association with the various organizations served by these emergency agencies after the Depression, and a number eventually rose to high places of authority.

The Depression also brought to the fore simple inexpensive pleasures, largely ignored in more affluent times. During Depression years recreational values were less likely to be rated on the basis of cost; increasing numbers of visitors to recreational areas discovered recreational interests that they had previously ignored or overlooked, and could enjoy them with minimum expenditure. Further, to an increasing degree Americans began to appreciate that environmental interest and beauty had practical values, that such values were worth protecting, and that their protection depended largely on carefully con-

---

[2] The high point in activities of various emergency agencies was approximately 1935. By 1942 all had been phased out, as their need was diminished by improved economic conditions and as the United States became deeply involved in World War II.

ceived long-range planning and the exercise of personal responsibility. Recreation as a logical part of life, as well as a profession, was on the way to coming of age.

Also during the Depression years, a number of recreation demonstration areas were developed by the National Park Service as examples of what might be accomplished for public benefit through most appropriate recreational use of certain types of wild lands. Some of these recreation demonstration areas were later incorporated into several state park systems.

Mission 66 and Operation Outdoors

Later noteworthy recreational planning activities were related to the Mission 66 program of the National Park Service [33], initiated in 1956, and the Operation Outdoors program of the U.S. Forest Service, initiated in 1958 [27]. Principal objectives of these programs were the rehabilitation, improvement, and modernization of recreational facilities in National Park Service areas and national forests, which had deteriorated badly during the years of World War II and were inadequate to meet the demands of rapidly increasing numbers of visitors.

National Outdoor Recreation Resources Review Commission

This commission was established [14] by authority of the Outdoor Recreation Resources Review Act (P.L. 85-470), approved June 28, 1958.[3] It represented the most tangible effort on a national level toward the study, planning, and coordination of varied public recreational needs and resources so that future as well as present Americans could be assured of outdoor recreational opportunities of adequate quality, quantity, type, and distribution.

The commission's report was published and presented to the President and the Congress in January, 1962 [14]. It was based upon twenty-seven specific published studies carried out by the commission staff and certain qualified

---

[3] The commission consisted of four members of the Senate Committee on Interior and Insular Affairs, appointed by the President of the Senate; four members of the House Committee on Interior and Insular Affairs, appointed by the President, who were "known to be informed about and concerned with the preservation and development of outdoor recreation resources and opportunities and experienced in resource conservation planning of multiple resource uses." One of the latter was appointed by the President as chairman of the commission.

The Outdoor Recreation Resources Review Act also made provision for an executive secretary and necessary personnel, as well as an advisory council to work with the commission in carrying out the purposes of the act. The advisory council consisted of liaison officers appointed by various Federal and independent agencies with a direct interest and responsibility in various phases of outdoor recreation, together with twenty-five additional members representing major geographical areas and group interests, appointed by the commission.

outside contractors. The report included recommendations of the commission, consisting of a national outdoor recreation policy; guidelines for management of outdoor recreation resources; expansion, modification, and intensification of existing programs to meet increasing needs; establishment of a Bureau of Outdoor Recreation in the federal government; and a federal grants-in-aid program to states.

Establishment of the Bureau of Outdoor Recreation

One of the first results of the National Outdoor Recreation Resources Review Commission's recommendations was the establishment of the Bureau of Outdoor Recreation[4] in the Department of the Interior on April 2, 1962 [29]. This new bureau was not designed as a land-management agency. Its responsibilities were coordination of related federal outdoor recreation programs; stimulation of and provision for assistance to the states in outdoor recreation; sponsorship and conduct of outdoor recreation research; encouragement of interstate and regional cooperation in outdoor recreation; conduct of recreation resources surveys; and formulation of a nationwide outdoor recreation plan on the basis of state, regional, and federal plans. Its various activities were subsequently aided by passage of the Land and Water Conservation Fund Act of September 19, 1964 (P.L. 88-578), as amended, 1968 (P.L. 90-401). The purpose of this act [30] was to create a revolving fund from which Congress could appropriate money for outdoor recreational areas and facilities. The program became effective January 1, 1965.

The Bureau provides staff services for the Recreation Committee of the Environmental Quality Council and for both the Advisory Council on Historic Preservation and the National Forest Reservation Commission.

Because of their close relation to and familiarity with local needs, the states have a pivotal role in outdoor recreation planning, acquisition, and development. The Bureau of Outdoor Recreation has developed guidelines for the preparation of comprehensive statewide recreation plans, including those relating specifically to various political subdivisions of the states. The Bureau assists the states with recreation planning, insofar as funds and personnel permit. To assist in federal-state cooperation, states have designated liaison officers to work with the Bureau of Outdoor Recreation. The states assume primary responsibility in allocating state grants-in-aid funds to their various political subdivisions and in assisting in recreation planning on local levels.

---

[4] Established Apr. 2, 1962, by order of the Secretary of the Interior; the Bureau's organic act (P.L. 88-029) was passed by Congress and signed by the President on May 28, 1963 [29].

Establishment of the National Wilderness Preservation System

On September 3, 1964, the President signed the Wilderness Act (P.L. 88-577), thus establishing the National Wilderness Preservation System [12,19,20]. Efforts toward this end, initiated by the Sierra Club and the Wilderness Society in the late 1940s, had resulted in the introduction of the first of a series of wilderness bills[5] into the Eighty-fourth Congress, second session, in June, 1956. No action was taken on any of these original proposals. During the following eight years several variations of them were considered by Congress, and numerous hearings on their merits were held in various parts of the country. The hearings evoked considerable, often bitter, controversy and debate, and none of the early bills received congressional approval. Eventually reasonable compromises were developed on major points of contention.[6] Although the compromises were not completely acceptable to everyone concerned, the legislation thus developed represents one of the more significant milestones in the history of recreational use of wild lands.

Basically the Wilderness Act provides maximum possible permanent statutory protection of natural qualities typical of certain federal lands with a minimum contiguous area of 5,000 acres. Wilderness areas, designated by Congress and approved by the President, cannot be modified except by congressional action. However, administrative responsibility for these lands is the same as before passage of the act; in addition, provisions were made for continuation of certain well-established activities and prior rights.

The Wilderness bill provided for the immediate inclusion of fifty-four existing wilderness and wild areas,[7] as well as the Boundary Waters Canoe Area,[8] within the national forests, aggregating 9,139,721 acres. It provided also for a ten-year study period to determine suitability or unsuitability for wilderness use of primitive areas[9] within the national forests, roadless portions of national parks and monuments, and similar undeveloped sections of national wildlife refuges and game ranges. Units of federal land in these latter categories are considered separately and, following completion of necessary study and public hearings on the nature of recommended disposition and management, may be added, in whole or part, to the National Wilderness Preservation System.

---

[5] S. 4013—Humphrey and others, June 7, 1956; H.R. 11703—Saylor, June 11, 1956; H.R. 11751—Metcalf, June 13, 1956; H.R. 11791—Reuss, June 14, 1956; H.R. 11806-Miller, June 18, 1956.

[6] Bill S. 4 was passed by the Senate, Apr. 9, 1963, and H.R. 9070 by the House, July 30, 1964.

[7] Previously administratively designated under USFS regulations U-1 and U-2.

[8] Previously classified as the Superior Roadless Area.

[9] Previously administratively designated under USFS regulation L-20.

Public Land Law Review Commission

Since our land laws were developed over many years as a result of independent action at various sessions of Congress in response to timely needs, they were not always properly related to one another. The expanding importance of varied benefits of wild lands, highlighted by controversies over different proposals of use, indicated that there was great need for better coordination of the objectives of the various land laws and the manner of their administration. The Act Establishing the Public Land Law Review Commission (P.L. 88-606), which became law on September 19, 1964, was intended to serve as a step toward this goal [17,18,21].

The Commission[10] was directed to (1) review the relation of existing public land laws; (2) determine the adequacy of the public land laws to meet current and future needs in providing maximum general public benefits; (3) identify and evaluate the division of administrative responsibility among various agencies of the federal government concerned with the public lands and public land laws; and (4) determine whether and to what extent revisions are necessary in the public land laws and relevant rules and regulations. Further, the Commission was directed to submit a report at a specified time[11] to the President and the Congress recommending both administrative and legislative actions which should be taken to assure "that the public lands of the United States shall be (a) retained and managed or (b) disposed of, all in a manner to provide the maximum benefit for the general public."

The magnitude of this assignment is emphasized by the fact that several thousand public land laws were in effect at the time this act was passed. While the effect of this legislation is expected to be significant, maximum benefits

---

[10] Though similar studies of our land laws were made in 1879, 1903, and 1930, the Commission was the first of these four groups to be composed of members of Congress [32]. It had nineteen members, consisting of six members from the Senate Committee on Interior and Insular Affairs, a like number from the House Committee on Interior and Insular Affairs (in each case equally divided between majority and minority parties), six members who were appointed by the President (not to include officers of federal agencies), and the nineteenth member and chairman of the Commission, who was elected by the other eighteen members.

The bill provided also for a full-time staff director, together with necessary personnel to carry out routine assigned tasks, as well as an advisory council to assist the Commission. The advisory council consisted of liaison officers from various interested federal departments and agencies, together with twenty-five members appointed by the Commission who represented various major citizen groups interested in public land law problems. Further, each governor was requested to designate a representative to work with the Commission and the advisory council.

[11] Original date of Dec. 31, 1968, was later extended.

cannot be expected for some time because of the many intricate complications involved.

The Commission's report, *One Third of the Nation's Land*, was presented to the President and the Congress in June, 1970, and published for the public by the Government Printing Office shortly thereafter [16]. In addition to the work of the Commission, the advisory council, and the Governor's representatives, the report was also based on data from public meetings held throughout the country and the results of thirty-three research studies related to the Commission's investigation.

In general the Commission made 137 specific recommendations, including the need for basic revisions in the land laws so that, in the future, lands disposed of would be only those lands where nonfederal ownership benefit to the general public would be maximum. It was suggested that Congress establish national policy on all public land laws. Reviews of public domain land withdrawals by Executive order and of lands not designated for any specific use were suggested, as were guidelines for land-use planning, statutory guidelines, and legislation concerning land-use management and future resource-use policy. A new federal department of natural resources, including the Forest Service within the Department of the Interior, was recommended. Categories of public groups involved in land policy and use were defined, and a recommendation was made that the interests of these groups be taken into account in public land decisions [16].

To improve recreational land use, recommendations were made concerning the role of the Bureau of Outdoor Recreation in national and state recreation planning, changes in the Land and Water Conservation Fund Act, the need for recreation user fees, federal responsibility for public accommodations on federal public lands. Unique public land areas of national significance were to be identified and protected, and guidelines were to be established for minimizing conflicting land uses on public lands. Private enterprise was to be encouraged to play a greater role in development and management of intensive recreation use on public lands not designated for concessionaire development. Further it was recommended that Congress provide guidelines for managing public land resources for recreation, revising the classification system suggested by the Outdoor Recreation Resources Review Commission (see Chapter 7). The need for rights-of-way across private lands to provide access to public land and limits on federal recreation land acquisition policy was indicated [16].

Since the Commission was concerned with all public land laws, there were of course overlaps between recreation recommendations and those for other land uses. If all or a major number of the recommendations became laws, federal land-use policy and management would be substantially altered. Would such wide-ranging changes in our land laws and policies be likely in the foreseeable future (set by the Commission as the year 2000)?

Conservation Organizations and Wild-land Recreation

Reference has been made earlier to John Muir and the Sierra Club and the fight for Hetch Hetchy Valley in Yosemite National Park. The Wilderness Society, which Bob Marshall, Aldo Leopold, and others founded, was instrumental in the passage of the Wilderness Act of 1964. The American Forestry Association, founded in 1875, and perhaps the oldest conservation organization, has long been concerned with the wise use and perpetuation of forests, including their use for recreation. The National Parks Association (now National Parks and Conservation Association), founded in 1919, partly with the aid of Stephen T. Mather, has worked for park establishment and preservation, more recently expanding its interests to broader environmental concerns, due to the interrelationship of park problems with pollution, population, and multiple resource planning. These are but a few of the older national organizations. There are numerous other national and local organizations concerned with recreational land use as it involves environmental protection and maintenance.

All these groups are volunteer organizations primarily made up of nonprofessionals, though the leaders are now professional managers. Often they are organized by people having a common interest, as was the Sierra Club (founded in San Francisco in 1892) to explore, enjoy, and preserve the Sierra Nevada and other Pacific Coast scenic areas [4]. Often there is a desire for protecting a particular area the group visits or for changing planning or policies concerning land use. A major cause, such as the struggle for the Wilderness Act, welds the groups together; the battle against a common foe, though not always clearly defined, strengthens the organization. When the goal is attained, the organization enlarges and prospers. The publications of all the above groups appeal to a wide range of people for support, though the work of the organization is usually done by a small group with the paid staff managing operations.

Though the paid executive secretary has almost always had major control in volunteer organizations, the expansion and development of the group society, especially since World War II, have also enhanced the power and growth of paid staff. The control once possessed by executive secretaries is now held by directors, executive vice-presidents, or presidents. With the support of loyal dedicated members, they often wield almost absolute power. The membership, so far largely from middle-class sections of society, with an infusion of younger students and outdoor enthusiasts, often sees the organization and its activities as a challenging diversion from somewhat mundane vocational chores.

The fight for a new park, the opposition to a large dam or road development or the push for legislation are all exciting activities requiring great dedication, loyalty, and effort. Members can feel they are contributing directly to social change. The diversity of the membership may make conservation groups more politically effective than professional organizations which may express a constant point of view or studied opinions conditioned by confirmed results.

There are many types of group organizations, with variations of emphasis, structure, and goals. Some are often at odds over one particular issue, or they may form coalitions to save large areas, as was the case in the fight to save the Florida Everglades from a jet airport and land development. There are also groups generally offering opposition to the older conservation clubs. Many of these groups view conservation primarily from the utilization, as opposed to the preservation point of view.

All these groups are important in their impact on recreation land policy and management. The land manager will encounter all of them in his work and should understand their objectives and goals.

Additional Events Important in Wild-land Recreation

Over many years other federal agencies, as well as commissions and related official bodies, have become involved, directly or indirectly, in outdoor recreation [8,9,31]. In some instances their activities have been authorized by specific laws, in others by extension of agency policy in response to public demand. In addition, certain significant legislative acts have recently been passed by Congress and have received Presidential approval.

Miscellaneous Federal Agencies and Related Official Bodies

The relations of several of the more important of these federal organizations are briefly outlined in the following paragraphs.

Bureau of Public Roads. For many years this agency, now included in the Department of Transportation, has cooperated with the National Park Service, the Forest Service, and other federal agencies in the construction of roads in various areas of federal land [8,31]. By authority of the Federal-Aid Highway Act of 1958 (P.L. 85-899), together with later supplements, the Bureau of Public Roads is responsible for federal aid to states in construction of the National System of Interstate and Defense Highways; it also cooperates with state highway departments in the development of access routes, subsidiary roads, and related highway services, including safety rest areas and parking places at scenic, historic, and related points of interest along highways. Good highway appearance is not overlooked. The Federal-Aid Highway Act includes a clause relating to the control of signs and displays along the Interstate Highway System [9]. In addition, a landscape development policy for the National System of Interstate and Defense Highways was adopted by the American Association of State Highway Officials on January 25, 1961 [8]. Further, scenic aspects of roads and parkways are subject to provisions of the Highway Beautification Act of 1965 (P.L. 89-285), as well as to consideration by the Environmental Quality Council and the Citizens Advisory Committee on Environmental Quality [29,31].

Indian Reservations. Many Indian reservations[12] have considerable outdoor recreational potential, but the Indians have traditionally been reluctant to permit any use, including recreational use, which might impinge upon its independent owner status. However, by 1960 tribal councils of a number of Indian reservations, recognizing general public interest in such areas as a source of employment and income opportunity for reservation residents, have sponsored various kinds of recreation developments [9,31]. These activities have been encouraged by the Bureau of Indian Affairs, and a revolving fund has been established by Congress to assist in necessary financing [9].

Environmental Quality Council and Citizens Advisory Committee on Environmental Quality. These two related organizations are descendants of several earlier bodies that had similar purposes.

A Recreational Advisory Council was established by the President on May 4, 1966, by authority of Executive Order No. 11278 [29,34].

The Council[13] was concerned with all phases of recreation and natural beauty. It was established to review recreation and natural beauty plans and programs of the federal agencies and to make recommendations to the President on matters of policy. It was also empowered to conduct studies in related fields and to encourage and assist federal agencies in coordinating their programs effectively.

The Citizens Advisory Committee[14] was made responsible for advising both the President and the Council on matters relating to (1) outdoor recreation and beautification of cities and the countryside, (2) correlation of natural beauty and outdoor recreation activities of federal organizations, and (3) local, state, and private outdoor recreation and natural beauty activities.

On May 29, 1969, the President's Council and the Citizens Advisory Committee on Recreation and Natural Beauty were superseded by the Environmental Quality Council and the Citizens Advisory Committee on Environmental Quality (Executive Order No. 11492). These more recent organizations have the same objectives, responsibilities, and membership as their predecessors. Changes in nomenclature indicate growing awareness that outdoor recreation is related to and dependent upon the nature of our total environment.

---

[12]Tribal Indian reservations are Indian property and, thus, private rather than public land. Such land is held in trust for the Indians by the federal government, with management on basic conservation principles supervised by the Bureau of Indian Affairs of the Department of the Interior, subject to consent of the Indian owners.

[13]A cabinet-level policy advisory body, with the Vice President as chairman, composed of the Secretaries of Defense; Interior; Agriculture; Commerce; Health, Education, and Welfare; and Housing and Urban Development; the chairman of the Federal Power Commission; the chairman of the Board of Directors of the Tennessee Valley Authority; and the administrator of the General Services Administration. The director of the Bureau of Outdoor Recreation serves as executive director.

[14]Composed of eleven members selected by the President for their interest in outdoor recreation and natural beauty.

Recent Significant Legislation

The Estuary Act of August 3, 1968 (P.L. 90-454), authorizes the Secretary of the Interior, in cooperation with the states, to conduct an inventory and study the nation's estuaries and their natural resources [22]. The Wild and Scenic Rivers Act of October 2, 1968 (P.L. 90-542), provides for the designation of portions of eight largely natural major streams as components of a National Wild and Scenic River System [23]. The National Trails System Act of October 2, 1968 (P.L. 90-543), designates the Appalachian Trail and the Pacific Crest Trail as initial units of a proposed National Trails System [24]. The National Environmental Policy Act of 1969 (P.L. 91-190) was signed by the President on January 1, 1970. This act declared a national policy concerning productive and enjoyable harmony between man and his environment, prevention of environmental damage, and better understanding of natural resource ecology; it also established the three-member Council on Environmental Quality, whose duties are to study and report on environmental matters [25,26].

General Comments and Concepts

At this point it may be helpful to the reader to bring major points together and focus on where we are. In Chapter 1 an organization framework was introduced, showing interrelationships of the parts of the book. We have seen that given more nonwork time, mobility, and income, plus changing attitudes and a taste for the outdoors, more urban people are seeking outdoor recreation in forests, parks, and other nonurban wild lands. A relationship has been shown between the manager of the recreation lands, the environmental resource, and the user. The role of interpretation as a catalyst has only been alluded to—so far.

This history of outdoor recreational use of wild lands has been closely associated with development of resource, particularly forest, conservation. Many of our great public parks and recreation areas are in the West, and the protection of these areas has required long and difficult struggles by inspired leaders, groups, and individuals. Planning thus far has not always been broadly conceived to include the interests of the visitor as well as those of the manager-planner. In an earlier period of much land, a small population, and slow transportation, individual rights in land use could more easily be gratified even if lands were developed. Today this is no longer the case. Research should provide insights for better planning and management.

The development of both the National Park System and the U.S. Forest Service were explained and elaborated upon. We found that recreation land-use policies of the two agencies are quite different. The Park Service is more nationally oriented, possibly due to the emphasis on seasonal visitation, from great distances. Management policy is toward protection and preservation of the natural environment while encouraging public use.

The Forest Service has a generally utilitarian policy toward its regular multiple-use forest lands, emphasizing support of local economies around or within national forests. Yet in the management of wilderness, Forest Service policy is perhaps more preservationist and limiting to development than that of the National Parks. Both organizations were founded by great leaders whose policies were most successful in the inception stages. Their organizational approaches have been models for similar federal, state, and local park and forest organizations.

After discussing the recreation visitor as described by Dr. Catton, we will return to an evolution hypothesis of park and forest organization that may provide reader insight for the future of recreation land management. Our growing, urbanized society provides the clientele for our parks and recreation areas. On public and to some extent private lands, consent of the people is necessary to area perpetuation. It is essential for the land manager to try to understand the goals and behavior of the visitor and to make certain the visitor understands managerial operation.

The visitor will view the recreation area manager, and other visitors, from the standards of his own group, not from those of the manager. Yet he may be directed by careful planning and adequate communication. Individual differences of age and sex also figure in visitor variance. Social class differences in taste, interests, and occupational roles have an effect on leisure patterns. Access to most of our big parks requires automobile use and often segments of leisure time not readily available to all. Are we perhaps too road-oriented?

Activities enjoyed in youth or with the family group may well persist into adult life, though it is also possible to learn new skills by observation and the enjoyment of others with whom we identify. Inferences as to motivation are difficult, but for some, as the mountain climber, uncertainty of outcome is important. For others, freedom from responsibility and minimal risks are thought to be part of a recreation camping experience. People visit areas for many reasons, varying along a continuum from social reasons, as enjoying the contact with others in the campground, to environmental reasons, as experiencing the beauty of nature. Interpretation can be useful in generating environmental interest, but will be more difficult with urban-oriented visitors unless it is stimulating and pleasurable. How could the manager use interpretation effectively?

A study of wilderness visitors in the Pacific Northwest found that post-college educated users had more wilderness purist attitudes and that more urban-bred people were wilderness purists than small-town or rurally raised respondents. In another study of campers in national forest and national park car campgrounds and backcountry, urban-bred people were found to be stronger differentiators of environments than rural-raised interviewees. Urban wilderness users preferred National Park Service backcountry to Forest Service wilderness.

Is it possible that support for wilderness and protected environments of parks will come largely from educated city dwellers? There are of course more urban than rural people, but what of the views of the city dweller generally? Why would people prefer National Park backcountry to Forest Service wilderness? What of the differences in agency policy and the range of recreation land-types?

An Evolutionary Hypothesis for Two Bureaus

Perhaps the historic agency development of the U.S. Forest Service and the National Park Service as described earlier may be used to give insights into present-day manager-visitor relationships in the use of wild-land environments for recreation. Anthony Downs, in "Inside Bureaucracy" [7], states that bureaus may be formed from existing bureaus by split-offs generated by zealots or charismatic leaders.[15] (Dr. Catton also mentions this theme in Chapter 5.) Both agencies were formed this way with Pinchot and Mather as the leaders. They dominated their small bureaus, selecting their associates carefully, pushing for their own forms of land management, obtaining bureau support from Presidents, congressmen, other political leaders, and businessmen outside the agency. We might call this the *inception stage*. The national forests and the national parks had the personal attention of leaders whose policies could be directly applied to field areas and to all personnel. Loyalty to the great leader was a hallmark of these agencies, morale was high, and they could usually rely on support of conservation organizations such as the American Forestry Association or the National Parks Assocation (and in Forester Pinchot's case, the Society of American Foresters, of which he was a founder). With much land and few resource users, inconsistencies in management or otherwise competitive uses were not so obvious as they are today. Demand for National Forest products was limited and locally oriented. Large National Park hotels served the life-style of most of the visitors and park supporters. Acquisition of new lands was an important agency function.

With the loss of the great men, leadership was passed to loyal lieutenants who carried on the founders' policies and successfully expanded the bureaus in the *planning, or organization, stage*. With the growth of the organization, the director's contact with individual forests and parks decreased. More emphasis went into building the organizational structure (regional organizations). Master planning, procedure manuals, and the like became important. In addition new functions were added (Emergency Conservation Work in the 1930s), and the types of resource users and visitors served expanded. Competition among resource users increased. Outside groups became more critical of agency policy.

As they grew the agencies began competing with each other, due partly to different concepts of land-use management and the desire to create national

---

[15]Anthony Downs. "Inside Bureaucracy," Boston, Little, Brown, a Rand Corporation Research Study, p. 6. Copyright 1966, 1967 by the Rand Corporation.

parks out of national forests (e.g., King's Canyon National Park, California; Olympic National Park, Washington). Also the agencies' emphasis shifted more toward timber production in the U.S. Forest Service and toward development for mass public use in the U.S. National Park Service (e.g., Mission 66). Today we seem to be in the *mass use—development stage*, in which organizations are very large with more administrative officers, and resource-management problems and allocation among competing clients are very complex. The initial goals of the agencies have been expanded to cover more resource uses (e.g., Multiple Use-Sustained Yield Act, 1960, for the U.S. Forest Service). Within the agencies the leaders are further removed from field problems by complex organizational frameworks, and the orientation of men of ambition is toward the position above them rather than to the resource-management tasks. At the same time, from the recreation point of view, both bureaus face increasing numbers of visitors with the complex characteristics developed above and those developed by Dr. Catton (see Chapter 5). Contact with organizations that once provided a great deal of support becomes more difficult and criticism of agency policy more frequent. Internal criticism of agency policy by staff is not encouraged.

This is just one point of view, and the reader is encouraged to study the organizational development in groups or bureaus of his knowledge to see if parallels exist. With as much diversity of areas, resource uses, types of visitors and groups, and with the need for flexible planning to provide a range of opportunities, how can bureaus in the mass use—development stage be adequately responsive to such variation? At least today's leaders usually are not so definite and specific in policy dictation as were the great founders of these organizations.

Summary

Current concepts of wild-land recreation and perpetuation of environmental quality evolved over many years; early efforts to speed up this process met with little success. Development of a national recreational plan was attempted as early as 1924, and during Depression years in the 1930s efforts were made to bring about the better coordination of recreational uses of different types of public lands. The Depression was responsible also for modifications in public attitude toward recreation on wild lands, which favored later development of improved policies and programs.

Progress was halted during World War II, but conditions afterwards, together with the population explosion and economic and social changes, brought increasing numbers of people to all types of recreational lands. The number of wild-land recreational areas and their facilities, which had deteriorated during the war years, was inadequate to meet accelerating demand.

Outdoor recreation became a major issue in 1958, when the Outdoor Recreation Resources Review Commission was established. The report of the

Commission, published in January, 1962, included recommendations for recreational land planning which were acted upon shortly afterwards. The Bureau of Outdoor Recreation was soon established. In 1965, passage of the Land and Water Conservation Fund Act made possible cooperation between the federal government, the states, and their political subdivisions on matters pertaining to outdoor recreation. In addition, the concept of a National Wilderness Preservation System, which had been a highly controversial matter for more than a decade, became reality on September 3, 1964, when the President signed the Wilderness Act. The Public Land Law Review Commission, designed to review the relations between existing public land laws and to make recommendations necessary to meet current and future needs, was also established in September, 1964. Conservations groups, such as the Sierra Club, have been important in the development and protection of parks, wilderness, and other wild lands. Their influence is very important for the land manager to understand. Later significant events were the establishment, by Executive order, of the Environmental Quality Council and the Citizens Advisory Committee on Environmental Quality, and the passage of the Estuary Act, the Wild and Scenic Rivers Act, the National Trails System Act (all in 1968), and the National Environmental Policy Act in 1969. This chapter concludes with general comments and concepts of materials presented thus far.

Selected References

1. Anonymous: For a National Outdoor Recreation Policy, *National Parks Bulletin*, no. 29, Apr. 30, 1924.
2. Anonymous: Organizing Recreation, *National Parks Bulletin*, vol. 7, no. 47, p. 8, January, 1926.
3. Anonymous: Recreation Resources of Federal Lands, *American Forests Magazine*, vol. 34, no. 418, pp. 606-607, October, 1928.
4. Brower, David (ed.): The Sierra Club, A Handbook, *Sierra Club Bulletin*, vol. 32, no. 10, November, 1947.
5. Clawson, Marion: "The Federal Lands Since 1956—Recent Trends in Use and Management," Resources for the Future, Johns Hopkins, Baltimore, 1967.
6. Doell, Charles E., and Gerald B. Fitzgerald: "A Brief History of Parks and Recreation in the United States," Athletic Institute, Chicago, 1954.
7. Downs, Anthony: "Inside Bureaucracy," Little, Brown, Boston, 1967.
8. Federal Interagency Committee on Recreation: "Role of the Federal Government in the Field of Recreation," no. 3, U.S. Government Printing Office, Washington, 1961.
9. Frederick Burke Foundation: "Federal Agencies and Outdoor Recreation," ORRRC Study Report No. 13, U.S. Government Printing Office, Washington, 1962.
10. Ise, John: "Our National Park Policy," Johns Hopkins, Baltimore, 1961.
11. LaGasse, Alfred B., and Walter L. Cook: Historical Development of Professional Education Programs for Outdoor Recreation, *Proceedings of the National Conference on Professional Education for Outdoor Recreation*, Syracuse, N.Y., 1964.
12. Nash, Roderick: "Wilderness and the American Mind," Yale University Press, New Haven, Conn., 1967.

13. National Conference on State Parks: "25th Anniversary Yearbook: Park and Recreation Progress," Washington, 1946.
14. Outdoor Recreation Resources Review Commission: "Outdoor Recreation for America: A Report to the President and to the Congress by the ORRRC," U.S. Government Printing Office, Washington, 1968.
15. President's Council on Recreation and Natural Beauty: "From Sea to Shining Sea," U.S. Government Printing Office, Washington, 1968.
16. Public Land Law Review Commission: "One-third of the Nation's Land," U.S. Government Printing Office, Washington, 1970.
17. U.S. Congress: "The Public Lands, Background Information on the Operation of the Present Public Land Laws," prepared by the Subcommittee on Public Lands for the Committee on Interior and Insular Affairs, U.S. Senate, Aug. 22, 1963, 88th Cong., 1st Sess., U.S. Government Printing Office, Washington, 1963.
18. U.S. Congress, Committee on Interior and Insular Affairs: "The Public Land Law Review Commission: Background and Need," Wayne N. Aspinwall, chairman, 89th Cong., 2d Sess., U.S. Government Printing Office, Washington, 1964.
19. U.S. Congress: "An Act to Establish a National Wilderness Preservation System for the Permanent Good of the Whole People, and for Other Purposes," P.L. 88-577, 88th Cong. S. 4, Sept. 3, 1964.
20. U.S. Congress: "National Wilderness Preservation System: Message from the President of the United States," 89th Cong., 1st Sess., H.R. 79, Feb. 8, 1965.
21. U.S. Congress, Committee on Interior and Insular Affairs: "Objectives, Functions and Operations of the Public Land Law Review Commission," Committee Print No. 21, 89th Cong. 2d Sess., U.S. Government Printing Office, Washington, 1966.
22. U.S. Congress: "Estuary Act," P.L. 90-454, 90th Cong., H.R. 25, Aug. 3, 1968.
23. U.S. Congress: "Wild and Scenic Rivers Act," P.L. 90-542, 90th Cong. S. 119, Oct. 2, 1968.
24. U.S. Congress: "National Trails System Act," P.L. 90-543, 90th Cong. S. 827, Oct. 2, 1968.
25. U.S. Congress: "National Environment Policy Act of 1969," 91st Cong. 1st Sess., Senate Calendar No. 287, Report No. 91-296, U.S. Government Printing Office, Washington, 1969.
26. U.S. Congress: "An Act to Establish a National Policy for the Environment, to Provide for the Establishment of a Council on Environmental Quality, and for Other Purposes," P.L. 91-190, 91st Cong. S. 1075, Jan. 1, 1970.
27. U.S. Department of Agriculture, Forest Service: "Operation Outdoors," U.S. Government Printing Office, Washington, 1957.
28. U.S. Department of the Interior: "Back of the Buffalo Seal," U.S. Government Printing Office, Washington, 1936.
29. U.S. Department of the Interior, Bureau of Outdoor Recreation: "Federal Focal Point in Outdoor Recreation," U.S. Government Printing Office, Washington, 1966.
30. U.S. Department of the Interior, Bureau of Outdoor Recreation: "Land and Water Conservation Fund Act, as Amended," U.S. Government Printing Office, Washington, July 15, 1968.
31. U.S. Department of the Interior, Bureau of Outdoor Recreation: "Federal Outdoor Recreation Programs," U.S. Government Printing Office, Washington, 1968.
32. U.S. Department of the Interior, Bureau of Land Management: Public Land Commissions, *Our Public Lands*, vol. 17, no. 2, Summer, 1967.
33. U.S. Department of the Interior, National Park Service: "Mission 66 in Action," n.p., n.d.
34. U.S. Government: Executive Order No. 11278: Establishing a President's Council and a Committee on Recreation and Natural Beauty, *Federal Register*, vol. 31, no. 87, May 5, 1966.

RESOURCES

chapter seven

NATURE OF WILD LAND RECREATIONAL RESOURCES

The dictionary defines a resource as something that lies ready for use.[1] Resources may be intangible (cultural, intellectual, aesthetic) or tangible (financial, natural), but they must be valuable in satisfying or providing for some human requirement. Their value varies with time, place, and individual preference. Many things considered as valuable resources today were not so regarded in the past; what may be highly valuable in one place may not be so elsewhere; and, for various reasons, things having great value to some people are often of little consequence to others. Resource values depend upon current desires or requirements; their importance is generally in inverse ratio to their abundance or availability. Scarcity enhances their value, confirming the truth of the old adage that one rarely worries about the water until the well goes dry.

Development of interest in conservation was related to wanton destruction of natural resources (forests, forage, soils, wildlife). Clean air and water, as well as environmental interest and beauty, were taken for granted until pollution, litter, or poorly planned or ill-advised development had caused deterioration of formerly attractive landscapes. Interest in the establishment of new parks and related reserves has grown with increased urbanization, reduction of open space, and overcrowding of existing areas. Public support of such establishment, necessitating certain sacrifices and costs, developed only when the value of some assets was enhanced by serious depletion.

---

[1] "Webster's New World Dictionary of the American Language" (College Edition), World Publishing Co., Cleveland, 1959.

Knowledge as a Recreational Resource

Outdoor recreation involves a multitude of interests and activities pursued on a great variety of areas, including both land and water. Individual capacity to appreciate the scope of such interests and activities contributes greatly to their maximum enjoyment, and to the exercise of responsibility in the perpetuation of values basic to such enjoyment. In turn, this is dependent upon background, training, and education with reference to:

1. Appreciation of the outdoors, especially the countless interests of complex associations and interrelations of the natural environment
2. Awareness of the importance of outdoor recreation and its inherent benefits to the individual and, thus, to society
3. Understanding of the relation of areas having different recreational functions as well as other uses
4. Understanding of the scientific, economic, political, and social factors basic to management, use, and perpetuation of values typical of different types of areas having recreational functions

The protection, proper use, and maximum enjoyment of wild lands used for recreation depend largely upon public understanding of the many interests and other factors involved. A well-informed public can be expected to relate recreation to the use of various areas of wild land in the most meaningful fashion. Both maximum enjoyment and perpetuation of the many interests of such areas are largely dependent upon a broad base of knowledge, understanding, and appreciation of their particular recreational values.

Development of such knowledge, understanding, and appreciation is the basic purpose of interpretive facilities and services (visitor centers or museums, nature trails, informative and educational programs, publications) now recognized as vital in recreational management of many types of wild lands. Public relations efforts aimed at development of public responsibility in the care and protection of wild lands (Smokey the Bear, Howdy Raccoon) have similar objectives. The considerable emphasis on biological and social sciences at all levels of our educational system is of great importance. In the future, increasing recognition of the value of such basic education in obtaining maximum value from leisure interests and activities pursued on wild lands will doubtless place even greater emphasis on less formalized indoctrination in fundamental concepts of biological, physical, and social sciences related to the outdoors.

However, since all things in the natural and man-made world are interrelated, much more than knowledge of assorted facts is necessary. Responsibility and good citizenship in the use and enjoyment of wild lands depend upon recognition of these intricate interrelations and an understanding of the implications and long-term effects of varied activities under different environmental conditions.

Land as a Recreational Resource

Many types of land, including lakes, reservoirs, streams, and related waters, are adapted to different kinds and combinations of recreational interests and activities. Areas other than wild lands are involved, including readily accessible and usually highly developed areas, such as urban neighborhood playgrounds and related city, county, and regional parks; though such lands receive only limited consideration in this book, their vital recreational function and their highly important relation to the use and protection of more remote, less-developed recreational areas should be recognized.

Most wild lands important for recreational use are administered by public agencies, though considerable acreage owned and operated for various purposes by private enterprise is increasingly important for recreation. It is important that these be managed, not only for the benefit and enjoyment of the current population, but in such manner that their basic values will be perpetuated for the future.

Recreational Lands Administered by Federal Agencies

The principal federal agencies which administer areas having diversified recreational interests, for varying recreational objectives, are listed in Table 7-1. For each of these, a more complete outline of its relation to recreation is provided in later chapters in this section.

Table 7-1
Principal federal agencies administering areas of varied recreation interests[a]

Area	Bureau or agency	Department
National parks and related units of the National Park System	U.S. National Park Service	Interior
National forests	U.S. Forest Service	Agriculture
Wildlife refuges; fish hatcheries	Bureau of Sport Fisheries and Wildlife, U.S. Fish and Wildlife Service[b]	Interior
Miscellaneous federal public lands[c]	U.S. Bureau of Land Management	Interior
Reservoirs, artificial lakes	U.S. Bureau of Reclamation	Interior
	Corps of Engineers, U.S. Army	Defense
	Tennessee Valley Authority[d]	d

[a]Not included are Indian lands and reservations, technically private lands held in trust for Indian owners through the Bureau of Indian Affairs of the Department of the Interior, and specifically designated wilderness areas administered by various federal land managing agencies as provided by the Wilderness Act.

[b]U.S. Fish and Wildlife Service consists of the Bureau of Sport Fisheries and Wildlife and the Bureau of Commercial Fisheries.

[c]Includes that part of the original public domain lands of the United States still under federal ownership which has not been set aside for such uses as national forests, parks, wildlife refuges, and other federal reservations.

[d]Independent agency.

In addition, over fifty other federal agencies and more than thirty federal commissions, boards, and related organizations have varying responsibilities to outdoor recreation, though they do not directly administer land [1,2,14]. Most important of these is the Bureau of Outdoor Recreation of the Department of the Interior, which, because of its singular position with respect to overall recreation throughout the United States has been outlined in Chapter 6 (p. 99).

Recreational Lands Administered by State, Local, and Private Agencies

Lands in each of these categories have varied important recreational functions and are outlined in later chapters.

Those administered by state agencies (parks, forests, wildlife areas, lands contiguous to highways, and public works developments) are similar in type to their federal counterparts, though they are generally more accessible and of more limited acreage [2,9]. Local recreational areas [2,5] are administered by municipal or county agencies, or by district or regional boards or commissions; though most readily accessible and usually typified by extensive man-made developments, a few are characterized by relatively large proportions of unmodified, natural sections. Among more important private lands used for recreation [4] are agricultural and industrial forest areas and those related to commercial recreation developments. However, quasi-public lands, such as Indian reservations, and areas owned or otherwise controlled by educational, scientific, outdoor, and philanthropic organizations are also noteworthy.

Classification of Recreation Resources

The Outdoor Recreation Resources Review Commission, in "Outdoor Recreation for America" [3], suggested a system for classifying outdoor recreation resources that would provide a common framework for management and recreation zoning that could be applied nationally. Six broad area classes were outlined with the concept that particular types of resources and areas would be managed for definite uses or combinations of uses (see Table 7-2).

Subsequently, the Bureau of Outdoor Recreation (BOR) adopted the classification system to provide uniformity in nationwide and state agency planning [9]. The BOR was concerned with the lack of consistency in systems developed by various states throughout the United States and adopted the six-class system recognizing that any one park or recreation area may have combinations of capability-use characteristics.

Table 7-2 shows the six classes and their characteristics of location, general types of recreation development activities, and physical characteristics. There are, of course, problems in application since different agencies have differing land-use patterns upon which the classes are imposed. For example, class III, natural environment areas, on national forest lands is applied to mixed recreation and production lands, while on national park lands class III lands are not open to resource production. Size of class units is also a problem, and there are

Table 7-2

Characteristics of ORRRC, Bureau of Outdoor Recreation land classes[a]

ORRRC-BOR class	Location	Developments	Recreation activities	Physical characteristics
I High-density recreation areas	Urban but may be in nat'l parks	Intensive; exclusively for recreation	Activity-oriented sports, games, etc.	Attractive; natural or man-made
II General outdoor recreation areas	More remote than I usually	Less intensive than I, but picnic, campgrounds, man-made facilities including hotels, stores, ski areas, etc.	Extensive; fishing, water sports, games, etc.	Attractive; natural to man-made
III Natural environment areas	More remote than I or II; largest acreage class	Limited—roads, trails, camping, picnic facilities; multiple-use management	Related to natural environment; hiking, camping, boating, hunting, etc.	Natural; attractive settings; varied landforms, lakes, etc.
IV Unique natural areas	Any place features found	Very limited; walks, trails, etc.	Study of natural features, sight-seeing	Outstanding natural features, scenic, scientific, geologic; part of a larger unit usually
V Primitive areas	V-A—where established under Wilderness Act; V-B—usually remote from cities	None to limited trails; usually no motor equipment	Wilderness hiking, camping, etc.	Natural, wild; *undeveloped*; away from civilization
VI Historic and cultural sites	Where sites exist	Limited—walks, interpretive centers, etc.	Sightseeing, study of sites	Associated with historic, cultural interests; national, state, local

[a]Adapted from USDI, Bureau of Outdoor Recreation Manual, part 241, Nationwide Plan, 1966 and ORRRC. "Outdoor Recreation for America," 1962 (see Chapter 6).

other complications which the reader is asked to consider based upon land-policy objectives developed so far in this text.

In addition, individual states have developed classification systems related to area designation. For instance, Minnesota state planners have proposed the use of such classes as state park, state recreation area, state riverway, etc. Nonetheless, the ORRRC-BOR classification system provides a convenient means of viewing recreation resource management considerations for analytical purposes. We will use it later in presenting a management framework.

Summary

Knowledge and areas of land and water are basic recreational resources. Maximum enjoyment of wild-land recreational interests and activities, as well as recognition of personal responsibility to the perpetuation of characteristics of areas which are basic to such interests and activities, are largely dependent upon knowledge, understanding, and appreciation of recreational land values. Many different types of areas are utilized for various recreational interests and activities. These areas are administered by public agencies (federal, state, local) as well as by private landowners (agricultural and industrial forest land, resort developments, lands controlled by special groups).

Seven principal federal agencies administer various types of areas which provide for the enjoyment of many wild-land recreational interests and activities. In addition, more than eighty other federal agencies, commissions, boards, and related organizations which do not directly administer land are directly or indirectly concerned with recreation.

The ORRRC-BOR recreation classification system of six land classes is a means of separating recreation resources by capability-use characteristics. Though it has weaknesses when broadly applied, it is useful in land-use analysis and planning.

Selected References

1. Frederick Burke Foundation: "Federal Agencies and Outdoor Recreation," ORRRC Study Report No. 13, U.S. Government Printing Office, Washington, 1962.
2. National Recreation and Park Association: "Recreation and Park Yearbook, 1966," Washington, 1967.
3. Outdoor Recreation Resources Review Commission: "Outdoor Recreation for America: A Report to the President and to the Congress by the ORRRC," U.S. Government Printing Office, Washington, January, 1962.
4. Outdoor Recreation Resources Review Commission: "Private Outdoor Recreation Facilities," ORRRC Study Report No. 11, U.S. Government Printing Office, Washington, 1962.

5. Outdoor Recreation Resources Review Commission: "The Future of Outdoor Recreation in Metropolitan Regions of the United States," ORRRC Study Report No. 21, U.S. Government Printing Office, Washington, 1962.

6. Recreation Advisory Council, Bureau of Outdoor Recreation: "Federal Executive Policy Governing the Reporting of Recreation Use of Federal Recreation Areas," U.S. Government Printing Office, Washington, 1965.

7. Shanklin, John F., and Edwin M. Fitch: Where Is the Outdoor Recreation Plan? *American Forests*, vol. 76, no. 3, March, 1970.

8. Stevens, Lawrence N.: Statement of Lawrence N. Stevens, Acting Director, Bureau of Outdoor Recreation, Department of the Interior, before the Subcommittee on National Parks and Recreation, House Committee on Interior and Insular Affairs, Apr. 21, 1969. (Duplicated.)

9. U.S. Department of the Interior, Bureau of Outdoor Recreation: "Manual," part 241, Nationwide Plan, Chap. 6, Washington, 1966.

10. U.S. Department of the Interior, Bureau of Outdoor Recreation: "Federal Focal Point in Outdoor Recreation," U.S. Government Printing Office, Washington, 1966.

11. U.S. Department of the Interior, Bureau of Outdoor Recreation: "Trails for America," U.S. Government Printing Office, Washington, 1966.

12. U.S. Department of the Interior, Bureau of Outdoor Recreation: "Index of Selected Outdoor Recreation Literature," vols. I, II, and III, U.S. Government Printing Office, Washington, 1967, 1968, and 1969.

13. U.S. Department of the Interior, Bureau of Outdoor Recreation: "Land and Water Conservation Fund Act, as Amended," U.S. Government Printing Office, Washington, 1968.

14. U.S. Department of the Interior, Bureau of Outdoor Recreation: "Federal Outdoor Recreation Programs," U.S. Government Printing Office, Washington, 1968.

15. U.S. Government: Executive Order 11278: Establishing a President's Council and a Committee on Recreation and Natural Beauty, *Federal Register*, vol. 31, no. 87, May 5, 1966.

chapter eight

THE NATIONAL PARK SYSTEM

T he National Park Service, a bureau in the U.S. Department of the Interior, is charged with the administration of national parks and related areas by authority of the act that established it. This act, passed by Congress and signed by President Woodrow Wilson on August 25, 1916, was designed to unify the administration of the national parks and national monuments then under the jurisdiction of the Department of the Interior. It stated that [11] :

The service thus established shall promote and regulate the use of the Federal areas known as national parks, monuments, and reservations hereinafter specified by such means and measures as conform to the fundamental purpose of said parks, monuments, and reservations, which purpose is to conserve the scenery and the natural and historic objects and the wild life therein and to provide for the enjoyment of the same in such manner and by such means as will leave them unimpaired for the enjoyment of future generations.

Extent and Diversity of the National Park System

The National Park Service administers several hundred areas of diverse sizes and types, widely distributed about the country, having an aggregate area of approximately 29 million acres (Table 8-1). National parks, although best known and having the greatest aggregate acreage and greatest travel, are only a part of the National Park System. Also included are a variety of other significant areas (national monuments and various types of parks and sites of historical interest),

Table 8-1
Summary of the National Park System (January, 1970)

Type of area	No.	Federal (acres)	Nonfederal (acres)	Gross (acres)
		Lands within exterior boundaries[a]		
National parks	35	14,275,007.52	184,589.07	14,459,596.59
National historical parks	13	36,000.70	8,689.08	44,689.78
National monuments	85	9,861,284.98	355,563.57	10,216,848.55
National military parks	11	30,394.96	1,588.40	31,983.36
National memorial parks	1	69,528.31	907.69	70,436.00
National battlefields	5	2,742.42	1,486.94	4,229.36
National battlefield parks	4	8,022.69	1,060.27	9,082.96
National battlefield sites	3	775.87	10.00	785.87
National historic sites	40	8,333.15	887.20	9,220.35
National historic sites (not federally owned or administered)	9	2.61	212.52	215.13
National memorials	21	5,487.49	178.27	5,665.76
National cemeteries	10	220.13	---	220.13
National seashores	7	231,758.32	213,246.91	355,005.23
National parkways	5	130,050.61	20,210.42	150,261.03
National capital parks[b]	1	7,024.05	---	7,024.05
White House	1	18.07	---	18.07
National recreation areas	13	3,595,102.62	213,901.38	3,809,004.00
National lakeshores	2	7,808.54	67,912.46	75,721.00
National scenic riverways	3	74,459.11	63,587.89	138,047.00
National scenic trails	1	17,000.00	33,000.00	50,000.00
National scientific reserves (not federally owned or administered)	1	---	32,500.00	32,500.00
"Other" parks[c]	5	24,056.31	1,549.16	25,605.47
International parks (not federally owned or administered)	1	---	10.50	10.50
Historic areas (not federally owned or administered)	1	---	7.00	7.00
Total	278	28,385,078.46	1,111,098.73	29,496,177.19

[a]Acreage as of June 30, 1969; areas added after that date: Florissant Fossil Beds National Monument and Lyndon B. Johnson and William Howard Taft National Historic Sites.

[b]Comprises 709 units within the District of Columbia and that part of the Chesapeake and Ohio Canal not included in the Chesapeake and Ohio Canal National Monument.

[c]Without national designation.

Note: Areas identified as living farms conduct appropriate farming operations all year. Areas identified as living history areas conduct appropriate historical and cultural activities. Depending on the area, these demonstrate Indian, Hawaiian, colonial, pioneer, frontier, together with certain other lands which embody high-quality scenic or recreational values whose protection is in the national interest.[1]

Legal Status of Areas in the National Park System

This diversity, coupled with various names applied to these lands, occasionally leads to some confusion as to the relation of various types of areas. Differences in name do not imply degrees of importance, significance, or size. Each unit in the National Park System has specific interests which are generally most typical of its area; each is nationally important in its own right. Size is a distinguishing characteristic of most, but not all, national parks, and of many national monuments. Two national monuments (Katmai and Glacier Bay, in Alaska) are both larger than the largest national park, Yellowstone National Park.

These areas differ primarily in the method of their establishment; in short, their legal status. The following paragraphs summarize the basic differences among the principal categories [17].

1. *National parks* are established only by specific act of Congress; likewise, enlargement or reduction of national parks is possible only by act of Congress.

2. *National monuments.* Most areas in this category have been established by Presidential proclamation, by authority of the Act for the Preservation of American Antiquities, which became law on June 8, 1906. The Antiquities act authorized the President to set aside, as national monuments, federal lands and waters which contain historic landmarks, historic or prehistoric structures, and other objects of historic or scientific interest. National monuments may be enlarged or reduced in size by Presidential proclamation, but only Congress can abolish them. A major result of the proclamation power was its success in setting aside vast areas of nationally significant lands and waters until Congress saw fit to make them national parks. Several national monuments have been reclassified as national parks. Congress may establish national monuments and did so in 1968 in authorizing Biscayne National Monument, Florida. Most national monuments, however, are the result of proclamation.

---

and military life, crafts, and transportation methods, generally using costumes and techniques of the historical periods.

Source: National Parks and Landmarks, Areas Administered by the National Park Service and related properties as of Jan. 1. 1970. (National Park System subject to change by addition of new areas and redesignation of existing units.)

[1] A generalized classification of the National Park System consists of three basic categories: *natural areas* (including most national parks and nearly half of the national monuments); *historical areas* (including Mesa Verde National Park, an archaeological area, together with most national monuments and varied historic parks and sites); and *recreational areas* (including national seashores, lakeshores, riverways, parkways, and related areas).

3. *National military parks, national battlefield parks and sites, national memorials and cemeteries, many national monuments, and the national capital parks* were originally administerd by various government agencies. On June 10, 1933, these areas were consolidated under National Park Service administration by authority of the Reorganization Act, which became law earlier in the same year.

4. *National historic sites.* The Historic Sites Act of August 21, 1935, provided for the establishement of national historic sites to be protected and preserved for public inspiration and enjoyment.

5. *Related scenic and recreational areas.* More recent legislation has been prompted by growing public interest in outdoor recreation and the need for environmental protection. Such legislation has provided legal basis for the acquisition or designation of various national seashores, national parkways, national recreation areas, and related protected lands.[2] Most of these areas (national parkways, national seashores, national lakeshores, and some national scenic riverways) have been placed under administration of the National Park Service; some national recreation areas are administered jointly with other agencies by interbureau agreement.

Organization of the National Park Service

The National Park Service organization includes a headquarters staff in Washington, D.C., six regional offices, several field offices, one planning and service

---

[2] *The Park, Parkway and Recreation Study Act, June 23, 1936,* authorized the National Park Service to conduct studies of park, parkway, and recreational area programs. Subsequently, the concept of national rural parkways was embodied in the *act of June 30, 1936,* providing for national park administration of the Blue Ridge Parkway. Cape Hatteras National Seashore, first area of its type, was established by the *act of Aug. 17, 1937,* thus paving the way for formation of similar areas under national park administration. Of particular importance in this respect was the *act of Aug. 7, 1961,* authorizing the establishment of Cape Cod National Seashore, including the use of appropriated funds for the purchase of large areas of land for public park purposes; previously, most National Park Service areas had resulted from designation of existing public lands, or from lands donated to the federal government for such purposes by private or other public interests. The *Surplus Property Act of 1944,* as amended, authorized the National Park Service to cooperate with the General Services Administration in investigating surplus properties for public park and recreation purposes. The *act of Aug. 7, 1946,* provided for administration of recreational aspects of areas under jurisdiction of other federal agencies. As a result cooperative agreements were developed between the National Park Service and the Bureau of Reclamation relative to provision for adequate public recreational use of certain reclamation projects, designed as recreation areas. Included are Lake Mead National Recreation Area, Arizona-Nevada; Glen Canyon Recreation Area, Arizona-Utah; and Coulee Dam Recreation Area, Washington. Although Flaming Gorge Recreation Area, Wyoming-Utah, began under joint National Park Service-Forest Service administration, full responsibility was transferred to the Forest Service in 1968.

center, two training centers, and personnel in each of the various national parks, monuments, historic sites, and related areas.

The principal administrative officer of the National Park Service is the Director, who is responsible to the Secretary of the Interior. Each of the six regional offices is in the charge of a Regional Director, who supervises National Park Service activities within a given region[3] and reports to the Director of the National Park Service in Washington, D.C. Each of the national parks, monuments, historic sites, and related areas is administered by a Superintendent who reports to his Regional Director.

The national headquarters in Washington consists of the offices of the Director, together with several Associate Directors and Assistant Directors, and other "key" headquarters administrative and policy-making personnel with their supporting staff who, at various levels, are responsible for different aspects of National Park Service activities and interests. Such activities and interests, organized under such basic categories as legislation, administration, operations, and professional services, are greatly diversified. They reflect the expanding importance and increasing responsibilities of the National Park Service in matters concerned with the protection, preservation, interpretation, and public use of National Park Service areas, as well as in cooperative efforts of the National Park Service with organizations of similar character concerned with national parks and equivalent reserves in other parts of the world.

An Assistant Solicitor, in charge of legal matters, is a member of the staff of the Solicitor of the Department of the Interior but attends, or is represented at, meetings of the staff of the Director of the National Park Service.

Regional offices are somewhat similarly organized. The Director of each region has several Associate and Assistant Directors and a staff of administrative and professional employees concerned with specific National Park Service activities within the region.

Various national parks, monuments, historic sites, and related areas complete the National Park Service organization. In each case the Superintendent is responsible for all matters pertaining to proper management and administration of his area, including general supervision of all planning and development therein.

The size and complexity of the staff in each unit of the National Park System are dependent upon the character of the area. The more complex organizations are divided into several principal departments: protection—under supervision of the Chief Park Ranger; fiscal, or varied business functions— in the charge of the Administrative Officer (in large areas) or the Administrative

[3] Names and headquarters of National Park Service regions (Figure 8-1) are *Northeast*, Philadelphia, Pa.; *Southeast*, Atlanta, Ga.; *Midwest*, Omaha, Neb.; *Southwest*, Santa Fe, N. Mex.; *Western*, San Francisco, Calif.; *Pacific Northwest*, Seattle, Wash.

Figure 8-1
The National Park Service, 1971; distribution of areas under its administration a

Voyageurs*
Grand Portage*   Isle Royale
Apostle Islands*   Pictured Rocks*

MINN.
Saint Croix*
WIS.   Wolf*   Sleeping Bear*
MICH.
Ice Age
Effigy Mounds   Chicago Portage   Indiana Dunes*
IOWA   Perry's Victory and International Peace Memorial
Herbert Hoover   NORTHEAST   OHIO
Johns Town Flood
Allegheny Portage Railroad
ILL.   IND.   Fort Necessity
MO.   William H. Taft*   Mound City Group   Eisenhower
George Rogers Clark   Lincoln Boyhood   KY.
Jefferson National Expansion Memorial   Abraham Lincoln Birthplace   Booker T. Washington   W.VA.   VA.
George Washington Carver   Mammoth Cave   Cumberland Gap
Wilson's Creek   Ozark   Fort Donelson   Andrew Johnson*
Pea Ridge   Stones River   Great Smoky Mountains   N.C.
Fort Smith   Shiloh   Carl Sandburg   Cowpens
ARK.   Brices Cross Roads   Russell Cave   Chickamauga and Chattanooga   Kennesaw Mountain   Kings Mountain
Hot Springs   Tupelo   TENN.   S.C.
Arkansas Post   MISS.   ATLANTA
LA.   Horseshoe Bend   GA.   Ocmulgee
ALA.   Andersonville   SOUTHEAST
Vicksburg
Chalmette   Gulf Islands*

Ft. Stanwix*   ME.   Saint Croix Island*
Saratoga   N.H.   Roosevelt Campobello
Ansley Wilcox House   Saint-Gaudens   Acadia
N.Y.   Minute Man   VT.   John Fitzgerald Kennedy
Vanderbilt Mansion   MASS.   Salem Maritime
Home of Franklin D. Roosevelt   Dorchester Hgts.   Saugus Iron Works
Edison   Federal Hall   Adams   Cape Cod
Delaware Water Gap   Sagamore Hill   Touro Synagogue
PA.   Morristown   CONN.   R.I.   Roger Williams*
Castle Clinton   Fire Island   General Grant
Hopewell Village   Hamilton Grange*
Gettysburg   Statue of Liberty
Philadelphia   Theodore Roosevelt Birthplace
Hampton   N.J.   St. Pauls Church
MD.   DEL.   Independence
Manassas   Gloria Del
Fredericksburg and Spotsylvania   Ft. Mc Henry
George Washington Birthplace   National Capital Parks
Shenandoah   Assateague Island
Appomattox   Richmond   Colonial
Petersburg   Yorktown
Poplar Grove   Jamestown
Wright Brothers   Fort Raleigh
Cape Hatteras
Guilford Courthouse
Moores Creek   Cape Lookout*
Fort Sumter
Fort Pulaski
Fort Frederica
Fort Caroline
Castillo De San Marcos
Fort Matanzas

ATLANTIC OCEAN

GULF OF MEXICO
De Soto
FLA.
Mar-A-Lago*
Everglades   Biscayne*

Legend
International Park
National Park
National Monument
National Lakeshore
National Seashore
National Historical Park
National Scenic Riverway or River
National Military Park
National Battlefield Site
National Battlefield Park
National Historic Site
National Battlefield
National Recreation Area
Regional Offices
National Memorial
National Memorial Park
National Cemetery
Parkway (---- not constructed)
National Capital Parks
National Scientific Reserve
Historic Area
National Scenic Trail
* No Federal Facilities

ATLANTIC OCEAN
St. Thomas*
Puerto Rico   Virgin Islands
Buck Island
St. Croix   Reef
Island   Christiansted

PUERTO RICO and the VIRGIN ISLANDS

s regional organization (National Park Service).

129

Assistant (in small areas); interpretation—supervised by the Chief of Interpretation or Chief Park Naturalist; maintenance—in the charge of the Chief of Maintenance. The organization of some areas also includes a sanitary department in the charge of a Sanitary Engineer. Some national parks also have a Park Landscape Architect, who is advisory to the Superintendent.

Administrative Policies of the National Park Service

The policy of the National Park Service was first defined approximately 1½ years after establishment of the agency in a letter dated May 13, 1918, signed by Secretary of the Interior Franklin Lane and addressed to Director Stephen T. Mather. The Secretary listed the following broad principles of national park management [3,15].

First, that the national parks must be maintained in absolutely unimpaired form for the use of future generations as well as those of our own time; second, that they are set apart for the use, observation, health, and pleasure of the people; and third, that the national interest must dictate all decisions affecting public or private enterprise in the parks.

A more detailed official statement of national park policy, prepared in conjunction with others interested in national park affairs, by Louis C. Crampton, special attorney for the Secretary of the Interior, was incorporated in the annual report of the Director of the National Park Service for the fiscal year ended June 30, 1931 [14]. The seventeen items in this policy statement emphasized that:

1. Supreme examples of scenic, scientific, or historic features, sufficient to justify national interest in their preservation, should characterize the greatly varied areas of the National Park System.

2. The twofold purpose of these areas is enjoyment and use by the present generation together with preservation unspoiled for the future—specifically these areas should be "spared the vandalism of improvement"; present use should not result in impairment of interests for the future.

3. Education (public understanding of significant interests typical of various areas) and inspiration are major aspects of use and enjoyment of the National Park System; recreation in its narrower sense ("having a good time") is a proper incidental use but exotic forms of amusement should not be encouraged, nor should anything that conflicts with or weakens enjoyment of inherent values be permitted.

4. Natural resources of these areas (forests, wildlife) should be considered from a noncommercial objective, emphasizing primitive or natural, rather than artificial, conditions.

5. Necessary developments (roads, buildings) should be in harmony with the environment, and their intrusion should be held to the absolute minimum.

6. The public welfare and best interests of park visitors should be considered in provision of necessary facilities and services, as well as in respect to federal control of land and federal jurisdiction over rules and regulations within boundaries of various areas.

Current Policy of the National Park Service

Since formulation of initial administrative policies for the National Park Systems, acts of Congress and Executive orders have greatly expanded the responsibilities and duties of the National Park Service. As a result, initial primary emphasis upon preservation of natural conditions was not relevant to certain more recently added areas which, by their nature and purpose, were noteworthy for other important values. In particular, recreational areas, and to a lesser degree areas of simple scenic quality (parkways), had already been variously modified; moreover, their significant features, where they existed, were of secondary importance. Further, public interest in and use of such areas emphasized activities and related necessary developments which often necessitated further environmental modification, even though such modification would not seriously impair their scenic attractiveness. Even significant archaeological and historical areas demand managerial procedures different from areas of truly natural character. Archaeological and historical interests relate primarily to man's past activities; hence natural conditions in such areas are usually modified in some degree.

Modern management of areas of the National Park System also had to consider recent and probable future technological innovations, as well as changes in social and economic conditions. These factors have been, and will continue to be, reflected in public recreational interests and demands, and consequent impact of rapidly accelerating use of all types of areas within the National Park System. In particular, there was increasing public concern over the effect of modern technology upon general environmental conditions; environmental relations, both within and without the National Park System, are delicately balanced and can be seriously damaged by inadvisable development or inappropriate activities.

A directive by the Secretary of the Interior, July 10, 1964, redefined National Park Service policy. While reaffirming the original principles relative to management of natural areas, this directive recognized that the modern National Park System contained three basic categories of areas (natural, historical, recreational) and outlined basic guidelines for the management, use, and development of each of them [17].

The Secretary's directive also approved the following six long-range objectives of the National Park Service, as recommended by the Advisory Board on National Parks, Historic Sites, Buildings, and Monuments [17]:

1. To provide for the highest quality of use and enjoyment of the National Park System by increasing millions of visitors in years to come

2. To conserve and manage for their highest purpose the natural, historical, and recreational resources of the National Park System

3. To develop the National Park System through inclusion of additional areas of scenic, scientific, historical, and recreational value to the nation

4. To participate actively with the organization of this and other nations in conserving, improving, and renewing the total environment

5. To communicate the cultural, inspirational, and recreational significance of the American heritage as represented in the National Park System

6. To increase the effectiveness of the National Park Service as a "people-serving" organization dedicated to park conservation, historical preservation, and outdoor recreation

Thus, despite social and economic changes, technological developments, and periodic modifications in the federal administrative structure [12], current National Park Service policies are basically like initial policies defined in 1918 and 1932. These concepts have been adapted to the management of the three principal types of areas in the National Park System.

Management of natural areas, most closely related to the 1918 policy guidelines, conforms to principles which provide for all appropriate public use and enjoyment that can be accommodated without impairment of natural values. Management of historic (including prehistoric) areas emphasizes preservation of the authentic character of primary features together with their appropriate public use and enjoyment. The primary function of recreational areas is active participation in outdoor recreation in an attractive setting; their management is guided by practices which will prevent deterioration of pleasing surroundings which contribute to the enjoyment of outdoor recreational activities and interests [17,20,21,22].

National Park Service policy emphasizes the necessity of continuing to maintain large sections of wilderness in natural areas [16]. It also notes that planned, orderly, harmonious development, required to serve future millions of visitors in each of the three categories, will be based upon minimum needs in each case, utilizing results of research as well as latest appropriate techniques. In addition, great emphasis is placed upon public understanding of varied significant interests, as a principal adjunct to public enjoyment of areas in the National Park System, particularly those of natural and historic quality. Further, expansion of the National Park System, cooperation with other organizations interested in environmental conservation both at home and abroad, and continued upgrading of personnel are featured in current National Park Service policy.

Relation of National Park System to Other Recreational Lands

Although the bill establishing Yellowstone National Park referred to that area as a "pleasuring ground," and although national parks are often referred to as outdoor playgrounds, the basic concept upon which most National Park Service areas were established, and upon which they are administered, differs greatly from that of other recreational lands. This is indicated in foregoing statements of National Park Service policy, which reveal that functional differences exist even between the three principal types of areas within the National Park System.

Though management of recreational areas in the National Park System leans toward the playground concept, care is taken to avoid unnecessarily disturbing their interests and attractiveness. The more remarkable natural and historical areas are, in essence, "outdoor museums." Though spectacular scenery is generally typical, scenic beauty for its sake alone is not necessarily a basic criterion; some of these areas are lacking in the scenic ingredient. Because of their significance the natural and historical areas of the National Park System are of such great value that the greatest return from their use is derived through maximum preservation, coupled with understanding of the great truths of natural and human history which they portray. Thus, the many distinctive waterfalls and the monumental granite cliffs typical of Yosemite Valley in Yosemite National Park are much more rewarding if one understands the reasons for their existence. Grand Canyon National Park is viewed in its true perspective when one knows something of the geological processes by which the great canyon of the Colorado River was formed. A knowledge of factors which contributed to the great age and size, even the very existence in modern times, of the giant sequoias adds zest to a visit to Sequoia National Park. Mesa Verde National Park may be truly enjoyed if one views its numerous cliff dwellings from the perspective of the original inhabitants of that area. Equally important is an understanding of events that took place in historical areas, such as Gettysburg National Military Park.

Evidences of significant geological processes, of plant and animal life and their intricate relations, of the remains of former civilizations, or of historical events typical of these areas qualify them for basically similar management objectives and unification under the same administration. Obviously, management and public use of these unique, significant recreational lands must necessarily be guided by criteria that are quite different from others that have recreational values, both within and without the National Park System.

Administration of such areas according to an outdoor-museum concept, however, does not rule out the possibility of fun and enjoyment; it seeks to guide related outdoor recreational interests and activities into channels which are in keeping with their outdoor-museum character. Further, it favors concentration of other types of outdoor recreational interests and activities not acceptable in national parks and related significant areas on lands of recreation value which are better able to accommodate them. Most people realize that commercial exploitation of natural resources cannot be condoned in areas of unique, significant quality. However, it is not as generally recognized that development of recreational facilities, or encouragement of recreational activities, that are at variance with preservation of unique, often fragile, interests is damaging and undesirable in significant recreation areas.

The term "outdoor museum," now widely recognized, was first introduced by Robert Sterling Yard of the National Parks Association. He made the following statement in an article published in the *Scientific Monthly* of April, 1923 [24]:

The primary use may be described sufficiently for present purposes by calling a national park a museum. Our national parks system is a national museum. Its purpose is to preserve forever, "for the use and enjoyment of the people," certain areas of extraordinary scenic magnificence in a condition of primitive nature. Its recreational value is also very great, but recreation is not distinctive of this system. Our national reservations are also recreational. Our national forest, set apart for scientific commercial utilization, is very highly recreational. The function which alone distinguishes the national parks system from the national forest is the museum function made possible only by the parks' complete conservation.

Earlier statements about the national parks, although they did not use the term "outdoor museum," suggested that concept. In his "Diary of the Washburn Expedition to the Yellowstone and Firehole Rivers in the Year 1870," N. P. Langford states that [6]:

... amid the canyon and the falls, the boiling springs and sulphur mountain, and, above all, the mud volcano and the geysers of the Yellowstone, your memory becomes filled and clogged with objects new in experience, wonderful in extent, and possessing unlimited grandeur and beauty. It is a new phase in the natural world; a fresh exhibition of the handiwork of the Great Architect; and, while you see and wonder, you seem to need an additional sense, fully to comprehend and believe.

The fiscal year ending June 30, 1916, marked the publication of the first annual report on the national parks. The following statement was included in this report [13]:

Clearly they are not designated solely for the purpose of supplying recreational grounds. The fostering of recreation purely as such is more properly the function of the city, county, and state parks, and there should be a clear distinction between the character of such parks and national parks.

Some Significant Interests of the National Park System

The National Park System embodies a national resource of tremendous value and importance; it represents a resource of culture and knowledge which will retain its value only so long as we protect and utilize it in such manner that its unique qualities will be available for public use and enjoyment in perpetuity [9,10]. Maximum value of a visit to significant natural and historic areas in the National Park System is derived from an understanding of the great truths of natural and human history which they embody, and which not only bear upon the nature of our own existence but will exert an influence on the lives of future generations. Such a visit is a cultural experience, one from which elements of compulsion typical of general processes of learning are absent. Visitors are challenged to fathom the apparent mysteries about them, and whatever their experience and background, they must seek their own means of answering the questions that present themselves in these unique superlative settings. Finding the answers on that basis is a test of initiative and ability; the tremendous satisfaction and enjoyment that are derived justify most adequately the effort and cost involved in protecting such lands and make a visit to one of these areas most rewarding. To help visitors enjoy these areas by understanding their significant features—to *see* them, instead of merely looking at them—the National Park Service has developed a corps of trained naturalists, archaeologists, and historians to interpret the significance of their varied features in an accurate and interesting fashion.

Much has been written about the national parks and their companion areas. No attempt to duplicate such efforts will be made here, but in the interests of completeness, and because the educational objective is sufficiently commanding to warrant constant repetition, the values to be discovered in significant National Park Service areas will be summarized briefly.

Some Geological Interests of the National Park System

Yellowstone National Park, with about 3,000 geysers and hot springs, is preeminent in the world as a region of hydrothermal activity. It was primarily because of these phenomena that this area was established as our first national park in 1872. Only two other areas, one of which is in Iceland and the other of which is in New Zealand, can compare with Yellowstone in its principal characteristic.

Mt. Rainier, rising 14,410 feet above sea level and with a base that covers approximately 100 square miles of territory, is our greatest volcanic cone. Although never in active eruption within the record of modern man, it is one link in a chain of volcanic mountains that rims the Pacific. Several other areas of the National Park System also are links in this series of Pacific volcanoes: Lassen Peak in Lassen Volcanic National Park and Lava Beds National Monument in

California, Mauna Loa and Kilauea in Hawaii Volcanoes National Park in Hawaii, and Crater Lake in Crater Lake National Park in Oregon.[4]

In sharp contrast to such volcanic areas are the rugged peaks of Glacier National Park, Montana. These mountains, as indicated by their layered appearance, are of sedimentary origin. Ages ago the numerous layers of sandstone, slate, and shale which compose them were sand, mud, and limy ooze on the floor of an ancient sea; later these sediments were folded, lifted, and changed to their present form by powerful forces accompanying the shrinkage of the earth's crust. In fact, so great were these pressures that the sedimentary layers were torn asunder and one section was pushed northeastward 15 to 18 miles over the adjoining portion. As a result one may observe older rocks overlying more recent geological strata, a feature that is world-famous to geologists as the Lewis overthrust.

Equally interesting are the peaks of the central Rockies along the Continental Divide in Rocky Mountain National Park and in the Sierra Nevada of California, as seen in Yosemite, Sequoia, and Kings Canyon National Parks. The mountains in these areas are composed largely of granite, rocks formed from once-molten lava which cooled and solidified very slowly beneath a former surface, originally at least 1 mile thick, which has since been largely destroyed by erosion. The granite peaks of Rocky Mountain National Park originally formed a portion of the core of a great dome of overlying sedimentary materials, uplifted by pressure from the sides. Remnants of these overlying sedimentary strata may be observed in the foothills as one approaches Rocky Mountain National Park. By contrast, the Sierra Nevada is composed of a great granite block, approximately 800 miles long, which was tilted bodily to the west. The precipitous eastern escarpment of this great range, together with its gradual westward slope, attests the nature of this upheaval.

In each of these specific examples the constructive forces which build these mountains were counteracted by destructive forces of erosion, which, over long periods of time, fashioned the present configuration of these areas.

As successive eruptions built Mt. Rainier's cone to greater heights, the moisture-laden winds from the Pacific, forced into cooler upper-air strata in passing over the Cascades, deposited great quantities of snow upon its flanks. This snow eventually compacted into ice and began moving slowly downward as glaciers. In various ways glacial ice modified the appearance of Mt. Rainier, forming large natural amphitheaters known as "cirques," giving rise to a myriad

---

[4] Eruptions of Mauna Loa and Kilauea are not infrequent. The terrain of Lava Beds National Monument, pitted with cinder cones, small craters, and fumaroles, and scored with deep, tortuous lava trenches, attests to the tempestuous past of this area. Lassen Peak is unique in being the only recently active volcano in the United States (1914 and 1917). The spectacular blue waters of Crater Lake are found in the *caldera* of a former volcanic cone, Mt. Mazama, thought to have been more than 12,000 feet high; it decapitated itself in a great eruption in prehistoric time.

of small but beautiful lakes known as "tarns," developing numerous broad U-shaped valleys, and depositing masses of rock debris known as "moraines." The numerous glaciers found on Mt. Rainier today are remnants of Rainier's greater ice fields of the past. Many of these glaciers, known as "living" glaciers, persist in downward movement. The surface of living glaciers is scored by many deep crevasses, many exposed rock surfaces are highly polished and striated, and, in summer, streams emerging from the glaciers are milky in color because of their burden of finely pulverized rock known as "glacial flour."

Mt. McKinley, Olympic, and North Cascades National Parks also possess extensive glaciers. The scenic quality of these areas, as in Mt. Rainier National Park, attests the erosive power of an even greater extent of glacial ice in the past.

Although Glacier National Park lacks an extensive glacier system, its scenery, featuring many-faceted peaks, broad U-shaped valleys, and spectacular lakes, is the result of erosive action of former glaciers on relatively soft sedimentary rocks. One finds small remnants of that region's once extensive glacier system nestled at the base of great cirques at high altitudes.

Similarly, the effects of past glacial erosion in granite, a much harder material then either the sedimentary rocks of Glacier or the extrusive volcanic material of Rainier, may be noted in Rocky Mountain National Park. Its scenery is replete with broad U-shaped valleys, glacial tarns, morainal deposits, and precipitous cliffs flanking glacial-carved cirques.

Perhaps the best known and most significant example of the erosive power of stream and ice action in granite is to be found in Yosemite National Park. The world-famous Yosemite Valley, principal topographic feature of this area, is noted for its level floor, its nearly vertical granite cliffs over ½ mile high, numerous waterfalls of great beauty, and such oddly shaped landmarks as Half Dome. These and related topographical characteristics are linked with the westward tilting of the Sierra block and the resultant acceleration in speed and erosive power of the prehistoric Merced River, as well as later erosion by glaciers which widened and deepened the previously formed V-shaped river-cut canyon to its present configuration. The nature of erosion in the Yosemite granite was determined by how this material fractured as it slowly cooled and solidified, long before it was exposed by removal through erosion of the original overlying material. Since the fractures in the Yosemite Valley region were largely vertical, many of Yosemite's cliffs, including the northern face of Half Dome, monumental El Capitan, and the cliff over which upper Yosemite Falls pours, are similarly formed. Where the fractures were horizontal or diagonal, greater resistance to erosion prompted the formation of ledges of various widths and sizes. Such differences in the fracture pattern are responsible for the "step" between the upper and lower Yosemite Falls[5] and the angled appearance of the

---

[5] Yosemite Falls, 2,565 feet high, consists of an upper fall of 1,430 feet, a lower fall of 320 feet, and an intermediate cascade of 815 feet.

Three Brothers. A number of trails by which one may climb from the valley floor to the rim also follow diagonal fracture patterns in the granite. The level floor of Yosemite Valley resulted from the filling of a lake which occupied the valley after the retreat of the glacier; sand, silt, and similar river-borne materials were carried into this lake by the Merced River and other streams.

That portion of the Grand Canyon of the Colorado River in Grand Canyon National Park, Arizona, presents still another significant example of the erosive power of running water. This great gorge, 217 miles long, 4 to 18 miles wide, and approximately 1 mile deep, was cut by the Colorado River as the vast plateau upon which it is located was slowly elevated above the surface of an ancient sea. Numerous layers of differently colored sedimentary rocks, once beds of mud, silt, or sand on a prehistoric ocean floor, reacted differently to the forces of erosion, accounting for the irregular pattern of numerous buttes, pinnacles, towers, and shelves which are comprised in the chaotic scene as viewed from vantage points on the rim. Some idea of the erosive power of the Colorado River can be obtained from the fact that it carries past any given point an average of nearly 1 million tons of sand and silt every twenty-four hours!

But the story of the Grand Canyon has other equally interesting features. We may learn something of plants and animals that existed there in past ages. Along several trails by which one descends from the rim to the Colorado River, one may observe fossilized remains of plants and see footprints of a prehistoric lizardlike animal, originally made in the sand along an ancient seashore, preserved in stone.

Colorful Zion Canyon of Zion National Park in southern Utah is also remarkable as an example of water erosion on sedimentary rocks, though the rocks of Zion National Park are of more recent geological origin than the strata of the Grand Canyon. Also in the same general vicinity is Bryce Canyon National Park, noteworthy for its multitude of fantastically eroded pinnacles, spires, and minarets in a variety of colors. These features resulted from the disintegration of still more recently formed sedimentary rocks by running water, rain, frost, wind, and chemical agents. In the formations of Grand Canyon, Zion, and Bryce Canyon National Parks one may read the story of the geological past encompassing a period of 1 billion years.

Erosion by underground water on limestone was responsible for the formation of Carlsbad Caverns National Park, New Mexico, and Mammoth Cave National Park, Kentucky. Fantastically beautiful stalactites and stalagmites found in the huge caverns are the result of later deposits of limestone on the ceiling and floor by percolating water.

Some Biological Interests of the National Park System. Equally significant are the varied biological interests of the National Park System. Best known are the giant sequoias (*Sequoia gigantea*) found in Sequoia, Kings Canyon, and Yosemite National Parks. The age of many of these arboreal giants, thought to be the largest living things, is estimated at between 3,000 and 4,000 years; thus, the largest and oldest of these trees date from the days of the Egyptian pharaohs.[6]

As shown by numerous fossilized specimens found in various parts of the world, many species of sequoia were once widely distributed. Today only two species exist—the giant sequoia, found only in a series of groves on the western slope of the Sierra Nevada, and the coast redwood (*Sequoia sempervirens*), native only to the coast of northern California and extreme southwestern Oregon. Within the National Park System the latter species is found in Redwood National Park and Muir Woods National Monument, both in California.

Also of special interest are the "rain forests" found at low elevations in several deep mountain valleys on the west side of Olympic National Park in the state of Washington. Here, where the annual precipitation is over 140 inches, is an extraordinary plant association of huge evergreen trees, many of which are over 10 feet in diameter and more than 200 feet in height, and a vast array of other plants. Of particular interest are many species of mosses, which thickly clothe the trunks of fallen forest monarchs and festoon the branches of living trees. These rain forests, ethereal in their somber, peaceful grandeur, offer an opportunity to observe and study a forest association found nowhere else in the country and, in addition, provide an insight into the character of Pacific Northwest coast vegetation before civilized man came to the region.

Similarly, the complex plant cover typical of Great Smoky Mountains National Park on the Tennessee-North Carolina border preserves a segment of the diverse vegetation of the southern Appalachian region, and Everglades National Park, Florida, embraces a subtropical area.

Many other units of the National Park System offer unique botanical interests. Among them are the bizarre Joshua trees (*Yucca brevifolia*) in Joshua Tree National Monument in southern California, and the organ pipe and saguaro cacti, unique desert plants, in Organ Pipe Cactus and Saguaro National Monuments, Arizona.

The National Park System also provides a habitat for a wide variety of native animals. Yellowstone National Park is well known for its bison, bighorn sheep, elk, moose, pronghorn antelope, grizzly and American black bear, many kinds of waterfowl, and numerous other less spectacular mammals and birds. Carlsbad Caverns National Park has its famous bat cave; the regular evening flight of countless bats is a never-to-be-forgotten spectacle. Everglades National Park is famous for avifauna, including several species of herons and egrets, the wood

---

[6] Some bristlecone pines (*Pinus aristata*) are thought to be older than the sequoias. The General Sherman tree in Sequoia National Park is considered the largest of the giant sequoias. It measures 101.6 feet in circumference at the base, has an average basal diameter of 36.5 feet, and is 272.4 feet tall. Its first limb, 130 feet above the ground, is 6.8 feet in diameter. *Sequoia gigantea* is now generally placed in a separate genus, *Sequoiadendron*.

stork (only American stork), white and brown pelican, white ibis, and roseate spoonbill. Also found in Everglades National Park is the rare aquatic mammal known as the manatee, or sea cow, and such spectacular reptiles as the alligator and crocodile. Mt. McKinley National Park, Alaska, besides having the highest mountain in North America, is noted for its wildlife, especially caribou, Dall sheep, moose, wolverine, grizzly bear, and timber wolf. Large bands of mountain goat inhabit both Glacier and Mt. Rainier National Parks. Ptarmigan, arctic grouse which change the color of their plumage with the season, are found in Mt. McKinley, Glacier, North Cascades, Mt. Rainier, Grand Teton, and Rocky Mountain National Parks. Grand Teton National Park and the adjacent Jackson Hole region have the largest elk herd in the country. Large bands of elk may be observed also in both Olympic and Rocky Mountain National Parks; in the latter area one may also find mountain sheep. Isle Royale National Park, Michigan, is noteworthy for its moose herd and timber wolves.

The foregoing are but a few examples of national parks providing a habitat for native animals; in most of the national parks and monuments animals form one of the principal attractions.

The great variety of plant and animal species typical of many National Park Service areas is due largely to the great differences in elevation within their borders. Changes in altitude are responsible for climatic differences, which in turn determine "life zones," each supporting typical associations of plants and animals. For instance, Grand Canyon National Park includes four life zones, ranging in climates, and consequently plant and animal forms, typical of latitudes from Mexico to northern Canada; and Yosemite, Sequoia, and Kings Canyon National Parks, each with five life zones, have climates typical of areas from northern Mexico to the Arctic. Similar striking climatic differences due to altitude are found in numerous other national parks.

Some Archaeological Interests of the National Park System. Among the units of the National Park System famous for their significant archaeological interests are the cliff dwellings and mesa-top pueblos in the Southwest. The most noteworthy of these are in Mesa Verde National Park, Colorado; Canyon de Chelly, Casa Grande, Montezuma Castle, Navajo, Wupatki, Tuzigoot, and Tonto National Monuments in Arizona; and Aztec Ruins, Bandelier, and Chaco Canyon National Monuments in New Mexico. In addition, the Effigy Mounds National Monument in Iowa and the unique remains of prehistoric towns in Ocmulgee National Monument, Georgia, and Russell Cave National Monument, Alabama, give us additional glimpses of peoples who occupied various parts of our land in bygone years.

Some Historical Interests of the National Park System. The National Park System also preserves areas which are linked with significant events throughout the entire range of the history of our country. The colonial period is featured in certain early Spanish forts and missions in Florida, Puerto Rico, Arizona, and

New Mexico, as well as at sites of early English settlements on the Atlantic seaboard. The birthplace of the "father of our country" is preserved at George Washington Birthplace National Monument, Virginia, and Independence Hall National Historical Park in Philadelphia is a shrine of American liberty.

Important events of the American Revolution become reality at Fort McHenry National Monument, Maryland; Saratoga National Historical Park, New York; and Kings Mountain National Military Park in South Carolina. Chalmette National Historical Park commemorates the American victory at New Orleans in the War of 1812. Epic chapters in the War between the States come alive at such places as Fort Sumter National Monument in South Carolina; Manassas and Richmond National Battlefield Parks in Virginia; numerous national military parks, such as Fredericksburg in Virginia, Shiloh in Tennessee, and Gettysburg in Pennsylvania; and Appomattox Court House National Historical Park in Virginia. In addition, the soul-stirring story of American exploration and settlement of the West may be brought into sharp focus by such national monuments as Custer Battlefield in Montana, Pipe Spring in Arizona, Scotts Bluff in Nebraska, Fort Laramie in Wyoming, Whitman and Fort Vancouver in Washington, and Homestead in Nebraska.

These and other historical areas of the National Park System serve to develop a better understanding of our American heritage, as well as greater pride in American hardihood, valor, and courage.

Public Use of the National Park System. Interest in the National Park System is reflected in the phenomenal public use of these areas. With the exception of a relatively few periods, such as during the years of World War II (1942-45) the number of visitors has mounted constantly. Excepting the national capital parks, use has risen from 120,690 visits in 1904 to 189,511,600 visits in 1971. Public use of the national capitol parks amounted to 10,971,700 visits in 1971.

Names of various National Park Service areas are not always indicative of their primary interests. Natural, historical, and recreational areas are included among a number of types. For instance, while most national parks are natural areas, Mesa Verde National Park is primarily of archaeological significance and is placed in the historical category by the National Park Service; in addition, most national monuments are primarily of historical interest, though nearly half of them are significant for their varied natural values. Thus, comparative-use data for various types, do not provide a completely factual indication of the recreation appeal of the natural, historical (including prehistorical or archaeological), and recreational interests of the National Park System. Public-use data [23] published by the National Park Service, December, 1968, provide a summary of visits to the principal categories of areas of the National Park System for the fiscal years 1967 and 1968. These data (Table 8-2) clarify the relation of basic interests of National Park Service areas.

Table 8-2
Summary of public use of National Park System, by categories, fiscal years

Category	Number of areas reporting	Visits, 1967	Visits, 1968
Natural areas	65	45,519,700	48,193,600
Historical areas	139	56,049,500	57,670,900
Recreational areas	20	26,561,200	31,831,600
National capital parks[a]	1	7,195,300	7,535,300
Total	225	135,325,700	145,231,400

[a]Administered as one unit; they include over 700 areas of various types.

Source: "Public Use of the National Parks; a Statistical Report," U.S. Department of the Interior, National Park Service, Washington, December, 1968.

Summary

Lands administered by the National Park Service, aggregating about 29 million acres, include several hundred areas of varying types, ranging from small historical sites to extensive tracts of many thousands of acres. Designations of various types of areas in the National Park System are often incorrectly interpreted as being indicative of the degree of relative importance, significance, or size. However, their basic differences are largely in their legal status, for all were established according to certain procedures defined by federal laws.

The National Park Service is a bureau in the Department of the Interior. The basic administrative structure of this organization consists of the headquarters in Washington D.C., a number of Regional Offices strategically located with reference to National Park Service areas of somewhat similar character, and various field offices and specific units of the Service. The principal administrative officer is the Director, who is responsible to the Secretary of the Interior. Each Regional Office is headed by a Regional Director, who reports to the Director. Each of the various units of the Service (national parks, monuments, historical, recreational, and related areas) is managed by a Superintendent, who reports to his Regional Director.

Current administrative policies of the National Park Service, founded upon basic principles first outlined in 1916, upon establishment of the National Park Service, have been adapted to the management of the three basic types of areas in the National Park System (natural, historical, recreational).

With the redefining of policy by Secretary of the Interior Stewart Udall in 1964, we see something of an expansion in mission of the National Park Service from that of 1918. This was due partly to increasing use of system areas and possible to a change in technology, access, and visitation problems. But also, it illustrates the expansion and growth of the bureau over time, and the statement of broader goals relates to a more diverse clientele. We also observe the concern for cooperation with foreign conservation organizations. Further, in 1971, Secretary of the Interior Rogers Morton directed the National Park Service to identify and create more parks in and near large urban complexes where people need them. These changes in National Park Service policy present a picture of agency evolution as mentioned in Chapter 6. A point of Anthony Downs in "Inside Bureaucracy" that "as bureaus grow older the breadth of functions they serve increases"[7] [4] is illustrated here.

National Park Service policy for natural areas provides for appropriate public use and enjoyment, consistent with minimum disturbance of natural values. The policy for historic areas emphasizes preservation of the setting of primary features and appropriate public use and enjoyment; and the policy for recreational areas relates to practices which favor active participation in outdoor recreational activities and interests in an attractive setting, without destroying the pleasant surroundings upon which these outdoor recreational activities and interests largely depend.

Within the National Park System are outstanding examples of the geological, biological, archaeological, and historical interests of our country. Selection of these areas for inclusion in this system is predicated upon their national significance in a particular field of interest and the dramatic, inspirational manner in which that interest is portrayed. Thus, in essence, most National Park Service areas are "outdoor museums," important because of their vital contribution to American culture and education. Maximum enjoyment of these areas, including "having a good time," is derived through understanding of their many significant interests. In that sense, they serve a somewhat different purpose from any other important recreational lands lacking in national significance.

Public use of the National Park System has grown phenomenally since 1904. More than 189,000,000 visits were reported for all types of areas in 1971 (exclusive of national capitol parks).

Selected References

1. Butcher, Devereaux: "Exploring Our National Parks and Monuments," (6th edition, revised) Houghton Mifflin, Boston, 1969.
2. Cameron, Jenks: The National Park Service: Its History, Activities and Organization, *Service Monographs of the U.S. Government*, no. 11, Institute for Government Research, Appleton-Century-Crofts, New York, 1922.
3. Crampton, L. C.: "Early History of Yellowstone National Park and its Relation to National Park Policies," U.S. Government Printing Office, Washington, 1932.

---

[7] Anthony Downs: "Inside Bureaucracy," Boston, Little, Brown, a Rand Corporation Research Study, p. 264. Copyright 1967 by the Rand Corporation.

4. Downs, Anthony: "Inside Bureaucracy," Little, Brown, Boston, 1967.

5. Frome, Michael: "National Park Guide," Rand McNally, Chicago, 1967.

6. Langford, N. P.: "The Discovery of Yellowstone National Park, 1870," J. E. Haynes, St. Paul, Minn., 1923.

7. Merriam, John C.: The Meaning of National Parks, *National Parks Bulletin*, vol. 10, no. 57, November 1929.

8. U.S. National Park Service and U.S. Forest Service: "The National Parks and the National Forests, Their Purposes and Management," U.S. Government Printing Office, Washington, 1969.

9. Tilden, Freeman: "The National Parks: What They Mean to You and Me," Knopf, New York, 1954.

10. Tilden, Freeman: "The National Parks," Knopf, New York, 1968.

11. Tolson, Hillary: "Laws Relating to the National Park Service, the National Parks and Monuments," U.S. Government Printing Office, Washington, 1933.

12. U.S. Department of the Interior: Secretary Hickel Announces Policy Guidelines for National Park System, Washington, D.C., June 22, 1969. (Mimeographed press release.)

13. U.S. Department of the Interior, National Park Service: "Annual Report of the Superintendent of National Parks to the Secretary of the Interior for the Fiscal Year Ended June 30, 1916," U.S. Government Printing Office, Washington, 1916.

14. U.S. Department of the Interior, National Park Service: "Annual Report of the Director of the National Park Service to the Secretary of the Interior for the Fiscal Year Ended June 30, 1932," U.S. Government Printing Office, Washington, 1932.

15. U.S. Department of the Interior, National Park Service: "Our Heritage: A Plan for its Protection and Use, Mission 66," Washington, n.d.

16. U.S. Department of the Interior, National Park Service: "The National Park Wilderness," Washington, n.d.

17. U.S. Department of the Interior, National Park Service: "Road to the Future," n.p., 1964.

18. U.S. Department of the Interior, National Park Service: "Parks for America: A Survey of Park and Related Resources in the Fifty States, and a Preliminary Plan," U.S. Government Printing Office, Washington, 1964.

19. U.S. Department of the Interior, National Park Service: "National Parks and Landmarks, Areas Administered by the National Park Service and Related Properties," U.S. Government Printing Office, Washington, 1968.

20. U.S. Department of the Interior, National Park Service: "Administrative Policies for Natural Areas of the National Park System," U.S. Government Printing Office, Washington, August, 1968.

21. U.S. Department of the Interior, National Park Service: "Administrative Policies for Recreational Areas of the National Park System," U.S. Government Printing Office, Washington, August, 1968.

22. U.S. Department of the Interior, National Park Service: "Administrative Policies for Historical Areas of the National Park System," U.S. Government Printing Office, Washington, August, 1968.

23. U.S. Department of the Interior, National Park Service: "Public Use of the National Parks; a Statistical Report [various periods]," Washington, v.d.

24. Yard, Robert S.: Historical Basis of National Park Standards, *National Parks Bulletin*, vol. 10, no. 57, November, 1929.

chapter nine

THE NATIONAL FORESTS AS OUTDOOR RECREATIONAL AREAS

The Forest Service, established as a bureau of the Department of Agriculture in 1905, administers over 186 million acres of land. Most of this area is occupied by 154 national forests; the remainder comprises nineteen national grasslands (3,808,767 acres) and fourteen miscellaneous areas (186,780 acres). Varying portions of the National Forest System lie in forty-four states, Puerto Rico, and the Virgin Islands. About 88 percent of these lands are in the West, including Alaska (see Figure 9-1).

The Forest Service does not control all land within the boundaries of national forests and grasslands. Intermixed with Forest Service lands are approximately 38 million acres of state, private, and other nonfederal lands.[1] The fragmentary ownership pattern typical of some areas of the National Forest System stems largely from early homestead and mining laws, together with federal grants from the public domain to certain states (for schools and other purposes) and railroads (to encourage Western development) and repurchase of lands in the Weeks Law forest of the East. To alleviate resultant administrative difficulties, and particularly to favor public interest through improved management of all resources of the national forests and grasslands, the Forest Service,

---

[1] In addition, certain areas administered by the National Park Service are partly or completely surrounded by national forest lands; in most cases these were formed by withdrawal and reclassification of former national forest lands by various federal legislative acts. Among such areas are Bryce Canyon, Crater Lake, Glacier, Grand Canyon, Kings Canyon, Lassen Volcanic, Mt. Rainier, Olympic, Rocky Mountain and North Cascades National Parks; Cedar Breaks, Chiricahua, Devils Postpile, Gila Cliff Dwellings, Great Sand Dunes, Lava Beds, Montezuma Castle, Saguaro, Sunset Crater, Timpanogos Cave, Tonto, Tuzigoot, and Walnut Canyon National Monuments.

Figure 9-1
Distribution of the national forests and regional organization of the Forest Service (Fore

U.S. Department of Agriculture Forest Service

National Forest System
and related data

Prepared in the Division of Engineering

0   50   100 150 200
Scale in Miles

▨ National Forests
☐ Purchase Units
▦ National Grasslands
▨ Land Utilization Projects
— Regional Boundaries*
● Regional Headquarters
• Supervisor's Headquarters
▲ Area Director State and Private Forestry Programs
✳ Forest Products Laboratory
○ Institute of Northern Forestry
  Institute of Tropical Forestry
▢ Area Director State and
  Private Forestry Programs

*Regional names and numbers shown for
  reference to accompanying tables

▲ Forest and range experiment stations

Northeastern - Upper Darby, Pa.
Southeastern - Asheville, N.C.
Pacific Southwest - Berkeley, Calif.
Intermountain, Ogden, Utah
Institute of Northern Forestry,
  Juneau, Alaska

North Central, St. Paul, Minn.
Pacific Northwest - Portland, Oreg.
Rocky Mountain - Ft. Collins, Colo.
Southern - New Orleans, La.
Institute of Tropical Forestry, Rio Piedras, P.R.

ervice).

147

wherever feasible, consolidates its control within boundaries of various units by a continuing program of land exchange and purchase.[2]

Legal Status of National Forests

National forests are based upon the act of March 3, 1891, which authorized the President to reserve, by proclamation, certain lands from the public domain and to designate such lands as forest reserves. The act provided [8] :

That the President of the United States may, from time to time, set apart and reserve, in any State or Territory having public land bearing forests, any part of the public lands wholly or in part covered with timber or undergrowth, whether of commercial value or not, as public reservations, and the President shall, by public proclamation, declare the establishment of such reservations and the limits thereof.

The primary purpose of this act was to effect a general revision of various laws concerning disposition of public lands, which had sometimes been characterized by irregular practices. The act contained twenty-four sections, the twenty-fourth providing for the establishment of forest reserves. Authority of the President to establish national forests from public lands, by proclamation, was withdrawn by Congress in 1907, largely because of Western opposition to such action. Other forests were created pursuant to the Weeks Law of March 1, 1911, as amended. The national grasslands are a result of the Bankhead-Jones Act of July 22, 1937, as amended.

Organization of the Forest Service

The Forest Service is organized in regional, decentralized form, permitting wide lattitudes in authority for Regional Foresters, Forest Supervisors, and District Rangers. Within a framework of broad national and regional policies, professional managers at different organizational levels make the on-the-ground decisions which guide the management of the national forests and grasslands.

The headquarters organization, in Washington, D.C., consists of the Chief Forester and his staff, various units of which are concerned with forest activities on a national level, including forest research and cooperative federal-state forest management programs for nonfederal lands. The National Forest System is divided into nine regions,[3] each in the charge of a Regional Forester; he and his

---

[2] Many exchange and purchase units include land with important recreational values.

[3] Names and headquarters of the nine regions of the Forest Service are *Northern*, Missoula, Mont.; *Rocky Mountain*, Denver, Colo.; *Southwestern*, Albuquerque, N. Mex.; *Inter-*

staff have regional responsibilities. Within each region are a number of national forests which, in turn, are composed of several ranger districts, averaging about 225,000 acres in area. National forests are in the charge of a Forest Supervisor, who is aided by staff assistants responsible for various activities on the forests. Ranger districts, the basic administrative units of the Forest Service, are in the charge of a District Ranger, who, with his assistants, directs and supervises all district activities.

Basic Forest Service Policy and Responsibilities

Multiple use and sustained yield for maximum, long-term public benefit have been a fundamental policy of the Forest Service in the protection, management, and development of national forest resources for timber, outdoor recreation, water, wildlife, and forage purposes. This concept was clearly defined in Secretary of Agriculture James Wilson's letter of February 1, 1906, shortly after the establishment of the Forest Service, to Chief Forester Gifford Pinchot. An excerpt from that document follows [9] :

. . . In the administration of the National Forests it must be clearly borne in mind that all land is to be devoted to its most productive use for the permanent good of the whole people, and not for the temporary benefit of individuals or companies. All resources of the National Forests are for use . . . and where conflicting interests must be reconciled the question will always be decided from the standpoint of the greatest good for the greatest number in the long run. . . .

Actually, this principle was inherent in the act of June 4, 1897, which outlined management policies of the initial forest reserves, even before the formation of the Forest Service. Provisions of this act, together with later amendments, as reflections of the wishes of the people in management of the national forests, are the basis of Forest Service administration policy. Current procedures adhere to statutory directives of the Multiple Use–Sustained Yield Act of 1960 (P.L. 86-517), of particular interest because it specifically mentions recreation as a national forest resource.

The authorization of certain uses of the national forests, such as mining, generation and distribution of electric power, highway construction, and defense needs, is the responsibility of other departments and agencies but is closely coordinated with the Forest Service. Law enforcement and management of fish and wildlife, including establishment of hunting and fishing regulations, are state responsibilities under a policy of concurrent federal and state jurisdiction.

---

mountain, Ogden, Utah; *California*, San Francisco, Calif.; *Pacific Northwest*, Portland, Ore.; *Southern*, Atlanta Ga.; *Eastern*, Milwaukee, Wisc.; and *Alaska*, Juneau, Alaska. (The former Lake States region has been incorporated into the Eastern region.) Also see Fig. 9-1.

In addition to responsibilities relative to the administration of the National Forest System, the Forest Service conducts a forest research and a cooperative forest management program. Its research program deals with all aspects of the protection, management, and development of forest and related wild-land resources—including recreation—as well as the utilization and marketing of resultant products. Research is conducted at eight forest and range experiment stations, the Forest Products Laboratory at Madison, Wisconsin, the Institute of Northern Forestry, at Juneau, Alaska, and the Institute of Tropical Studies in Puerto Rico, under the direction of the directors of those units. The Forest Service also administers a program of grant and contract research for universities and others. The Cooperative Forest Management Program of the Forest Service seeks to have other federal, state, and private landowners apply multiple use-sustained yield forest management to their forest lands.

Recreational Policy of the Forest Service

The importance of recreation in national forest administration varies according to the management situation in various sections of the country. It may differ from one national forest to another. All national forest lands have some recreational value, but this aspect of their management is given a greater degree of importance on some areas than on others; on a number of national forests, recreation receives the most emphasis, but all resource uses receive equal consideration in development of management plans.

Basic Forest Service recreational policy emphasizes (1) integration of recreation with all other uses of national forests by careful and coordinated resource management, and by designation of specific areas for certain types of recreation not compatible with other national forest uses; (2) maintenance and perpetuation of an attractive and appropriate environment for forest recreation, with emphasis on spaciousness, including preservation of rare and fragile flora, fauna, and other features; (3) major attention to the interests of the general public, rather than those of special groups or individuals; (4) participant rather than spectator activities, favoring those requiring a minimum of cost, special equipment, and ability; (5) minimum restrictions on users, consistent with protection of environment, public health and safety, and rights of others; and (6) cooperation with other agencies and organizations, both public and private, in the most economical development of a wide range of complementary recreational opportunities in a given locality.

The "Forest Service Manual" describes these basic policies in greater detail as follows [17,18]:

Coordination:
1. The Recreation resources of the National Forests will be managed in conjunction with all the other forest resources under the principles of multiple

use. This does not mean that specific areas may not be devoted principally to recreation. In general, however, over any area large enough to be classified as an administrative unit, such as a ranger district, recreation use will take its place with grazing, mining, and water storage, timber production, and other uses.

2. The recreation developments on the National Forests are planned to complement those available on other public lands.

National Forest recreation developments in the vicinity of National Parks and along park approach roads will be planned in consultation with the National Park Service in relation to developments in National Parks—the objective being to obtain coordination between the two Services as far as practicable so that developments on the two types of area may complement each other.

3. In planning the development of the recreation resource and the necessary adjustments with other uses, the viewpoints of interest groups will be considered.

Preservation of the Natural and the Primitive:

4. One of the distinctive characteristics of forest recreation is that it is enjoyed in a natural environment. Every effort will be made to preserve this quality and the atmosphere of spaciousness in the planning and development of recreation opportunities.

Further than this, suitable provision will be made for the establishment of areas which will preserve primitive conditions of transportation or vegetation, and where possible, a combination of the two.

Developments:

5. The Forest Service will develop or permit the development of such facilities as will aid in the enjoyment of those types of recreation appropriate to the forest. It will especially discourage developments which tend to introduce urbanization into the forest.

6. The Forest Service will install or permit the installation of facilities only to the extent required to serve public needs so as to keep to a minimum the introduction of artificial developments in the forest environment.

7. The basic objective in designing National Forest developments is to have them perform their intended function and at the same time harmonize as much as possible with the natural environment.

8. Preference will be given to recreation developments which emphasize opportunities for participant rather than spectator enjoyment of forest recreation activities.

9. When Federal funds are expended on recreation developments, the objective should be to provide recreation opportunities for relatively large numbers of people and not for the exclusive use of individuals or small groups. The determination of priorities in the expenditure of funds under this policy requires consideration both of the quantity and quality of recreation enjoyment made possible by a development. It also requires that any development should be considered in relation to other developments so that a well-balanced system of recreation facilities will be provided.

Use:

10. The recreation use of the National Forest will be handled with the fewest possible restrictions on users, consistent with the protection of the forest against damage, the observance of essential sanitary and safety measures, and the prevention of actions by individuals or groups which unduly interfere with the enjoyment of others.

11. Uses which require exclusive private occupancy, such as summer homes and limited membership clubs, have a proper place in the National Forests, but will be granted only where it appears certain that the desired areas will not be needed for more general public uses. In determining the public need, future as well as present requirements must be considered and the estimates of future needs should be liberal.

12. Charges will be made at public recreation areas for special services such as (1) charcoal, (2) electricity, (3) checking clothes, renting suits and towels, (4) boat rental, (5) use of ski tows and lifts, (6) hot showers (if artificially heated), and (7) any special services of similar character.

13. Permit fees for resorts, services, and summer homes will be based on the fair value of the land, as determined by the rental charges for comparable privately owned land, with due allowance for all differences between the conditions associated with the use of public and private land.

Recreation Planning and Administration of the National Forests

Recreation values of the national forests receive equal consideration with the other resource values. Their planning, development, use, and maintenance are handled, in varying detail and degrees of responsibility, at all levels of the Forest Service organization from the office of the Chief to that of the District Ranger.

Fundamental policies of national forest recreation use, on the national level, are established by the Chief as authorized by the Secretary of Agriculture, subject to provisions of legislation passed by Congress and to Executive directives. Regional recreation plans are prepared within this broad framework by various Regional Foresters. Planning objectives set forth in state recreation plans and the plans of others are also considered in preparing recreation plans for the National Forest System.

More detailed planning of recreation opportunities is done for each national forest. The plans are prepared by staff in consultation with the Supervisor. He works with recreation specialists from the regional headquarters, as well as with various District Rangers on the forest. District Rangers also may make recommendations to the Forest Supervisor as to recreational features, policies, and needs. Such recommendations, after proper consideration, may be included in the national forest recreation plan.

The smallest unit of recreation planning in the National Forest System is the recreation management composite. This is a small geographical area usually consisting of a complex of recreation-developed sites and dispersed areas that have sufficiently strong interrelations to require further amplification of the national forest plan. Management composites are made only for situations with significant use and enjoyment.

Basis for Recreation Plans

The national forest recreation plans are guides for further management actions. As such, they are an assemblage of current management objectives and policies with the necessary descriptive material and factual data for understanding the situation and for arriving at decisions as to the best courses of action to meet the objectives. Plans are continuously monitored and updated as necessary to reflect changes by the following factors [17,18] :

1. *Current recreation resources of the forests.* These are listed in an inventory of varied recreational values of the forest and include a determination of specific areas best suited to different types of recreation use. In addition, the human capacity for each type of recreation use, as well as for each type of recreation area, is estimated, and an outline of recreation developments in the vicinity, other than those on the forests, is prepared.

2. *Constraints on recreation use on the forests.* Consideration is given to other needs that can be supplied by the forests, which may receive emphasis equal to or greater than that on recreation (forage, water supply, timber, and other resources).

3. *The potential recreation demand of the area of which the forest is a part.* Future public recreation needs and their relation to national forest management are important in planning. Factors such as present and probable population trends, technological developments affecting recreation, and probable trends in private and public recreation development must be carefully weighed in arriving at decisions.

In consideration of the foregoing factors, various areas selected for recreation development are allocated on the basis of their particular value or combination of values to specific types of recreation activity. The current status of such areas is indicated on the recreation base map as "developed and in use" or "reserved for future development." In the latter case, areas scheduled for immediate future development are separated from lands to be held in reserve.

Actual development of each recreation area, as provided for in the recreation plan, is preceded by the preparation of action lists and detailed tract plans showing the location and design of all improvements, together with necessary specifications. Such plans are prepared by landscape architects in the Regional Forester's office or the Supervisor's office, upon the advice of the Forest Supervisor or District Ranger.

Distinction between National Forests and National Parks [3]

Since national forests and national parks often have common characteristics (forests, scenic beauty), and since both receive heavy recreation use, the basic purposes served by these two types of public land often appear to be similar. Therefore, distinctive differences in their recreation functions and management objectives are not always clearly understood.

National forests are basically utilitarian. With few exceptions (oil, gas, minerals), their resources are renewable and, in the multiple use-sustained yield concept of management, can be periodically harvested and reestablished on the same land. Outdoor recreation activities in the national forests are integrated with the management of other resources. Included are those lands which are compatible with the production of timber, those requiring development for the accommodation of large crowds, and in addition, those which demand privacy, such as wilderness. This relatively liberal recreation policy is possible in national forests because of their extensive area and physiographic variation, plus the action taken to coordinate uses and to disperse users over wide areas.

By contrast, national parks, as well as many other areas of the National Park System, are managed as outdoor museums. The highly significant and often fragile character of the features in these areas demands a more restrictive policy of recreational use. Preservation of their highly significant natural, scientific, and inspirational qualities is a basic concern. Thus, in national parks public hunting is not permitted; timber and other resources are not utilized commercially; and certain recreation activities and facilities are not included.

Both these philosophies of wild-land management, concerned with different aspects of conservation, fulfill vital and specific needs. Properly coordinated, they supplement one another in the provision of a wide variety of highly necessary public benefits and services.

Recreational Resources of the National Forests [2,13,15]

Diversity of outdoor recreation opportunities, in all seasons, is one of the principal characteristics of the national forests. Somewhere in their vast acreage climbers, hikers, horsemen, skiers, canoeists, or boatmen find varied opportunities to test their skill or stamina. There are also outlets for the interests of both amateur and professional photographers, artists, naturalists, and historians. And those who merely seek a scenic drive, a picnic, a visit to a lake, or similar casual relaxation in a pleasant environment can also be rewarded. Since hunting and fishing are permitted in the national forests, subject to state laws and regulations, these areas play a vital role in such forms of outdoor recreation. Through its Division of Wildlife Management, the Forest Service works closely with state fish and game departments on lands under its jurisdiction.

National forests include most types of North American forest environment with their related plants and animals. Included are varied coniferous forests of the West, coniferous-broadleaved forests in the Lake States and southern Appalachians, and, to the south, subtropical and a medley of tropical regions. Some of these forest regions are noted for seasonal beauty of flowers or fall foliage. National forests also include the largest specimens of many native North American tree species. Arboreal communities of particular interest receive special protection. For example, the Ancient Bristlecone Pine Botanic Area in the Inyo National Forest, California, includes America's oldest living vegetation.

More than one-third of the big game population of the United States, as well as many small mammals and numerous species of birds, inhabit the national forests. They are managed to maintain an adequate population-environment balance.

Equally diverse are facilities to aid visitors in enjoyment of national forest recreation opportunities. These range from a variety of readily accessible, developed sites to remote primitive and wilderness areas [2,14] completely lacking in modern conveniences. The concept of wilderness and primitive areas of the national forests originated with the establishment in 1924, by administrative order, of the Gila Primitive Area in New Mexico. With passage of the Wilderness Preservation Act in 1964, fifty-four then-existing areas were incorporated into our National Wilderness Preservation System.

Numerous opportunities are available to serve almost every personal interest, with due consideration of available time, physical condition, family responsibilities, or financial status. In addition to many federal, state, and county highways which serve the national forests, there are many miles of forest development roads open to the public.[4] Roads in the national forests offer scenic views or panoramas, or provide access to points from which journeys into remote areas by trail, on foot or on horseback may be initiated. The thousands of miles of trails in the national forests include substantial portions of the famous Appalachian Trail in the East and the Pacific Crest Trail in the Far West. A wide choice in picnicking or camping experience is possible in numerous picnic areas and campgrounds strategically located along both main highways and remote byways. More sophisticated accommodations include modern motels or hotels, as well as "rustic" cabins or lodges and dude ranches, in equally varied accessible or remote locations. Establishment of organized camps by youth, church, and other groups offers opportunities for group activities.

Coordination of Use of National Forest Lands

To effect proper coordination of the most logical uses of the national forests, lands are grouped under a zoning approach. Generalized and special zones, as needed, are utilized. They include:

1. Water influence zones: areas for existing or anticipated significant public outdoor recreational occupancy, use, and enjoyment along streams and rivers and around lakes, reservoirs, and other bodies of water; areas in which uses and activities are oriented to overwater travel and outdoor recreation

2. Travel influence zones: areas for existing or anticipated significant public outdoor recreational occupancy, use, and enjoyment along existing and planned

---

[4] Under certain conditions, such as periods of extreme fire hazard, closures may be invoked.

overland routes of travel; areas in and around existing or planned developed recreation sites

3. Special management zones: areas formally designated by the Congress, Secretary of Agriculture, Chief of the Forest Service, or Regional Forester

4. Other management zones: developed as necessary to meet the needs of the resources, topography, types of present and proposed use, and access

The foregoing classification is based on careful resource inventory and appraisal which must necessarily consider a wide variety of interrelated factors. Among the more important of such considerations are the physical characteristics and quality of sites suited to different types of recreation, trends in recreation needs and interests, present and future demand and degree of use, development costs, and relative importance of recreation and other national forest uses.

Intensive and Dispersed Recreation Uses

Recreation use of the national forests is characterized by two phases, intensive and dispersed.

Intensive recreation use activities require facilities and developments for the comfort and convenience of users or to protect the environment. To accommodate these activities, the Forest Service provides developed sites. These include observation sites, camp and picnic grounds, playground park and sport sites, swimming and boating sites, organization camps, commercial public service sites, winter sports sites, recreation residence sites, and visitor centers.

The dispersed phase is characterized by relatively low-density use, well distributed over broad expanses of land and/or water. It encompasses the entire land and water resource base not included in the intensive phase. Development in support of the dispersed phase typically consists of roads, trails, parking places, and rather simple facilities designed more for protection of the environment than for the convenience of the user.

National forest lands that are primarily valuable as developed sites are designated on recreational plans. The establishment, development, and co-ordination of such necessary public recreational facilities, carried out with due regard for the maintenance of varied recreational interests, public health, and safety, are determined by District Rangers, Forest Supervisors, and Regional Foresters under broad authority granted by the Chief Forester.

Practically all national forest lands are open and available to the public for some type of outdoor recreation. Many recreation uses are thoroughly compatible with scientific management of other resources. Some recreation activities are favored by such management; for instance, hunting is improved by proper timber harvest, which enhances the habitat for deer and certain other game animals. However, certain interests and activities are of such nature, or enjoy such wide popularity, that maximum recreation use and enjoyment, as well as environmental protection and proper relation of recreation with other forest uses, are achieved by designating specific areas for them. Various experience levels ranging from primitive to modern are currently recognized in national forest recreation management (see Table 9-1). Integrated environmental treatment and facility designs are a part of the planning processes. Thus, the national forests offer a range of opportunities for recreation experiences providing a high degree of personal challenge and privacy and minimum development, as well as areas having recreation potential for larger crowds, which can be most advantageously realized by maximum development.

Table 9-1
National forest recreation experience levels[a]

Level	Description
Primitive	Recreation opportunities to satisfy basic needs to the maximum degree. A maximum degree of outdoor skills required. Unmodified natural environment and an absence of man-made developments and comfort or convenience facilities are dominant consideration. Feeling of adventure, challenge, and physical achievement, in the absence of obvious controls, important to the user.
1.	Recreation opportunities to satisfy basic needs to a nearly maximum degree. High degree of outdoor skills involved. Little-modified natural environment is dominant consideration. Modifications for comfort and convenience are minimal. Feeling of physical achievement at reaching opportunities without mechanical access is important to the user. Adventure and challenge afforded through minimum controls.
2.	Recreation opportunities to satisfy basic needs to nearly maximum degree except as tempered by motorized access. Little-modified natural environment is dominant consideration. Modifications for comfort and convenience are few. Some feeling of achievement for reaching the opportunity through challenging motorized access is important. Minimum controls evident to the user.
3.	Recreation opportunities to satisfy basic needs to an intermediate degree. Moderate degrees of outdoor skills are involved. Natural environment dominates, but some modifications for comfort and convenience are also important to the user. Controls and regimentation afford sense of security although some taste of adventure is still important to the user.
4.	Recreation opportunities to satisfy basic needs to only a moderate degree. Moderate degree of activity skills suffices. Natural environment important, but modifications for comfort and convenience are more important. Sense of security afforded the user. Regimentation and fairly obvious controls important to the user.
5.	Recreation opportunities to satisfy basic needs to a modest degree. Skills required for outdoor activities are minimal. Natural environment is important but dominated by man-made modifications. Feeling of security is very important to the user. Learning or beginning skills suffice when supplemented by administrative controls.

[a]Degrees of outdoor recreation activities satisfying basic needs of people including needs: to find isolation; to socialize; to achieve self-fulfillment; for identity; for compensating experiences; for aggression outlets and others.

Source: U.S. Forest Service, Washington, D.C.

Recreation land classifications recommended by the Bureau of Outdoor Recreation[5] [4,5] are, in general, applicable to various types of areas on the national forests which are specifically designated for different recreation interests and activities.

Brief comments on various types of specifically designated areas, recognized by the Forest Service as offering special recreation opportunities, follow [17]. Bureau of Outdoor Recreation classifications are indicated by roman numerals in parentheses.

Wildernesses and Primitive Areas (V).   Prior to enactment of the Wilderness Act of 1964 (P.L. 88-57), the national forests contained four kinds of areas specifically designated for wilderness purposes: *primitive, wilderness, wild,* and *canoe areas.*[6] The first category was retained, at least pending further study, but

---

[5] The classes are I, High-density; II, General; III, Natural; IV, Unique; V, Primitive; and VI, Historic and Cultural Sites (see Chapter 7, p. 119).

[6] *Primitive areas.* Designated modified, or eliminated by the Chief Forester, under regulation L-20, adopted in 1930. Under this regulation, seventy-three primitive areas were established by 1939; some were later redesignated as wilderness areas under the more restrictive regulation U-1. Primitive areas still in existence retain this classification until determined otherwise by Congress.

Wilderness areas. Designated, modified, or eliminated by the Secretary of Agriculture, upon recommendation of the Chief Forester, under regulation U-1, which replaced L-20 in 1939. Regulation U-1 stipulated that wilderness areas were to have a minimum area of 100,000 acres; it also provided a greater degree of protection to wilderness qualities than did regulation L-20.

Wild areas. Designated, modified, or eliminated by the Chief Forester, under regulation U-2 also adopted in 1939. Regulation U-2 stipulated that the same protective restrictions applicable to wilderness areas applied to wild areas, although their size was smaller (5,000 to 100,000 acres).

Canoe areas. Designated, modified, or eliminated by the Secretary of Agriculture under regulation U-3, adopted in 1930. Regulation U-3 provided for maintenance of the natural quality of such areas in the vicinity of streams, lakes, and portages without unnecessary restrictions on other uses (including timber harvest) at a distance from these key recreational locations. Since passage of the Wilderness Act, "no cut zones" have been extended by the Secretary of Agriculture, upon recommendation of a special citizens review committee, which was formed in 1964. The Boundary Waters Canoe Area is the only one in this category. It is on the Superior National Forest in northern Minnesota, contiguous with Quetico Provincial Park in Ontario, and was formed in 1958 by consolidation of three smaller, earlier, specially designated "roadless areas" (Caribou, Little Indian Sioux, and Superior).

Since the foregoing areas were established by administrative regulation rather than by law, the stability of their boundaries and the protection afforded their wilderness quality was not so permanent as many felt would be desirable. This fact prompted initial interest in federal wilderness legislation in 1955, which, in 1964 culminated in enactment of the Wilderness Act and establishment of the National Wilderness Preservation System. One of the stipulations of the Wilderness Act was that all wilderness, wild, and canoe areas were to be automatically blanketed under its provision as the nucleus of the National Wilderness Preservation System, with administrative authority over these areas remaining with the Forest Service.

the Wilderness Act provided for immediate inclusion of the last three categories as wildernesses in the National Wilderness Preservation System.

In 1970, the national forests contained 61 wildernesses with an aggregate area of nearly 10 million acres, and 27 primitive areas aggregating over 4 million acres.

Except for the Boundary Waters Canoe Area in Minnesota, the Great Gulf Wilderness in New Hampshire, and the Linville Gorge Wilderness in North Carolina, the designated Forest Service wildernesses and primitive areas are in the West. Among the largest of these are: Mazatzal Wilderness, Arizona (205,346 acres); John Muir Wilderness, California (504,263 acres); Salmon Trinity Alps Primitive Area, California (285,756 acres); San Juan Primitive Area, Colorado (240,000 acres); Idaho Primitive Area, Idaho (1,232,744 acres); Selway-Bitterroot Wilderness, Idaho-Montana (1,243,659 acres); Bob Marshall Wilderness, Montana (950,000 acres); Gila Wilderness, New Mexico (433,916 acres); Eagle Cap Wilderness, Oregon (221,355 acres); High Uintas Primitive Area, Utah (237,177 acres); Glacier Peak Wilderness, Washington (464,471 acres); and Teton Wilderness, Wyoming (563,500 acres). These are gross acreages; those for the primitive areas are subject to change, such lands are classified under the Wilderness Act of 1964.

Both types are essentially similar in quality and outdoor recreation value. Modern developments (roads, mechanized transportation, structure) and commercial utilization of natural resources are prohibited or greatly restricted, either by law, as in wildernesses, or by administrative regulation, as in primitive areas. Both types are characterized by expansive, often highly scenic, undisturbed terrain. Those who use these areas must do so "on their own." Travel is on foot, with horses and pack stock, or, in the case of the Boundary Waters Canoe Area, by canoe. Self-reliance, an ability to live with nature, and an understanding of its hazards as well as its interests are necessary for safe and pleasurable use of these undeveloped lands.

As their titles imply, there are certain differences between wildernesses and primitive areas,[7] related primarily to the original conditions of their estab-

---

[7] In national forest wilderness, commercial enterprise, structures and installations, roads, and all forms of mechanized transportation are prohibited by provisions of the Wilderness Act, except as specifically permitted and as subject to existing private rights on such lands. The specific exceptions in the Wilderness Act include (1) temporary truck trails or mechanized access in emergencies concerned with health and safety of visitors, or in the control of forest fire, destructive insects, and disease; (2) prospecting for purposes of obtaining information on resources including minerals after 1983, if carried out in a manner compatible with preservation of wilderness environment; (3) until 1983, location, development, and operation of mining claims, subject to reasonable regulations governing ingress and egress and restoration of the surface as prescribed by the Secretary of Agriculture; (4) investigation, establishment, and maintenance of reservoirs and power plants which are in the public interest, as authorized by the President; (5) grazing of livestock, where such activity was established prior to enactment of the Wilderness Act; (6) fishing

lishment, their current status, and the degree of protection applied. Wildernesses on the National Forests are units of the National Wilderness Preservation System. They receive maximum practical protection of their wilderness quality, backed by law, as defined in the Wilderness Preservation Act of 1964. Primitive areas are not included in the National Wilderness Preservation System but were given legal status pending a decision by Congress concerning the suitability or nonsuitability of these lands for wildernesses. The Wilderness Act stipulated that, by 1974, all primitive areas on the national forests were to be evaluated as to their suitability or nonsuitability for inclusion, in whole or in part, in the National Wilderness Preservation System.[8]

Solitude and a feeling of self-sufficiency, prime ingredients in the appeal of wilderness recreation, are not limited to specifically designated wildernesses and primitive areas. There are extensive undesignated areas of backcountry in the national forests, often managed for timber production, which provide very challenging recreation experiences. A recent concept is management of certain small, relatively accessible portions of such undesignated lands for limited-access recreation areas. These fulfill the needs of many users, particularly those who lack the necessary time, experience, and physical stamina required in extensive wilderness travel.

Geological, Archaeological, and Historical Areas (IV).   These areas vary in size but are of sufficient extent to protect and preserve specific interests found on the national forests.

Scenic Areas (IV).   Specifically designated lands of this type are characterized by unique or outstanding beauty. Their size varies, and they are often smaller than 5,000 acres. They are maintained, as nearly as possible, in an undisturbed condition; hence, development of roads, trails, and other facilities is permitted only to the minimum extent required to make the area accessible.

Observation Sites (I, II, or III).   The recreation activity of viewing outstanding scenery is normally associated with travel. Where opportunities exist for providing sight-seeing, particularly scenes possessing qualities of beauty or inter-

---

and hunting, subject to state laws; (7) continued management of the Boundary Waters Canoe Area in accordance with established Forest Service policy, as authorized by the Secretary of Agriculture.

Primitive areas are administered according to 36 CFR 251.86, in effect at the time the Wilderness Act was passed. Provisions of this regulation are not very far removed from the more severe stipulations of the Wilderness Act; further, great care has always been, and continues to be, exercised by the Forest Service in preventing disturbance of their natural character. Regulations governing primitive areas and the boundaries of the areas were given legal status by the Wilderness Act. All lands within primitive areas must continue to be managed under regulations in effect at the time the Wilderness Act was passed until Congress determines otherwise.

[8] The Wilderness Act provides also for similar evaluation, by 1974, of undeveloped portions of lands, with a minimum area of 5,000 acres, administered by the National Park Service and the Fish and Wildlife Service, for possible inclusion in the National Wilderness Preservation System.

est which make lasting impressions, the Forest Service develops overlooks or observation sites. These sites usually are turnouts along routes of travel and include parking and sanitation facilities. Some have tables, benches, and stoves to promote picnicking and other day-use activities. The Forest Service maintains more than 400 observation sites.

Winter Sports Areas (II).   Recreation use of the national forest is not limited to the summer season. Approximately 200 winter sports areas with necessary facilities and services are found in national forests of New England, the Lake states, the Rocky Mountain region, the Southwest, the Cascade area, and the Sierra Nevada region [13]. Although emphasis is placed upon skiing, provisions for other winter sports activities, such as skating, tobogganing, and snowshoeing, is consistent with the demand for them.

In order to administer this extensive winter sports program, the Forest Service has formulated certain well-defined policies and has established procedures necessary to provide adequate facilities and protect visitors from hazards.

Special facilities for the highly proficient are of secondary importance on national forest winter sports areas; instead the areas are planned for the enjoyment and use of the average participant with specific portions designated for skiers of varying abilities. Such facilities as warming shelters, lunch counters, rope tows, and ski lifts are generally available, and some of the larger and more isolated developments offer regular hotel and meal services. Tows and ski lifts, lunch or meal services, hotel accommodations, and the like are installed and operated by private parties, subject to the full administrative control of the Forest Service. Since national forest objectives under law are different from those for parks, national forest winter sports developments need not be subject to the severe restrictions applicable in National Parks; hence permanent ski lifts of varying types can usually be provided. The Forest Service is mindful of the need for preserving the scenic beauty of areas in its charge, however, and so permanent ski lifts cannot be erected without its permission. Further, hotels for overnight accommodation are not encouraged unless an area lacks such facilities in the immediate vicinity and unless the ski area is located at a distance from population centers.

Qualified Forest Service personnel known as Snow Rangers are stationed at individual winter sports areas to supervise various aspects of these operations. Research in such matters as avalanche hazard removal has been conducted [11], and on areas located along main highways the Forest Service has the cooperation of state highway departments in removing snow from roads and parking areas and of state highway patrols in controlling traffic. Further, the National Ski Patrol cooperates with the Snow Rangers in supervising winter sports activities; this is of particular importance in the rescue of lost or injured skiers and in the provision of competent first aid. In addition, at many winter sports areas on the national forests ski instruction is provided, by instructors certified by the National Ski Association, for beginners and those not yet thoroughly proficient in this outdoor sport.

Organization Camp Areas (II).   Facilities (lodging, meal service) necessary for the accommodation of organized groups are developed on organization camp areas. Such areas are specifically designated for development by nonprofit organizations and public agencies, and they are generally used by those who cannot afford expensive accommodations or costly camping equipment. Opportunities of this kind are often favored by such groups as Boy Scouts, Girl Scouts, Campfire Girls, the YMCA, 4-H clubs, churches, and welfare agencies. Administrative control of these areas, allotted on the basis of need, remains within the Forest Service.

Approximately 400 organization camps, most of which are privately owned, operate within the national forests. These units can serve a maximum of about 40,000 people at one time.

Concession Sites (II).   Specifically designated areas of this type on national forest land include various public accommodations (hotels, motels, resorts, trailer sites) that are more elaborate than campgrounds and organization camps and are incidental to the enjoyment of the national forests. They also provide for the establishment of related necessary public services (restaurants, stores, gasoline stations, horse and boat liveries).

Facilities of this type must be in keeping with the forest environment and are constructed with private funds, except where essential services cannot otherwise be obtained.[9] Full administrative authority over resort areas is retained by the Forest Service.

Recreation Residence (Summer-home) Sites (II).   Units of national forest land which are not needed or suitable for uses of higher priority have been designated on some national forests. On such areas individuals have been permitted to lease lots for summer residences at an annual rate determined by appraisal. Buildings erected conform to Forest Service architectural and construction standards. Over 19,000 summer homes are found in the national forests. The pressures of increasing demands for public-use areas preclude the establishment of additional sites.

National Recreation Areas.   A number of areas of this type, characterized by outstanding combinations of outdoor recreational interests and opportunities, have been established by Congress. If they involve national forests, administration is by the Forest Service.

Public Recreational Use of the National Forests

There has been rapid development of public interest in the diversified recreational advantages offered by the national forests (Table 9-2). Such interest began

---

[9] Two hotels within the national forests, Timberline Lodge in the Mt. Hood National Forest, Oregon, and Magazine Mountain Lodge, in the Ouachita National Forest of Arkansas, were built with federal funds and are owned by the federal government. They are operated by private concessionaires under Forest Service supervision.

Table 9-2
Summary, public recreational use of the national forests[a]

Year[b]	Total	Year[b]	Total	Year[b]	Total	Year[b]	Total
1924	4,460,389	1936	10,781,094	1948	24,010,964	1960	92,594,500
1925	5,622,206	1937	11,832,658	1949	26,080,255	1961	101,912,500
1926	6,044,267	1938	14,495,276	1950	27,367,799	1962	112,762,200
1927	6,136,813	1939	14,331,861	1951	29,950,252	1963	122,582,000
1928	6,550,317	1940	16,162,967	1952	33,006,885	1964	133,762,300
1929	7,132,058	1941	18,004,785	1953	35,403,050	1965	151,751,900
1930	6,910,924	1942	10,407,120[c]	1954	40,304,047	1966	150,728,900[d]
1931	8,073,917	1943	6,274,659[c]	1955	45,712,868	1967	149,647,100[d]
1932	7,895,843	1944	7,151,953[c]	1956	52,556,084	1968	156,655,300
1933	8,165,521	1945	10,074,089[c]	1957	60,957,273	1969	162,838,100
1934	8,580,806	1946	18,240,677	1958	68,449,500	1970	172,554,500
1935	9,718,330	1947	21,330,751	1959	81,521,000		

[a]Unit used from 1924 to 1964 is "visit" (entry of a person for an undetermined length of time); since 1965 unit used is "visitor day" (person-presence, either individuals or groups, for twelve visitor hours; there is no predictable relation between the visitor and visitor-day figures). See Recreation Advisory Council, Bureau of Outdoor Recreation, "Federal Executive Policy Governing the Reporting of Recreation Use of Federal Recreation Areas," U.S. Government Printing Office, Washington, 1965.

[b]Data for 1933 through 1939 on fiscal year basis; balance on basis of calendar year.

[c]Does not include visits from armed forces personnel (1942: 345,526; 1943: 283,084; 1944: 310,142; 1945: 121,235).

[d]Decrease in reported use due to improved sampling method and more reliable figures. Actual use estimated to have increased at rate of approximately 7 percent each year.

Sources: 1924-1940 from summary provided by Forest Service, Washington; 1941-1952 from Statistical Supplements to Report of the Chief of the Forest Service, U.S. Government Printing Office, Washington; 1953-1954 from Annual Statistical Report, "Recreation Visits," Forest Service, Washington; 1955-1970 from Report of the Chief of the Forest Service, U.S. Government Printing Office, Washington, various dates.

many years ago, even before the Forest Service gave formal official recognition to recreation as a valid resource of these areas. Since 1924, when records were first taken, growth in recreational use of the national forests has paralleled that of other types of public lands; except for the Depression years of the 1930s and during World War II, recreational patronage of the national forests has shown a constant and rapid acceleration which gives no indication of abating.

Summary

The Forest Service, a bureau in the Department of Agriculture, administers over 187 million acres of land, the major portion of which is included in 154 national forests. Headquarters of the Forest Service, including the office of the Chief Forester, is in Washington, D.C. There are nine regions, each in the charge of a

Regional Forester. National forests, each administered by a Forest Supervisor, are divided into ranger districts, which are the basic administrative units of the Forest Service. Ranger districts are administered by District Rangers. This decentralized administrative framework permits delegation of authority to varied levels of the Forest Service organization in making decisions concerning uses of national forest lands.

The basic policy of the Forest Service is multiple use and sustained yield for maximum, long-term public benefits in the protection, management, and development of National Forest resources for timber, outdoor recreation, water, wildlife, forage, and related values. Forest Service recreation policy emphasizes integration of recreation with other uses of the national forests and the maintenance and perpetuation of an attractive environment for varied forest-oriented outdoor recreational interests and activities. This policy includes preservation of rare or fragile flora, fauna, and other features.

Diversity of outdoor recreational interests at all seasons is one of the principal characteristics of the National Forests. These reserves embrace large portions of our principal mountain ranges noted for rugged scenic beauty. They also include sections of the Pacific Coast and portions of the lake country of northern Minnesota. And they include most types of North American forest environment with their typical plants and animals. Facilities necessary for public enjoyment of these varied interests include thousands of miles of trails, modern highways and subsidiary roads, and many areas for skiing and related winter sports. There are numerous picnic areas and campgrounds; those which are readily accessible and equipped with modern facilities contrast with more remote, less developed sites. There are also similarly varied hotel and lodge accommodations, usually privately operated. The national forests also include extensive, completely undeveloped primitive and wilderness areas; the latter are the core of our National Wilderness Preservation System. Development of public interest in the recreational advantages of the national forests began long before the Forest Service gave formal recognition of recreation as a valid national forest resource. Since 1924, when records were first taken, recreational use of the national forests has, in common with other uses of wild lands, grown phenomenally.

Though basically the national forests and the national parks complement each other in providing recreational opportunities, there are also overlaps and areas of competition. Many of the national parks were created from, or are adjacent to, national forests, causing some cases of possible conflicts of interest between the primarily preservationist land-use policy of the Park Service and the basic utilitarian policy of the Forest Service. Where attempts are made to coordinate planning and management involving both agencies, as in the case of efforts made on the North Fork of the Flathead River, Montana, between Glacier National Park, Flathead National Forest, related state agencies, and owners [1], harmonious relationships can develop.

The Forest Service, in its recreation policy, ranges from highly developed areas, involving many recreation and resource uses, to the almost natural wilderness. And there are overlaps in recreational (BOR) classes. Management of such a spectrum of opportunity areas requires great skill, particularly where competitive uses overlap. With the increasing number of visitors, the expanding number of resource producers, and the growing complexity of the organizational structure, the problems of multiple use of the national forests become more difficult. Various interest groups push for their particular interest in hearings and in the media.

Selected References

1. Bolle, A. W.: The Cooperative Study of Multiple Use of Natural Resources in the North Fork of the Flathead Valley, *Montana Business Review,* vol. 12, no. 3, March, 1960.
2. Freeman, Orville L., and Michael Frome: "The National Forests of America," Putnam, New York, 1968.
3. U.S. National Park Service and U.S. Forest Service: "The National Parks and the National Forests, Their Purposes and Management," U.S. Government Printing Office, Washington, 1969.
4. National Recreation and Park Association: "Recreation and Park Yearbook, 1966," Washington, 1967.
5. Outdoor Recreation Resources Review Commission: "Outdoor Recreation for America: A Report to the President and to the Congress by the ORRRC," U.S. Government Printing Office, Washington, 1962.
6. Outdoor Recreation Resources Review Commission: "Multiple Use of Land and Water Areas," ORRRC Study Report No. 17, U.S. Government Printing Office, Washington, 1962.
7. Recreation Advisory Council, Bureau of Outdoor Recreation: "Federal Executive Policy Governing the Reporting of Recreation Use of Federal Recreation Areas," U.S. Government Printing Office, Washington, 1965.
8. U.S. Department of Agriculture: "The Principal Laws Relating to the Establishment and Administration of the National Forests and to Other Forest Service Activities," Miscellaneous Publication No. 135, U.S. Government Printing Office, Washington, 1939.
9. U.S. Department of Agriculture, Forest Service: "Our National Forests," Agriculture Information Bulletin No. 47, U.S. Government Printing Office, Washington, 1951.
10. U.S. Department of Agriculture, Forest Service: "The Work of the U.S. Forest Service," Agriculture Information Bulletin No. 91, U.S. Government Printing Office, Washington, 1952.
11. U.S. Department of Agriculture, Forest Service: "Avalanche Handbook," U.S. Government Printing Office, Washington, 1954.
12. U.S. Department of Agriculture, Forest Service: "Our Forest Resources: What They Are and What They Mean to Us," Agriculture Information Bulletin No. 131, U.S. Government Printing Office, Washington, 1954.
13. U.S. Department of Agriculture, Forest Service: "National Forest Vacations," U.S. Government Printing Office, Washington, 1955.
14. U.S. Department of Agriculture, Forest Service: "Wilderness," U.S. Government Printing Office, Washington, 1967.

15. U.S. Department of Agriculture, Forest Service: "Outdoor Recreation in the National Forests," Agriculture Information Bulletin No. 301, U.S. Government Printing Office, Washington, 1968.

16. U.S. Department of Agriculture, Forest Service: "Recreation Information Management," In-Service Training Guide, U.S. Government Printing Office, Washington, 1968.

17. U.S. Department of Agriculture, Forest Service: "Forest Service Manual; National Forest Protection and Management, Recreation, Vol. III," Washington. (Multilithed.)

18. U.S. Department of Agriculture, Forest Service: "Forest Service Manual—Title 2300, Recreation Management," Washington, January, 1969. (Multilithed.)

19. U.S. Department of Agriculture, Forest Service: "Report of the Chief of the Forest Service [various dates]," U.S. Government Printing Office, Washington, v.d.

chapter ten

OTHER FEDERAL AGENCIES

Other federal agencies that provide varied outdoor recreational opportunities are the Bureau of Sport Fisheries and Wildlife, the Bureau of Land Management, and three agencies important in water-based recreation—the Bureau of Reclamation, the Corps of Engineers, and the Tennessee Valley Authority.

Bureau of Sport Fisheries and Wildlife

This federal agency is one of two bureaus of the Fish and Wildlife Service.[1] Headquarters, including the office of the Director, are in Washington, D.C. There are five regions,[2] each supervised by a Regional Director, who reports to the Director. Within each region are various wildlife refuges, fish hatcheries, and wildlife and sport fishery research stations. Field installations, except for those engaged in fundamental sport fishery and wildlife research, report to their own Regional Directors. Those engaged in fundamental research report directly to their Division Chiefs in the Washington, D.C., headquarters.

---

[1] Both the Bureau of Sport Fisheries and Wildlife and the Bureau of Commercial Fisheries are headed by a Director and have a number of divisions and branches dealing with varied aspects of their operation. General responsibility for the direction and supervision of activities of the Fish and Wildlife Service, including coordination of programs and operations of the two bureaus and their divisions and branches, rests with the Commissioner of the Fish and Wildlife Service, with headquarters in Washington, D.C. [1,7,8,9].

[2] Names and headquarters of the five regions are region I, *Pacific*, Portland, Ore.; II, *Southwest*, Albuquerque, N.M.; III, *North-central*, Minneapolis, Minn.; IV, *Southeast*, Atlanta, Ga.; and V, *Northeast*, Boston, Mass.

Figure 10-1
National Wildlife Refuge System (Bureau of Sport Fisheries and Wildlife).

Legend
- ● Migratory Bird
- □ Big Game
- ■ Game Range
- ✳ Wildlife Range

Activities of the Bureau of Sport Fisheries and Wildlife

Activities of the Bureau of Sport Fisheries and Wildlife relate to various recreational uses of wild lands; they include:

1. Essential research in fish and wildlife biology and related matters for solution of various sport fish and wildlife problems in the most adequate and economic manner. Research concerns improvement of management techniques; alleviation of animal damage; classification, distribution, and life history studies; prudent use of wildlife resources; pesticides, including surveillance and registration; fish nutrition and disease; endangered species research; wildlife disease studies; and anadromous fisheries work.

2. Management of numerous refuges for mammals, birds, and fishes, together with their environment, to maintain adequate numbers in vigorous condition in typical surroundings, with minimum disruption of other necessary land uses. The extent and quality of wildlife environment in relation to changes attributed to modern technology and land-use pressures, and protection and restoration of rare or vanishing species and their environment are vital concerns of the refuge program.

3. Administration of appropriations provided by laws in the interest of wildlife conservation.[3]

4. Cooperation with other federal agencies, state agencies, and foreign governments on fish and wildlife matters. Such cooperation involves law enforcement; technical wildlife management on projects where wildlife is an important resource, or where developments affect wildlife populations; investigation and importation of foreign wildlife for trial release; training of personnel; management or studies of international faunal resources (migratory birds, fur seal, whale, certain fisheries) as prescribed by treaty or agreement with other nations.

5. Development of public interest in and understanding of the importance of fish and wildlife resources through interpretation, conservation education programs, the mass media, and technical reports and publications.

The National Wildlife Refuge System [1,9,38,39]

The National Wildlife Refuge System is the largest and most diversified in the world (Figure 10-1). The aggregate area is about 28½ million acres, with over 300 units ranging in size from a few acres to 9 million acres. They are in every state but four (Connecticut, Rhode Island, New Hampshire, West Virginia), as well as in Puerto Rico. Various areas occur from the Arctic to the tropics and from below sea level to nearly 10,000 feet in elevation. They include ocean

---

[3] These include the Pittman-Robertson Act, regarding federal aid to states in wildlife restoration; the similar Dingell-Johnson Act, regarding sport fish restoration; and the Wetlands Loan Act and the Migratory Bird Hunting Stamp Act, which provide funds for the establishment of flyway refuges.

beaches, shoreland and salt marshes, offshore islands, swamps, deserts, prairies, and forests. Within each of these generalized environments are more detailed habitats adapted to particular needs of various species. As a result, faunal interests of these areas are highly significant and noteworthy (Table 10-1). Practically all of nearly 800 species of North American birds may be found during at least one season on the National Wildlife Refuges. These lands also provide suitable environment for essentially all North American big-game animals, as well as most smaller mammals and many reptiles. Many refuges provide

Table 10-1
Examples of areas and interests of the National Wildlife Refuge System[a]

Name	Acres	Interests
Arctic National Wildlife Range, Alaska	8,900,000	Caribou, polar and grizzly bears, Dall sheep, waterfowl, shorebirds
Aleutian Islands, Alaska	2,720,235	Sea otters, geese, seabirds, ptarmigans
Cabeza Prieta Game Range, Ariz.	860,000	Desert bighorns, Sonoran pronghorns, peccaries
Farallon, Calif.	91	Seabirds, sea lions
Bombay Hook, Del.	14,854	Snow geese, other waterfowl, shorebirds
Loxahatchee, Fla.	145,524	Waterfowl, herons, egrets, spoonbills
National Key Deer, Fla.	6,745	Key whitetail deer, West Indian birds
Blackbeard Island, Ga.	5,617	Sea turtles, waterfowl, shorebirds
Okefenokee, Ga.	330,973	Alligators, black bears, various birds
Sabine, La.	142,716	Waterfowl, spoonbills, ibises, alligators
Seney, Mich.	95,455	Waterfowl, sandhill cranes, grouse, otters
Creedman Coulee, Mont.	2,728	Waterfowl, prairie chickens, sage grouse
National Bison Range, Mont.	18,541	Buffalo, elk, bighorns, deer
Red Rock Lakes, Mont.	39,946	Trumpeter swans, moose, grayling
Fort Niobrara, Nebr.	19,122	Buffalo, Texas longhorns, elk, prairie chickens, sharp-tailed grouse
Desert Game Range, Nev.	2,188,055	Desert bighorns, mule deer
Brigantine, N.J.	15,122	Waterfowl, shorebirds, gulls
Great Swamp, N.J.	1,870	Waterfowl, deer, otter
Malheur, Ore.	180,850	Whistling swans, white pelicans, sage grouse, waterfowl
Cape Romain, S. C.	34,697	Waterfowl, shorebirds, sea turtles, alligators, deer
Santa Ana, Tex.	1,980	Tree ducks, red-billed pigeons, chachalacas, green jays
Aransas, Tex.	47,261	Whooping cranes, shorebirds, waterfowl, turkeys, deer, peccaries
Bear River, Utah	64,895	Waterfowl, shorebirds, muskrats
National Elk Refuge, Wyo.	23,754	Elk, moose, trumpeter swans, sandhill cranes

[a] Unless otherwise noted, areas are national wildlife refuges.

Source: "1966 List of National Wildlife Refuges," U.S. Department of the Interior, Fish and Wildlife Service, Bureau of Sport Fisheries and Wildlife, Washington, 1966. (Multilithed.)

virtually the only places where some of the rarest of North American wildlife species now exist. Many refuges are remote and difficult of access, but others are located close to centers of population.[4]

About 250 refuges with 3,500,000 acres are primarily waterfowl habitat. About forty more, containing 420,000 acres, are used mainly by other migratory birds, especially those with colonial nesting habits. At least twenty were set up as threatened-species territory; these total about 8,750,000 acres. A few especially large refuges, amounting to about 15 million acres, were set aside for their outstanding and extensive multiwildlife environments; much of this acreage is in Alaska.

In addition, the National Wildlife Refuge System includes about 677,400 acres in waterfowl production areas, small but excellent duck-producing wetlands in North and South Dakota, Minnesota, and Nebraska. Of this total, 147,578 acres were purchased in fee and the rest is covered by protective easements.

General Land Management Policy of the National Wildlife Refuge System

Refuges and related lands administered by the Bureau of Sport Fisheries and Wildlife are managed on a multiple-use basis [1,7,9,11,38,39], consistent with maintenance of desirable wildlife habitat required to support optimum variety and abundance of species. Refuges for migratory waterfowl are not necessarily natural areas. Many have been developed by improving marshes or farmed-out land. Even on some "wild" refuges natural processes are often modified to favor the requirements of certain species. Cultural operations (agricultural crop production, domestic stock grazing, trapping or hunting of surplus animals, timber cutting) may be permitted when in the interest of wildlife populations or the purpose of the area involved. As a result, by-products of refuge management include income from sale of hay, grazing fees, wildlife-benefiting timber operations, sale of pelts of surplus fur-bearing animals, and oil and gas leases.[5]

As stipulated by the Wilderness Act of 1964, refuge lands are being evaluated as to their suitability or nonsuitability for inclusion in the National Wilderness Preservation System; this review is to be progressively completed by 1974. In addition, as directed by the Land and Water Conservation Fund Act, access to some areas designated by the Secretary of the Interior is subject to an admission fee.[6]

---

[4] One of the most noteworthy is the Great Swamp National Wildlife Refuge in New Jersey, which is only about an hour's drive from New York City.

[5] Section 401, act of June 15, 1935, known as the Revenue-Sharing Act (49 Stat. 383), as amended by the act of Aug. 30, 1964 [78 Stat. 701; 16 U.S.C. 715(s)], calls for payments to the county in which a refuge is located, amounting to three-quarters of 1 percent of the adjusted value of acquired lands, or 25 percent of refuge receipts, at the option of the county.

[6] In 1968 refuges charging entrance fees included Aransas, Tex.; Bear River, Utah; Parker River, Mass.; Brigantine, N.J.; Bombay Hook, Del.; Blackbeard Island, Ga.; Cape Romain, S.C.; and the National Bison Range, Mont.

Recreation Policy and Public Use of National Wildlife Refuge System
[1,7,11,39]

Recreation on national wildlife refuges is confined almost entirely to wildlife-oriented activities.[7] General recreational activities, services, and facilities suited to large concentrations of people, though appropriate on a few refuges, are not encouraged by the Bureau of Sport Fisheries and Wildlife. Observation and study of flora and fauna, general sightseeing, fishing, and picnicking are among the principal recreational uses. Camping, however, is generally discouraged, except on specially designated lands sometimes provided for that purpose. Lodge accommodations, operated by concessionaries, are available on only a few refuges. Fishing is permitted on many of these areas, and others may occasionally be opened to controlled or managed hunting. Where appropriate, boating and swimming are allowed. A number of refuges feature self-guiding wildlife trails and designated auto tour routes. Wildlife interpretive centers, now available in only a few areas, will be increased in number in the future; these contain exhibits explaining the establishment and operation of refuges and the interests of local animal and plant life. Despite the limitations, recreational use of the National Wildlife Refuge System rose from nearly 3.4 million visits in 1951 to over 19.2 million visits in 1971.

Adjacent to Okefenokee National Wildlife Refuge a small section of swamp habitat, designated as Okefenokee Swamp Park, is operated by a non-profit organization which has leased land from the state of Georgia. From here boat trips, conducted by licensed guides, may be made for a short distance into the Okefenokee National Wildlife Refuge for the benefit of visitors who wish to experience the feeling of solitude engendered by this interesting area.

National wildlife refuges have a particular appeal to individuals with definite interest in wildlife and related natural history. Sportsmen's clubs, bird and garden clubs, school and service groups, and professional and scientific societies find them especially attractive. Many refuges are the locale for Christmas Bird Counts, sponsored throughout the country for many years by the National Audubon Society.

Bureau of Land Management

This bureau of the Department of the Interior[8] has jurisdiction over more than 452 million acres of federal land in twenty-four states, mostly in the West

---

[7] Authorized by act of Sept. 29, 1962 (75 Stat. 653), as amended [19 U.S.C. 460(b)-460(k)(4)].

[8] Formed in 1946 by consolidation of the General Land Office (established 1812) and the Grazing Service (established 1934), the Bureau of Land Management inherited responsibility for multipurpose management of about 2.6 million acres of forested O & C revested railroad lands in Oregon as stated in the O & C Sustained Yield Forestry Act of 1937.

(Figure 10-2); more than half, approximately 262 million acres, is in the state of Alaska [24].[9]

Current Basic Responsibilities and Policy

The Bureau of Land Management is both a land management and a land disposal agency, having assumed most of the functions of its two predecessor agencies. Its basic responsibility is the administration of public lands under its jurisdiction in a manner that will result in maximum public benefit [3,4,7,11,24].

Lands retained by the Bureau of Land Management are those having natural resources of such character and quality that the public interest is served best by retention in federal ownership. Such natural resources include forage, minerals (including outer continental shelf), forests, water, fish, and wildlife, plus outdoor recreation, wilderness values, natural beauty and open space, and other public values (including unique or scarce features of our environment) that would be lost if the land passed from federal ownership. No overall priority has been assigned to any specific use, though certain uses may be dominant in some areas. Lands are managed on a multiple use-sustained yield basis for optimum production of various products and services for which they are best suited, in consideration of (1) existing and future demand; (2) coordination and coopera- tion with resource use and management by other federal, state and local government agencies, public organizations, and private landowners; (3) consis- tency with national programs; and (4) compatibility of possible uses.

Lands disposed of by the Bureau of Land Management are those in which the public interest can be served best by subsequent appropriate management and use by other public agencies (federal, state, local), private organizations, or individuals. Disposal, as authorized by various land laws, is accomplished in the most efficient manner by sale, exchange transfer of jurisdiction, or lease. Such transactions involve a fair return in money, lands, or other property, or the assurance of bona fide, substantial development or use—tangible or intangible— which is in the public interest.

Organization of the Bureau of Land Management [24]

Bureau of Land Management headquarters are in Washington, D.C. The principal administrative officer is the Director. The headquarters staff includes various administrative and technical personnel who deal with different aspects of the Bureau's far-flung, complex operations (land classification, outdoor recreation, wildlife, minerals, public land surveys, forest management, range management, resource conservation and development, protection, legal matters, administra-

---

[9] This area represents the remaining portion of the original public domain. Public lands managed by the Bureau of Land Management in the forty-eight contiguous states include lands reserved by the Taylor Grazing Act of 1934 and Executive orders of the President in 1934 and 1935; they are reserved from most forms of private acquisition, until classified. Unreserved public lands exist only in Alaska, where various settlement laws apply.

tion, and finance). There are eleven state offices,[10] each in the charge of a state director and staffed with administrative and technical personnel who deal with various Bureau of Land Management activities in the states concerned.

Recreational Resources of the Public Lands

Lands administered by the Bureau of Land Management provide for a multiplicity of outdoor recreational interests and activities [26] . They contain spectacular desert, canyon, and mountain country; glaciers and other noteworthy geological features; river, lake, and ocean frontage; and archaeological and historical sites. They may be large expansive areas or small scattered tracts. Large portions of these lands are still generally inaccessible except by the most hardy, resourceful individuals, but some sections are more readily reached. In many instances they border routes of recreational travel or are adjacent to national and state parks, national forests, wildlife refuges, and related recreational areas. Occasionally they are near towns or cities.

The recreational potential of the public lands was not of imperative interest until growing urbanization and expanding leisure-time interests and activities prompted consideration of environmental interests and beauty, and need for additional outdoor recreational areas to accommodate increasing crowds. The importance of outdoor recreational use of public lands administered by the Bureau of Land Management is growing rapidly, and facilities are being expanded every year to meet increasing demands. From 1964 to 1971 the number of visits increased from 14.5 million to over 69.2 million.

Current Recreational Land-use Policies

Current recreational policy of the Bureau of Land Management emphasizes public recreation on lands under its jurisdiction in its multiple use-sustained yield management program [24] . Where authorized by law it cooperates with federal, state, and local efforts in providing for critical recreational needs, facilities, and services. Legislative acts basic to this recreational policy include:

1. *Taylor Grazing Act of 1934* (P.L. 73-482; 48 Stat. 1269), as amended.[11] This act is the basic legislative authority governing the management and protection of the vacant public lands of the United States, exclusive of Alaska. Included in its

---

[10]State offices are located in Anchorage, Alaska; Phoenix, Ariz.; Sacramento, Calif.; Denver, Colo.; Boise, Idaho; Billings, Mont.; Reno, Nev.; Santa Fe, N.M.; Portland, Oreg.; Salt Lake City, Utah; and Cheyenne, Wyo. Bureau of Land Management matters in the state of Washington are handled by the Portland office, in North and South Dakota and Minnesota by the Billings office, in Kansas and Nebraska by the Cheyenne office, and in Oklahoma by the Santa Fe office; in other states they are administered by a land office at Silver Springs, Md.

[11]1936 (49 Stat. 1976), 1939 (53 Stat. 1002), 1947 (61 Stat. 630), 1947 (61 Stat. 790), 1948 (62 Stat. 533), and 1954 (68 Stat. 151).

Figure 10-2
Public lands in the Western states administered by the Bureau of Land Management (Bureau
of Land Management).

broad powers are provisions for access to lands administered by the Bureau of
Land Management, the right to hunt and fish on them (subject to state laws), the
conservation of wildlife, and the classification of land for recreational purposes
in connection with their lease or sale under the public land laws.

2. *O & C Sustained Yield Forestry Act of 1937* (P.L. 75-405).[12] This act directs
that O & C timberlands in western Oregon be managed for permanent forest

---

[12]Three other important legislative acts which affect O & C lands have been passed. The act
of July 31, 1939, provides authority to exchange O & C lands for others of approximately

production and the protection of watersheds and regulation of stream flow, vital to the economic stability of local communities and industries, and that recreational facilities be provided.

Primary emphasis under the O & C Act is on encouraging state and local government agencies to assume initiative and responsibility in developing, maintaining, and operating public recreational areas under lease or permit. However, counties with O & C lands in Oregon have approved a proposal that a proportionate share of receipts from timber sales which would otherwise be returned to counties be expended by the Bureau of Land Management in the development of public recreational facilities on O & C lands.

3. *Recreation and Public Purposes Act of 1926* (P.L. 69-386; 44 Stat. 741), as amended.[13] This act provides an improved opportunity for state and local governments, as well as nonprofit private organizations, to acquire lands for public recreational, educational, health, or other public purposes. Vacant and unreserved lands suitable for public recreation areas and not needed for multiple-use purposes ordinarily are made available for purchase under this act, subject to conditions and terms which ensure their use for public recreation and at prices commensurate with the use of the land for a public purpose. Lands needed for multiple-use purposes may be made available by lease, rather than by purchase and transfer of title [22].

The term "recreation" is interpreted broadly by this act, and there are no area limitations on the amount of land that may be leased; area limitations on purchases are determined by the nature of the particular recreational use. Numerous types of recreational areas have been acquired through provisions of the Recreation and Public Purposes Act. Among them are state, county, and municipal parks, picnic areas and campgrounds, beaches and boat-launching sites, historical sites, highway waysides, wildlife refuges, and various recreational areas of an essentially public character obtained by sportsmen's organizations and civic, service, and youth groups.

4. *Small Tract Act of 1938* (P.L. 75-577; 52 Stat. 609), as amended.[14] This act authorizes the lease or sale of certain classes of public lands classified as

---

equal acreage value held in private, state, or county ownership either within or contiguous to the grant limits. The act of Apr. 8, 1948, reopened O & C and CBWR lands, except power sites, to exploration, entry, and disposition under the mining laws; it also validated mineral claims, if otherwise valid, located on O & C lands during the period from Aug. 28, 1937, to Apr. 8, 1948. The act of June 24, 1954, declared approximately 463,000 acres of unselected and unpatented, odd-numbered sections within the indemnity limits of the O & C grant, which were included within the boundaries of various national forests, to be revested O & C lands; these lands continue to be administered as national forest lands though the proceeds go to the O & C fund (personal communication, BLM, Portland, Oreg., Apr. 22, 1970).

[13]1954: 68 Stat. 173, 1959: 73 Stat. 110, 571, 1960: 74 Stat. 899; 43 U.S.C. 869; 869:1-5.

[14]43 U.S.C. 682 (a) (3).

particularly valuable for various purposes, including recreation. Individual tracts are 5 acres or less in size [30].

5. *Public Land Sale Act of 1964* (P.L. 88-608; 78 Stat. 988; 43 U.S.C. 1421-1427). This act authorizes the sale of public lands, in tracts not exceeding 5,120 acres, that have been classified for sale in accordance with a determination that they are required for orderly growth and development of a community, or that they are chiefly valuable for residential, commercial, agricultural (not including grazing or forage production), industrial, and public uses and development. Sales are made at fair market value to qualified governmental agencies and through competitive bidding to individuals and organizations.

6. *Classification and Multiple Use Act of 1964* (P.L. 88-607; 78 Stat. 986; 43 U.S.C. 14111-1418). This act authorizes the classification of public lands administered by the Bureau of Land Management, including those in Alaska, for determining which portions of them can properly be sold and which portions will provide greater public benefits if retained in federal ownership. Lands classified for eventual sale are those required for orderly growth and development of a community, or those particularly valuable for residential, commercial, agricultural (not including grazing of forage production), industrial, or public uses and development. Lands classified for retention in federal ownership, at least for the time being, will be managed for domestic livestock grazing, fish and wildlife development and utilization, industrial development (including power production), mineral production, occupancy by useful structures, outdoor recreation, timber production, watershed production, wilderness preservation, or preservation of public values that would be lost if the land passed from federal ownership.

Current Recreational Land Management Program [28]

In order for the Bureau of Land Management to place proper emphasis on coordination and correlation of its plans with those of other agencies at different levels of government, as well as with those of private landowners, the land classification system used by the Bureau of Outdoor Recreation [11,12] is generally followed. Within this frame of reference the Bureau of Land Management has defined four types of recreational land units, as follows:

1. *Recreation lands.* A tract of public land (usually several thousand acres in size) on which outdoor recreation or wildlife has been determined to be the primary use. Recreation lands may have facilities for intensive recreation use, or they may remain in a relatively undeveloped condition for extensive forms of use. Where wilderness values predominate, an area may be preserved in a primitive, roadless condition. Thus, these areas may include all classes in the Bureau of Outdoor Recreation classification system.

2. *Recreation site.* A tract of BLM land, generally less than 500 acres, on which recreation use is the primary value. Such lands are generally characterized by, or adapted to, concentrated development and use (camping, picnicking, sightseeing, fishing, swimming, organization camps, summer-home site leases), though in some cases they may contain significant archaeological or historical features requiring careful protection. Recreation sites may be retained for management by the Bureau of Land Management, developed and managed jointly by the Bureau and other agencies, transferred to other federal agencies, or sold or leased under provisions of the Recreation and Public Purposes Act and related pertinent legislation. Depending upon their type of attraction, these areas may fall into any of the six recreational land classes of the Bureau of Outdoor Recreation. By 1967 over 3,500 recreational sites with an aggregate area of over 1 million acres had been designated. Designated archaeological and historical sites numbered nearly 700, with an aggregate area of over 90,000 acres.

3. *Transfer tract.* A tract of BLM land which has been sold or leased to a state or local government agency, or to a qualified nonprofit organization, for recreation purposes. Such tracts are usually transferred or leased under provisions of the Recreation and Public Purposes Act and are reviewed periodically by BLM to determine whether use is in compliance with the terms and conditions.

4. *Buffer or scenic zones.* Designated protective areas of BLM lands surrounding or partly surrounding recreation sites, transfer tracts, and similar developments; or adjacent to highways and roads commonly used by recreationalists; or adjacent to lakes, reservoirs, or major streams. These zones are dedicated to protection and enhancement of scenic beauty, vegetation, water supply, privacy, or other factors that contribute to recreational values. They may be of varying widths according to circumstances, but ordinarily they will not be less than 200 feet or more than ½ mile wide. Nonconforming uses[15] are prohibited; after official approval they are noted prominently on maps, marked on the ground, and otherwise protected against the possibility of inadvertent damage. Nearly 200 areas of this type, with an aggregate area of over 3 million acres, had been designated by 1967.

Water-based Recreational Areas

The Bureau of Reclamation, Corps of Engineers, and Tennessee Valley Authority administer areas consisting of reservoirs and other artificially impounded waters, together with their contiguous lands, resulting largely from construction of dams. These multipurpose projects, developed primarily for irrigation, hydroelectric power, flood control, and similar objectives, are extensively used for such outdoor recreational activities as boating, swimming, water skiing, picnick-

---

[15] Clear-cutting of timber (carefully conducted light selective cutting may be permissible), mining, road building (permitted in some situations), homesite leases, advertising signs, and certain other types of developments.

ing, camping, fishing, and hunting. Many people are attracted to these areas also to enjoy their scenic qualities, which are noteworthy in some cases, or to marvel at the engineering aspects of the dams themselves. Since many of these projects are located in arid sections of the West, where there are few natural lakes, or in the Appalachian Southeast, they have a tremendous effect on outdoor recreation in such regions, including economic benefits.

Bureau of Reclamation [7,10,11,13,31-37]

Reclamation projects developed by this bureau of the Department of the Interior include 227 reservoirs and related recreation use areas in seventeen Western states. They have an aggregate surface water area of over 1½ million acres and a total shoreline of over 11,000 miles, together with contiguous lands aggregating more than 4 million acres. Public recreational use of these areas has grown rapidly since 1950, when a total of 6 million visitor days was recorded to 1970 when there were 54,237,639 visitor days used.

Jurisdiction relative to the engineering aspects and primary project functions (irrigation, hydroelectric power, flood control), usually is retained by the Bureau. However, except in certain cases, the Bureau of Reclamation does not assume direct responsibility for development and management of recreation. Though recreation is included in project planning, responsibility for outdoor recreational development and management is transferred to other federal agencies or comparable state or local interests, largely through cooperative agreement, pursuant to the Bureau's authority (act of August 7, 1946) for appropriate utilization of project resources. Prior to 1965, recreation development of new projects was included in project plans only as specifically provided for by Congress in individual project-authorizing acts. However, the Federal Water Project Recreation Act of 1965 (P.L. 89-72) provides general authority for recreation on new developments and limited authority to develop and expand recreational opportunities on existing projects.

The National Park Service assumes responsibility for outdoor recreational development and administration on certain Bureau of Reclamation reservoirs which have recreational values of national importance. Outdoor recreational administration on reservoirs within or adjacent to national forests is handled by the U.S. Forest Service, and on national wildlife refuges by the Bureau of Sport Fisheries and Wildlife of the Fish and Wildlife Service. Qualified state and local agencies with comparable responsibilities on many reservoirs developed by the Bureau of Reclamation include state park and fish and game departments, regional or county parks, water and irrigation districts, and municipal park and recreation departments or water and irrigation authorities.

Matters relevant to the protection and management of fish and wildlife resources of Bureau of Reclamation reservoirs and contiguous lands are handled by the Bureau of Sport Fisheries and Wildlife of the Fish and Wildlife Service, or comparable state organizations, by authority of the Fish and Wildlife Coordination Act of 1934, as amended (1958: P.L. 85-642; 72 Stat. 563).

In addition to recreational resources of its reservoir areas under organized development and management programs, reclamation development creates significant recreational values in its irrigated project land areas. The total area irrigated on all projects in 1967 was 8,441,000 acres. The recreational values result primarily from the change from a desert type to an irrigation type of environment for fish and wildlife. Important recreational activities benefiting from this change include upland game bird hunting (primarily pheasants), waterfowl hunting, and fishing.

Corps of Engineers

The current extensive civil works program of the Corps of Engineers contributes to outdoor recreation through construction, operation, and maintenance of reservoirs and stabilizing pools, harbors, and waterways, and the protection and improvement of coastal beach areas. There are more than 300 such projects located in over forty states [5]. The original purposes of these projects are improvement of navigation, flood control, hydroelectric power, and related objectives. However, today recreation is given full consideration in their planning and in the development of maximum outdoor recreational potential [6].

Recreational resources of Corps of Engineers projects aggregate over 8 million acres of water and contiguous land, together with many miles of waterways and beaches, having a total shoreline of approximately 28,000 miles [5]. Wherever suitable, they are open to public use for all forms of recreational activities associated with water (boating, swimming, water skiing, fishing and hunting, picnicking, camping). Facilities include more than 600 swimming beaches, over 2,000 picnic areas, more than 1,000 campgrounds with about 35,000 tent and trailer spaces, and several hundred organization campsites used by youth groups and related organizations. In 1944 the recreational use of these projects was estimated at 4 million visits; since that time such use has increased phenomenally. By 1971 some 299,750,000 visits were recorded at Corps projects.

Authority for recreational development and public use of projects developed by the Corps of Engineers is contained primarily in the Flood Control Act of 1944, as amended (1946, 1954, 1962: P.L. 87-874; 68 Stat. 1266), and the Fish and Wildlife Coordination Act of 1934, as amended (1958: P.L. 86-642; 72 Stat. 563). Two other acts pertinent to recreational use of these projects are the Land and Water Conservation Fund Act of 1964 (P.L. 88-578; 78 Stat. 897) and the Federal Water Project Recreation Act of 1965 (P.L. 89-72; 79 Stat. 213).

The Corps of Engineers does not have authority to construct water-resource projects primarily for recreational use; however, it does operate many recreational facilities on projects under its jurisdiction. It cooperates with other interested federal, state, and local governmental agencies in relevant recreational planning, development, and administration. Many state parks and related recreation areas have resulted from this practice. Water-resource development projects within or adjacent to national forests are planned, developed, and administered in cooperation with the Forest Service. Similar cooperation is carried out with the Bureau of Sport Fisheries and Wildlife on national wildlife refuges and with state game departments on state wildlife management areas. Management of fish and wildlife is the responsibility of the Bureau of Sport Fisheries and Wildlife or comparable state agencies.

Basic facilities necessary for public use, enjoyment, health, and safety are usually constructed by the Corps of Engineers (access roads, water supply, sanitary facilities, overlooks, signs, guardrails, marker buoys, simple picnic and camp areas). Further developments are provided by cooperating governmental agencies or by nonprofit organizations, which are granted long-term leases without monetary consideration. These agencies are also responsible for recreational administration on such areas. Recreational lands not required for public use may be leased to private individuals or organizations for commercial development, including appropriate services not provided by public agencies, under terms negotiated with the Corps of Engineers.

Tennessee Valley Authority [7,11,13,15-17,31]

Since its establishment in 1933 the Tennessee Valley Authority has built or acquired thirty-six reservoirs. These have an aggregate water surface area of approximately 600,000 acres and a total shoreline of about 11,000 miles. In addition, there are thousands of acres of contiguous lands which either are being used for various types of outdoor recreation or have potential recreational value related to water.

Development of the recreational potential of varied projects of the Tennessee Valley Authority, recognized by this agency at the time of its inception, has been guided by a carefully formulated recreational policy adapted to its broad multiple-use program. It has encouraged recreational use primarily by making land with an identified recreational potential available to other federal agencies, state and local agencies, and private organizations and individuals through transfer, lease or license, or sale; TVA has also provided technical assistance for development of these lands. The agencies, organizations, and individuals involved are made responsible for recreational administration and proper coordination of their activities.

This policy prompted the establishment of fourteen state parks, a number of state wildlife refuges and public shooting areas, and over eighty county and municipal parks. In addition, more than 124,000 acres of land have been transferred by the Tennessee Valley Authority to the National Park Service, Forest Service, and Bureau of Sport Fisheries and Wildlife for some form of recreation or wildlife management. Thirty-eight camps for various youth groups and other specialized nonprofit organizations have been established on the shores of reservoirs, and 340 privately operated resorts and 14,000 private recreation residences have been developed. With the exception of lands transferred to other federal agencies, all capital required in development of these recreational facilities came from other than TVA sources; total investment, both public and private, exceeds 254 million dollars.

Today, the Tennessee Valley Authority is engaged in a basic recreation program that has three primary functions: (1) research to examine the characteristics of recreation supply and demand in both water- and nonwater-oriented situations; (2) technical assistance to public agencies, private organizations, and individuals in the Tennessee Valley; and (3) comprehensive planning and development.

The renewed emphasis on recreation indicates that TVA's program continues to place high value on sharing the development responsibility with other agencies and individuals in the Tennessee Valley. However, TVA is now beginning a program of development of basic recreational facilities on its reservoirs to assure safe and adequate opportunities for recreational access to and use of these lakes.

One of the more noteworthy of TVA projects is Land Between the Lakes. This project involves an area of 170,000 acres, about 8 miles wide and 40 miles long, in western Kentucky and Tennessee, situated between TVA's Kentucky Lake on the Tennessee River and Lake Barkeley on the Cumberland River, developed by the Corps of Engineers. It is intended as a demonstration of multiple-use management on a single area of land which will provide maximum social and economic benefits for present and future generations. Provisions are also made for cooperative programs with state and local agencies to help guide development of surrounding areas.

In addition, TVA is proposing a different kind of demonstration project in recognition of the renewed need for guidelines to meet changing demands on resource uses. Jointly with the state of Tennessee, TVA is proposing to create the Buffalo Scenic Riverway to protect the beauty of this outstanding 120-mile pastoral stream in middle Tennessee, and, at the same time, to provide public opportunity for enjoyment of the stream and its environment.

Recreational resources associated with developments of the Tennessee Valley Authority are close to large population centers in the eastern United States. This has prompted heavy recreational use of TVA reservoirs and contiguous lands. In 1947, when collection of recreation-use data for the entire reservoir system was undertaken, 7,338,755 recreation visits were recorded. Since that time such use has greatly expanded. By 1970 recreation visits, not including visits made to the Land Between the Lakes, were over 47,000,000. Land Between the Lakes visits rose from 597,267 in 1965 to about 1,700,000 in 1971.

Summary

Various opportunities for outdoor recreation available on lands administered by the National Park Service and the Forest Service are augmented by those on other types of federal lands. National wildlife refuges, administered by the Bureau of Sport Fisheries and Wildlife; public lands administered by the Bureau of Land Management; and reservoirs and contiguous lands under the jurisdiction of the Bureau of Reclamation, Corps of Engineers, and the Tennessee Valley Authority all provide for appropriate recreational uses, consistent with specific agency policies. In large measure, recreational uses are coordinated with multipurpose management programs designed to fulfill the primary objectives and purposes for which each of these five federal agencies were established.

The reader will note that there are similarities between the land-management policies of the U.S. Forest Service and those of the Bureau of Sport Fisheries and Wildlife and the Bureau of Land Management. Recreation use on lands of the latter two agencies is somewhat more restrictive and less developed than on Forest Service land. Also the Bureau of Land Management is somewhat lacking in the needed legislation for recreation policy and is subject to land disposal provisions. Both the Bureau of Reclamation and the Corps of Engineers view recreation generally as a secondary mission, sharing responsibilities with other agencies where possible.

Selected References

1. Butcher, Devereux: "Exploring Our National Wildlife Refuges," Houghton Mifflin, Boston, 1963.
2. Carson, Rachel: "Guarding Our Wildlife Resources" (Conservation Action No. 5), Fish and Wildlife Service, U.S. Department of Interior, Washington, 1948.
3. Carstensen, Vernon (ed.): "The Public Lands: Studies in the History of the Public Domain," University of Wisconsin Press, Madison, 1963.
4. Clawson, Marion: "Man and Land in the United States," University of Nebraska Press, Lincoln, 1964.
5. Corps of Engineers, Department of the Army: "Recreation," n.p., n.d. (Brochure.)
6. Denny, Peter P.: "The History of Recreation as a Corps of Engineers Function," n.p., January, 1968. (Mimeographed.)
7. Frederick Burke Foundation: "Federal Agencies and Outdoor Recreation," ORRRC Study Report No. 13, U.S. Government Printing Office, Washington, 1962.
8. Laycock, George: "The Sign of the Flying Goose," Natural History Press, Garden City, N.Y., 1965.
9. Murphy, Robert: "Wild Sanctuaries, Our National Wildlife Refuges—a Heritage Restored," Dutton, New York, 1968.
10. National Recreation Association: "1956 Recreation and Park Yearbook: A Nationwide Inventory of the Public Recreation and Park Services of Local, County, State and Federal Agencies for the Year Ending December 31, 1960," New York, 1961.
11. National Recreation and Park Association: "Recreation and Park Yearbook, 1966," Washington, 1967.

12. Outdoor Recreation Resources Review Commission: "Outdoor Recreation for America: A Report to the President and to the Congress by the ORRRC," U.S. Government Printing Office, Washington, 1962.

13. Outdoor Recreation Resources Review Commission: "Mutiple Use of Land and Water Areas," ORRRC Study Report No. 17, U.S. Government Printing Office, Washington, 1962.

14. Recreation Advisory Council, Bureau of Outdoor Recreation: "Federal Executive Policy Governing the Reporting of Recreation Use of Federal Recreation Areas," U.S. Government Printing Office, Washington, 1965.

15. Tennessee Valley Authority: "Land Between the Lakes, Annual Report, 1966," Knoxville, Tenn., n.d.

16. Tennessee Valley Authority: "Outdoor Recreation for a Growing Nation," Knoxville, Tenn., 1961.

17. Tennessee Valley Authority: "Extent of Recreation Development and Use of TVA Lakes and Lake Frontage Property: Comparative Gains, 1947-1968," Knoxville, Tenn., n.d. (Multilithed tabulation.)

18. U.S. Department of the Interior, Bureau of Land Management: Secretary Seaton Approves Policy Statement of Bureau of Land Management on Recreational Land Use, April, 1958. (Mimeographed press release.)

19. U.S. Department of the Interior, Bureau of Land Management: "The Public Land Records—Footnotes to American History," U.S. Government Printing Office, Washington, 1959.

20. U.S. Department of the Interior, Bureau of Land Management: *Our Public Lands*, vol. 11, no. 4, April, 1962.

21. U.S. Department of the Interior, Bureau of Land Management: "Landmarks in Public Land Management," U.S. Government Printing Office, Washington, 1963.

22. U.S. Department of the Interior, Bureau of Land Management: "Community Recreation and the Public Domain," U.S. Government Printing Office, Washington, 1963.

23. U.S. Department of the Interior, Bureau of Land Management: "The Public Domain," U.S. Government Printing Office, Washington, 1966.

24. U.S. Department of the Interior, Bureau of Land Management: "Public Land Statistics, 1966, 1967, 1968," U.S. Government Printing Office, Washington, 1967, 1968, 1969.

25. U.S. Department of the Interior, Bureau of Land Management: "What Are the Public Lands?" U.S. Government Printing Office, Washington, 1967.

26. U.S. Department of the Interior, Bureau of Land Management: "Room to Roam—a Recreation Guide to the Public Lands," U.S. Government Printing Office, Washington, 1968.

27. U.S. Department of the Interior, Bureau of Land Management: Red Rock Canyon Recreation Lands, *Our Public Lands*, vol. 18, no. 1, Winter, 1968.

28. U.S. Department of the Interior, Bureau of Land Management: "Bureau of Land Management Manual (Subjects No. 6000, Recreation Management; No. 6231, Management of Antiquities)," Washington, 1968. (Mimeographed.)

29. U.S. Department of the Interior, Bureau of Land Management: Title 43—Public Lands, Interior (Chapter II, Subchapter A, Circular No. 2216), *Federal Register*, Doc. 66-11792, U.S. Government Printing Office, Washington, 1966.

30. U.S. Department of the Interior, Bureau of Land Management: Title 43—Public Lands, Interior (Chapter II, Subchapter B, Circular No. 2201), *Federal Register*, Doc. 65-10787, U.S. Government Printing Office, Washington, 1965.

31. U.S. Department of the Interior, Bureau of Outdoor Recreation: "Federal Outdoor Recreation Programs," U.S. Government Printing Office, Washington, 1968.

32. U.S. Department of the Interior, Bureau of Reclamation: "Reclamation Accomplishments and Contributions Report of the Library of Congress Legislative Reference Service,

Printed for Use of the Committee on Interior and Insular Affairs, House of Representatives," Committee Print No. 1, U.S. Government Printing Office, Washington, 1959.

33.   U.S. Department of the Interior, Bureau of Reclamation: "Reclamation's Recreational Opportunities," U.S. Government Printing Office, Washington, n.d. (Brochure.)

34.   U.S. Department of the Interior, Bureau of Reclamation: "Recreation Areas on Reclamation Projects [various dates]," Washington, v.d.

35.   U.S. Department of the Interior, Bureau of Reclamation: "Utilization of Recreation Areas on Reclamation Projects," Washington, v.d.

36.   U.S. Department of the Interior, Bureau of Reclamation: "Lake Powell, Jewel of the Colorado," U.S. Government Printing Office, Washington, 1965.

37.   U.S. Department of the Interior, Bureau of Reclamation, Division of Water and Land Operations: "Federal Reclamation Projects: 1967 Crop Report and Related Data," U.S. Government Printing Office, Washington, 1968.

38.   U.S. Department of the Interior, Fish and Wildlife Service, Bureau of Sport Fisheries and Wildlife: "1966 List of National Wildlife Refuges," Washington, 1966. (Multilithed.)

39.   U.S. Department of the Interior, Fish and Wildlife Service, Bureau of Sport Fisheries and Wildlife: "National Wildlife Refuges," U.S. Government Printing Office, Washington, v.d.

chapter eleven

STATE AND LOCAL RECREATIONAL LANDS

Recreational areas administered by various state and local agencies provide recreational opportunities of great importance and considerable diversity. Because state lands are generally larger and have a more truly natural character, they are particularly important to wildland recreation.

State Recreational Lands

State recreational lands serve a purpose midway between the generally more remote federal lands and the readily accessible municipal and county areas, supplementing and accentuating public outdoor recreational opportunities to varying degrees in different sections of the country. They are most important in the more populous states, particularly those with rather small proportions of federal land. In the East, where they are especially vital, they serve as major outdoor recreational outlets.

Large numbers of people find many federal recreational areas too distant for regular or convenient use; and in the more readily accessible municipal and county areas, limited size, greater physical development, larger crowds, and the largely modified conditions usually typical of them militates against outdoor interests and activities which require more expansive and less artificial terrain. To a large degree, state recreational lands bridge this gap. They provide reasonably accessible outlets for those who wish a more natural setting than is customarily available in local areas but, for various reasons, do not desire or are not demanding of unmodified, primitive surroundings, or for those who cannot afford the time and expense of a journey to more remote federal lands.

Geographic location within a state or region is an important consideration in the establishment of state recreational lands, for availability to large numbers of people is one reason for their existence. Many such areas provide for high-density use; in others, absolute maintenance of undisturbed natural conditions is not a primary consideration; and some are sufficiently large and of such character that localized development for large crowds can be undertaken without materially damaging their attractiveness. Mounting pressures of expanding use of state recreational land are a mixed blessing, for they have resulted in improved planning and management which modify the effects of overcrowding and serve to protect the interests, appearance, and environmental quality.

Types and Characteristics of State Recreational Lands

Among state recreational lands are state parks, forests, fish and wildlife areas, areas along roads and highways or related to reservoirs and other public works developments, and miscellaneous natural-resource lands. Some of these areas were established and are managed primarily for recreation; on others recreation is coordinated with their primary function.[1] State parks are the best known and most heavily used of state recreational lands, and reliable long-term data about them are available. State parks are discussed in greater detail later in this chapter.

Information published by the National Recreation and Park Association [15], derived from data collected by the Bureau of Outdoor Recreation, indicates that all six recreational land classifications adopted by the Bureau of Outdoor Recreation [15,19] are represented in state recreational areas. Of the total acreage, about 87 percent is class III, Natural Environment, most of which is included in fish and wildlife and forest areas. The remainder consists of class II, General Outdoor Recreation, approximately 6 percent, represented largely in fish and wildlife areas; class V, Primitive, about 4 percent, with fish and wildlife and parks areas most strongly represented; class IV, Outstanding Natural Feature, roughly 2 percent, found largely in park areas; and class I, High-density Recreation, and class VI, Historic and Cultural Sites, each with a fraction of 1 percent, are represented primarily in park areas (Table 11-1).

As indicated previously these six recreational classes are useful as guides in recreation planning and will be used later on in this book as a basis for comparison of management approaches. Nevertheless, it must be pointed out again that the classes are not applicable to all areas nor is any classification so adaptable. Some states (e.g., Minnesota) do not use this classification system.

---

[1] Management policy of state forests is generally similar, on a state level, to that of national forests. In some states, particularly in the Great Lakes region and New York, recreation is a primary use of state forest land. Management of state fish and wildlife areas (including refuges, sanctuaries, public hunting areas, fish hatcheries) is not unlike that of areas administered by the Bureau of Sport Fisheries and Wildlife of the U.S. Fish and Wildlife Service.

Table 11-1
State outdoor recreation areas and acreages by Bureau of Outdoor Recreation classification system, 1964[a]

	Number of areas[b]	Class I: High-density recreation, acres	Class II: General outdoor recreation, acres	Class III: Natural environment, acres	Class IV: Outstanding natural feature, acres	Class V: Primitive area, acres	Class VI: Historic and cultural site, acres
Park	1,677	28,435	625,669	1,310,262	305,978	603,146	29,855
Forest	925	6,076	101,891	12,297,756	18,061	137,716	51
Fish and wildlife	5,410	10,731	1,128,813	11,091,836	42,389	659,424	2,661
Historic	142	--	147	6,783	--	--	3,147
Highway	7,856	1,850	8,353	2,646	16	--	113
Other	2,352	20,199	417,054	5,433,015	304,914	92,510	3,445
Total	18,353	67,291	2,281,927	30,142,298	671,358	1,492,796	39,272

[a]For explanation of classification system see references 15 and 19 at the end of this chapter; also Chap. 7, p. 119.

[b]Does not include areas of less than 10 acres.

Source: "Recreation and Park Yearbook, 1966," National Recreation and Park Association, Washington, 1967.

There is also difference of opinion as to the separation of classes within a particular park.

Salient Information on State Recreational Lands

Authoritative, long-term data concerning areas and acreages, public use, personnel, operational costs and revenues, and related relevant information are important in assessing recreational values of different types of state land, in comparing these values to those of lands administered by other public and private agencies, and in evaluating trends in public recreational demand and use. However, except for state parks, reliable, long-term comparable data concerning state lands are lacking.

Most of the authoritative, all-inclusive information has resulted from studies of the Bureau of Outdoor Recreation in its development of a nationwide recreational land inventory [15,25]. Though the result of only a few years' investigation and, thus, subject to later modification, data concerning state recreational lands are impressive. A brief analysis of these data follows.

Administrative Agencies. Over 200 agencies are involved in the administration of state lands which provide opportunities for varied outdoor recreational interests and activities. Such fragmented administrative responsibility poses difficulties in developing reliable, comparative, long-term data.

Areas and Acreage.   There are about 30,000 state recreational areas, aggregating approximately 50 million acres. Relatively small areas adjacent to highways are greatest in number, but their total area is exceeded by most other categories, particularly fish and wildlife, forest, and park areas. Fish and wildlife and forest areas have the largest total acreage among all categories listed.

Public Use.   Annual attendance at all state recreational areas exceeds 400 million, about 90 percent of this patronage representing day use. State park areas account for about 70 percent of the use of all state recreational lands, though highway, fish and wildlife, and forest areas are greater in number, and both fish and wildlife and forest areas have greater total acreage.

Personnel.   Nearly 30,000 employees are directly concerned with recreation on all types of state lands, about 60 percent being employed throughout the year. In addition, more than 10,000 employees are concerned with recreation on a part-time basis. However, the relation between year-round and seasonal personnel differs with various agencies; for instance, because of seasonal nature of state park use, seasonal personnel are in the majority in state parks.

Costs and Revenues.   Total expenditures, including operation and maintenance (salaries and wages, supplies and equipment) and capital outlays (lands and improvements), exceed 225 million dollars annually.

Total expenditures are partly offset by total revenue from operations (facilities, concessions, entrance and parking fees, and such miscellaneous sources as special leases and sale of special products). Total annual revenue from operations amounts to between 30 and 40 million dollars.

Total funds available for expenditure, derived from appropriations and various other sources (operational revenue, sale of hunting and fishing licenses, carry-over funds, and miscellaneous sources) was about 348 million dollars in 1962. Since that year, growing public interest in and awareness of the recreational value of state lands has, in an increasing number of states, resulted in the approval of bond issues as a means of financing outdoor recreational programs on state lands [15]. In addition, the Land and Water Conservation Fund Act [26] has, under certain restrictions, provided for matching grants for planning, acquisition, and development of recreational areas and facilities.

Acquisition of State Recreational Lands

Until passage of the Land and Water Conservation Fund Act of 1965, state acquisition of adequate acreage of land for outdoor recreational purposes was often difficult. Basically, this had two causes. First, except for Texas, the states had no public domain lands from which to form areas comparable to the parks, forests, and wildlife refuges established by the federal government.[2] Second,

---

[2] The residue of original public domain lands is the property of the federal government, subject to sale or other transfer under federal laws; most national parks and national forests were established from the public domain either by congressional action or by Presidential proclamation. Unoccupied and unappropriated lands within the present boundary of Texas, following its annexation, remained as public lands of that state instead of becoming part of the public domain [4,5,24].

private acquisition of extensive areas of land throughout much of the nation had taken place long before the need for state recreational areas became acute. The nature of development and rising costs often made it impossible to reestablish certain areas of prime recreational value under public ownership.

Early state recreational areas, particularly state parks, were acquired largely by the following methods:

1. *By gift from private citizens.* Gifts varied from small contributions of money from numerous individuals, accumulated for the purchases of specific areas, to extensive acreage given by one person. Gifts involving extensive land areas have been important in the development of state recreational resources in New York, Maine, Michigan, Texas, Iowa, Washington, Wisconsin, Minnesota, Kentucky, and Indiana [16,23].

2. *Transfer of federal lands to state ownership* [16]. Outstanding examples of such transfers include the Yosemite Grant, entrusted to the state of California by the federal government in 1864, and Mackinac Island, acquired by the state of Michigan from the federal government in 1885. Originally such transfers had to be accomplished by specific congressional action, but in 1927 Congress passed the Recreational Act,[3] eliminating that necessity in connection with such transfers. Later, additional laws passed by Congress relative to the disposal of surplus federal lands provided further assistance in the development of state recreational systems. Of greatest significance was the amending, in 1948, of the Surplus Property Act of 1944. As amended, this act provided for the transfer of federal lands declared surplus previous to July 1, 1948, at 50 percent of their fair, appraised value, to states and local governments for use as public parks and recreational areas. The amended Surplus Property Act of 1944 also made possible the transfer, without monetary consideration, of lands having historic value, the provision being that lands were to be administered as historic sites [6].

3. *Exchange of school lands* [16,23]. Sections 16 and 36 of each township were originally given by the federal government to all but the original thirteen states, as well as the states created from them, and Texas, for support of schools. Many of these school sections were scattered throughout the western national forests. To promote efficient administration of the national forests, Congress authorized the Forest Service to negotiate with the states for the exchange of school sections within national forest boundaries for a consolidated, equivalent national forest area within the same state. Some exchanges of this nature were prompted by the recreational values of lands derived from the Forest Service. Custer State Park in South Dakota was formed largely in this manner [16].

4. *Purchase, through funds derived in a variety of ways.* In some states land for state parks and related recreational areas has been purchased from a percentage

---

[3] The Recreational Act permits a discount by the Bureau of Land Management of up to 70 percent for land only; timber involved must be acquired at full value. This act also permits a 50 percent discount for land and timber by the General Services Administration.

of fish and game receipts reserved for that purpose.[4] Recreational lands have been purchased also from funds derived from tax levy, or by authority of legislative action and appropriation.[5] Increasingly, bond issues have provided funds for purchase of state recreation lands.[6] This procedure was at first justified on the basis of the relation of outdoor recreation to public health and welfare, but in recent years the general public has shown an increasing willingness to invest in outdoor recreation by such means. Today nearly one-half of the states have either bond financing or the authority to issue bonds to finance outdoor recreation programs [15]. Bonds were generally authorized by voters in a referendum or by legislative action alone. Some states do not view this method of fund raising for recreational purposes with favor. In Indiana, for instance, statutory provisions prohibit the sale of bonds by the state for such purposes [8,16]. However, the Indiana Division of State Parks will assume responsibility for development and administration of lands purchased by individual counties, through county bond issues, for state park purposes. This procedure is based upon the philosophy that local demonstration of interest in state parks is indicative of the need of such areas, since citizens of various counties assume the financial burden involved in the acquisition of necessary area.

The most important recent source of finances for acquisition of recreation lands has been the Land and Water Conservation Fund, which has materially added to the extent of state recreational lands [26].

State Parks

All states have some form of state park system. These areas are managed for the conservation and public enjoyment of the scenic, geological, biological, historic and prehistoric, and recreational resources characteristic of various states. Though they vary widely in type and size, they may be logically grouped into the three following categories:

1. *Utilitarian areas* (class I, high-density). Developed primarily to foster physically active recreational interests (swimming, boating, picnicking, camping, winter sports, and related activities), generally without areas of significant interests. Many state parks are in this class.

2. *Significant areas* (classes III, natural environment; IV, outstanding natural areas; V, primitive; and VI, historic and cultural sites). Contain unique or important geological, biological, archaeological, or historical features typical of a particular state. Such state parks are designed to foster public understanding of the primary interests of such areas; physical facilities are usually held to a

---

[4] An important source of funds in Missouri, Nebraska, and Kansas [16].

[5] A number of state parks in Iowa, Massachusetts, and Washington owe their origin to funds provided by special legislative appropriation [16].

[6] The states of New York, Illinois, New Hampshire, Rhode Island, and California were pioneers in financing purchase of land for state recreational areas [23].

minimum. State parks such as Ginkgo Petrified Forest (Washington), John Day Fossil Beds (Oregon), Spring Mill (Indiana), and Valley Forge (Pennsylvania) fall in this class.

3. *Scenic or dual-purpose areas* (class II, general). Owing to their larger size, these often combine the qualities of the two former types. Generally they offer opportunity for various outdoor recreational activities (hiking, camping, horseback riding, swimming, boating, and the like) in a scenically attractive and usually natural setting. Development of necessary physical facilities is conducted with regard to preservation of scenic beauty and natural environmental interests. Such state parks as Moran (Washington), Fall Creek Falls (Tennessee), Matthiesson (Illinois), Turkey Run (Indiana), Bear Mountain (New York), and Custer (South Dakota) are in this class.

Administration of State Parks

State park systems generally operate within bounds of well-defined policies which, although they vary in detail owing to differences in local conditions, are somewhat similar to the policy of the National Park Service, though on a state rather than national level [1,7-11,18,22,23,33]. Various state park policy statements indicate:

1. A definite recognition of the value of preserving areas containing typical state scenery

2. A definite recognition of the value of preserving significant historical, geological, or biological interests characteristic of the state

3. That development of state parks should be carried out under a carefully considered plan, and that their public use should be governed by regulations which will ensure perpetuation of the values which make them interesting

4. That, consistently with the preservation of inherent interests, development of state parks should be guided by the policy that, if such development is not compatible with public use of certain state parks, other areas adapted to such needs should be provided

5. That a definite minimum size limit exists for state parks having interesting or unique scenic values

6. That, wherever possible, accessibility to centers of population should be given adequate consideration in selection of various types of state park lands, particularly those designed for high-density use

7. That, while the greater effort will be made for citizens of a particular state, the interests of out-of-state visitors should not be neglected

Over the years state park organizations have assumed positions of importance equal to other state agencies in state government. Inadequacies of state park organizations which often typified early years of their existence, if, indeed, such organizations existed at all, have been largely remedied. Most state park organizations now operate upon a higher professional level of efficiency. There are, of course, exceptions.

However, responsibility for state park administration is variously assigned in different states [12,23,25]. Local needs, together with historical and political considerations have largely determined the relation of state park organizations to other agencies of state government. Although there are differences in specific details, in most states state parks are administered by one of two or more separate divisions within a major department concerned with management of several other natural resources (forests, fish and wildlife, land, waters).[7] Such organization reflects the close affinity between outdoor recreation and other land values. The importance of recreation to economics is inferred from the close relation that exists in some states between state park departments and state agencies concerned with economic development or tourism.[8] In Oregon inclusion of the Division of State Parks in the Highway Department is considered conducive of efficient and economical maintenance of state park areas by existing highway department personnel skilled in and equipped for such activity. A variation of this plan exists in Rhode Island where the Division of Parks and Recreation is under the Department of Public Works. State parks in a number of states are administered by an autonomous department independent of other state agencies.[9]

It should be noted, however, that park agencies operated as adjunct divisions of larger nonrelated agencies often suffer loss of identity and subordination of goals to the overpowering drive of the major department. For example, park lands administered by highway organizations are likely to be good sources of inexpensive rights-of-way for new road construction.

In some states certain specific state parks, or areas closely related to them, are separately administered by recognized historical, scientific, or educational bodies, or by special commissions established particularly for such purposes.[10]

---

[7] E.g., Alabama, Alaska, California, Colorado, Connecticut, Hawaii, Illinois, Indiana, Iowa, Kansas, Maryland, Massachusetts, Michigan, Minnesota, Montana, Nebraska, Nevada, New Jersey, New York, North Carolina, Ohio, Pennsylvania, South Dakota, Tennessee, Texas, Utah, Vermont, Virgnia, West Virginia, and Wisconsin.

[8] E.g., Arkansas, New Hampshire, Oklahoma, and South Carolina.

[9] E.g., Arizona, Delaware, Florida, Georgia, Idaho, Kentucky, Louisiana, Maine, Mississippi, Missouri, New Mexico, North Dakota, Washington, and Wyoming.

[10] Examples include the State Historical Society of Colorado, Franklin D. Roosevelt Warm Springs Memorial Commission in Georgia, Kansas State Historical Society, Baxter State Park Authority in Maine, two specific reservation commissions in Massachusetts, the Mackinac Island State Park Commission in Michigan, Minnesota Historical Society, Palisades Interstate Park Commission in New Jersey, East Hudson Parkway Authority in New York, Division of Historical Sites of the North Carolina Department of Archives and History, State Historical Society of North Dakota, Ohio Historical Society, Will Rogers Memorial Commission in Oklahoma, two independent commissions in Pennsylvania, and the Wisconsin State Historical Society.

This accounts for the fact that pertinent state data are recorded from more than fifty agencies (Table 11-2).

Importance of State Parks

Comparative data relative to the extent and public use, number of personnel, costs, and other important operational information have been compiled for state parks for several decades. These data (Table 11-2) show trends that are typical of all aspects of state park administration; they are also indicative of the importance of state parks in outdoor recreation and the increasingly vital role which these areas are destined to play in the future. In the absence of similar reliable, long-term statistics concerning other types of state recreational areas, these state park statistics are often regarded as a barometer of public interest in the recreational values of state lands. The summary of state park data (Table 11-2) indicates the following:

Areas and Acreage.   In 1967 the number of state parks was nearly 2½ times that of 1941, having increased from 1,335 to 3,202. During the same period the aggregate acreage of these areas nearly doubled: from 4,259,899 to 7,352,322 acres.

Public Use.   Attendance in 1967 (391,062,694 visits) was about four times as great as in 1941 (97,488,528 visits).

Although most of the total attendance has always consisted of day visits, the percentage of day visits has declined from 97 percent in 1941 (94,570,487 visits) to 89 percent in 1967 (354,819,049 visits). Campers have always accounted for the majority of overnight visits, and there has been a noticeable increase in the percentage of use by campers over the years—from 55 percent of total overnight visits in 1941 (2,918,041 visits) to 88 percent in 1967 (36,243,645 visits). A growing problem in many state park areas designed for overnight use has been finding ways to accommodate increasing numbers of campers.

Personnel.   Rapid increase in the number and aggregate acreage of state parks, and even greater expansion of public use, is reflected in increased personnel. State parks had more than five times as many employees in 1967 (29,254) as in 1941 (5,486). The number of seasonal employees, always in the majority, increased from a little over 50 percent in 1941 (2,856) to slightly more than 60 percent in 1967 (17,777). In most state parks throughout the country the busiest period is during the summer months, when regular park staffs are augmented by additional seasonal help.

It should be pointed out that the foregoing data on personnel tell only part of the story. Opportunities for meaningful professional careers with state park agencies, once dubious by comparison with better-established federal and municipal organizations, have greatly improved. Conditions typical of earlier years, which were largely responsible for low salary schedules, job insecurity, and lack of public and official recognition of personal initiative, have been altered. Complex biological, social, and economic problems have developed as a result of expanding use of state parks. Solution of these problems has demanded

Table 11-2
Comparative summary of state park statistics

	1941	1946	1951
Number of reporting agencies[a]	100[b]	67	78
Areas and acreages:[c]			
Total number of areas	1,335	1,531	1,750
Total acreage	4,259,899	4,634,365	4,877,178
Total attendance	97,488,528	92,506,662[d]	120,722,423
Day visitors	94,570,487	88,922,723	114,024,207
Overnight visitors	2,918,041	3,138,929	6,698,216
Total number of employees	5,486	6,650	11,413
Year-round	2,630	2,771	4,476
Seasonal	2,856	3,879	6,937
Total expenditures	$10,022,146[d]	$15,144,680[d]	$38,545,051
Salaries and wages	4,186,433	5,556,029	15,141,739
Supplies and equipment	2,755,702	3,160,649	7,698,854
Lands	1,559,721	3,204,384	3,314,161
Improvements	1,449,319	2,303,636	12,390,297
Funds available for expenditure	$10,372,213	$20,710,995	$62,859,125
Appropriations	7,093,234	17,123,148	37,290,456
Other	3,278,979	3,587,847	25,568,669
Total revenue from operations	$3,176,504[d]	$4,117,906[d]	$7,652,243
Operated facilities	1,091,023	1,585,743	4,128,149
Concessions	298,636	681,513	1,530,787
Entrance and parking fees	625,386	305,194	1,016,839
Other	105,360	365,477	976,468

[a]The same park agencies have not always reported each year.

[b]Includes reports partially covering state forests, wildlife areas, waysides, etc., that have not been included in subsequent tabulations.

[c]Area and acreage figures for 1941, as well as for subsequent years, do not include state forests, wildlife areas, and waysides not administered by state park agencies.

[d]Totals do not equal the sum of component parts because some agencies reported no breakdown of total figure.

[e]Does not include grants made to local agencies from the Land and Water Conservation Fund; in 1967 such grants totaled $15,625,847.

higher and higher standards of performance in planning, development, protection, and improvement of public understanding of these areas. These demands have placed a premium on professional competence in a variety of fields relevant to administration of state parks. As a result, the number of both year-round and seasonal employees with varied types of professional education in wild-land recreational management has steadily increased.

Costs and Revenues. Increases in the number, aggregate acreage, and degree of public use of state parks are reflected in increases in costs, operational revenues, and public interest in providing for expansion of recreational opportunities on state parklands.

Total state park expenditures in 1967 ($279,520,488) were nearly thirty

1956	*1960*	*1961*	*1962*	*1967*
89	95	101	89	80
2,100	2,664	2,792	2,479	3,202
5,156,125	5,601,542	5,799,057	5,763,142	7,352,322
200,705,045[d]	259,001,001	273,484,442[d]	284,795,025	391,062,694
185,325,197	238,431,744	249,185,801	260,744,994	354,819,049
12,642,073	20,569,257	22,998,641	24,050,031	36,243,645
14,932	17,537	18,126	17,621	29,254
6,048	7,412	7,984	7,075	11,477
8,884	10,125	10,142	10,546	17,777
$65,843,582[d]	$87,372,621	$110,101,338	$108,880,516[d]	$279,520,488[e]
27,705,841	37,137,261	41,076,031	42,694,166	77,087,172
13,304,603	19,132,139	19,904,837	18,420,419	36,934,706
5,987,080	12,077,069	13,035,245	12,295,857	57,410,420
21,520,424	19,026,152	36,085,225	34,004,393	107,923,198
$88,254,728	$131,419,241[d]	$133,672,787	$144,611,230	$472,511,927[f]
49,609,999	69,294,155	89,851,622	98,734,045	174,428,819
38,644,729	61,793,983	43,821,165	45,877,185	298,083,108[f]
$14,927,567	$22,641,254	$23,363,524	$26,466,250[d]	$50,083,874
8,473,557	13,266,949	12,649,134	15,600,638	28,226,604
2,240,498	2,804,353	3,429,558	3,270,247	5,709,534
2,854,292	3,838,925	5,569,875	4,690,308	12,813,623
2,359,220	2,731,027	1,714,957	2,813,972	3,334,113

[f]Includes grants to state agencies from Land and Water Conservation Fund, totaling $14,082,181.

Sources: "State Park Statistics, 1956 to 1960," National Park Service, Division of Recreation Resource Planning, Washington, 1957-1961. "State Outdoor Recreation Statistics, 1962," Report No. 1, Statistical Series,,Bureau of Outdoor Recreation, Division of Research and Education, Washington, December, 1963. "1967 State Park Statistics," National Conference on State Parks, National Recreation and Park Association, Washington, June, 1968.

times as great as in 1941 ($10,022,146). As related to total expenditures for 1941 and 1967, the amount spent on salaries and wages dropped from 40 percent ($4,186,433) to about 24 percent ($77,087,172), and the total amount spent for supplies and equipment dropped from 27 percent ($2,755,702) to slightly more than 13 percent ($36,943,706). However, expenditures for land rose from 15 percent ($1,559,721) to about 20 percent ($57,410,420), and costs of improvements increased from 14 percent ($1,449,319) to nearly 35 percent ($107,923,198).

Partially offsetting expenditures are total revenues derived from state park operations; these were nearly seventeen times as great in 1967 ($50,083,874) as in 1941 ($3,176,504). As related to revenues received in 1941 and 1967, revenue from operated facilities rose from about 33 percent in 1941

($1,091,023) to slightly more than 55 percent in 1967 ($28,226,604). Returns from concessions showed a slight increase from a little less than 1 percent in 1941 ($298,636) to slightly more than 1½ percent in 1967 ($5,709,534). The amount received from entrance and parking fees jumped from about 2 percent in 1941 ($625,386) to 24 percent ($12,813,623). Other revenue, including income from such miscellaneous sources as special leases (air beacons, radio and television towers erected on state park lands) and sale of special products (sand, gravel, coal, salvage timber), remained fairly constant, rising from a little less than ½ percent ($105,360) to slightly more than ½ percent ($3,334,113).

There has been a striking rise in cost per visit since 1941, due largely to inflationary trends reflected in increases in all operational and capital expenditures. Net *total* cost per visit[11] was about eight times as great in 1967 as in 1941, rising from 7 to 58 cents. However, net *operational* cost per visit[12] has not climbed as rapidly; this was about four times as great in 1967 as in 1941, rising from approximately 4 to 16 cents per visit.

Funds available for expenditure increased over forty-fold between 1941 ($10,372,213) and 1967 ($472,466,927). It is significant to note that the percentage of these funds derived from appropriations dropped from about 70 percent in 1941 ($7,093,234) to approximately 37 percent in 1967 ($174,428,819), while the percentage of funds derived from other sources rose proportionately—from 30 percent in 1941 ($3,278,979) to about 60 percent in 1967 ($298,083,108). Funds derived from these miscellaneous sources include proceeds from bond issues and, particularly in recent years, grants from the Land and Water Conservation Fund.

Local Recreational Lands [15]

These include different types of public lands administered by agencies of municipal or county governments and by various regional or district authorities.[13] Such recreational areas are briefly mentioned here, for although usually lacking in conditions generally associated with wild lands, they are vital in the broad range of outdoor recreation. In one way or another outdoor recreation at the community level affects more people to a greater degree than recreational opportunities provided by any other type of land.

All types of recreational lands have certain similar basic objectives and

---

[11] Total operational (salaries and wages plus supplies and equipment) and capital (lands and improvements) expenditures less total revenue from operations, prorated among total visits.

[12] Total operational expenditures (salaries and wages plus supplies and equipment) less total revenue from operations, prorated among total visits.

[13] In addition to parks and related lands, certain public recreational activities are permitted on municipal power reservoirs, city forests, and, in certain cases, municipal watersheds. Local recreational lands also include areas controlled by private philanthropic organizations.

problems. However, the administration, management, and public use of local recreational areas are a highly specialized field. Programs and procedures are based upon long experience, historical perspective, and professional performance; they are essentially socioactivity-oriented. Wild-land recreation, however, has only recently developed a truly professional perspective, and it is largely resource-oriented. Although these two recreational policies are related only indirectly, workers concerned primarily with recreational use of wild lands should clearly recognize that proper coordination of urban and rural recreation yields many reciprocal values. Understanding the important role of local recreational areas is definitely relevant to the success of wild-land recreational workers.

Local areas are important because they are located near concentrations of people. They are readily available for short daily periods of use, often coordinated with job and other responsibilities, by individuals, families, and special groups. The opportunities they provide range from sports to cultural interests, and the areas themselves vary from rough and undeveloped to carefully maintained. They are especially adapted to simple forms of outdoor recreation within the interests and capabilities of people of both sexes, all ages, varying family responsibilities, and different social and economic backgrounds. Though they generally have high-density use, their attractiveness is maintained by carefully planned development and modification. Thus local recreational areas, as vital units of open space in crowded urban and metropolitan districts, aid in the maintenance of an interesting, attractive, and livable environment. To many people who lack time, money, and experience necessary for recreational use of more distant wild lands, they offer the major—often the only—contact with the outdoors. It is primarily because of the foregoing factors that expansion of local recreational acreage is recognized as one of the more critical outdoor recreation needs.

Adequate, properly related local recreational areas also protect the interests of wild lands, particularly in cases where administrative policy emphasizes maintenance of natural conditions. By providing readily accessible outlets for interests and activities which may be inappropriate on the more natural wild lands, they disperse recreational use, relate activities to areas best able to accommodate them, and reduce public pressure for development of unsuitable facilities.

Basically, recreational land management relates broadly to the protection and perpetuation of the beauty and varied interests of our environment, together with continued enjoyment of that environment through a diversity of appropriate activities. The readily accessible neighborhood plot equipped with minimum facilities for simple activities and personal relaxation is as important as more extensive, more famous, distant outdoor recreational areas. Properly coordinated, each unit of land serving some outdoor recreational function has its particular role. Each supplies particular needs for different people at different times, supplementing and protecting the basic values of other areas.

Local Recreational Area Statistics

The importance of local recreational areas is shown by the accompanying statistical summary (Table 11-3). Since there is no practical way of determining attendance, no accurate indication of their patronage is available. However, some idea of the magnitude of the use of local recreational areas can be deduced from the fact that, in 1938, the total use of areas of this type was estimated to exceed 600 million annually [13]. More recent data [14] also point to phenomenal public use. For twenty-six of the more popular recreational facilities best adapted to taking attendance,[14] the number of visits in 1955 totaled nearly 300 million. In 1960 attendance at the same type of facilities had increased to 415 million.

Summary

State recreational lands fall midway between the readily accessible and generally more highly developed municipal areas and the many federal areas which usually are undeveloped as well as almost inaccessible for many people. There are various types of state recreational lands, including state parks, forests, wildlife areas, areas bordering highways and about various public works, and miscellaneous natural-resource lands. Some have been established primarily for recreational use; in others recreational uses are coordinated with their primary purposes. Though state park organization policy is similar to that of the National Park Service, there are many variations ranging from highly organized programs, as in California, to custodial holding operations.

Data concerning all types of state recreational lands have become available only recently. Though the result of only a few years' investigation, these data are, nevertheless, impressive. Most state recreational land acreage is classed as natural environment. In addition, there are about 30,000 areas of different sizes and types, aggregating more than 50 million acres; total annual patronage exceeds 400 million.

Best known and most heavily used of state recreational lands are state parks; on these parks statistical data have been collected for many years. These data indicate a constant increase in the number and aggregate acreage of state parks, the amount public use, number of employees, and cost of operation. There are more than 3,000 state parks with a total area of more than 7 million acres; their combined annual public use is nearly 400 million visits.

---

[14]These included arboretums and special gardens, athletic fields and related facilities (archery ranges, handball and tennis courts, golf courses), bathing beaches and pools, picnic areas, camps and campgrounds, winter sports areas, boating facilities, museums, nature trails, stadiums, outdoor theaters, and zoos.

Table 11-3
Summary, local outdoor recreational areas

Year	Number of agencies	Number of areas	Aggregate acreage	Expenditures Operations	Capital expenses	Year-round paid personnel
1925-1926[1]	--	--	316,092	--	--	--
1940[2,3]	--	--	641,471	$ 25,761,113	$ 5,000,000	--
1950[2]	2,277	17,142	644,067	178,657,800	88,996,729	--
1955[3]	2,939	20,417[a]	748,701[a]	284,771,151	92,995,363	45,396[b]
1960[4]	2,968	24,710[c]	1,015,461[c]	414,255,738	151,339,136	52,542[d]
1965[5]	2,696	30,509[e]	1,496,378[e]	611,100,000	290,200,000	65,213[f]

[a]Does not include approximately 7,500 school areas with about 50,000 acres usable for recreation.

[b]Includes 8,387 recreation leaders employed full time.

[c]Does not include 13,160 school areas with 86,152 acres used for recreation.

[d]Includes 9,216 recreation leaders employed full time.

[e]Does not include 16,539 school areas with 116,706 acres used for recreation.

[f]Includes 19,208 recreation leaders employed full time.

Sources: [1]U.S. Department of Labor, Bureau of Labor Statistics, "Park Recreation Areas in the United States," U.S. Government Printing Office, Washington, 1928.

[2]National Recreation Association, "Recreation and Park Yearbook, Mid-Century Edition: A Review of Local and County Recreation and Park Developments, 1900-1950," New York, 1951.

[3]National Recreation Association, "1956 Recreation and Park Yearbook: A Nationwide Inventory of the Public Recreation and Park Services of Local, County, State and Federal Agencies for the Year Ending December 31, 1955," New York, 1956.

[4]National Recreation Association, "Recreation and Park Yearbook, 1961: A Nationwide Inventory of the Public Recreation and Park Services of Local, County, State and Federal Agencies for the Year Ending December 31, 1960," New York, 1961.

[5]National Recreation and Park Association, "Recreation and Park Yearbook, 1966," Washington, 1967.

In the past, acquisition of land for state recreational areas was often difficult, but in recent years citizens in many states have become more willing to finance purchase of land for recreational purposes through bond issues. Grants derived from the Land and Water Conservation Fund also have favored such purchases.

Local recreational lands administered by municipalities, counties, and regional or district authorities also are important to recreational use of wild lands. Being most readily available to large numbers of people, they provide for many types of recreational activities and interests which may be inappropriate on other more distant and more truly natural lands.

Selected References

1. California Department of Parks and Recreation: "California State Park System," Sacramento, Calif., 1967.

2. California Department of Parks and Recreation: "Organization Plan for the Department of Parks and Recreation," Sacramento, Calif., 1967. (Multilithed.)

3. California Department of Parks and Recreation: "California State Park System Plan," Sacramento, Calif., 1968.

4. Carstensen, Vernon (ed.): "The Public Lands: Studies in the History of the Public Domain," University of Wisconsin Press, Madison, 1963.

5. Clawson, Marion: "Man and Land in the United States," University of Nebraska Press, Lincoln, 1964.

6. Emerson, Ralph W.: Disposal of Surplus Federal Property for Parks and Recreation, *1949 Yearbook, Park and Recreation Progress*, National Conference on State Parks, Washington, n.d.

7. Illinois Department of Conservation, Division of Parks and Memorials: "Illinois State Parks and Memorials," Springfield, Ill., n.d.

8. Indiana Department of Conservation, Division of State Parks, Lands and Waters: "Description of Properties and Facilities," n.p., n.d. (Mimeographed.)

9. Maine State Park and Recreation Commission: "Outdoor Recreation for Maine, 1966," University of Maine Press, Orono, Maine, 1966.

10. Michigan Department of Natural Resources, Parks Division: "Your Michigan Department of Conservation, What It Is and What It Does," Lansing, Mich., 1966.

11. National Conference on State Parks: Suggested Statement of State Park Policy: Wildlife Policy for State Parks. State Park Policy on Vegetation Management, and Suggested Park Management Standards and Practices in Historical and Archaeological Areas, *Planning and Civic Comment*, vol. 22, no. 2, June, 1956.

12. National Conference on State Parks, National Recreation and Park Association: "1967 State Park Statistics," Washington, June, 1968.

13. National Recreation Association: "Recreation and Park Yearbook, Mid-Century Edition: A Review of Local and County Recreation and Park Developments, 1900-1950," New York, 1951.

14. National Recreation Association: "1956 Recreation and Park Yearbook: A Nationwide Inventory of the Public Recreation and Park Services of Local, County, State and Federal Agencies for the Year Ending December 31, 1960," New York, 1961.

15. National Recreation and Park Association: "Recreation and Park Yearbook, 1966," Washington, 1967.

16. Nelson, Beatrice: "State Recreation," National Conference on State Parks, Washington, 1928.

17. New York, State of: "An Act to Amend the Conservation Law (with Reference to State Council of Parks and Related Provisions)," Laws of New York, chap. 665, Albany, N.Y., 1967.

18. New York State Conservation Department, State Council of Parks and Outdoor Recreation: "New York State Parks," Albany, N.Y., n.d.

19. Outdoor Recreation Resources Review Commission: "Outdoor Recreation for America: A Report to the President and to the Congress by the ORRRC," U.S. Government Printing Office, Washington, 1962.

20. Outdoor Recreation Resources Review Commission: "The Future of Outdoor Recreation in Metropolitan Regions of the United States," ORRRC Study Report No. 21, U.S. Government Printing Office, Washington, 1962.

21. Tennessee Department of Conservation, Parks Division: "Rules and Regulations Governing the Use of Tennessee State Parks," Nasvhille, Tenn., n.d.

22. Tennessee Division of State Parks: "Tennessee State Parks," Department of Conservation, Nashville, Tenn., 1969.

23. Tilden, Freeman: "The State Parks: Their Meaning in American Life," Knopf, New York, 1962.

24. U.S. Department of the Interior, Bureau of Land Management: "Landmarks in Public Land Management," U.S. Government Printing Office, Washington, 1963.

25. U.S. Department of the Interior, Bureau of Outdoor Recreation: "State Outdoor Recreation Statistics, 1962," Report No. 1, Statistical Series, Department of Research and Education, U.S. Government Printing Office, Washington, 1963.

26. U.S. Department of the Interior, Bureau of Outdoor Recreation: "Land and Water Conservation Fund Act, as Amended," U.S. Government Printing Office, Washington, 1968.

27. U.S. Department of the Interior, National Park Service, Division of Resources Planning: "State Park Statistics, 1956-1961," Washington, June, 1957-1962.

28. U.S. Department of the Interior, National Park Service: "Parks for America: A Survey of Park and Related Resources in the Fifty States, and a Preliminary Plan," Washington, 1964.

29. U.S. Department of Labor, Bureau of Labor Statistics: "Park and Recreation Areas in the United States," Miscellaneous Publication No. 462, U.S. Government Printing Office, Washington, 1928.

30. Washington Game Department: "L. T. Murray Wildlife Recreation Area," Olympia, Wash., n.d.

31. Wisconsin, State of: "Public Parks and Places of Recreation," chap. 27, Wisconsin Statutes, Madison, n.d.

32. Wisconsin Department of Natural Resources: "State Parks, State Forests, and Other Departments of Natural Resources Lands," Wisconsin Administrative Code, chap. WCD 45, Madison, 1969.

33. Wisconsin Department of Natural Resources: "Wisconsin Parks, Forests and Historic Sites," n.p., n.d.

chapter twelve

PRIVATE LANDS AND A PLANNING-MANAGEMENT FRAMEWORK

Though public lands serve as the major base for outdoor recreation, they cannot continually accommodate all the rapidly growing recreational demands. For many reasons, private lands are destined to play an increasingly vital role in providing additional and more diversified opportunities for outdoor recreational interests and activities.

Approximately 60 percent of our land is privately owned [9]. Further, large portions of private land are more readily accessible from population centers than much of our public land. In themselves, these conditions indicate why the private sector will be increasingly involved in providing for many public outdoor recreational needs.

Many public recreational areas are overcrowded and overused, causing problems of public health and safety, vandalism, and antisocial behavior. Overcrowding also promotes conflicts of interest among different groups of recreationalists, resulting in public improvements which may not be appropriate to certain types of public recreational lands. In particular, excessive physical development in areas of fragile features endangers their existence. The high cost of extensive developments on public lands necessary for accommodation of large crowds is also a problem, especially when it is borne by public funds and there is little or no provision for charges to cover investment costs.

A wide variety of outdoor recreational needs can be satisfied on private lands, some of which are better adapted to certain outdoor recreational uses than are public lands. In many cases such uses offer opportunity for profit, as well as other benefits, to landowners. If readily accessible from high-quality public recreational areas, private lands are often the most logical sites for the more elaborate facilities required by many people, such as hotels, trailer parks, and highly developed campgrounds. Thus, disturbance of high-quality public land nearby is minimized. Further, cost of these more elaborate facilities is appropriately borne by patrons through normal charges for their use. Thus public funds may be freed for investment in basic facilities and services necessary for protection and enjoyment of high-quality public areas.

For these reasons it is most important to have carefully coordinated planning of public land uses and developments involving adjoining private owners to provide complementary operations. Each type of ownership may thus contribute to a balanced system with a minimum of competitive overlaps.

On certain types of private lands, recreation and commercial production of food and fiber are complementary, or at least nonconflicting uses. Many forms of simple outdoor recreation, such as driving for pleasure and walking, are favored by maintenance of open space provided by well-managed farms and forests, though the lands themselves may not physically be used for recreation. In many instances private landowners, or groups of them, are as considerate of public recreational interests as are public land management agencies. Private landownership may even result in stricter control of public recreational use, particularly if education and scientific investigation are considered as aspects of recreation.

Factors Influencing Recreational Use of Private Lands

Important factors which influence use of private lands for outdoor recreation include:

1. The desire of landowners to earn a profit, either from some form of exclusive recreational operation (resorts) or from a part-time adjunct of some major land management program (fees for varied outdoor recreational privileges on farms, ranches, industrial forests)

2. Provision of facilities, services, and recreational opportunities adapted to special groups' interests (hunting, outdoor, or boating clubs; fraternal, church, union, or youth organizations; large industrial enterprises)

3. Philanthropic programs of protection, management, and use which, although in the public interest, relate to various types of land not administered by public agencies (privately organized scientific, educational, and conservation organizations)

4. Provision of public recreational facilities and services for public relations purposes, or the improvement of the "image," of an industry (industrial forest lands and tree-farm parks)

Privately Owned Commercial Resorts

Commercial resorts on private land are the oldest and most familiar type of outdoor recreational operations. They range from simple developments, sometimes but a few acres with a campground, to elaborate, extensive areas with varied types of overnight accommodations, related food services, entertainment, and subsidiary recreational facilities. Most commercial operations are conducted by individuals or families, though the more extensive are generally controlled by companies or corporations. They exist in all sections of the country but are most common in regions where climate is favorable for a maximum period of productive, long-term operation. Practically all offer a variety of scenic or related interests (mountains, deserts, ocean or lake shores, regions of prime hunting, fishing, or winter sports), and many are near well-known public recreational areas, such as national and state parks and forests. Most private enterprises of this sort rarely own, or lease, more than the minimum area necessary for housing and related physical facilities for their patrons. Certain recreational facilities may be provided (swimming pools, tennis courts, golf courses), but principal attractions and the site of most recreational activities of visitors are nearby peripheral lands which, in most cases, are publicly owned.

Accurate data on the size and importance of the commercial resort industry on private lands are unavailable. Associations of certain types of similar operations exist, largely for exchange of ideas and solution of common problems, but there is no centralized body from which complete data may be obtained. The private resort industry is too diverse in type, size, and objective of its varied units; it is too widely scattered geographically; and many operators do not regard information about their business as public property. However, it is obvious that the aggregate land area, investment, and patronage involved are considerable. It is equally obvious that the private resort industry plays an important role in serving a wide variety of necessary and desirable outdoor recreational activities, and that it offers important economic benefits. The commercial outdoor recreational industry is a major economic base for numerous towns, cities, and even entire regions.

Outdoor Recreation on Agricultural Land

Private agricultural land is of increasing importance for many kinds of outdoor recreational interests and activities, for it includes extensive acreage involving most of the open space which is readily accessible from areas of heavy population concentration. Attractive, well-managed farmland offers opportunity for many types of outdoor activities which, if properly developed and operated, can provide an important source of supplementary farm income through charges made for fishing and hunting, in season, as well as picnicking, camping, swimming and boating, winter sports, and holidays at vacation farms and dude ranches. A growing number of agricultural landowners are developing their recreational resources and offering them to the public for a fee. Recent actions of Congress are aimed at encouraging this tendency.

Good agricultural practices are productive of conditions conducive to adequate numbers of fish and game species. Many farms are adjacent to public lakes or rivers, or have fishing streams running through them. In others, ponds and artificial lakes, developed primarily for other purposes, are stocked and managed by the landowners for fishing. To prevent overcrowding, public patronage of such privately stocked ponds, as well as privately controlled fishing spots on public waters, can be regulated by charging a fee, which many fishermen are willing to pay. Agricultural land also provides habitat for many kinds of birds and mammals, particularly waterfowl and upland game birds. Although game species are public property, landowners have the right to control access to their property; thus, payment of fees to owners is for the privilege of access to and use of the area for hunting rather than for any game which may be secured. Even if the landowner does not elect to make charges for hunting or fishing privileges on his land, control of such activities serves to reduce damage to private property.

The extent of such activities, as well as the nature of landowner charges and restrictions, depends upon hunting and fishing pressure and consequent demand for privileges, as well as the nature and abundance of fish and game species. Most agricultural landowners, aware of the potential of supplementary income, work closely with state game departments for the improvement of local game populations by following prescribed agricultural practices, habitat improvement, and propagation of game species. Groups of properties are often managed cooperatively. In some cases lodging, meals, equipment, supplies, and services are provided.

Farm interests and activities themselves have assumed recreational significance, largely as a result of urbanization of our population and ignorance of how our food is produced. This has resulted in a growing number of vacation farms and dude ranches catering to paying city guests. Their operations may be strictly commercial, with guests merely as observers, or the guests may assume varying degrees of responsibility in actual farm or ranch tasks. The dude ranch concept has the longer history, since it is related to the romanticism of the "Old West," which began to decline about the turn of the century. Thus, it is more firmly established and better defined than that of vacation farms, and supports several associations which have been in existence for many years.

Retention of rural open space as green belts within and adjacent to rapidly expanding urban centers is important in regional planning. The beauty of a well-managed rural countryside is an important aspect of our environment, and it is basic to enjoyment of the outdoors.

Difficulties

Development of recreational opportunities on privately owned agricultural land is a venture that should not be approached carelessly. Like any business enterprise it requires special abilities, interests, and aptitudes, and it demands attention to detail. It is not an easy road to riches. In granting permission to use his land, with or without payment of a fee, the owner assumes certain definite responsibilities. To most agricultural landowners these present numerous, unfamiliar, and often vexing problems.

Also, not all agricultural land is suitable for use as a recreational enterprise. It may lack basic physical attractions or established agricultural uses plus size may preclude public use (e.g., a turkey farm).

An element of any recreational enterprise on private agricultural land is the owner's interest in the general public along with his tolerance of urban people's unfamiliarity with the rural environment, which may require patience and diplomacy. There are also many problems relative to adequate financing, planning and development, maintenance of health and safety standards, legal matters, liability, and varied requirements of the general operation of the recreation business. In addition, the possibility of vandalism and carelessness, as well as behavior problems, common on any area catering to strangers, cannot be disregarded.

Assistance

Awareness of likely problems, provision for their solution, and advance planning of all aspects of the operation are the best guarantee of success. The federal government, recognizing that well-conducted recreational enterprises and production of agricultural products can be compatible activities, and thus of economic importance to individual landowners and the economic stability of rural areas, provides varied assistance to interested landowners. The Food and Agriculture Act of 1962 (P.L. 87-703), as amended, provides for cooperation by the U.S. Department of Agriculture through the Rural Areas Development program. Principal agencies of the U.S. Department of Agriculture which are involved are the Agricultural Stabilization and Conservation Service, Farmers Home Administration, Soil Conservation Service, Office of Rural Areas Development, and Forest Service. Assistance can be obtained also from agencies of other federal departments, such as the Area Redevelopment Administration of the Department of Commerce, the Small Business Administration, and the Bureau of Outdoor Recreation, National Park Service, and Bureau of Sport Fisheries and Wildlife of the Department of the Interior. The nature of the assistance, involving both loans and technical advice, is set forth in a variety of government publications [10-12,15-18,20].

Lands Owned or Controlled by Special Groups

It is impossible to determine accurately the total acreage of certain lands that are owned or otherwise controlled by various private organizations for their members' recreational use. Among them are outdoor and mountaineering clubs (Sierra Club, Appalachian Mountain Club); fraternal and union organizations; churches and religious denominations; groups catering to youth (Boy Scouts, Girl Scouts, Campfire Girls, 4-H) or elderly people; privately sponsored social service bodies (Salvation Army); private game, hunting, fishing, yacht or boat, and ski clubs; and various scientific, educational, and conservation associations (Audubon Society). Some large industrial concerns also sponsor diversified recreational programs for their employees, some of which involve areas of wild land.

Quasi-public Lands

Some privately owned areas are operated for public benefit and offer various types of recreational interest and use. Among noted examples of such areas are Mount Vernon, George Washington's home near Washington, D.C., owned and operated by the Mount Vernon Ladies Association, and the colonial city of Williamsburg, Virginia, restored by funds provided by John D. Rockefeller, Jr. Areas more relevant to the scope of this book, however, are the wild quasi-public lands that include Indian reservations as well as reserves owned or otherwise controlled by the Nature Conservancy.

Indian Reservations [7,19,20]

Indian lands, totaling about 53 million acres, are those granted to various Indian tribes by treaty with the United States Government. They are essentially private lands, administered by tribal councils with technical assistance provided by the Bureau of Indian Affairs of the U.S. Department of the Interior, for the benefit of Indian residents. All recreational activities on Indian lands, including hunting and fishing, are dependent upon permission of the Indians. These lands, especially large reservations, have a wide variety of outdoor recreational interests. Many reservations are highly scenic and contain significant geological, biological, or archaeological and historical interests. In addition, traditional activities of the Indians themselves are highly appealing. Though Indians have been reluctant to share recreational potentials of their reservations with non-Indians, obvious economic advantages derived from such activities have prompted a more liberal point of view on the part of some tribes in recent years.

There are a number of noteworthy examples. Public hunting and fishing are permitted on the Fort Apache Reservation in Arizona, but conditional on the purchase of a reservation as well as a state license. Recreational facilities (motels, boat rentals, gas stations, guide services, campgrounds) have been developed at Lake Hawley and Tonto Lake. A large part of the highly scenic Monument Valley on the Utah-Arizona border has been designated a tribal park by the Navajo tribe; the Navajos have designated also a number of other tribal parks and have established a Navajo Park Commission, which has plans for the improvement of public recreational facilities on their large reservation. Recreation facilities are operated also on the Warm Springs Reservation in central Oregon, the Pyramid Lake Indian Reservation in Nevada, the Colorado River Reservation north of Blythe, California, and the Cherokee Indian Reservation adjacent to Great Smoky Mountains National Park.

The Bureau of Indian Affairs encourages such interests on the part of various tribes, and a revolving fund of 20 million dollars provided by congressional appropriation (P.L. 87-250) assists in financing such operations, which are economically beneficial to various tribes, provide opportunity for employment and individual enterprise of local residents, and aid in improved relations between Indians and non-Indians. Though the recreational potential of Indian reservations is as yet not fully understood or utilized, it offers great opportunities for the future if properly handled.

Nature Conservancy [5,8]

This is a nonprofit organization, incorporated under the laws of the District of Columbia. It is interested in many aspects of natural-resource conservation and environmental preservation, and is primarily concerned with the acquisition and protection of outstanding natural areas. It has been instrumental in having between 80,000 and 100,000 acres set aside as sanctuaries and preserves. Most areas involved are rather small[1] but nonetheless important. They are representative of unique or interesting biological environments involving forests, prairies, swamps, seashores, and islands which, because of ownership complications, isolated location, or related reasons have not been included in larger public reservations.

Financial support of its activities is derived entirely from gifts from individuals, grants from foundations, and dues from various membership grades. Lands are acquired by gift or purchase. Gifts may be by deed or legacy; purchases are made from funds raised by local chapters or committees, often with the help of loans from a revolving fund administered by the national office in Washington, D.C.

Once land is acquired, it may be protected and managed by the Nature

---

[1] One to several thousand acres; a number exceed 1,000 acres and the largest is 12,000 acres. 12,000 acres.

Conservancy through committees of interested people (usually associated with some type of educational or scientific institution) or, in a few cases, by paid personnel. A number of areas, however, have been acquired and transferred to some existing public land-managing agency for administration and protection, subject to certain restrictions relative to public use, protected by a "reverter clause" in the transfer agreement.

Areas acquired by the Nature Conservancy, including those transferred to other organizations or agencies, are maintained so that the natural character of the land endures. Nondestructive uses (nature photography, hiking, canoeing) may be permitted. Scientific research and outdoor education are nearly always encouraged and, where necessary to protect and maintain threatened animals or plants, habitat manipulation is practiced. However, construction of artificial features (roads, dams, buildings) is not generally permitted.

Public Recreational Use of Private Forest Lands

Privately owned industrial timberlands have long been open to public hunting and fishing, in season. However, recent years have witnessed extension, refinement, and more scientific management of these activities, together with establishment of specific recreational areas designed for more general types of outdoor recreational activities [6,10-12].

Surveys conducted by the American Forest Institute[2] in 1956, 1960, and 1968 indicate an increasingly important role for industrial forest lands in public outdoor recreation [1-4]. Data developed are summarized in Table 12-1.

In spite of ever-present and growing vandalism, the majority of industrial forest concerns, whose main objective is the continued production of timber from their lands, continue to provide for a wide variety of public recreational uses of their properties. It is estimated that the value of recreational improvements provided by companies involved in these surveys exceeds 13 million dollars and that they spend over 7 million dollars annually on recreation improvements. A number of firms employ professional wildlife managers and engage in cooperative management activities with relevant public agencies, including the operation of public hunting grounds controlled by the state. The number of employees responsible for recreational planning and management has increased.

Industrial forest lands are used for a wide variety of outdoor recreational interests and activities—both diversified (trapping, berry picking, and hiking in addition to hunting and fishing) and concentrated (picnicking, camping, swimming, boating, winter sports). Since the concept of the tree-farm park in 1941

[2] Previous to 1968 known as American Forest Products Industries.

Table 12-1
General recreational use of industrial forest lands

	1956	1960	1968
Number of companies surveyed	370	518	234
Acreage surveyed	46,263,852	58,140,936	65,688,333
Percentage of lands surveyed	68.3	86.2	88.2
Recreational visits	1,533,795	6,057,660	a
Est. value rec. improvements	--	--	$13,371,127
Est. annual rec. expenditure	--	--	7,083,850
Est. annual loss (vandalism)	--	--	436,070
Number companies operating parks, picnic areas, campgrounds	65	107	121[b]
Aggregate acreage of above	3,432	19,690	--
Visitor day capacity	--	--	28,994[c]
Recreation areas operated and maintained by others; by permission, no charge	--	582[d]	741[d]
Aggregate acreage of above	--	16,392	12,011
Recreation leases	--	7,345[e]	28,906[e]
Aggregate acreage of above	--	710,256	53,198
Number of companies employing recreational planners	7	7	12
Acreage open to hunting	42,737,538	53,654,702	61,409,031
Number of companies employing professional wildlife managers	31	24	37
Number of companies charging for hunting	--	--	32
Acreage open to fishing	44,567,341	56,646,326	63,787,359
Number of companies requiring permit for fishing	--	46	41

[a]Accurate number of visitors impossible to ascertain.

[b]In 1968 there were 122 parks, 175 campgrounds, and 191 picnic areas. Previous to the 1968 survey, little or no differentiation was made among parks, campgrounds, and picnic areas. In 1967 the following minimum standards were adopted:
Picnic area   minimum of one table and bench, garbage can, fireplace (optional); overnight camping not permitted
Campground minimum of one table with bench, garbage can, fireplace, toilet facilities, water (optional); overnight camping permitted
Park facilities provided in picnic areas and campgrounds, plus other recreational attractions; contain a minimum of six table units and a potable water supply; overnight camping may or may not be permitted.

[c]Visitor day adopted to conform to Bureau of Outdoor Recreation System [13].

[d]Includes picnic areas and camping sites.

[e]Includes summer homes, hunting and fishing camps, miscellaneous.

Sources: American Forest Institute, "Recreation on Forest Industry Lands in the United States, 1960," and "1968 Forest Industry Recreation Survey," Washington, 1960, 1968.

there has been a steady growth in the number of specifically designated parks, campgrounds, and picnic areas. Moreover, both the aggregate acreage and the number of companies that have established such areas have increased. In addition to basic facilities, some parks on industrial forest land have covered shelters or outdoor kitchens, children's playground equipment, nature trails, ski lifts, and related winter sports facilities, and where bodies of water are involved, swimming floats, bathhouses and boat ramps. Expansion of the number and acreage of recreational areas in industrial forest land has necessitated some form of standardization of facilities and use of units classed as parks, campgrounds, and picnic areas. Recent nationwide outdoor recreational developments have also required standardization of data on capacity and degree of use of all types of recreational areas and facilities. Consequently, recreational capacity and the use of industrial forest lands and facilities are now related to the visitor day concept [13] adopted by the Bureau of Outdoor Recreation for federal recreational areas.

In most cases there is still no charge made for use of facilities or for recreational privileges enjoyed on industrial forest lands. However, because of rising costs (including taxes), increasing public recreational use, increasing responsibilities of the landowner with respect to that use, and the more sophisticated character of facilities expected by recreationalists, the number of companies placing commercial value on the recreational qualities of their land is increasing. Sometimes a charge is made for use of company recreation facilities. Also in recent years there have been an increased number of leases of land to recreationists for summer-home sites and hunting and fishing camps.

Private Recreation Summary

Private lands, amounting to about 60 percent of the land area of the United States, are becoming increasingly important for public recreation use. In addition, many private lands are better adapted to some forms of outdoor recreation than many types of public lands, presently the major base for outdoor recreation. Also, by providing recreational facilities and activities desired by many people, they free public funds for expenditure on more basic needs. Further, well-managed private lands not directly used for recreation are important in providing open space, or green belts, for environmental interest and beauty.

The reader can see the importance of the interrelationship between public and private lands in planning for recreational use. Coordination is essential here to avoid duplication of effort and to provide complementary relationships between public and private efforts.

Increasing use of wild lands for recreation is prompted by the desire for profit, to gain the services needed by particular groups and organizations, for fulfillment of philanthropic interests in environmental protection and use, and for improving the image of an industry. Many types of commercial resorts serve as the backbone of the tourist industry, which is of great economic importance to many communities and regions. Agricultural and ranch lands are characterized by expanding recreational use involving payment of charges for a wide variety of activities, ranging from hunting and fishing privileges to guest accommodations. Since management of such activities is often unfamiliar to landowners and thus beset with unseen difficulties, certain federal agencies are legally permitted to provide technical and financial assistance. Youth groups, outdoor clubs, church and fraternal organizations, and related bodies own or lease various kinds of recreational land for the benefit of their membership and friends. Scientific, educational, and professional societies often acquire lands for public benefit for philanthropic reasons. Certain quasi-public agencies, such as Indian reservations and lands owned or controlled by the Nature Conservancy are also important. Industrial forest lands, long used by the general public for dispersed recreational activities, such as hunting, are being made increasingly available for camping, picnicking, and other types of more general recreational uses, largely as a public relations gesture.

A Framework for Recreation Planning and Management

Up to this point we have presented the recreation policies of a wide range of public, quasi-public, and private organizations. The reader again is referred to the organization framework in Chapter 1. We are now about to enter a discussion of economics, and then go into planning, development and management. A new framework for planning and management using the ORRRC-BOR land classification system should be helpful to reader understanding. The following framework (Figure 12-1) is used, recognizing the limitations of a single classification system.

In this arrangement management responsibility (public agency or private owner) is related to ORRRC-BOR guideline class, land categories, characteristics and uses, and finally management techniques (tools). This is a simplified version and should be viewed as merely a guide or as one approach to recreation planning and management matters. There are, of course, overlaps between classes, agency approaches, and techniques.

To illustrate the use of this framework, ORRRC class III (natural environment areas) is indicated as the land zone. There are many public and private agencies concerned with class III lands. Some are indicated in the diagram. The U.S. Forest Service in the Department of Agriculture is chosen as the example. The other column entries expand on examples of Forest Service class III lands.

Among possible categories on these natural environmental lands might be: (1) Special zones as along highways, streams, and lakes (these may overlap into

Figure 12-1
Framework for recreation planning and management

Management responsibility	ORRRC-BOR classes	Owner-agency land categories	Charac- teristics and uses	Management techniques (tools)
Local County park, etc.	(Zoning)[a] I. High density recreation areas			
State State forestry State parks Fish and game, etc.	II. General outdoor recreation areas	Special zones [roadside, lake, stream, overlap to classes I–II]		(Environmental manipulation) Biotic community management Recreational timber
Federal U.S. Forest Service National Park Service	III. Natural environment areas	General forest multiple- use area	Larch, Douglas- fir forest	management wildlife mgt. Logging– watershed interrela-
U.S. BLM Fish and Wildlife Service, etc.	IV. Unique natural areas	Near unique areas [overlap to class IV]	Picnicking, Hiking, Simple camping, fishing, hunting	tionships (Development) Maintenance of limited facilities
Private Owners Company Individual Group, etc.	V. Primitive areas	Wilderness Buffer [overlap to class V]		(Rules, interpretation) Visitor contact and control
	VI. Historic and cultural sites			(Public relations) Local owner relations (Research) Related to mgt.

Possible group pressure at these points

[a]Tools of recreation management are shown in parenthesis (see also Chapter 15).

ORRRC classes I and II also); (2) general multiple-use forestry zone where many types of resource production, including timber harvest, occur; (3) near unique areas with outstanding scenic features, such as waterfalls, glaciated valleys, etc. (overlap to class IV); and (4) wilderness buffer (higher or remote) nondesignated land that is primitive in character and where resource use because of access or topography is limited (this might overlap with ORRRC class V, primitive areas). These land categories are most typical of western forest lands and would vary somewhat in the central and eastern parts of the United States. The general multiple-use area has been selected as the example. If we had used the National Park Service natural areas in class III there would be no timber harvest.

In our example, we have chosen for the heading characteristics and uses one of several forest-type possibilities—a larch and Douglas-fir forest where recreation activities might include picnicking, hiking, simple camping, fishing, or hunting. These naturally vary with season. Nature study, photography, summer-home visitation, and other activities could be added to the list, as well as variations in camping types, etc. This forest association is typical of the Northern Rocky Mountains.

User and conservation groups may exert pressure about the points of classification and the allocations for various types of recreation activities and uses, as well as for certain management techniques. This example is therefore a static one of a dynamic situation. At any stage conflict may develop within management circles, between user and management, between users and potential users that would alter management proposals. Through such conflict the original area purposes, or objectives, may be threatened or changed.

In the management techniques column are listed those matters that might generally be associated with recreation management in this type of U.S. Forest Service, (zone) class III, Northern Rocky Mountain forest of larch and Douglas fir. The techniques, or tools, listed concern environmental manipulation, development, rules, interpretation, public relations, and research. These will be covered in greater detail in Chapter 15.

Selected References

1. American Forest Products Industries: "Recreation on Forest Industry Lands in the United States," Washington, 1957. (Mimeographed.)

2. American Forest Products Industries: "Forest Industry Recreation Survey," Washington, 1958. (Mimeographed.)

3. American Forest Products Industries: "Recreation on Forest Industry Lands; Results of a Survey by AFPI, 1960," Washington, 1960.

4. American Forest Institute: "1968 Forest Industry Recreation Survey," Washington, 1968. (Mimeographed.)

5. Buchinger, Maria: "Saving Natural Areas," Nature Conservancy, Washington, March, 1968. (Mimeographed.)

6. Cordell, Harold K., and Stephen J. Maddock: Survey of the Recreational Policies of the Major Pulp and Paper Companies in the South, *Journal of Forestry*, vol. 67, no. 4, April, 1969.

7. Frederick Burke Foundation: "Federal Agencies and Outdoor Recreation," ORRRC Study Report No. 13, U.S. Government Printing Office, Washington, 1962.

8. Nature Conservancy: "Questions and Answers about the Nature Conservancy," Washington, n.d. (Brochure.)

9. Outdoor Recreation Resources Review Commission: "Outdoor Recreation for America: A Report to the President and to the Congress by the ORRRC," U.S. Government Printing Office, Washington, 1962.

10. Outdoor Recreation Resources Review Commission: "Hunting in the United States—Its

Present and Future Role," ORRRC Study Report No. 6, U.S. Government Printing Office, Washington, 1962.

11. Outdoor Recreation Resources Review Commission: "Sport Fishing—Today and Tomorrow," ORRRC Study Report No. 7, U.S. Government Printing Office, Washington, 1962.

12. Outdoor Recreation Resources Review Commission: "Private Outdoor Recreation Facilities," ORRRC Study Report No. 11, U.S. Government Printing Office, Washington, 1962.

13. Recreation Advisory Council, Bureau of Outdoor Recreation: "Federal Executive Policy Governing the Reporting of Recreation Use of Federal Recreation Areas," U.S. Government Printing Office, Washington, 1965.

14. U.S. Department of Agriculture: "Rural Recreation: A New Family Farm Business," U.S. Government Printing Office, Washington, 1962.

15. U.S. Department of Agriculture: "Rural Recreation Enterprises for Profit," Agriculture Information Bulletin No. 277, U.S. Government Printing Office, Washington, 1963.

16. U.S. Department of Agriculture: "Rural Recreation, New Opportunities on Private Land," Miscellaneous Publications No. 930, U.S. Government Printing Office, Washington, 1963.

17. U.S. Department of Agriculture, Federal Extension Service: "Bibliography of Selected Publications on Rural Recreation as a Business," with periodic supplements, U.S. Government Printing Office, Washington, 1963.

18. U.S. Department of Agriculture, Forest Service: "Forest Recreation for Profit," Agriculture Information Bulletin No. 226, U.S. Government Printing Office, Washington, 1962.

19. U.S. Department of the Interior: "The Race for Inner Space," U.S. Government Printing Office, Washington, 1964.

20. U.S. Department of the Interior, Bureau of Outdoor Recreation: "Federal Outdoor Recreation Programs," U.S. Government Printing Office, Washington, 1968.

ECONOMICS

chapter thirteen

ECONOMICS OF OUTDOOR RECREATION[1]

To many who are interested in outdoor recreation the subject of economics is distasteful. To perform an economic analysis of outdoor recreation is even worse. Economists are preoccupied with prices, profits, markets, supply, and demand. The outdoor recreation enthusiast is likely to be inspired by natural beauty, and the peace and serenity to be found far-removed from commercial activity. Bridging the communications gap between these two worlds is a difficult task. Some of the most knowledgeable noneconomists, who are responsible for the outdoor environment and its recreational use, have difficulties understanding the contribution economists might make in analyzing their problems.

Economists have much to offer in deciding how to obtain maximum benefits from land and other resources allocated to outdoor recreation. If their talents are to be utilized efficiently, however, a meaningful dialogue must be established. The purpose of this chapter is to discuss recreation as an economic problem; to provide a *basic introduction* to the role of economics in the recreational management of wild lands. This involves discussion of what an economic problem is, institutional frameworks within which economic choices are made, and some of the consequences of making economic choices.

Why Economics?

The emergence of outdoor recreation as an economic problem is a rather recent occurrence. Most of the literature on the subject has been published within the

---

[1] Prepared by Dr. Barney Dowdle, Associate Professor of Economics and Forest Resources, University of Washington.

past twenty years. Indeed, a number of disciplines have allocated increasing time and effort to outdoor recreation as public demand for outdoor recreation has increased. Reasons for growing interest in outdoor recreation are well understood, but worth emphasizing. In the past we had fewer people than today, less leisure time, and less income to spend on outdoor recreational activities. Translated into economic terms, this meant there was less demand for outdoor recreational facilities and services. Lower demand on the relatively fixed supply of resources considered suitable for providing recreational services meant we were less concerned with deciding how our resources would be used. If there is no demand, there is no economic problem. Placed in an economic context, outdoor recreation is not a problem for which we will find a solution in the usual sense of the term. The economic problem will become larger as population grows, and as our income and leisure time increase.

The fundamental cause of the outdoor recreation problem is scarcity. In other words, nature has not provided us with sufficient resources to provide all the recreational activities we would like. When the recreational desires of all the people are summed, they far exceed what is available. Additionally, many recreational activities are incompatible with each other; e.g., water-skiing and swimming. Some recreational areas are incompatible with nonrecreational activities; e.g., wilderness and logging. The nature of the dilemma is often publicized as a "crisis," and the search for "solutions" is correspondingly frenzied. Not uncommonly, greed and selfishness are cited as contributory causes, and the proposed solution is to overcome these somewhat undesirable human traits.

To be sure, if we could overcome the pursuit of self-interests, perhaps the problem in outdoor recreation might be resolved. One should note, however, a "cure" of this kind might be worse than the disease. Self-interest motivates people to produce many of the items we consume daily, such as food, clothing, books. These items are usually taken for granted. Much of the prosperity of our nation depends upon the acquisitive efforts of its citizens. If we overcame self-interest, what would happen to our prosperity?

The pursuit of self-interest, and its glorification by economists, appears to be a divisive issue in the dialogue between economists and specialists from other disciplines interested in outdoor recreation. This is unfortunate. Economists are preoccupied with the market economy, an institutional framework within which people pursue self-interest and serve society in the process. They do recognize that other institutional arrangements are necessary for some kinds of economic problems. Moreover, some of these problems are in the area of outdoor recreation.

Part of the economic problem in outdoor recreation is to determine the optimal set of institutions for producing optimally various recreational facilities and activities. If the activities people desire are not being provided in appropriate quantities, or places, perhaps our institutions need changing. There is nothing sacred about an institutional arrangement that has no useful social function. An economist is interested in the costs and benefits of making institutional changes.

The economic approach is different from disciplines which often attribute bad outcomes to human misbehavior and suggest that solutions lie in educating people to behave in a more socially responsible manner. The economist accepts human nature as a constraint and attempts to design an institutional framework, the penalty and reward system, which results in individual behavior contributing to social welfare.

Institutional Frameworks for Making Economic Choices

The basic economic problem which necessitates choice is scarcity. Resources which can be used to produce goods and services are limited in supply; man's desires are insatiable. Even in the most affluent societies there is little evidence to suggest that man's appetite for more diminishes as he obtains more. Quite the contrary appears to be true in spite of numerous philosophical and religious questions continually being raised about the propriety of such behavior. If we always want more, we are always living in a state of scarcity. In other words, we do not have enough to fulfill our desires.

The implication of scarcity is that we must make choices regarding the use of our limited resources. Many outdoor recreational activities are dependent upon the use of rather large acreages of land. Hunting, camping, and wilderness hiking are good examples. If land is used only for these activities, it cannot be available for homesites, highways, or many agricultural uses. How should society use land that is suitable for both purposes? If desires change, what kinds of arrangements should be made to facilitate changing land from one use to another? One of the more important problems in outdoor recreation results from the fact that society is not a homogeneous mass of people all of whom have similar desires. Some like highly accessible, commercially developed facilities. Others prefer that areas remain inaccessible and that development be kept to a minimum. Whose preferences will prevail? Who will get the benefits? Who will pay the cost? The latter two questions are especially important to the economist because of his interest in whether or not the same people who benefit also pay. If not, socially undesirable inequities may be perpetrated.

An obvious outcome of having to answer the questions posed is competition. Because of scarcity we have limited alternatives; hence we must compete with each other for the alternative—or alternatives—best suited to our interests, however selfish or altruistic they may be. Mankind has evolved a number of institutional frameworks within which this competition can take place.

Market

In Western societies most choices regarding the use of scarce resources are made within the framework of a market economy. A market economy, alternatively called a capitalistic, or free enterprise, economy, has a number of characteristics which are essential to its operation. Among the most important, from the standpoint of understanding the economics of outdoor recreation, are private property and freedom of choice on the part of both consumers and producers.

None of the characteristics listed is absolute. Private property rights are subject to numerous restrictions including easements, the power of the state to condemn private property for alternative uses, and zoning regulations. Creation of parks from private property is an example relevant to outdoor recreation. Freedom of choice is limited by legal restrictions on certain kinds of consumption, although restrictions vary widely by area and the extent to which laws are enforced. Examples include gambling and the use of alcoholic beverages. For the most part, however, each individual is endowed with the right to use his income as he pleases. He can purchase goods offered on the market, divide his income between savings and consumption, and incur debt.

Regulations on production include the type of technology that may be used, pollution-control measures, workers' benefits, and the location of plant and facilities. Within the limit of these and other restrictions production is directed by management, which is free to acquire resources by purchase, rental, or hire. They are also free to organize these resources to produce what they desire. They may also choose to produce nothing. Permitting land to lie fallow is an example. Producers may sell their output when and where the objectives of the firm are best served.

Numerous products and services, either directly or indirectly associated with outdoor recreational activities, are produced and organized within the framework of a market economy. Equipment for hunting, fishing, skiing, and camping is produced almost exclusively within the private sector of the economy. Most tourist facilities and overnight accommodations are privately owned and operated. Market-produced recreational activities extend into the area of hunting and fishing rights.

In economic theory the objective of each decision maker in a market economy is to maximize his welfare—to pursue his self-interests. By doing so he promotes the public interest. A producer is assumed to maximize expected returns from buying and hiring resources, and producing and selling output. Consumers are assumed to maximize satisfaction received from spending their income and allocating their time between work and leisure. How well they achieve these objectives is determined by the rules of the game.

The ability of decision makers in a market economy to perform correctly and efficiently is the basis of the penalty and reward system. Profits are especially important in production for judging the soundness of decisions regarding investment, innovation, and the efficiency of management of an enterprise. Poor performance on the part of producers means losses. Low profits, or losses, are the punishment for inefficiency. They are assumed eventually to drive inefficient producers out of business.

The rules of the private market are not absolute, and economists have spent considerable time and effort evaluating exceptions, flaws, and qualifications. It is well known, for example, that many companies are not single-purpose profit maximizers. Other objectives commonly pursued include long-run security, welfare of employees, and service to the community. Many companies in the forest products industry, which have large land holdings useful for recreational activities, are under public pressure to open their lands for recreational use. Many have responded and are permitting use of their lands without user fees. It would be difficult to explain these actions in terms of profit maximization. Perhaps the desire to contribute to community welfare may have some bearing on this demonstration of corporate statesmanship.

The elimination of inefficiencies which result from poor performance in a market economy may be delayed for numerous reasons. Nevertheless, the rules discussed above generally predominate, and exceptions are limited where competition exists. Competition forces producers to seek improvements, to introduce innovations, to experiment, and to take risks. Producers who neglect the pursuit of profits in a competitive situation are eliminated. Their performance is constantly being tested, and failure to pass the test cannot be continued long. If competition does not exist, producers may enjoy security and relax in their task to produce goods which satisfy human desires.

Planning

The importance of state planning as an alternative to the market for making decisions is especially significant in outdoor recreation because of the large ownership of public land. Approximately 24 percent of the land area of the continental United States is in some form of federal ownership. Most federal ownership is in the western United States: 56 percent of the Mountain states and about 46 percent of the Pacific Coast states. Within this area federal ownership ranges from a low of 36 percent in Washington to a high of 84 percent in Nevada.

Federal ownership in the eastern United States is very small. In the New England states federal ownership ranges from a low of 1.2 percent in Connecticut to a high of about 4.4 percent in New Hampshire. Most of the states on the Atlantic coast have very little federal ownership.

The significance of federal ownership for outdoor recreation should be obvious. Many public lands are used primarily for recreational purposes. These include national parks and related areas of the National Park System, wildlife refuges, and numerous areas of the national forests. If lands are publicly owned, decisions regarding their use will generally be made within the framework of the planning processes. Central planning is thus very important in the western United States because of the heavy concentration of public lands in the West. In the Eastern states, on the other hand, where most of the land is privately owned, outdoor recreational activities will be largely produced and organized within the framework of a market economy.

In contrast to the market economy, where producers serve the public interest by pursuing their own self-interest, the objective of public officials (planners) is to serve the public interest directly. Much of the ideological dispute over the merits of the two systems is over this difference. Unfortunately, if the debate is conducted at this level, the most likely result is to raise blood pressures.

Agreement is often lacking among public officials on the best way to promote the "public interest." Indeed, ambiguities and controversy in the literature of public administration provide ample evidence of how elusive the concept is. Some suggest the public interest is no more than the sum of private interests. Others regard it as something that transcends the desires of the community.

In spite of the difficulties indicated, the planning process, however organized, can be assumed to serve the public interest. In the United States most planning is done within the executive and legislative branches of government and various administrative agencies. The Department of the Interior, the Department of Agriculture, and numerous other federal and state agencies play a major role in making decisions in the field of outdoor recreation. Viewed as a producer of goods and services, they interpret consumer demands, both present and future, and prepare budgets which provide the resources for meeting these demands. Alternatively, decisions regarding what to produce can originate within the executive or legislative branch of government.

In the market, purchasing power and dollar expenditures dictate what is produced; but in the political and administrative processes, votes and political power largely dictate the kinds of decisions that will be made. As noted earlier, the planning process is like the market in the sense that it serves as an arena within which competition takes place over the use of scarce resources. Not all members of society have similar desires; hence they would have scarce resources used to produce different goods and services. The production of one good may preclude producing another. People with similar desires form groups or lobbies to bring maximum pressure to bear on the political decision-making process in order to serve the interests of their groups. The extent of these pressures and their degree of sophistication is obviously dependent upon the amount of benefit involved and the resources of the pressure group. Not all groups in society have power proportional to their numbers. Herein lie some of the inequities of the planning process.

The role of lobbyists in the field of outdoor recreation has grown more or less proportionately with outdoor recreation activities. In the past, for example, administrators of public lands faced little opposition in making decisions which today would have them embroiled in controversy. Land was relatively less scarce, because demands were lower or nonexistent; therefore, decisions were relatively less important. Given the fixed supply of land and the expected rise in the demand for outdoor recreation activities, controversies over land use can be expected to increase. Unfortunately, increased controversy is likely to consist of more sophisticated hypocrisy and inconsistency in argument. Policies will increasingly be advocated, ostensibly to serve the public interest, which will serve primarily to benefit special-interest groups.

Public and Private Goods and Services

Whether to use the market or the planning process for making resources allocation decisions is fundamentally related to whether or not goods and services are "public" or "private." The distinction is not related to the producer; rather it is characteristic of the good itself. In general, public goods will not be produced efficiently within the framework of a market economy.

The market involves exchange. For example, a man exchanges a day's work for a day's pay. He exchanges $10 for a fishing rod. In order for this exchange to be satisfactory to both sides, the benefits and the costs must be restricted to the two parties involved. In economics, this is known as the exclusion principle. The exclusion principle is the basis of private property rights, the right to control a good in one's interest, and the right to enjoy it while in one's possession.

If the costs and benefits involved in exchange are not restricted to the two parties involved, the market exchange system begins to break down. At the extreme, where people can benefit from production without having to pay, we have what economists have labeled public goods. Economists have long been aware of the difficulties of getting public goods produced in a market economy. Adam Smith devoted considerable attention to these problems in his "Wealth of Nations," a classic treatise in economics published in 1776.

Commonly cited examples of public goods are law and order, national defense, and flood control. Examples with some relevance to outdoor recreation include fire, insect, and disease prevention activities, and landscaping. An individual could benefit from all these activities without paying anything for their production.

Private industry is the source of numerous goods and services to which the exclusion principle does not apply. In Table 13-1 examples of public and private goods, whether produced by public or by private industry, are listed.

It should be emphasized that the listings in Table 13-1 are primarily illustrative. Some of the public goods listed are restricted to a particular region. Residents of New England benefit very little from flood-control projects in the Columbia River basin. TV signals can be transmitted through a cable, in which case they are private goods. The person who does not pay does not receive the signal.

Landscape beauty is more directly related to outdoor recreation. The general public is not excluded from enjoying landscaping produced by, say, a home owner or a timberland owner. The private owner bears the cost of producing the beauty, and the general public can enjoy it as they drive by. If one has a neighbor who keeps a beautiful yard and home, quite possibly this will result in an increase in the price of adjacent property. The reverse would be true if one had a neighbor who neglected his property and it became unsightly.

Private goods produced by public industry include timber used in the forest products industry and electricity. Both represent products the consumer will not receive if he does not pay the price. The price paid is on a per unit use basis. The more one uses, the more one pays.

There are numerous reasons for public involvement in the production of private goods. Government ownership and management of timberlands has its roots in land disposal policies of the past and historical attitudes regarding conservation of natural resources. Public power is quite different. As previously noted, flood control is a public good. If a dam is constructed to produce flood-control benefits, it may as well be used to produce power too; it may also provide for varied outdoor recreational benefits. The additional cost of equipment to generate electricity or to provide for outdoor recreation is relatively small. Indeed, resources are not likely to be used efficiently if electricity is not produced.

Much of the controversy over public versus private power has to do with the way the costs of the dam are allocated between flood control and power production. Proponents of private power are inclined to allocate much of the cost of constructing the dam to electricity. Proponents of public power are inclined to allocate the cost of constructing the dam to flood-control benefits. The decision on how to allocate these joint production costs is somewhat arbitrary; hence, it is difficult to make a definitive statement about whether public power or private power is the more economical.

The categories listed in Table 13-1 do not include a number of goods and services which have both public and private good characteristics. Examples more commonly cited include educational and health benefits.

An educated, healthy individual is an asset to society, and so the argument is made that society should bear part of the cost. Similarly, outdoor recreational

Table 13-1
Producers of public and private goods

	Type of Goods or Service	
Producer	*Private use*	*Public use*
Private industry	Skis, fishing rods, camping equipment	Radio and television signals and landscape beauty
Public industry	Timber, electricity, irrigation water	National defense, law and order, flood control, etc.

facilities contribute to emotional stability by providing a place to release the frustrations of urban living; therefore, they should be provided by the public. It is difficult, of course, to evaluate statements of this kind empirically, or to reach agreement on the ethical issue of how far society should go in providing these services. Most people might agree on the desirability of parks and playgrounds in urban areas; there would be much less agreement on the appropriate size to make a wilderness area.

Changing Role of Government in Outdoor Recreation

We have sketched an outline in which the market and the political processes are alternative systems for making decision in the use of scarce resources. Additionally, we have indicated the market will not function efficiently in the production of certain kinds of goods and services. Even the most staunch supporter of a laissez faire economy will assign certain activities to government.

The role of government in outdoor recreation is becoming increasingly important for two reasons. Consumers are demanding relatively more goods that are of a public-good nature. Pressures for more parks and a cleaner environment are good examples. Secondly, public ownership of large acreages of land places public agencies in the position of having to arbitrate increasingly controversial conflicts in land use. The latter may or may not be related to the public versus private goods issue.

Whatever the reason, public agencies do require more resources to carry out their functions. This raises the question of government finance. Should government activities be financed by charging users where feasible, or should they be financed through government powers of taxation?

The distinction between these two means of providing benefits is much more subtle than might appear. Consider the issue of landscaping logging operations on public forest lands. Landscape beauty, as noted earlier, is a public good in the sense that once it is produced, viewers do not have to pay to look. Not all people will be viewers, however, and some of the nonviewers will be consumers of wood products. Decisions to landscape may, therefore, result in a redistribution of income from the latter group to the former. Is this equitable or in the public interest? Numerous "answers" that sound authoritative are given to questions of this kind. None can be objective. If direct taxation is used, policy makers must face the issue of whether to tax users or people who have the ability to bear heavier tax burdens.

An additional consideration facing policy makers is whether or not government entry, or expansion of activities, in the field of outdoor recreation will adversely affect private efforts in these areas. Public campgrounds are clearly substitutes for private campgrounds. If public facilities are available at zero, or a low price, this may preclude private investments in these activities.

Pricing Decisions

In the private sector of the economy prices serve the dual role of allocating scarce resources, or output, among competing users, and generating the revenues necessary to continue or expand production. Profits and losses are different, and a private producer without some form of subsidy who fails to cover production costs from sales revenues is not likely to continue in business.

In the public sector this is not the case. Many public agencies, such as the National Park Service and the U.S. Forest Service, have no responsibility to show a profit from their activities. If revenues collected from users of the goods and services these agencies provide fail to cover operating costs, deficits are covered by tax revenues. As long as taxpayers are willing to bear the burdens of these deficits, economic survival is not an issue. Moreover, willingness on the part of taxpayers to cover these deficits in the past appears to have established precedents against pricing certain kinds of output. Recreational use of public lands is one of the best examples. Another reason for not pricing recreational activities on public lands is the difficulty of controlling access. In many cases, the cost of administering a pricing system would exceed revenues collected.

In addition to generating revenues to offset production costs, prices serve the important function of rationing use. As demands for outdoor recreational activities have increased, the problem of rationing, or restricting, the use of recreational facilities has become increasingly troublesome. How does one control the crowds? Past precedents of not pricing now plague public administrators who must meet ever-increasing demands with limited recreational facilities. If supplies cannot be expanded, as would be the case of unique natural resources, demands must be controlled. Recreational facilities do have capacity limits, even though they may not be very rigid. If prices are not politically feasible, congestion, queuing, and deterioration of facilities generally result.

Unless funds are available to expand the capacity of recreational facilities, public administrators are hung on the horns of a dilemma. Charging, or raising prices, to control intensity of use is hardly popular with the using public. Users are also likely to be dissatisfied with congestion, waiting, and deterioration in the quality of facilities. The plea for more funds to solve this recreational "crisis" is hardly surprising. It is a predictable reaction of one who does not like to make painful decisions. Moreover, it will have the full support of users who stand to benefit from an expansion of output of services they prefer. The benefits are even greater if the cost of expanded output is borne primarily by others.

If scarce resources are to be used to produce goods and services which will maximize long-run social welfare, there is a major difficulty in the above approach. One of the virtues of the price system is that it generates information regarding consumer preferences. Even though this information may be imperfect, it does provide reasonably good guidelines. If consumers are willing to pay twice as much for one good as another, there is a reasonably good presumption they get twice as much satisfaction from it. Expenditures for altruistic motives would be included in these calculations.

If the price system is not used to generate information regarding relative consumer demands, information with which to plan production decisions must be obtained in some other way. Methods of collecting information for use in making public decisions range from congressional and public agency hearings to consumer surveys. Sociological and statistical research in the field of outdoor recreation is partially a manifestation of increased use of surveys to determine what people want in the way of recreational services. In the private sector price offerings serve this function. A major objective of marketing research is to determine the consumer's willingness to pay. If he does not have to pay, his desires are very likely to exceed the productive possibilities of limited resources. To the extent that this is true, survey information will be inadequate to make the marginal choices among competing resources necessary to achieve maximum social welfare. Perhaps more important, there is no assurance that public officials will use all the information given to them. History provides ample evidence of public decisions made on the basis of faulty information and disregard of accurate information.

A technique commonly used by public agencies to evaluate benefits for which prices are not available is benefit-cost analysis. Many public investment funds are allocated on the basis of analyses of this kind. Increasing use of benefit-cost analysis as a guide for making public investment decisions has resulted in considerable effort being devoted to the development of techniques for estimating the "value" of various kinds of benefits. What is the value of the beauty provided by, say, a timbered hillside if the alternative is to look at a logged area? What is the value of fly-fishing in a stream if the alternative is to construct a dam and flood the area? Numerous questions of these kinds continually arise in the field of outdoor recreation, particularly in making decisions regarding competing land uses.

Economic analysis can provide insights into these problems; it does not provide answers. Value is a measure of satisfaction and will vary among individuals according to their preferences. Even though two individuals may pay the same price for an item, they may value it quite differently. Cost is a measure of the sacrifice made if one alternative is selected rather than another.

Placing a monetary valuation on nonpriced recreational benefits is necessarily arbitrary and puts a rather severe strain on the objectivity of those who make these estimates, as well as those who use them. The major contribution of analyses of nonmarket costs and benefits is that they provide guidance in making decisions by identifying the relevant factors which should be considered. A dollar measure of the quality of human life, and the benefits people enjoy, may be imaginary. Nevertheless, it can be a useful first approximation for making difficult choices, where sacrifices (costs) must be made if one alternative is chosen rather than another. Some guidelines are necessary unless the choices are to be made on the basis of political expediency, personal whim, or perhaps even random selection.

The economist's preoccupation with prices in making decisions of these kinds arises because of two fundamental economic considerations: (1) all costs should be counted, whether they are easily countable or not, and (2) all benefits should be evaluated, however difficult this may be. The crude yardstick used for this purpose is merely scaled in monetary units. It is to be expected that different estimates would be obtained by different people. As long as the relevant cost and benefit variables are considered in the analysis, different numerical estimates may be useful in negotiating agreements.

Summary and Conclusions

The demand for outdoor recreational facilities in the United States, as well as most other countries of the world, will surely increase as incomes rise and people exchange additional income for more leisure time. Resources suitable for supplying recreational demands are both publicly and privately owned. The institutional frameworks for making public and private decisions are quite different with respect to immediate objectives and the means of achieving objectives. Private enterprise must pursue profits for reasons of survival. Presumably, the public interest will be served in the process. Governmental ownership and control of the means of production is presumably to serve the public interest directly.

If society's demand for public goods increases, which is apparent in increased public concern over the quality of the environment, the role of government must necessarily expand. The kinds of public policies and programs adopted will have significant effects on the efficient utilization of both public and private resources. Where public ownership of land is relatively negligible, as in the eastern United States, private enterprise can be expected to respond to certain kinds of increased recreational demands. Other kinds may have to be provided by government purchase of land, or restrictions being placed on the management of private lands. Which approach is used will be largely dependent upon whether goods are public or private, that is, whether or not the exclusion principle applies and the extent to which the general public will accept encroachments on private property rights.

Where large amounts of land are in public ownership, such as the western United States, the impact of public actions on private efforts in providing outdoor recreational activities will be considerably different from that in the eastern United States. Many public activities will involve the production of recreational services for which the exclusion principle would apply; campgrounds are an example. In other words, private producers would be expected to respond and provide facilities. Prices would be charged, and the revenues collected would be expected to cover cost of production. If public agencies supply services of these kinds without charge, and costs are covered through tax revenues, private incentive to provide facilities could be adversely affected. Consumers can hardly be expected to patronize private facilities, where they must pay a fee, if zero, or lower-fee, publicly operated substitutes are available. Adverse effects of this kind could distort resource use by placing a heavier burden on public lands than would be necessary.

A further problem in public management is the possible adverse redistributive effects that may occur largely as a result of the effects of political pressure groups who are able to obtain a disproportionate share of public benefits. This problem is particularly difficult to resolve because administrators must weigh conflicting values. Given the impossibility of doing this objectively, there is a tendency to bow to political pressures. It is not obvious that decisions made in this manner are always consistent with maximum social welfare.

The contribution of economics to outdoor recreation is primarily to provide insights and to raise relevant questions. Even though answers may not be immediately forthcoming, this should lead to greater efficiency and equity in allocation of resources to outdoor recreation.

Selected References

1. Alchian, Armen A., and William R. Allen: "Exchange and Production: Theory in Use," Wadsworth, Belmont, Calif., 1964.

2. Clawson, Marion, and Burnell Held: "The Federal Lands: Their Use and Management," Johns Hopkins, Baltimore, 1957.

3. Clawson, Marion, and Jack L. Knetsch: "Economics of Outdoor Recreation," Johns Hopkins, Baltimore, 1966.

4. Kohler, Heinz: "Welfare and Planning: An Analysis of Capitalism versus Socialism," Wiley, New York, 1966.

5. Mundell, Robert A.: "Man and Economics," McGraw-Hill, New York, 1968.

6. Musgrave, Richard A.: "The Theory of Public Finance," McGraw-Hill, New York, 1959.

7. Rourke, Francis E.: "Bureaucracy, Politics and Public Policy," Little, Brown, Boston, 1969.

8. Shonfield, Andrew: "Modern Capitalism: The Changing Balance of Public and Private Power," Oxford, New York, 1965.

9. Sirkin, Gerald: "The Visible Hand: The Fundamentals of Economic Planning," McGraw-Hill, New York, 1968.

10. U.S. Congress: "The Analysis and Evaluation of Public Expenditures: The PPB System," compendium of papers submitted to the subcommittee on economy in government, Joint Econ. Comm., U.S. Cong., vol. XVII, 1969.

PROVIDING RECREATIONAL OPPORTUNITIES

chapter fourteen

RECREATIONAL LAND-USE PLANNING

S ince outdoor recreation involves many diverse interests and activities no one area can provide opportunities for all types. Many outdoor recreational interests and activities are incompatible, and some can be engaged in only in certain areas with suitable terrain. Thus, different kinds of areas for different basic recreational purposes are desirable; their number, distribution, character, and size in various sections of the country depend upon public demand and the availability of land suited to different recreational uses.

Recreation represents but one aspect of land use [5,7,28,43]. Modern technological society requires consideration of other needs as well. Industry must have a continuing source of raw materials (timber, minerals, hydroelectric power). Production of food for expanding populations depends upon adequate agricultural and range land. Expanding metropolitan areas require space for homes, businesses, and a multiplicity of supporting services and utilities. On lands where such needs are dominant, outdoor recreation may be minimized, developed on an urban pattern, or, in some cases, even eliminated from consideration. Conversely, on some kinds of wild lands outdoor recreational benefits are dominant; under such conditions commercial use of natural resources, however well managed, should be materially reduced or even totally excluded. Between these two extremes are lands with resources of such character that, by proper planning and subsequent careful management related to the nature of the environment, both recreational and nonrecreational needs can be served without serious consequences in either case.

Recreational Land-use Planning

For our purposes, planning concerns advanced preparation of policies, procedures, or designs to achieve desired goals. With recreation lands this varies from comprehensive planning relating land uses and developments to public needs over a large region, such as a state or county, down to the design or arrangement of specific facilities on a particular piece of land, or site. As Dr. Dowdle indicated in Chapter 13, in the eastern United States with private lands predominant, outdoor recreation may be organized and produced largely under the market economy framework. For the large public land areas of the West, central planning by public agencies is very important.

The *plan* may be a publication of policies, programs, and priorities, such as a comprehensive state recreation plan. It may also be a specific design and drawing for development of a tract of land—a site plan. Also the *plan* may be a combination of the above, as a park feasibility study.

Planning is a continuing process dealing with present conditions in terms of projected future needs, allowing for flexibility and revision with the evolution of new socioeconomic concerns and technological change [12]. There is also a control implication in planning as directions and procedures are formalized, restricting use to some areas (e.g., class V—primitive or wilderness lands) and concentrating activities in others (e.g., class I—high-density recreation areas). Thus recreation planning ideally should involve latest knowledge, all concerned parties—public administrators, owners, plannees (visitors, local residents, interest groups, resource users), as well as others affected by the plan. Planning will be effective to the extent that it is comprehensive and coordinates all concerned groups and affected resources. It is limited by those aspects excluded, or overlooked, and may impose undue control on those omitted.

Basic land planning coordinates various uses of land, on either the same or separate areas. Proper coordination among agencies and landowners with concern for the plannee maximizes the net benefit to society on a sustained basis. This basic principle applies when recreation is the primary concern of land planning, when lands have both multipurpose recreational and nonrecreational values, or when they have other primary functions which exclude recreation.

Basic Elements of Recreational Land-use Planning

Proper recreational land planning is fundamental to efficient recreational land management. When applied to specific areas, planning and management are closely interrelated. Management implements the planning. Such planning:

1. Identifies varied benefits derived from wild-land use, clarifies objectives for recreational use of different types of land, identifies recreational land-use problems, and outlines future recreational land needs
2. Develops guidelines for making decisions concerning allocation of land for various kinds of recreational use and development, and establishes priorities for meeting recreational needs on various types of land

3. Defines the purpose and scope of different types of recreational areas in an overall recreational program for a given region

4. Maximizes user satisfaction by developing diversified recreational opportunities for varied spare-time interests and activities for all classes of society on areas of suitable type and size, properly distributed in accordance with need

5. Ensures proper coordination of various types of recreational areas with each other, as well as with nonrecreational lands, thus encouraging perpetuation of intrinsic recreational interests, economy in recreational land management, and the satisfaction of nonrecreational requirements

6. Allocates public and private funds to specific recreational land-use problems

7. Provides guidelines for private persons contemplating an outdoor recreational enterprise as a source of income

8. Includes site design and layout of facilities and uses in specific recreation areas

Important Considerations in Recreational Land-use Planning

Recreational land-use planning, at its several levels, is circumscribed by a number of variables and constraints which are related to final decisions in land allocation. These variables and constraints include:

1. The nature of basic recreational characteristics of areas in question; that is, both the physical characteristics of such lands and the primary recreational qualities

2. The amount of demand for and use of various recreational interests and activities, together with trends indicative of probable future changes in demand and use

3. Population density, dispersal, and increasing or decreasing trends, particularly in regions from which areas derive the major proportion of potential users

4. Means of access; the nature of both present and probable future transportation to and within existing and proposed recreational areas

5. Socioeconomic factors affecting recreational use and demand.

6. Variations in land-use patterns other than recreational

7. Modifications in the nature and ideology of political institutions

8. Degree of cooperation of public and private landowners and between planner and plannee

9. Budgetary limitations of the planning process

Careful consideration of the foregoing factors aids in relating the most suitable recreational uses to different types of land. Acceptable size and degree of development can be defined, ranging from small, readily accessible, highly developed areas for large numbers of people to remote areas of wild land typified by extensive size, lack of physical development, and freedom from modern distractions.

Incompatibility of recreational interests and activities adapted to varied multipurpose management with nonrecreational uses can be identified, and the activity assigned to appropriate multipurpose lands. The influence of activities distracting to recreational uses on nearby lands can be eliminated or modified by establishment of restrictive buffer zones, or related techniques. Thus, a variety of recreational resources will be perpetuated, in both quality and quantity, for the benefit of future generations, with minimum cost and disruption to the economy.

Nature of Basic Recreational Resources

Basic recreational characteristics of wild land serve as principal attractions for varied recreational interests and activities. These are: (1) the physical character of the land including climate, topography, soils, and water resources; and (2) inherent recreational land values, such as significant geological, biological, archaeological, or historical interests, scenic quality, natural or primitive conditions with varying degrees of solitude and the necessity for self-sufficiency, and conversely, various factors which lend themselves to mass recreational use. These characteristics vary widely with different lands in various sections of the country. They react differently to the impact of different types and intensity of recreational use. They are variously adapted to multipurpose management in conjunction with nonrecreational uses. They are also affected differently by activities carried out on adjacent lands.

The physical character of land affects both the type and the quality of recreational service which can be rendered best by different areas. Climate, as a major factor in the distribution of plant and animal life, strongly affects the characteristics of various recreational areas. Climate also affects the cultural patterns of people; consequently, ethnological and archaeological interests vary widely in different sections of the country.

Topography is related to scenic interests, the nature of recreational activities and development, and the degree of hazard involved in recreational use. Mountain climbing, riding, skiing and related winter sports, boating and other water-oriented activities are dependent upon the character of the terrain. Topography is also important in determining the location of roads, trails, campgrounds, hotels, and similar developments. Topographical characteristics are also responsible for numerous public dangers which must be recognized, understood, and guarded against.

Various kinds of soils react differently to varying degrees and intensity of use. Water resources are also important. The presence of lakes, streams, expanses of salt water, or interesting waterfalls, can be responsible for both the interests and the hazards of recreational areas. Further, water resources are a determining factor in the nature of specific developments; campgrounds, hotels, sanitary facilities, and similar needs are dependent upon an adequate water supply.

The inherent recreational values typical of different types of wild land must also be carefully considered in recreational land planning. As noted in a few following examples, these primary values largely determine the character and intensity of public use. Some areas can accommodate large numbers of people without serious, irreparable loss of recreational interests. Their basic attractions may be more durable, may respond more readily to suitable maintenance and repair, or may simply not embody the irreplaceable unique qualities that demand restricted use and development. High-density areas are generally so characterized. On other types of recreational lands varying degrees of restriction in development and use may apply; their more delicately balanced qualities are more easily damaged by highly concentrated public use and accompanying physical development. On such lands the nature of permissible modifications and intensity of use varies from moderate to nil. In addition, some areas are typified by recreational values which can be more readily coordinated with nonrecreational uses (timber harvest, development of multipurpose reservoirs). Other areas managed primarily for recreation are often characterized by severe restrictions as to numbers of users and nature of physical development. In particular, areas typified by unique, irreplaceable geological, biological, archaeological, or historical interests, as well as wilderness values, fall in the latter category. Therefore, it is imperative that recreational land planners correctly evaluate the primary recreational values of different types of land and understand the complex ecological relationships and related conditions which are basic to maintenance and perpetuation of inherent recreational benefits.

Where recreational benefits are dependent upon the maintenance of natural conditions, planners of recreational areas must give particular attention to ecological relations, weighing the values to be maintained against possible public hazards. For instance, extensive snag removal in a forest eliminates the nesting sites of many birds; indiscriminate clearing of brush and debris from the forest floor destroys elements of food, cover, and other conditions necessary to the survival of certain animals; the flooding of lands, and conversely, the draining of swamps or bogs damage conditions upon which other plants and animals are dependent.

Public Recreational Interests and Trends

Recreational land planners should understand and be able to correctly estimate the relative importance of various public recreational interests and activities. They must also be able to evaluate changes in trends. Studies such as those conducted by the Outdoor Recreation Resources Review Commission and the Bureau of Outdoor Recreation are significant guides [30,31,39,40].

Many activities now regarded as recreation, such as hunting and fishing, were not so considered in pioneer times [24,25]. Other activities, previously unknown or having little popular appeal, have developed phenomenally. Winter sports, particularly skiing and snowmobiling, have extended the use of many established wild-land recreational areas and have prompted development of others specifically for their pursuit. Expanding public interest in winter sports has prompted a number of perplexing problems, such as visitor safety and the propriety of permanent winter sports developments in significant areas like national parks.

There has also been a rapid growth in water-related recreational interests, including those of wild rivers [36]. Increasing popularity of boating, water skiing, and skin and scuba diving has created the need for marinas, boat-launching ramps and related developments, as well as more rigorous application of water safety rules and regulations. In addition to more extensive use of natural coastal and inland waters for such activities, many reservoirs, developed primarily for other public benefits, are widely used for water-related recreation. Further, a number of recreational areas have been established primarily because of their underwater interests; some of these feature underwater nature trails.

Changes in recreational interests and activities are closely related to improvements in means of travel, modernization of recreational equipment, and changes in types of recreational accommodations. These influence, to a considerable extent, the nature and degree of recreational use of wild lands.

Areas formerly difficult to reach are now more readily accessible by four-wheel drive vehicles, trail bikes, and snowmobiles. Resultant problems are minimized by zoning of appropriate areas for the use of such vehicles. Better highways and automobiles, as well as faster and more versatile aircraft, have made formerly distant areas more accessible to visitor use. The greater mobility of recreationists has resulted in less need for permanent summer-home sites on public land and for a greater variety and number of overnight accommodations for transients. For instance, compact motels and hotels have largely replaced the monstrous structures typical of many recreational areas several generations ago. In addition, with improved technology, camping has increased in popularity, resulting in expansion in the number of campgrounds. Even backpacking into remote areas is rendered less difficult by lightweight equipment and palatable dehydrated foods. Such changes have created problems as well as benefits, particularly with respect to changing character of campgrounds.

Increased use of trailers affects campground design and use. Modern campers insist on certain campground refinements which may be beyond budgetary limits of public agencies, or may result in such highly concentrated sophisticated use that natural conditions and related basic interests of an area are destroyed. Planning can minimize such difficulties by correlating type of campground with type of camping experience. In addition, planning is important in encouraging greater participation by private industry in the provision of the more sophisicated camping facilities, for the use of which adequate charge can be made.

Over the years the term "last frontier" has been applied to progressively more remote wild lands. Increased recreational use of wild lands has indicated that criticism of the number and "excessive size" of wild-land recreational areas, often voiced when they were established, was not always valid. Deterioration of many such areas, including those remotely located, has resulted from improperly planned coordination of use and environment. Should current planning repeat such errors or fail to anticipate the constant changes in recreational needs and interests, future generations can expect continued depreciation of both the diversity and the quality of wild-land recreational experience.

Population as Related to Recreational Use of Wild Lands

The population pattern of various regions (density, dispersal, increase or decrease) affects all aspects of land use, including that for wild-land recreation. The greater the number of potential users of recreational lands; the greater the need for recreational areas of adequate size, proper distribution, and suitable diversity of interests; and the greater the difficulty of perpetuating relevant recreation quality. In particular, problems of congestion and overuse are intensified.

Each region has singular land-use problems that must be solved upon their own merits if all vital public needs, social as well as economic, are to be most advantageously served. Sections of the country with a highly concentrated population, as in parts of the eastern United States, have particularly difficult land-use problems. Where population is rapidly expanding, different but equally difficult problems develop. Many western areas exhibit evidences of "growing pains." Their complicated and controversial land-use problems can be reduced only by timely consideration of, and planning for, all varied public needs, recreational and otherwise, in proper relation to one another.

Severe fluctuations in the use of some recreational areas, particularly sudden weekend expansion of visitor population, which as quickly subside, can be very troublesome. All types of recreational lands accessible to large centers of population are characterized by this kind of use pattern. Prohibitive costs make it unsound and uneconomic to gear the operation of such areas to their maximum patronage. As a result, they are plagued by overtaxed facilities and inadequate personnel during peak periods and by incomplete utilization at other times. Moreover, the physical character of most areas places definite limits on the extent and kind of physical development.

Many recreational interests and activities are compatible with commercial utilization of wild-land resources [28]. In such instances, multiple-purpose use is not only feasible but desirable. Current or potential recreational use may be so great, however, that its benefits preclude, or at least severely limit, any other use. Additionally, recreational interests and activities themselves are not always compatible. Large concentrations of people and certain types of equipment (firearms, motorized trail bikes, snowmobiles) are not compatible with recreational uses demanding privacy or solitude. Planning minimizes such conflicts by confining noncompatible interests and activities to different areas.

Large concentrations of people invariably cause deterioration of recreational interests in the outdoors. Besides increasing the likelihood of vandalism, the mere presence of large crowds has a wearing effect upon recreational lands. Hazard from fire is increased; shrubs and vegetation may be literally tramped out. Certain soil types require definite limitations on the degree and type of public use [34].

Any particular type of recreational land, if based on carefully planned use, and environmental characteristics with respect to long-term public needs, will attract people of kindred interests. Thus, congestion can be alleviated, controversy over competing interests will be largely avoided, and duplication of costly services and facilities will be minimized.

Means of Access

The public use of different types of recreational lands both affects and is affected by the nature of related transportation facilities, both without and within such areas. In some cases established or impending future transportation patterns predispose certain areas to specific kinds of recreational uses. For instance, existing or definitely planned roads or customary mechanized equipment (aircraft, trail bikes, snowmobiles) may predispose an area to certain uses; or if several areas are being considered for winter sports development, lower operational costs of a location adjacent to a highway regularly maintained for winter travel may outweigh certain minor deficiencies in terrain.

The nature of transportation facilities also affects the character and the degree of patronage typical of different recreational lands. Where visitors come from, their background, economic status and interests, the distance they travel, the length of their stay, and the type of accomodations and services required are all related to the type of available transportation.

Increasing use of four-wheel drive vehicles, trail bikes, and snowmobiles, as well as light aircraft for reaching remote places, poses serious recreational land management problems. Many recreational land planners contend that, under certain circumstances, roads are more damaging to scenic beauty and environmental interests, as well as more costly, than the various types of cableways, funiculars, or lifts that are common in mountainous areas in Europe; their use in the United States will undoubtedly be more widespread in the future.

Socioeconomic Factors Affecting Recreational Use and Demand

Population patterns relating to age, sex, marital status, race, religion, national origin, educational background, and economic status are important determining factors in the demand for and use of wild-land recreational areas. Differences in maturity and physical and emotional characteristics associated with various age groups and the sexes promote typical recreational interests. Recreational preferences of young people differ from those of older groups. Recreational objectives and requirements of families differ from those of unattached individuals; there are differences in financial restrictions, and family recreation is generally oriented toward the needs and interests of children. People of different races, religions, or national origin often reflect their specific heritage in recreational interests and activities.

Variations in Land-use Patterns Other Than Recreation

Wild lands have been increasingly invaded by expanding industrial and urban developments and their various supporting services and facilities. It is unlikely that the rapidity of urban expansion will be checked. In the future fewer acres will have to supply increasing amounts of food as well as necessary raw materials for industry (timber, minerals) if high living standards, basic to enjoyment of modern recreational opportunities, are to be maintained.

The Outdoor Recreation Resources Review Commission reported that inadequate variety and distribution of recreational opportunities were due, not to lack of land area, but rather to lack of adequate planning for proper use of available land. There is a growing realization that man can and must adapt his activities to his environment, rather than subjugating his environment to his activities [10,15,32,37,38]. The latter policy, acceptable in pioneer times, when land and its varied resources were seemingly unlimited, is now recognized as both economically and socially shortsighted. In this connection we can learn from European concepts of land planning and natural-resource utilization.[1] There, where necessary intensive uses are properly related to environmental characteristics, many amenities as well as productivity and relatively high living standards have been maintained. Conversely, where past land use has ignored environmental limitations, both social and economic values and, consequently, general living standards have suffered. The latter situation applies in parts of Europe, as well as Asia and Africa, on the perimeter of the Mediterranean.

Changes in Nature and Ideology of Political Institutions

A variety of legislation, ranging from establishment of various types of parks and reserves to restrictive controls relative to water and air pollution, has brought about radical changes in policies of land use and natural-resource management since pioneer times. Old agencies have been reorganized or reoriented, new

---

[1] The following is a policy statement of the State Forestry Administration, Bavaria, Germany, in 1914:

Considering landscape appearance and the educational role of the forest, it is desirable, at least in the vicinity of larger cities and favored travel points, to abstain from creating large, aesthetically offensive clear-cuts, and from producing only artificial forests of too-uniform appearance; moreover it is desirable to guide economic management so as to conform to the appearance and essence of an area, sustaining its appeal, and maintaining or, if necessary, recreating the character of the natural forest scene, with its varied plant community. [W. Mantel (ed.), "Wald und Forstwirtschaft in Bayern," p. 12, BLV Verlagsgesellschaft, München, 1963.]

agencies have been formed, and deeply rooted institutional and personal concepts have been considerably modified. Many of these alterations reflect changing public attitudes toward the importance of recreation in proper use of spare time and the maintenance of environmental quality.

Legislators and other public officials are understandably sensitive to the changing attitudes of their constituents [9,35]. Through the democratic process, resultant legislation bearing on such subjects reflects increasing public concern for the interests of the majority as opposed to individual privilege.

Since land planning activities must be conducted within the framework of enabling legislation, the intent and purpose of relevant legislation, particularly its ambiguities and limitations, must be thoroughly understood. The underlying causes, as well as the history or events that brought such legislation into being, must also be recognized. There are always several sides to every question involving radical departure from accepted procedure.

Cooperation of Public Agencies, Private Landowners and Plannees

Recreational planning at all levels generally involves a variety of lands controlled by different public agencies (federal, state, municipal) and private owners with varying primary management objectives. These objectives largely determine what the nature and degree of public recreational uses will be and how they may be coordinated to provide for a wide variety of interests and activities, thus favoring economy of operation as well as perpetuation of recreational values of different areas.

Planners usually have advisory rather than administrative functions in developing ideas and proposed courses of action. As planners develop ideas, it is important, where possible, to involve the recipients of the planning (plannees). Though the process is complicated by increased variety of opinions and interests, plans have a better chance of being accepted if plannees help in their creation.

Budgetary Limitations

If inadequate, available funds, whether derived from public or private sources, place obvious limitations on recreational land-planning activities.

It is important to recognize that financial aid from the Land and Water Conservation Fund, as well as many similar sources, is not the sole support of recreational developments. Such a fund, supplied on a matching basis, in effect serves as a catalyst in developing local interest and responsibility in the assumption of the planning task.

Levels of Planning

Individual recreational areas, whether small urban neighborhood playgrounds or extensive, remote wilderness areas, are not completely independent entities. Each type of area has singular importance, featuring some particular recreational opportunity important to large segments of the population. Though ideal situations are not common, planning seeks to provide varied types of recreational areas, suitably developed; adequate in number, size, and distribution; and appropriate to the need so that they will supplement one another in kind and quality of recreational opportunities. Such coordination offers maximum variety for the largest number of people, at minimum cost, and with maximum consideration for environmental maintenance.

The complex recreational land-planning process involves a number of steps of varying detail [6] including:

1. Broad, comprehensive planning on a national, regional, state, or local (county, municipal) level.
2. Specific planning of individual areas, including detailed planning of sites within individual areas.

Comprehensive Planning

Although comprehensive recreational land planning on a local level typified a number of more heavily populated sections of the country at an early date, it was not until after publication of the Outdoor Recreation Resources Review Commission report in 1962 that planning on a broader scale was undertaken. Development of a national recreational plan was delegated to the Bureau of Outdoor Recreation. Parallel programs were developed by various states as a prerequisite for securing financial assistance from the Land and Water Conservation Fund for acquisition of necessary lands and for development of suitable recreational programs. County and municipal needs as presented by various appropriate local agencies were incorporated in various state plans. It is the intention of these operations to coordinate typical recreational opportunities, and to provide for such modifications as future conditions and demands may require.

The Bureau of Outdoor Recreation coordinates planning with states and also local governments through administration of the Land and Water Conservation Fund. Thus recreation planning at state and local levels is, in part, directed by the national government [39].

Both public and private lands are considered in comprehensive planning conducted on a national, regional, state, or localized basis. Comprehensive planning can promote cooperation between public and private agencies relative to coordinated recreational use of various types of land, together with development of legislation and administrative decisions with respect to such coordinated use. Though we are far from Utopia with relation to adequate coordination in recreational use of public and private lands, a framework for such coordination is slowly developing. The primary steps in recreation planning are (1) to identify recreational resources of public and private areas—supply, (2) to relate these resources to assumed public need for outdoor recreation, and (3) to develop a program of action relative to the funding and fulfillment of outdoor recreational opportunities which will most adequately satisfy necessary requirements.

There are several steps in the comprehensive planning process once a project is funded, as by a state legislature, special grant, or through the Land and Water Conservation Fund. Here are the major steps followed, though not necessarily in this way. Complications are added to suggest the difficulties of the planning process.

Inventory—supply.   For this step objectives must be clearly defined. Though planners often must take existing conditions as given, it should be understood how various land resources fit into a workable and interrelated system. What role do you want existing parks and other lands to play in serving the public? What of adjoining lands serving many uses? Can recreation lands complement each other, each serving somewhat independent functions, rather than a series of areas all with similar picnic and camping sites, view points, and hiking trails? The mere gathering of data on numbers of parks, acres of forest land, miles of shoreline, or number of climbable mountains may not be useful unless it is related to planning goals, means of access, location, and public acceptance.

Perhaps a scenic waterfall in a narrow gorge has no suitable service area other than for limited parking and a vista point. Nearby private land or a public park a few miles away may offer picnic and toilet facilities. This case is an example of a physical limitation. In "A Systems Approach to Park Planning" [11], the author, William J. Hart describes three basic factors controlling the location, size, and management of parks and related areas. These are biological, physical, or social, depending upon species or habitat considerations, site location of physical features, or sociopolitical concerns.

In reference again to ORRRC-BOR land classification and the framework given in Chapter 12, these classes can be used as a means of inventorying recreation resources in planning. A judgment must be made as to how classes are applied to various lands; and there may be overlaps between say class I, high-density recreation areas, and class II, general outdoor recreation areas. There will be differences in management of classes if lands in question are already under the administration of specific agencies (e.g., the U.S. Forest Service management of class III, natural environment areas, differs from that of the National Park Service). Interest-group pressure may be expected to affect use of classes. Also, there will be differences in the size and application of classes. Planners will have to determine the size of class units and how they are to be applied to multiple ownerships in a physiographic region or designated park. Nevertheless, the classes do serve as beginning reference categories for the planner, and they can be altered as supply is related to public use.

Public Use.   In this step, assessment is made of public use of recreation lands, or use patterns. We avoid the use of the term "demand," though it is often used in the literature and guides on recreation planning. As Dr. Dowdle indicated in Chapter 13, in recreation we are dealing with public land opportunities as public goods, not private goods priced in the market. Hence the use of participation rates to determine needs or demand where the use is related only to what is available does not give a measure of choice for varying opportunities. Use figures, however, can be an indication of impact on existing areas, though they may not be too helpful for unused proposed areas.[2]

An analysis of use as to types, origin-destination data, the relation of use to population, trends of use and user social characteristics can be helpful to the planner. Use patterns reflecting changing technology and thus related to design for future use may be significant. For example, the recent great increase in the number of snow machines, all-terrain vehicles, and motorized trailers has affected legislation, trail construction, and campground design.

The above statements suggest the need for research results to guide the planning process. The results of user behavior and perception studies may provide planning insight, as Dr. Catton mentioned in Chapter 5, into differences in concepts of wilderness or public campground behavior. It is possible to obtain from user studies good indications of recreation concepts and desires which are often different from those usually generated by the planner when dealing with technical standards and past use. The user is the plannee.

Evaluation of Alternatives. Evaluation is the sticky part of planning, but it is often passed over as following logically from inventory-supply and use data; however, it does not. Usually there are several alternatives, which in broad comprehensive planning may not be as clear as when dealing with one area.

As an example, suppose that gathered inventory and use data suggest the creation of three state parks—all with equally attractive physical features, but there is only money for two. The published plan could simply indicate all three areas without choice. In practice this is often done. Types of recreation areas and needed activity developments are listed in an order of priority established by the planners, based on collected cost and use data. It is then up to political bodies, legislatures, county boards, etc., to make final allocation decisions. To the extent that elected officials consult the public via interest groups, hearings, or public forums, decisions for action may be made workable by adjustment of planning suggestions to sociopolitical realities.

1. Economic Analysis—Returning to our three state-park example given above, let us assume that one park (A) is near the city and will serve a large population with adequate development area, but land prices are high and a detracting industrial plant adjoins the property. The second proposed park (B) is distant from population centers, but the land is to be donated and there are no known resource conflicts. Adjoining land use complements the park and vice versa. The

---

[2] It should be pointed out here that participation rates and related demand formulas are much in use by the Bureau of Outdoor Recreation and state planning groups in statewide plans.

third area (C) is in between with respect to population served. The land is public, but there are resource use conflicts in the area and on adjoining lands. It contains quality merchantable timber, and the adjoining owners wish to harvest timber on their land.

Dr. Dowdle in Chapter 13 mentioned the use of benefit-cost analysis as a means of valuing trade-offs between various benefits and resource uses. For park A the costs of land, development, adjoining industrial plant purchase, or process change to protect park values can be balanced against listed user benefits at an assumed value per user. For park B cost of development at a distant location can be balanced against benefit or possibly limited visitation.

A different approach could be used for park C where the market value of timber resource lost in park designation and development of facilities, as well as the costs of adjoining owners, would be computed. These opportunity costs would be a marginal indication of area value in park use. There are other economic analysis methods that could be used here, such as least-cost ranking or marginal analysis. All merely provide a basis for comparison, not a decision itself, but they do indicate costs often overlooked in planning.

2. Plannee Involvement and Education—Involving the recipient of planning (plannee) in the process before the final report may produce a consensus which will lead to the acceptance and implementation of the finished plan. Very possibly the planners will learn as much as the plannees, and information inputs on the areas of concern may surface and cause plan changes. In our examples an interest group might work with the industrial owners next to park A to alleviate mutual problems. It might develop in working with larger groups that park B is not really attractive to its potential clientele; while at park C the park proponents and resource producers have common interests that could complement each other.

The process has been most simplified for illustration. Actually the plannee-involvement approach can be complicated by militant unyielding interest groups, strong dominant individuals, unintentional omission of concerned groups, and planner desire to retain original ideas intact.

However, after completing all these steps the comprehensive plan can be put together and published for public and legislative review. If recommendations of the plan are implemented, more detailed planning of specific areas and sites is necessary.

The master planning of a particular designated park is one approach. It is similar to area planning, perhaps in larger and varied use areas, as in a national forest, where lands of several public agencies and owners may overlap. After master or area planning comes planning and design of definite sites such as campgrounds, picnic areas. Each site will reflect its relation to other sites in overall master or area plan.

Master Plans for Specific Areas

Detailed master plans for specific recreational areas (national, state, or local parks; reclamation developments; seashores; wildlife refuges) are developed within a more generalized format. Master plans include narrative and graphic materials. They define the function and purpose of individual areas, relate them to current and anticipated recreational needs of the region as defined in comprehensive plans discussed previously. Necessary facilities and services are indicated. Legislation and executive orders generally establish policy and serve as the framework of these master plans, especially in the case of public land. In some instances, particularly private lands, management policies are based upon institutional or personal objectives.

In effect, the master plan is a guide in dealing with the specific details of management. It prescribes the kind of recreational activities that are compatible with the area's primary purpose. It outlines procedures for use and protection of recreational values (plant and animal life, scenic and environmental interest and beauty, archaeological and historical features). It establishes standards for the degree and character of necessary physical development and public service (access, accommodation, health and safety, interpretation). It defines recreational objectives of each area in relation to other lands considered in the overall recreational program for the region, ensuring maximum economy of operation by elimination of expensive duplication of facilities and services through coordination of effort, wherever practical. And, while allowing for possible future changes as a result of unforeseen developments or public demands, the master plan provides for continuation of a well-balanced program and the preservation of intrinsic recreational values.

Preparation of the master plan should be preceded by examination of public recreational needs of the region and the general relationship of the proposed recreational area to them. These data should be available from state or local comprehensive plans, previously discussed.

First steps in the master plan include: (1) determination of proper size and boundaries of the proposed area, (2) predevelopment inventory, (3) acquisition or other ways of controlling necessary land by means suited to anticipated recreational use (transfer of jurisdiction, purchase, lease, easement), and (4) cost data. It is recognized that these steps may not always follow in this order. Master plans may be developed before land is acquired, to explain feasibility to legislators or present ideas to plannees.

The predevelopment inventory should include a narrative report with maps of water areas, soil evaluation, vegetation, and topography as needed. It should note the character of various features of recreational interest (plant and animal life, geological importance, topography, scenic quality, archaeological and historical values, climate, soil conditions, adaptability to water- or winter-oriented activities and physically active sports). The predevelopment inventory also should include the relation of the proposed recreational area to others of similar or different types and sizes in the region, so that proper coordination of recreational opportunities can be developed consistent with public demand. Data on location and accessibility of the area in relation to population provide a basis for estimating probable degree and character of use. Preliminary land designation by Bureau of Outdoor Recreation class (I to VI) at this point is helpful to indicate the interrelation of uses and activities. Definition of land ownership is also essential; this is directly related to costs and acquisition of necessary acreage suited to the anticipated program of development and use. In the case of areas on which certain modifications to enhance recreational use is permissible, the adaptability of the areas to planned modifications should be noted.

A statement on lands to be acquired, their costs, and conditions of purchase should be presented and also an estimate of costs of development and maintenance relative to probable recreational use.

In final form the master plan may be presented as a single complete unit, or as several separate but coordinated parts. Regardless of the final format, it includes a variety of necessary maps, charts, diagrams, and drawings developed in varying detail, augmented by explanatory text and complete specifications.

The complexity of the master plan depends on the size and type of area involved. Small areas, especially those related to a single type of activity (swimming, physically active sports), can usually be planned as single units. Larger, more complex areas involving numerous types of recreational interests, activities, and facilities (national parks, national recreation areas) must necessarily be broken down into coordinated units in order to include required detail. The complete recreational master plan includes:

1. An investigative or administrative statement. This statement, one of the more important parts of the plan, sets forth all necessary facts supporting the functions of the proposed area. It includes and may expand the predevelopment inventory developed through in-depth studies of basic features of recreational interest, relation to other recreational areas in the region, location and accessibility of the area in relation to population and travel facilities, land ownership, adaptability of modification, and costs of development and maintenance. It also relates probable use to sources of attendance, differences in character of probable users, probable future trends in recreational interests and activities, and possible land-use problems. Location, and space requirements of planned facilities (roads, trails, accommodations) are noted, together with special considerations relevant to planned physical development (soil stability, water supply, waste and sewage disposal, public utilities) and control of visitor use and activities (visitor circulation within the area, enforcement of rules, regulations, and laws).

2. Maps of varied types relevant to the investigative statement. These include (1) regional outline maps illustrating relation of various recreational areas in the

region, population concentrations, and major transportation facilities (roads, airports, docks, and similar pertinent data); (2) topographic or aerial map of the area showing proposed boundaries and relief, location of streams, lakes, and similar details important in use, development, and protection of the area; (3) plat map indicating landownership together with dates of transfer, purchase, or other modifications in land control (easements, etc.); (4) soil and vegetation maps; (5) topographic maps of planned development, including roads, trails, centers of public concentration, administrative facilities, public utilities, and facilities for protection.

Except for regional outline maps, it is advisable that these be prepared on the same scale for easy correlation. A good plan is to use the topographic map as a base and to prepare the others on plastic overlays. For large areas, general maps are supplemented by more detailed maps, on a larger scale, of principal sections of the area which involve most if not all of the foregoing considerations.

3. Site plans, prepared in accordance with the predetermined purpose to be served (transportation, visitor accommodations and services, administration, protection) complete the recreational plan. These include detailed working drawings of larger scale (e.g., 1 in to 20 ft) together with complete specifications.

Site plans show detailed layout, siting of specific facilities (e.g., roads, tables, waterlines, latrines, trails, etc.). They should also be useful for actual construction of facilities with items located on the ground. Cost data should be furnished and alterations necessary to site development should be noted.

In certain instances (independent campgrounds or other areas which serve some single type of recreational activity) sites may be considered as distinct recreational areas and planned as independent units. Such plans, however, are improved to the extent they are related to other nearby units or a larger comprehensive plan.

Summary

Wild lands in great variety are required for various types of recreational interests and activities, as well as for nonrecreational uses. Not all such uses are compatible with one another, or with particular types of land. Planning seeks to correlate various uses on the same or separate units of both public and private lands to which they are best adapted in order to maximize net benefit to society on a sustained basis.

Land planning for recreation and other public needs is a complex operation; it is not a one-man project and planners are only advisors. It involves expertise in a wide variety of fields including basic scientific knowledge of areas considered; socioeconomic factors related to the nature, degree, and variations of public use; legal and political considerations concerning land ownership patterns and philosophy of use; and budgetary limitations of the planning process.

In addition to determination of supply of lands and opportunities and data on current and proposed visitations, it is helpful to make economic analyses of proposed recreation alternatives and their impact on other resource uses. As planning develops, involvement of planners and broad groups of concerned people, though complicated, is a positive step toward plan acceptance and implementation. Broad comprehensive planning on a national, regional, state, or local level generates data for more detailed planning of individual areas, including that for specific sites within particular areas. Development of master plans for each individual area serves as a basic guide in management, aimed at perpetuation of recreational and other values, and proper coordination with the purposes of other lands serving different needs. Bureau of Outdoor Recreation land classes may be used to designate lands within the planning unit or to show interrelationships.

The master plan may be developed as a single unit or, for larger, more complex areas, as several coordinated parts. Its development is preceded by an examination of broad recreational and other needs in the vicinity, a complete inventory of recreational values of the area, and determination of boundaries and adequate means of control of lands within boundaries. In final form the plan includes all relevant information concerning the function, nature, and degree of use of the area, including maps, charts, statistical data, detailed specifications of necessary physical developments, budgetary outlines, and supporting explanatory text.

The planning process has been explained here in a series of steps. They are not always followed in this order. Planning means restricting some uses and allowing others. To the extent that all concerned (planners and plannees) are involved in the process, planning should result in optimum land use and perhaps maintenance of environmental integrity. However, perfect planning is seldom done; the result is damage to people and environments. Good planning provides for flexibility with recurring evaluation and change. Management stems from and is related to planning.

Selected References

1. Alden, Howard R., and Ralph S. Sampson: "So You're Planning an Outdoor Recreation Business," University of Idaho, College of Agriculture, Idaho Agricultural Extension Service Bulletin No. 493, Moscow, February, 1968.

2. Amidon, Elliott, and E. M. Gould, Jr.: "The Possible Impact of Recreation Development on Timber Production in Three California National Forests," U.S. Forest Service, Pacific Southwest Forest and Range Experiment Station Technical Paper 68, Berkeley, 1962.

3. Burch, Wm. R., Jr.: Wilderness—the Life Cycle and Forest Recreation Choice, *Journal of Forestry*, vol. 69, no. 9, September, 1966.

4. Burch, Wm. R., Jr., and W. D. Wenger, Jr.: "The Social Characteristics of Participants in Three Styles of Family Camping," U.S. Forest Service, Pacific Northwest Forest and Range Experiment Station, Research Paper PNW-48, Portland, Oreg., 1967.

5. Coffman, John D.: How Much and What Kind of Forest Land Should Be Devoted Exclusively to Recreation and Aesthetics? *Journal of Forestry*, vol. 35, no. 2, February, 1937.

6. Doell, Charles E.: "Elements of Park and Recreation Administration," Burgess, Minneapolis, Minn., 1963.

7. Frank, Bernard: When Can Forest Recreation Be Considered as Exclusive or Dominant? *Journal of Forestry*, vol. 50, no. 4, April, 1952.

8. Gilligan, James P.: The Contradiction of Wilderness Preservation in a Democracy, *Proceedings of the Society of American Foresters Annual Meeting*, Milwaukee, Wis., October 24-27, 1954, Washington, 1955.

9. Green, Arnold: "Recreation, Leisure, and Politics," McGraw-Hill, New York, 1964.

10. Harris, F. B.: The Sanctity of Open Spaces, *Living Wilderness*, vol. 22, no. 60, Spring, 1957.

11. Hart, William J.: "A Systems Approach to Park Planning," IUCN, Morges, 1966.

12. Hawkes, A. L.: Coastal Wetlands—Problems and Opportunities, *Thirty-first North American Wildlife and Natural Resources Conference*, Pittsburgh, Pa., 1966.

13. Hendee, John C., Wm. R. Catton, Jr., L. D. Marlow, and C. Frank Brockman: "Wilderness Users in the Pacific Northwest—Their Characteristics, Values and Management Preferences," U.S. Forest Service, Pacific Northwest Forest and Range Experiment Station, Research Paper PNW-48, Portland, Oreg., 1967.

14. James, George A.: "Recreation Use Estimation of Forest Service Lands in the United States," U.S. Forest Service, Southeast Forest Experiment Station, Research Note SE-79, Asheville, N.C., 1967.

15. Jackson, Henry M.: An Appeal for a Law of Environmental Rights, *Seattle Times*, May 25, 1969.

16. Leopold, Aldo: Wilderness Values, *1941 Yearbook, Park and Recreation Progress*, U.S. National Park Service, Washington, 1941.

17. Lucas, Robert C.: "The Recreational Capacity of the Quetico-Superior Area," U.S. Forest Service, Lake States Forest Experiment Station, Research Paper LS-15, St. Paul, Minn., September, 1964.

18. Marshall, Robert: The Problem of Wilderness, *Scientific Monthly*, vol. 30, no. 2, February, 1930.

19. Murie, Olas J.: Wild Country as a National Asset, *Living Wilderness*, vol. 18, no. 45, Summer, 1953.

20. Outdoor Recreation Resources Review Commission: "Public Outdoor Recreation Areas—Acreage, Use, Potential," ORRRC Study Report No. 1, U.S. Government Printing Office, Washington, 1962.

21. Outdoor Recreation Resources Review Commission: "Wilderness and Recreation—A Report of Resources, Values, and Problems," ORRRC Study Report No. 3, U.S. Government Printing Office, Washington, 1962.

22. Outdoor Recreation Resources Review Commission: "Shoreline Recreation Resources of the United States," ORRRC Study Report No. 4, U.S. Government Printing Office, Washington, 1962.

23. Outdoor Recreation Resources Review Commission: "The Quality of Outdoor Recreation: As Evinced by User Satisfaction," ORRRC Study Report No. 5, U.S. Government Printing Office, Washington, 1962.

24. Outdoor Recreation Resources Review Commission: "Hunting in the United States—Its Present and Future Role," ORRRC Study Report No. 6, U.S. Government Printing Office, Washington, 1962.

25. Outdoor Recreation Resources Review Commission: "Sport Fishing—Today and Tomorrow," ORRRC Study Report No. 7, U.S. Government Printing Office, Washington, 1962.

26. Outdoor Recreation Resources Review Commission: "Water and Recreation—Values and Opportunities," ORRRC Study Report No. 10, U.S. Government Printing Office, Washington, 1962.

27. Outdoor Recreation Resources Review Commission: "Private Outdoor Recreation Facilities," ORRRC Study Report No. 11, U.S. Government Printing Office, Washington, 1962.

28. Outdoor Recreation Resources Review Commission: "Multiple Use of Land and Water Areas," ORRRC Study Report No. 17, U.S. Government Printing Office, Washington, 1962.

29. Outdoor Recreation Resources Review Commission: "Participants in Outdoor Recreation: Factors Affecting Demand among American Adults," ORRRC Study Report No. 20, U.S. Government Printing Office, Washington, 1962.

30. Outdoor Recreation Resources Review Commission: "Trends in American Living and Outdoor Recreation," ORRRC Study Report No. 22, U.S. Government Printing Office, Washington, 1962.

31. Outdoor Recreation Resources Review Commission: "Prospective Demand for Outdoor Recreation," ORRRC Study Report No. 26, U.S. Government Printing Office, Washington, 1962.

32. President's Council on Recreation and Natural Beauty: "From Sea to Shining Sea," U.S. Government Printing Office, Washington, 1968.

33. Recreation Advisory Council: "A National Program of Roads and Parkways," RAC Circular No. 4, U.S. Government Printing Office, Washington, 1964.

34. Stevens, M. E.: Soil Surveys as Applied to Recreation Site Planning," *Journal of Forestry*, vol. 64, no. 5, May, 1966.

35. Smith, F. E.: "Politics and Conservation," Pantheon, New York, 1966.

36. U.S. Department of Agriculture and U.S. Department of the Interior: "Wild Rivers," Washington, 1965.

37. U.S. Department of the Interior: "Quest for Quality," U.S. Government Printing Office, Washington, 1965.

38. U.S. Department of the Interior: "The Race for Inner Space," U.S. Government Printing Office, Washington, 1964.

39. U.S. Department of the Interior, Bureau of Outdoor Recreation: "Federal Focal Point in Outdoor Recreation," U.S. Government Printing Office, Washington, 1966.

40. U.S. Department of the Interior, Bureau of Outdoor Recreation: "Outdoor Recreation Trends," U.S. Government Printing Office, Washington, 1967.

41. U.S. Department of the Interior, Bureau of Outdoor Recreation: "Recreation Land Price Escalation," U.S. Government Printing Office, Washington, 1967.

42. U.S. Department of the Interior, National Park Service: "Parks for America," U.S. Government Printing Office, Washington, 1964.

43. Wagar, J. V. K.: Some Major Principles of Recreational Land Use Planning, *Journal of Forestry*, vol. 49, no. 6, June, 1951.

44. Woodbury, Coleman: Land Economics Research for Urban and Regional Planning, in *Land Economics Research; Resources for the Future*, Washington, 1962.

45. Zahnizer, Howard: The Need for Wilderness Areas, *Living Wilderness*, vol. 21, no. 59, Winter-Spring, 1956-57.

chapter fifteen

RECREATIONAL LAND MANAGEMENT

There is often much confusion as to the meaning of the words "management" and "administration." Management is frequently thought of as the carrying out of specific projects or functions in accordance with a definite plan or objective. Administration, on the other hand, concerns the organization of management tasks, supervision, direction, and control of personnel in management jobs. Thus management and administration overlap. For purposes of this book the term management will be used to include both administrative and managerial activities. Management also involves managerial activity, functional organization (staffing, direction, control, organizing), and operational processes [22].

The primary objectives of the management of wild lands for recreation are the provision of maximum variety of most rewarding recreational opportunities for the greatest number of people at the lowest possible cost and, at the same time, the perpetuation of recreational land values for the future. Attainment of these management objectives involves a variety of activities ranging from routine maintenance to research. They can be most effectively carried out through provisions set forth in a concise but comprehensive master plan developed for each recreational area.

At this point the reader is referred to the framework of the book in Chapter 1. We are now discussing management with an overlap to development as a part of the large management job. Also the framework for recreation planning and management introduced in Chapter 12 concerns differences in management approaches by agencies and landowners according to ORRRC-BOR recreation land class or zones. Here we introduce the framework again (Figure 15-1), changing it to class V, primitive area, example under National Park Service management. Note the limitations in management techniques under primitive

Figure 15-1
Framework for recreation management

Management responsibilty	ORRRC-BOR classes (zoning)	Owner-agency land categories	Character-istics and uses	Management tools and techniques[a]
State State forests State parks Fish and Game etc.	I. High-density recreation areas II. General out-door rec-creational areas III. Natural envi-ronment areas			
Federal U.S. BLM U.S. Forest Service National Park Service Fish and Wildlife Service	IV. Unique natural areas V. Primitive areas VI. Historic and cultural sites	Overlap to class IV, VI Wilderness threshhold Wilderness areas, back-country Overlap to developed zones (I, II), adjoining ownerships Natural envi-ronment area (III)	Larch and Douglas fir to Spruce, Subalpine fir forests; streams; lakes; hik-ing; fishing; camping; nature study	(Development) trail mainte-nance (Environmental manipulation) Fire control **(Rules, public** relations) Visitor contact and patrol Wilderness shelter-camp; maintenance (Interpretation) Naturalist hikes (Research)

Possible group pressure at these points

[a]Tools of recreation management are indicated by parentheses.

area classification as compared to class III (Figure 12-1). Areas classified wilder-ness under the Wilderness Act of 1964 usually would have more use and management restrictions than nonclassified areas. Also techniques and uses will vary with agency and owner policies. As various management tools are discussed in this chapter, consider possible differences in application under various owners or agencies and with different land classes.

"Tools" of Recreational Management

Various methods, and combinations of methods of controlling the nature and degree of recreational use, as well as activities of users, are necessary to the perpetuation of outdoor recreational values of different types of lands. The methods involve:

1. Zoning and related controls, of both land and user groups
2. Facility development—type, location, and design
3. Environmental manipulation
4. Rules and regulations
5. Public relations
6. Interpretation
7. Research

Zoning and Related Controls of Both Land and User Groups

The recreational land classification adopted by the Bureau of Outdoor Recreation (BOR) can be usefully applied to both local and regional control problems. Zoning of specific recreational areas, especially large ones for particular types of outdoor interests and activities, is an accepted management technique. Proper dispersal of acceptable uses on different types of recreational lands is important for protecting recreational values. At the same time, use of the BOR class V (primitive area) designation, for example, is limited as to resource uses. This class defines standards of access and type of use.

Varied environmental characteristics of an area (soils, plant and animal life, scenic interests and natural beauty, unique features) are affected in different ways by ecological laws and other natural changes. Different parts of recreational areas have varying degrees of durability against the impact of different uses. Further, recreational interests and activities themselves have varying degrees of compatibility. Examples of groups of users with conflicting recreational interests, objectives, and needs are campers and picnickers; campers with different types of camping equipment (tents versus trailers); skiers of varying degrees of proficiency; water skiers and fishermen; hunters and those who simply observe wildlife; hikers, horsemen, and users of motorized trail equipment. Zoning, if accomplished with due consideration of all factors involved, enhances the enjoyment and safe use of wild-land recreational areas and the perpetuation of values basic to such use and enjoyment [65,83].

Some important means of controlling recreational lands and user groups are boundary definition; consolidation of management objectives through ownership, easements, leases, or land exchange; and fees or rationing of patronage [1,7,32,47,48,55,64]. Clearly defined boundaries are vital; where possible, these should follow recognizable topographical features (ridge crests, streams). In addition, all lands within boundaries should be subject to unified control and comparable management policies; otherwise troublesome complications are inevitable. Outright ownership is most desirable. However, this is not always possible; high costs and various other factors may prohibit purchase of necessary areas. Problems of ownership have been solved through negotiation of easements, particularly with respect to access, leases, and, in certain cases, exchange of lands of equal value.

Fees charged for use of recreational areas and facilities have occasionally been suggested as a means of controlling use. However, their primary function is to provide a portion of financial support for recreation. On that basis they can be justified, even on public lands supported by taxes collected from the population at large. Since tax revenue pays only a portion of the cost of recreational management, it is not illogical that those who actually utilize specific recreational areas and their facilities should assume a larger portion of the cost by paying additional charges. But when such charges, established in accordance with desired use of recreational lands, are used as a means of controlling numbers of users, the ultimate effect of control is negative rather than positive. For example, doubling the entrance fee of a particular area to reduce the number of visitors may, in truth, accomplish that purpose. Those who can afford the higher cost in time as well as in money, are not deterred from making use of the area, but use by less affluent visitors, who may have greater need for benefits of an outdoor recreation experience, may be severely limited. Affluence is not necessarily a guarantee that the user is qualified to derive maximum benefits from a recreational experience.

Rationing, if conducted on a "first come first served" basis, is a less discriminating means of use control. The use of campgrounds within many recreational areas is already subject to varied means of rationing. The number of days of consecutive occupancy may be strictly limited, or the number of clearly defined individually developed sites may be restricted to the maximum carrying capacity of the environment. After maximum periods of consecutive use, or when all sites are occupied, visitors must seek accommodations elsewhere. Increasing use of recreational lands may force further extension of such restrictions by requiring advance reservation, as in the case of hotel accommodations.

Most positively, restriction in degree of use may be accomplished by limiting facilities and services to the ones most appropriate to the basic purpose of an area and character of its environment. Extraneous developments are omitted or, if in the public interest, are provided on nearby lands better able to accommodate them.

Restriction will vary, of course, with the type of area. Using the BOR classification for illustration, there would be less restriction in class I high-density recreation areas devoted primarily to recreation activities than in class V primitive areas—depending upon agency or owner policies.

In class V areas designated under the Wilderness Act of 1964, though there are variations between say the U.S. Forest Service and the National Park Service, uses are simpler and related to natural conditions. Since no motorized vehicles (except motor boats and canoes in part of the Boundary Waters Canoe Area (BWCA), Minnesota) or roads are allowed, visitors must use horses, paddle canoe, or walk to enter. There are also limitations in types of material they can carry into wilderness (e.g., no cans or bottles are allowed in the BWCA). Also in many areas permits are required for wilderness campfires or travel.

Such restrictions limit area use and define standards for development. Thus improvements may include trails; simple campsites with latrine, table, stove and tent space; outfitter camp and pasture sites; signs, simple shelters and administrative structures required for area maintenance. There are some problems as to the amount of maintenance and related structures needed for trail and campsite upkeep, visitor contact, fire control, area administration, and research. The trend is toward minimal facilities wherever possible, though policy varies with the agency. At the same time there are philosophical questions about the limitations in wilderness participation by some groups of society and the degree of visitor control with increasing use.

To maintain diversity of opportunity for many interests, class III natural environment area lands, which are usually less restrictive in forms of access and development, provide for uses in between wilderness and more highly developed class I and II areas. Here visitors may pursue natural setting activities without the limitations of designated wilderness, though there may be other uses like timber harvest or grazing and perhaps more people. Again, within designated national or state parks, activities are usually more restricted than on national or state forests.

Facility Development—Type, Location, and Design

The nature and degree of physical development of an area are a strong indication of the basic recreational purpose recognized by its management [37,43,62,65]. For instance, development of a number of national parks reflects the concept of an "outdoor playground" or "resort," rather than an area having unique recreational qualities. Under these circumstances, it is not surprising that the hordes of people attracted to such areas largely fail to understand the distinctive values of national parks as contrasted to other types of recreational areas with quite different recreational purposes. Psychologically, the type, design, and location of facilities reflect interests and values of an area favored by management; these, in turn, develop public attitude toward an area and influence the character and degree of use. Such use may or may not be in accord with environment and related values or in the best long-term public interest. Thus, it is important that basic values of an area, whether they involve wilderness or other unique qualities or features suited to varying degrees of development, be properly related to primary values and environmental conditions. If they are, management difficulties resulting from inappropriate public attitude and use can often be minimized. It may be, as suggested in the discussion of bureau evaluation in Chapter 6, that over time bureau leaders have changed management emphasis toward new goals. Thus naturalistic preservation goals embraced by founding director Mather for the national parks, though still stated in publications, in fact may be followed only to a limited degree in response to pressures for extensive development.

Further, where environmental conditions typical of different parts of a recreational area are suited to different types and intensity of use, the distribution of development serves to channel various uses into most appropriate portions of the area. More vulnerable environments receive maximum protection through proper dispersal of impact of use. Use of BOR land classes in the planning stage can set priorities and limitations on development.

However, many recreational land managers consider dispersal of use merely as dispersal of problems, as a workable method in the past when land for recreation was plentiful and the number of users was relatively limited. They now lean more strongly toward concentration on carefully selected sites as a more likely method of preserving recreational qualities of wild land. At any rate, the nature of development may either confine impact of use to limited sections of an area or control user patterns of movement. For instance, in high-use areas, properly located hard-surface trails protect adjacent, attractive wild-flower meadows; visitors in "city" footgear find it unnecessary to wander indiscriminately in avoiding mud, water, excessive dust, and related unpleasant conditions. Similarly, pleasure driving in scenic areas is favored by properly located one-way roads free from dangers and distractions of oncoming vehicles.

Development need not be destructive to recreational interests of wild lands. If properly related to the basic purpose of an area and the nature of environment, development may favor perpetuation of an area's features of interest with minimum restriction on public use.

Many facilities and services are necessary to the development and proper public use of different types of recreational lands. Included are roads and trails, signs, campgrounds and picnic areas, commercial overnight accommodations and related requirements, organized camps, provision for such activities as water and winter sports, and varied structures required for administration and maintenance. These facilities and services are variously integrated with such basic needs as water supply, sanitary facilities, sewage and waste disposal, and enforcement of laws and rules and regulations; these essentials are particularly relevant to the protection of public health, safety, and property.

Some basic considerations concerning principal facilities and services of recreational areas follow. These are intended merely as guides in such matters; limited space does not permit presentation of details, which are available in selected references at the end of the chapter.

Roads and Trails.   Although roads in recreational areas should conform to sound engineering principles, they should be so located, designed, and constructed as to avoid extensive modification of scenic beauty or damage to natural features of interest. The same principle applies to trail development.

Extensive cuts and fills should be avoided if possible, especially if they result in scars visible from a distance. If scars are unavoidable, they should be rehabilitated by suitable plantings of native trees and shrubs. The road surface, bridges and culverts, walls and guard rails, and similar features should blend with natural surroundings so as to be unobtrusive. Roads and trails in recreational areas are a means to an end, rather than an end in themselves. Their primary function is to facilitate proper mobility, circulation, and distribution of visitors, and to bring visitors in contact with representative attractions.

Roads, and to a lesser degree, trails, are no longer considered the sole means of visitor access to points of interests within recreational areas. Highway construction and maintenance are costly. Available roads invariably attract crowds which often seriously damage or modify the environment. Crowded conditions typical of many recreation areas, together with anticipated future use, have prompted studies and experiments which, hopefully, will verify expected advantages of other means of access. Overhead lifts and tramways, as well as public vehicles rather than private cars, in areas of high quality are receiving careful consideration. In addition, surfacing of heavily used trails is generally accepted; the more pleasant walking surface encourages visitors to remain on established routes, minimizing indiscriminate wandering and resultant damage.

Signs.   Public use of recreational areas necessitates a variety of signs. These serve to direct public movements, designate features and facilities, identify hazards, caution against improper actions or activities, define rules, and regulations, or point out particular attractions [9,12,69].

In large measure signs indicate the motif of recreational areas. Proper placement, scale, design, materials, nature and clarity of text, size and relation of letters, and length and spacing of lines are important features of their serviceability; decisions on these factors come from careful consideration of the purpose to be served. The location of signs should be related to the average sight distance for various rates of travel, varying from a few feet for stationary viewing or for foot or horse travel to approximately 300 feet for fast motor traffic on main highways [9]. Scale, design, and materials used should be in accord with the character of the region, cost of maintenance, and cost of occasional replacement. Except in special cases text should be positive; emphasis should be placed upon desirable actions rather than prohibitions. Long lines and all capital letters should be avoided. The size of letters and the nature and extent of the text depend on the purpose. A few words in large, readily visible letters serve directional or cautionary needs; regulatory or informational signs require more extensive text. In any event, brevity, consistent with clarity and completeness, is paramount. Unnecessarily wordy signs are ineffective. The possibility of vandalism should also receive careful attention.

Campgrounds and Picnic Areas.   The location and development of campgrounds should conform to their primary purpose [17,23,77,79]. Their clientele may consist of motorists, horsemen, canoeists, or hikers. A variety of types of campgrounds provide for differing visitor needs. The traveler stopping for one night has different needs from the long-term camper. Simple campgrounds would be found on BOR class III lands, with primitive camps on class V, and the majority of developed campgrounds on class I and II lands. Some campgrounds serve as centers of operation from which attractions of a given region may be conveniently explored within a specified time. Others serve to accommodate overflow crowds during peak-use periods or to satisfy transient visitors en route to more distant objectives. They may be accessible to large numbers of people and developed for accommodation of large crowds or located in more remote places to serve those few who desire greater privacy or more primitive conditions.

Campgrounds serve to control and guide public use of the outdoors, thus aiding overall preservation of the attractiveness of recreational lands without too great a limitation of visitor use and enjoyment. Limiting camping to specific, well-defined sections within an area, however, often results in large concentrations of people in a relatively small space. Unless campgrounds are properly planned, designed, and developed, such concentrations will bring about serious modification of campground features.

Destruction of vegetation is one of the first indications of campground overuse. In extreme cases herbaceous plants, even shrubs, may be literally tramped out. Excessive packing of soil, from trampling and unregulated use of motor vehicles, affects tree vitality through reduced soil aeration and increases the probability of damage by destructive insects and fungi. Camping refuse, such as piles of ashes from numerous fires and oil and grease from cars, adversely affects the health of shrubs and trees. The likelihood of deliberate vandalism is increased by added numbers of people.

Proper planning, design, and development of campgrounds are vital. Good planning not only preserves recreational features for use by future generations but also ensures everyone an equal opportunity for enjoyment, provides the maximum number of camp spaces consistent with the character of a given area, and fosters maximum efficiency and economy of operation as well as public safety. In campgrounds designed and developed for large numbers of people, portions of more heavily used camp spaces may be paved with some appropriate hard-surface material. Though this introduces an element of artificiality into the camping experience, it has the advantage of preventing adjacent environmental damage.

Proper selection of an area for a campground depends upon a number of important factors: the interests of the area, its topography (including hazards), proximity and nature of water supply, the type of soil and vegetation, climate, accessibility, expected public use and its seasonal or periodic variations, the requirements of users (including kind of vehicles or mode of transportation), and the proximity of the campground to public needs (food and automotive supplies) and points of interest.

The attractions of a campground (vegetation and forest cover, nearby lakes and streams and other topographic interests, scenic beauty or outlook, animal life) may be hazardous as well as charming. Consideration must be given to fire hazard, public health and safety, possible depredations of certain animals (American black bear), and, in some cases, the existence of poisonous plants or reptiles. Although level terrain simplifies campground layout and facilitates greater economy of space, selection of a level site is not obligatory; a reasonable degree of irregularity in topography often lends itself to development of a plan which provides maximum individual privacy. The nature and proximity of water supply are important to economy of operation and public health. The reaction of soils and types of vegetation to different degrees of use must be understood, for they react variously to similar conditions; further, some types of vegetation can be more easily replaced than others, if excessive use of an area necessitates rehabilitation. Climatic conditions (including elevation, temperature, prevailing winds, rainfall, and snow quantity) and accessibility to centers of population bear strongly upon the degree and fluctuation of campground use. Such factors, in addition to topography, are important in determining the location, size, and arrangement of camping facilities.

The mode of transportation generally used by campers must also be considered. For instance, use by trailers requires certain modifications in campground design, and campgrounds in remote areas for those traveling on foot or horseback or by canoe must obviously be laid out differently from those adjacent to primary highways. Increased use of pickup trucks with campers and growing demand for utility connections (water, power) further complicate the problems of campground planning.

It is vital to examine the relation of campgrounds to interesting features or activities in the immediate vicinity, as well as the nature of other developments in the area.

An adequate site plan is basic to proper development of campgrounds, particularly those of large size. This is necessary because roads, campsites, and related developments must be tailored to the terrain and associated characteristics. One effective form of layout embraces a system of one-way roads which should be 10 feet wide, with an additional 3-foot width to accommodate bordering gutters [12]. The resultant traffic pattern eliminates congestion and minimizes the damage to vegetation and trees that is almost inevitable in a two-way system. If two-way roads are necessary, a 16-foot width, with an additional 3 feet for shoulder is required [12]. Short individual parking spurs branching from the primary campground road give access to single campsites which, in addition to a parking spur for the car, provide a fixed tent site, table, and outdoor fireplace; approximately 750 square feet of space is required. Trailer camp units occupy about 1,200 square feet of space, though newer trailer types need less. Campgrounds combining trailer and tent sites in various arrangements are now in general use [9,12]. Maximum efficiency of such individual campsites is accomplished by definitely locating units in proper relation to each other, to existing vegetation, and to prevailing winds. Spacing between individual campsites will be dependent upon topography, vegetation, and the degree and character of expected use. Maximum privacy may be provided by placing each unit behind screens of vegetation; in areas where growth is sparse or lacking, an illusion of privacy can sometimes be accomplished by greater spacing between units. Each camp unit should be within 200 to 250 feet of safe drinking water, no more than 300 to 400 feet from sanitary facilities [9,12].

Protection of trees and other vegetation from damage through undesirable movement of automobiles can be effected by the erection of solid log or rock barriers at critical locations bordering roads and parking spurs. Trees and shrubs which unnecessarily interfere with proper visitor movement in campgrounds should be removed; otherwise the damage which will inevitably occur to such vegetation will set a pattern for more extensive, undesirable modification of the area [28].

Where space is not a major problem, large campground developments sometimes can be planned in distinct but harmonious sections that are separated by suitable buffer zones. This permits ready increase or decrease of available camp space according to fluctuations of seasonal travel. Also, under some conditions use of entire sections may be rotated annually in order to minimize the likelihood of damage by distributing public pressures over a wider camping area.

Since those who utilize the outdoors for picnicking are more transient than campers and have different objectives, it is advisable to provide separate areas whenever possible. This not only avoids temporary, periodic overcrowding of campgrounds, with resultant ills, but also eliminates possible friction between campers and picnickers.

In many cases, because of the larger number of picnickers, natural conditions are more likely to be sacrificed in planning adequate picnic areas than in developing campgrounds. Further, design and arrangement of picnic areas are different from those of campgrounds. The one-way road pattern still applies, and for the same reasons, but group rather than individual parking facilities are the rule. These should be located within easy walking distance of permanent tables, outdoor fireplaces, water, and sanitary facilities. The size of parking areas required for a number of cars is computed on the basis of 300 square feet per car; this allows a 10- by 20-foot space for static parking plus the necessary room for backing and turning [9]. Individual picnic spaces, suitable for small groups not exceeding eight individuals and including a table, camp stove, and trash can, require an area of 225 square feet [10].

Utility, economy of construction and maintenance, and a design which is in harmony with the region are guiding principles in the construction of tables, camp stoves, and other necessary items in campgrounds and picnic areas [2,3,4, 9,10,12,71,72,73].

Picnic or camp tables made of sawed or native wood products, different forms of masonry or metal, or various combinations of the two are suitable to **many types of terrain and conditions of use.** Dragging tables from place to place not only damages ground cover but materially increases the cost of table maintenance. This practice may be discouraged by using materials of considerable weight or, preferably, by anchoring tables in a fixed position. In campgrounds the fixed table is particularly useful, but less so in picnic areas. Wooden facilities should be adequately protected from the weather by proper preservatives. Where weather conditions make seasonal storage necessary, tables should be constructed so that they can be handled by two men or so that they can be dismantled and reassembled readily.

Camp stoves must be economical to construct and maintain and must be planned for ease and economy of operation. As in the case of tables, the type and design of camp stoves are largely a matter of local determination and should be based upon the nature and degree of their use, as well as the character of the region. Increasing use of gasoline stoves by campers does not necessarily eliminate the need for camp fireplaces. Not all people have gasoline equipment, and a fire is often a necessity as well as a pleasure in outdoor living. The same principle does not always apply to picnic areas, especially those of excessive use, where camp stoves are often replaced by community kitchens with wood stoves or metered gas ranges.

Pure water supplies, proper refuse disposal, and adequate sanitary facilities are vital to campgrounds and picnic areas [2,8,9,12,45,70,72,73,76]. An uncontaminated water source must be maintained by proper development and regular inspection, and the design of taps and drinking fountains should conform to modern sanitary requirements. A verticle pipe fitted with an upturned tap is the simplest form of drinking fountain. The basic feature of this device can be elaborated in a variety of ways to appear more attractive and to provide for greater utility and better sanitation. For instance, proper disposal of waste water eliminates muddy ground about a drinking fountain, a separate tap for filling pails can be added, and steps can be enclosed by masonry of suitable design and roofed for protection from the weather if necessary. The nature and degree of development depends upon local conditions. An estimate of water requirements per person per day for picnickers is 3.1 gallons; for campers, 5.5 gallons; for occupants of cabins, 18.4 gallons; and for those in organized camps, 15 gallons.

Adequate refuse and garbage disposal requires a sufficient number of properly placed containers, the development of public responsibility in the proper use of such facilities, and a system of frequent, regular servicing.

Sanitary facilities, whether they are of a modern flush type or not, should conform to regulatory laws governing such features. They should be adequately lighted, properly ventilated, and designed for easy regular cleaning and maintenance. Where there is danger of freezing in winter, adequate provision must be made for complete draining of all pipes and related equipment, unless there is sufficient use to justify heating of the buildings. When the foregoing conditions have been met, thought should be given to the development of an attractive exterior in harmony with the surroundings.

Facilities Necessary to Operators of Commercial Services on Public Lands.
Among the more difficult problems of recreational land management are those concerned with the location and design of buildings required by concessionaires. These apply to extensive developments (hotels, lodges, cabins, and associated facilities for overnight use) or minor needs (food stores, photo and souvenir shops, and refreshment stands). Harmonious relations between administrators and concessionaires enhance the quality of public service. To remain financially solvent, a concessionaire must attract sufficient patronage. It is to his advantage to seek and obtain a location for his enterprise which is alongside visitor traffic or which commands strategic viewpoints, and to conduct his operations in buildings which readily proclaim the nature of their specific service.

Although varied types of commercial services and facilities are necessary on many recreational areas, the best long-term interest of both the public and the concessionaire will be served if commercial activities do not usurp the primary values of such lands. While the financial solvency of those who provide necessary commercial services must be considered by the administration, concessionaires must also recognize that the existence of their enterprise depends upon the maintenance of the attractions of an area. To this end administrators of recreational lands should:

1. Permit establishment of only those commercial facilities that are in keeping with the character of a given area, and only if they are definitely necessary to its proper public use. For instance, overnight accommodations should not be provided if they merely offer a convenient stopping point in an extended itinerary, or if adequate services of this kind are available nearby.

2. Give proper consideration to all factors concerned in preparation of an operating contract. If a given commercial development is acceptable on an area, the administration and the operator should understand their particular responsibilities clearly.

3. If possible, locate, design, and construct necessary commercial facilities for lease to suitable operators. By assuming responsibility for capital investment and holding title to buildings, the administration can better control the location and design of commercial buildings, as well as the character and propriety of the operation which they are designed to serve.

Hotels and other commercial structures in recreational areas should be planned so as not to detract from natural features; their design should reflect the character of the region. Native materials are usually preferred, but their use must be carefully gauged for economy of construction, since much handwork entails higher costs than commercial materials. This factor is important, since commercial buildings must pay their way; their cost is reflected in charges for the public services which they provide. Proper design and skillful use of less expensive materials can often produce attractive results, since cost may rule against more expensive native materials.

Organized Camps. Camps designed for organized groups have an important place in outdoor recreation. Sponsored by a wide variety of organizations (churches, lodges, schools, youth groups, clubs, and even towns and cities), they serve diverse purposes, catering to specific age groups, boys or girls, families, the infirm, or the underprivileged.

The nature and the extent of facilities, as well as the camp layout, should be in accord with the purpose to be served. For instance, the facilities and layout of family camps differ from those of youth groups. Further, many camps must necessarily be used consecutively by several organizations; in such cases it is necessary that they be designed to satisfy diverse needs.

Proper layout of an organized camp is important for efficiency of operation, maximum enjoyment of the recreational interests of an area, and proper care of the health and physical well-being of its patrons [12]. Regimented arrangement of barracklike structures, promoting close confinement of many individuals on a small area, is impractical and undesirable; instead, large camp populations are broken up into small groups having similar interests or abilities. This is accomplished best by an arrangement consisting of a central headquarters in which all campers have a common interest and supplemented by a number of separate but closely coordinated sleeping units. Occupants of different sleeping units engage in activities as specific groups, frequently joining in overall camp programs.

The camp headquarters include the main lodge (including dining hall, kitchen and related facilities, camp store, office, and the like), the service road, visitor parking area, and the central washhouse and laundry. In large camps a separate administration building may be needed. The lodge kitchen should be so related to the service road that refuse and bulky supplies may be handled conveniently, unobtrusively, and with dispatch. Parking space for visitors should be so located that a pleasing approach to the camp is provided. Two or more units of sleeping accommodations, each with necessary sanitary facilities and with responsible supervision and leadership, augment camp headquarters; small specific units of from four to eight tents or cabins, each housing four individuals, are recommended as a means of reducing behavior problems, especially in youth camps. Each of these group facilities should be located so as to provide satisfactory privacy and yet be convenient to the central lodge and features of special interest. Finally, the infirmary should be suitably isolated from the main body of the camp.

The development and operation of camps for organized groups should give careful consideration to the following:

1. *Adequate, experienced leadership and supervision.* This is extremely important. Qualified leadership should be provided for the development of all values typical of the region wherein the camp is located, including various forms of physical activity (swimming, boating, hiking, riding) and cultural interests (nature study, handicrafts, dramatics). Poor, unqualified, or inadequate administrative supervisory personnel greatly reduce the value of individual camping experience.

2. *Character of buildings.* Building design should be attractive and, insofar as possible, should reflect the spirit of the region. Permanent structures should be designed for economy of operation and ease of maintenance. The main lodge, at least, should be well constructed, since it is a permanent building generally used for winter storage of equipment. The use of tents for sleeping quarters, although desirable in many ways, has the disadvantage of high maintenance cost. Small buildings and tent platforms should be provided with masonry foundations and should be sufficiently elevated to provide ready access to the area beneath them.

3. *Fire hazard.* Electrical wiring, flues, and other details of building construction should conform to accepted safety regulations. If it is necessary to use lanterns, they should be carefully controlled, and campfires should be permitted only in safe, designated places.

4. *Health and safety.* Clean, healthful surroundings, personal cleanliness, good food, and proper supervision of activities are basic to the health and safety of any group. Adequate sanitary facilities (one toilet for a maximum of ten individuals) and showers (one for eight campers) are required [12]. Hazards should be eliminated or guarded against. Experienced first-aid and medical attention, if not provided in camp, must be readily available.

Facilities for Swimming and Boating. An understanding of the hazards involved, proper supervision, and provision of adequate equipment for public health and safety are necessary wherever swimming, boating, and related water sports are made available on public lands.

Bathhouses must be designed in accordance with proper sanitary practice and for numerous public needs. Where beaches and pools are used by large numbers of people, temporary private dressing rooms are provided (at least for women), together with some suitable method of safeguarding wearing apparel and valuables, such as small individual lockers or containers to be checked at the bathhouse office.

Adequate shower facilities are also necessary, particularly when swimming is done in pools, for bathing with soap and water before entering the pool is mandatory. In all cases, sanitary facilities should be located so that their use may be encouraged before the swimmer enters the water.

The degree to which these basic requirements are expanded depends upon local conditions. Staff lockers and dressing rooms and first-aid provisions are desirable; in addition, drinking fountains, public telephones, wringers, hair dryers, a shop for the sale or rental of equipment, and refreshments may also be necessary.

Floats for swimming should be mobile so that they may be moved and securely anchored at various locations; they may also be removed from the water, if necessary, for repair or winter storage. Docks and piers should be designed in some sort of enclosed form in order to limit the activities of children or those of different abilities.

The construction of docks, for use by either swimmers of boating enthusiasts, should be accompanied by careful selection of proper materials. This applies particularly to the foundations of the docks, which should be treated with suitable preservatives to prolong life. Fluctuating water levels, ice, marine animals, and many other factors which affect the serviceability of docks should also be taken into account [46].

In areas subject to excessive changes in water level, such as tidal marine locations, it is convenient to have an attached float that connects to the dock platform by a ladder, which is readily available to those using boats. Where water levels do not fluctuate so severely, a hinged dock with the outer end floating on the surface will usually suffice. Broad shallow beaches call for use of a floating dock connected to the shore by a catwalk. Another system employs inclined railed runways into deep water; a wheeled cart operating on these rails transports the boat to the necessary depth by gravity. Boats are returned, after being maneuvered into position on the cart, by a cable from the boathouse.

Since canoes and racing shells must be removed from the water when not in use, suitable storage racks are necessary. Transportation of this equipment, to and from the water, whether for current use or for seasonal storage, is made easier by large overhead or barn-type boathouse doors.

Winter Sports Facilities. Skiing dominates the winter sports picture, but snowmobiling, skating, tobagganing, sledding, sleighing, and ski jumping are also important. Besides, many people simply enjoy the beauty of the winter landscape or watching various activities. Children especially like to play in the snow, often with various types of informal sliding equipment.

The basic requirements of a ski area are proper terrain, snow conditions, and climate. Ski areas usually fall in BOR class I or II areas, plus class III on slopes and long runs or trails. Snow must be of dependable depth and quality. In order to reduce accidents, topography should allow development of different sections for beginner, intermediate, and expert skiers; the ratio of steep to gentle slopes depends upon the number and proficiency of users. Specific zones, defined by topographical boundaries or patches of trees, separate groups of skiers of varying ability, "snow players," and others attracted to such areas. Patch cutting on heavily timbered terrain sometimes provides a suitable substitute for natural ski slopes, though the timber may not always be readily marketable.

Climate, in addition to affecting visitor enjoyment of ski areas, is responsible for numerous hazards. Storms and heavy fog create considerable danger. Extremes of temperature or prolonged periods of high wind often develop a dangerous surface crust on snow slopes. Wide variations in altitude have equally diverse snow conditions owing to differences in temperature and wind velocity at varying levels. The probability of avalanches or slides is increased by certain combinations of climate, snow conditions, and topography [63] .

Careful evaluation of proposed ski areas should be made by experienced skiers before development is undertaken. Further, before a final decision is reached, areas under consideration should be examined carefully during the summer as well as during winter. Often the presence of large stumps, boulders, and related ground debris makes it impossible to use an area safely except during the relatively limited period of greatest snow depth.

Accessibility of ski areas and types of transportation used in reaching them will largely determine the character and degree of their development. Access roads should be located and constructed so as to minimize the difficulty, hazard, and expense of snow removal. Highways which ascend a slope by a series of switchbacks, one above the other, are almost impossible to maintain, since snow cleared from the upper sections accumulates in recently cleared portions below. Cost of road maintenance due to winter sports developments may be materially reduced by locating ski areas along or near highways which are regularly maintained for general winter travel. Where ski areas are adjacent to busy main highways, access to parking areas and related facilities should be provided by spur roads. Parking on main highways interferes with normal traffic and increases traffic hazards.

The ski area itself will require parking areas, various buildings to serve public needs, some sort of uphill transportation for skiers, and adequate, experienced personnel. Since parking an individual car requires a space of 10 by 20 feet, an additional width of 20 feet on each side of the highway will provide for single rows of cars parked at right angles to the flow of traffic. Parking space for more than one row of cars in a specific area is not advisable, since this increases the difficulty of snow removal. Roads and parking areas, invariably bordered by precipitous snowbanks, should not be immediately adjacent to the center of activity, as they represent a serious hazard to unwary skiers.

Necessary buildings, although located conveniently to the ski area, should be sufficiently removed from ski runs to avoid any danger of collision between skiers and buildings or between skiers and groups of spectators gathered about them. Buildings should also be constructed with full regard to snow depths and prevailing winds in order to ensure accessibility and easy maintenance at all times. It is usually advisable to provide such basic needs as shelter, comfort stations, and a first-aid rooms under one roof in order to use one heating plant.

Overnight accommodations are necessary only if ski areas are located at a considerable distance from centers of population and if such facilities are not already available nearby.

Some form of uphill transportation, varying from a simple rope tow to some type of permanent lift, is necessary on most modern ski areas. Rope tows are sufficient on areas where there is not enough patronage to justify more extensive development or where it is necessary to preserve significant or scenic values in summer, as in national parks. Such less elaborate developments can be installed each fall and removed at the end of the winter season.

Personnel concerned with the public use of ski areas should be experienced skiers with a thorough, first-hand knowledge of the area and its hazards; they should also be able to perform first aid and rescue work.

Environmental Manipulation

Because of the nature and rapidly expanding use of wild land for recreation, some sort of environmental management is generally necessary. Environmental manipulation serves purposes both of preservation of the attractions and values of the area and of public health and safety. Its activities include:

1. Hazard removal, particularly in campgrounds and picnic areas, along roads and trails, and similar areas of public concentration [49,82]

2. Judicious plantings to ensure or to develop privacy [25,28,53,54]

3. Supplementary watering, fertilizing, and related cultural treatments to maintain or to enhance vigor and character of vegetation [10,21,23,29,51,52,75,77-80]

4. "Vista cutting," especially along roads and trails in heavily forested areas, to open up views or to improve scenic quality of strategic locations [44,56]

5. Maintaining animal populations in balance with environment, or stabilization of ecological succession at a particular stage

6. Control of destructive insects and fungi, especially if not indigenous to the area

Environmental management varies with agency or owner policy and also with BOR recreation land class. More intensive efforts would be applied in classes I and II, areas where recreation development and activity are of primary concern. In these classes vegetation plantings and cultural practices would be followed to maintain and enhance recreation sites. In class III (natural environment areas) emphasis would be on natural conditions, but various forms of forest harvest might be practiced on areas or in adjoining recreation sites on national or state forest lands. In some park areas hazard, dead and down trees would be salvaged on class III lands, as well as classes I and II. Vista cutting might also be applied in these areas.

On class IV (unique natural areas), class V (primitive areas) and class VI (historic and cultural sites), natural conditions usually would be altered as little as possible. This might mean not disturbing blow down, disease, or insect killed forests as they occur from natural rather than man-induced forces. Such practices, of course, present problems. It is often difficult to tell what is man-caused and what is natural or where conditions occur as a result of man's artificial interference. For example, where parks or wilderness areas are protected from all fires, there is evidence that potentially more hazardous fire conditions may develop than if periodic fires had occurred. This is the case in some of the *Sequoia gigantea* groves in Sequoia-King's Canyon National Park in California [20].

Currently many research studies are being conducted in various parks and wildernesses (e.g., Sequoia-King's Canyon National Park, California, and Boundary Waters Canoe Area, Minnesota) on the role of fire in natural ecosystems. Also some ameliorative practices are followed in restoring wilderness camp sites after vegetation and soil loss due to heavy wilderness visitation [15,25,26, 43,59,75].

The procedures in hazard removal, salvage operations, and vista cuttings are quite important to adequate maintenance of the natural environment, particularly when done by private contractors. Careful measurement and evaluation of the material to be removed are the first step. Area boundaries and removal material should be carefully marked, as should any access routes, loading zones, or temporary roads. Special operating conditions should be carefully enumerated in a legal contract to include limitations on rubber-tired loading equipment, size of tractors, preparation of site, weather limitations, cleanup, and planting. Performance bonding of operators is recommended as is very careful supervision of all operations from beginning to end.

Because this process is very demanding, some managers prefer to use special contractors with whom sales can be negotiated or to do the work with their own personnel. Maintenance of the quality of the forest or wild-land environment should be the main consideration rather than the return from sale of forest products. The application of the above procedures has been used successfully in the Pacific Northwest [35].

Rules and Regulations

Definite guidelines of use, among the first tools of recreational land management, are important to area administration. Regulatory restrictions, some of which may be irksome, will be increasingly necessary as greater numbers of people engage in outdoor recreation. Greater emphasis is placed upon a positive approach, the objective being to encourage public cooperation in the proper use of an area through greater understanding and appreciation of the values involved, and the development of individual responsibility in their perpetuation for the future. The effectiveness of rules and regulations is enhanced by use of other relevant methods such as interpretive programs, which guide user interest and activities into channels appropriate to specific recreational areas, or even parts of a particular area.

Deliberate vandalism is attributed to only a small percentage of users. In large measure, improper or destructive actions result from unfamiliarity with requirements in the use of an area and the lack of understanding of the ultimate effects of improper behavior on environmental interests. Dr. Catton, in Chapter 5, has discussed the concerns and recreation patterns of social groups and the need for understanding differences in visitor goals.

However, the phenomenal expansion in the use of recreational areas has, unfortunately, been accompanied by a rise in various acts of antisocial behavior [5,6,18,57]. Such acts range from nuisances to serious crimes. Rules and regulations should define the legitimate uses of an area and clearly indicate varied restrictions of such uses. Those guilty of infractions must be dealt with promptly and firmly, but fairly, in such manner as defined by law.

Of even greater importance is a well-organized interpretive program which, besides developing greater enjoyment of an area, also fosters public understanding of different hazards and how to recognize, anticipate, and cope with them [69]. They explain the vagaries of nature, identify poisonous plants, and give information on patterns of animal behavior dangerous to man. The interpretive program, coupled with public relations and general public education programs, bridges the gap in understanding between visitor and manager. Hopefully, the manager will also learn from the visitor-resource user as a part of these educational efforts.

Public Relations

The importance of proper, well-coordinated management policies that are understood and supported by the general public is apparent in the increasing need for all products and services of wild lands. Among the more troublesome results are problems induced by the rapid growth in recreational use of land, including protection of environmental features and beauty. As a result, attention has been focused upon all available types of land suited to varied, rapidly expanding, and increasingly diverse recreational interests and activities.

Various types of both private and public lands are involved. Many conflicts of interest have developed among vociferous and politically effective groups who champion numerous land-use philosophies. Many techniques of natural-resource extraction and use, acceptable when land was plentiful and use competition less severe, have become outmoded and require reevaluation and improvement.

The number of agencies concerned with recreation has greatly increased. Their responsibilities to recreation are not always completely clear; personnel trained for development of other objectives are often puzzled by unfamiliar requirements of recreational management. In some cases the language of legislative acts establishing and defining the purposes of certain areas is outmoded. Titles applied to some areas may be somewhat ambiguous; "wilderness area," "recreation area," and "wildlife refuge" are definitive, but the term "park" is subject to various interpretations, especially when applied to areas of unique quality (national parks). Both biological and economic principles upon which different types of land use are based are often misunderstood by the general public. Many recreational interests and activities, in addition to being incompatible with some other forms of land use, are incompatible with one another. The necessity to promote equable division and control of recreational land use must be more generally recognized, for we can no longer afford unrestricted access to and use of wild lands. Some people find it hard to accept the trend toward modern-type design of facilities which are planned for use by great numbers of people with minimum environmental damage.

Properly organized public relations programs assist in the solution of such land-management problems [11]. All forms of communications media are utilized. Proper signing of an area and distinctive uniforms of key personnel, psychologically related to the nature of recreational uses and values, are also useful. The objective of public relations efforts is to enlarge public support of logical land-management policies so that development and use of various recreational and other values of wild land may be properly related to one another and to the environment. However, they are effective only if based upon factual information presented in a manner both interesting and understandable to laymen, and if supported by appropriate management practices in the field. Also, there may be some danger of implied authoritarian control in the use of public relations methods.

Interpretation

Interpretative activities (visitor centers or museums, nature trails, guided field trips, campfire programs, publications) were initiated primarily to enhance public enjoyment of outdoor recreation through appreciation of the areas involved. It was soon apparent, however, that such activities were of equal importance in directing recreational land use into proper channels and in developing public responsibility in environmental protection. In brief, public interest in perpetuation of recreational values is increased by understanding and appreciation of the interests involved [3,60,69]. Interpretation is on-the-spot contact which stimulates the visitor to explore beyond the talk or visitor center. It is based on a well-organized, accurate, and appealing presentation—although it is not primarily entertainment. The successful interpreter likes people, is interested in their thoughts, and can project his ideas to them.

Specifically, if the archaeological importance of a remarkable cliff dwelling is understood and its value to mankind is recognized, one's approach to it, both physically and psychologically, will be more in keeping with the dignity which should characterize such treasures, and wear and damage will be minimized. Similarly, flora, fauna, and ecological interests will be less subject to modification by selfish removal of plants, disturbance of animals, or thoughtless meandering from developed trails. Moreover, the danger of fire or acts of vandalism which ravage the beauty of unique forests will be materially reduced. Even features of geological excellence, generally more resistant to damage, will be more likely to escape defacement if their importance is recognized. At some national parks (e.g., Rocky Mountain National Park), entering visitors stopping at the administration building may see a movie of the park, its attractions and means of access. This presentation serves as a guide to the visitor, highlighting important points, introducing rules preparing the user for his trip. It may have the effect of directing use, though not all visitors attend.

Interpretation as a management tool is not limited to areas of highly unique quality, such as national parks, where early developments took place [3]. Today interpretation is an accepted technique on many other types of recreational lands, including national forests, state parks and forests, county and municipal parks, and even some recreational areas on privately owned, commercial forest land. Visitor centers, museums, and displays are generally located on BOR class I, II, VI, or near class IV lands. On classes III and V lands simple trails with or without guides would be the case.

Interpretive Facilities and Services. Interpretive activities are designed primarily to enhance visitor enjoyment of outdoor recreational areas by developing public understanding of their varied interests [3,12,14,60,67,68]. A good interpretive program also contributes to the protection of recreational lands, since it develops an awareness of visitors' responsibilities in preserving a recreational heritage by fostering recognition of its values.

Interpretation may embrace such items as visitor centers or museums, roadside and trail-side exhibits, self-guiding nature trails, wild-flower gardens, informative lectures or campfire programs, field trips, libraries, and the publication of material pertinent to a given region for distribution and sale.

Visitor centers or museums are generally but one part of a broader interpretive program.[1] They are to a recreational area what a table of contents is to a book or a display window is to a department store; they inform and stimulate interest in an area. Well-planned exhibits in a strategically located and attractively designed building present, outline, and briefly explain the significance of an area's interests, thus encouraging people to go afield and observe such interests at first hand. Exhibits should not be so complete that the visitor becomes jaded or feels no need to explore further on his own. The features of an area are its primary interests; visitor centers or museums should encourage responsible public use and enjoyment of recreational areas through understanding. Consequently, the scope of the exhibit "story" should not go beyond the immediate area involved except where necessary for perspective or in the interest of reasonable completeness. Extraneous material should not be included; for

---

[1] The term "visitor center" is now more widely used in recreational areas than "museum," mainly because the general public often associates the latter term with old-fashioned and often unattractive, boring displays of conglomerate, poorly arranged subjects. However, modern museums utilize advanced techniques in arrangement, color, and materials which dramatize factual data and excite public curiosity.

instance, regardless of the interest or value under other conditions, a display of weapons of modern warfare would be inappropriate in an area of unique biological significance.

A successful visitor center or museum project in a recreational area is dependent upon the following:

1. The quality of the scientific foundation of the project or the character of the research program which develops such a foundation. Misrepresentation of an area's factual interests in an interpretive program cannot be condoned; for this reason the visitor center or museum, especially in more significant recreational areas, often serves as a center of research activities and contains adequate facilities necessary to such a program (library, laboratory, study collections).

2. An understanding of public psychology by those who plan and prepare the exhibits. Since the displays will be available to people of all ages, interests, and backgrounds, their effectiveness will depend greatly on how scientific fact is simplified and dramatized. Modern museum displays borrow considerably from good advertising technique, for their objectives are similar in spite of radically different "products." The objective of advertising displays is to "sell" some type of commercial product; that of museum displays is to arouse interest in and understanding of the significance of scenery and related attractions. Eye catching arrangements and judicious use of color have great value. Careful preparation of explanatory texts, often given too little attention, is very impor- tant; no matter how attractive an exhibit, it will not completely fulfill its purpose unless necessary labels are concise and couched in language understand- able to the layman.

3. The location of the building. Since visitor centers or museums are designed to foster public understanding of an area, they must be strategically located in relation to public activity.

4. The design and plan of the building. In addition to an attractive appearance, a visitor center or museum should have public display rooms arranged to foster proper visitor circulation. Adequate space for necessary staff activities must also be provided. It is extremely important that the design and plan of the building be adapted to the exhibit plan; reversal of that procedure will invariably result in lowered efficiency in the presentation of the story of an area.

Roadside and trailside exhibits are actually small-scale visitor centers or museum developments applied to detailed, on-the-spot interests. They vary from simple, attractive, informative signs to more elaborate semienclosed structures; the latter contain exhibit cases with interpretive displays concerning specific localized interests (fossil remains, a biological association of particular note, or a geological feature). Since, by comparison with museums, these developments are relatively inexpensive, they often shoulder the entire burden of interpretive programs in many types of recreational areas.

Self-guiding nature trails involve so little cost and effort and are so adaptable that they should be included in recreational areas wherever possible. A short trail that is readily accessible to centers of public concentration, offers typical views of the area, and provides opportunity for observation of special features of interest usually serves this purpose. Two systems of development prevail. In one system individual features of interest along the way (trees, flowers, and the like) are marked by small signs attached to movable stakes. In the other a small, attractive leaflet describes specific interests at points along the trail, marked by permanent, numbered posts. The descriptive leaflets are made available in a container located at the beginning of the nature trail; these may be purchased on the honor system (box for coin deposit is attached to container) and retained by visitors or returned to the container after they have served their purpose.

The latter system has many advantages. A minimum of maintenance is required. The leaflets are appropriate souvenirs. Such nature trails are always available during daylight, at the convenience of the visitor; thus, the number of people served is often greater than on officially conducted nature walks. In addition, visitors have greater privacy than is possible in large crowds usually typical of conducted walks. They can also proceed at their own pace, and if leaflets are carefully prepared, answers to questions may be obtained more readily than in the confusion normally typical of large groups. Further, personal investigation of points of interest is encouraged, and the information gained has maximum, more lasting value.

Many areas contain a wide variety of habitats, and consequently plants, not readily accessible to the public. To make these interests more readily available to visitors, wild-flower gardens are sometimes developed to simulate the natural setting of varied plant associations. Many plants, however, are not adapted to such treatment; this, together with the cost of development and maintenance, usually militates against wild-flower gardens as an interpretive facility.

Informal lectures or campfire programs on varied interests of recreational areas are often important features of interpretive programs. Such activities generally require campfire circles or outdoor amphitheaters of different type and design. These should be readily accessible but in a setting which will inspire the visitor and arouse interest in the topics discussed. Surroundings should be typical of the area and emphasize its principal interests. The site should be as free as possible from distractions which will destroy the mood of the program; forests, topographical features, water surfaces, and other characteristics of a natural setting have varied acoustical properties which must be taken into account. Since it is desirable to illustrate such programs, proper visibility to the audience is essential, and provision must be made for convenient use and safe storage of projection equipment. If large crowds are the rule, an amplifying system may be necessary. Seating arrangements and stage, usually informal, should blend into the surroundings. If parking space is necessary and programs are given during the evening, care should be taken that headlights from cars do not impair the quality of projection.

In certain instances programs may have to be given indoors. In such cases community buildings and related suitable structures, or even hotel lobbies, may be utilized.

Guided field trips may vary in duration from one hour to several days; they may involve a hike on foot or a trip by auto caravan, bus, boat, or horseback. The success of such ventures is largely dependent upon the qualifications and experience of the leader; his background in the scientific aspect of interests along the way, his understanding of people, and his technique of presenting various subjects to his group are vitally important. Each type of trip involves specific problems. Since the audience is a mobile one, a running commentary is out of the question. The leader should confine explanations to specific points, properly spaced along the way in accordance with the capabilities of the group or the location of special attractions. While the main purpose of such trips is interpretation, it is also necessary that the group be impressed with the importance of good outdoor manners. The leader should also understand the hazards of the route to be taken, see that his party has proper respect for safety precautions, and in the event of accidents, know how to cope with emergencies.

Libraries are of value to the general administrative staff. They function as a research tool for interpretive work, and they are a source of information to special visitors.

While most people who use and enjoy outdoor recreational areas have merely a casual interest in various detailed features, a small percentage have a much deeper perception. For these people, as well as for the administrative and interpretive staff, a well-chosen collection of books about the region is of great value. However, a general library is seldom necessary unless considerable numbers of people remain in an area for long periods.

Publication, distribution, and sale of literature dealing with the area may also be desirable, particularly where recreational lands have diverse interests. In addition to serving as acceptable souvenirs, such publications promote a broader understanding of a region and contribute to the visitor's continual interest after his return home. In some cases such activities may be handled directly by the administrative agency; in others by approved subsidiary organizations established specifically for such purposes.

Various natural history and museum associations which operate in many national parks and monuments are outstanding examples of such subsidiary organizations. In addition to selling more elaborate books obtained at the regular bookseller's discount from established publishers, these organizations also publish small, popular, inexpensive booklets on specific subjects (wild flowers, animal life, geology, history). These organizations are organized so that accumulated small profits derived from their operation accrue to the benefit of the local interpretive program rather than to the park in general or to any individual.

Research

Both basic and applied research are important "tools" in the solution of wild-land recreational management problems and the improvement of wild-land recreational services. However, except in certain instances, research is not generally the province of management personnel [13]. Research and management are distinct activities which appeal to people of quite different interests and qualifications. Further, the multitude of details to be dealt with by management personnel usually leave them no time for significant participation in various research tasks. Therefore research is generally conducted by staff personnel who are especially motivated, trained, and qualified for their duties. Specialized research personnel may be permanently or seasonally employed,[2] or they may be engaged on a cooperative or consulting basis through universities or similar institutions. The latter procedure is often the rule when specific, long-term projects are being considered, though cooperative ventures between regular research personnel and consultants sometimes give promise of best results. In some instances research proposals initiated by qualified graduate students or faculty can be modified to conform to needs of management so that purposes of both groups can be served.

Though their role in research is indirect, management personnel nevertheless have an important function in such activity. They are close to the practical grass roots of the problems and thus are in a singular position to aid in establishing the direction and emphasis of research efforts. Often they can assist in projects by carrying out certain assigned tasks, particularly when the results of a program depend upon regular, periodic recording of data by someone other than the project leader. Management personnel should also be cognizant of how the effectiveness of their operations can be improved by the results derived from scientifically oriented investigations. The validity of conclusions based upon experience can often be substantiated and strengthened by research results; or research may expose important factors which bear upon the solution of problems which might have been overlooked, ignored, or misinterpreted. In particular, it is important that management personnel be capable of evaluating research results and subsequently applying them to direct action in the field. And, in certain cases, suitably qualified management personnel may contribute to the research requirements of special wild-land recreational areas.

One way in which research and management might be coordinated was suggested by the Advisory Board on Wildlife Management (Leopold Committee)

---

[2] U.S. Forest Service research personnel connected with various forest and range experiment stations serve as examples.

in its report to the Secretary of the Interior ("Wildlife Management in the National Parks," 1963) [24].

Speaking about park management from the biological standpoint, the Committee suggested the following steps for national parks where the objective is maintenance or restoration of original biotic associations:

The first step in park management is historical research, to ascertain as accurately as possible what plants and animals and biotic associations existed originally in each locality. Much of this has been done already.

A second step should be ecological research on plant-animal relationships leading to formulation of a management hypothesis.

Next should come small scale experimentation to test the hypothesis in practice. Experimental plots can be situated out of sight of roads and visitor centers.

Lastly, application of tested management methods can be undertaken on critical areas.

By this process of study and pre-testing, mistakes can be minimized. Likewise, public groups vitally interested in park management can be shown the results of research and testing before general application, thereby eliminating possible misunderstanding and friction. [24].

Since 1965 the National Park Service has been working on implementation of the recommendations of the Leopold Report.

Summary

The objectives of administration and management of recreational lands are to provide opportunities for the greatest number of people at the lowest cost and, at the same time, the perpetuation of varied recreational interests and values. Control and manipulation of both the environment and its users are involved. Management tasks are difficult, often frustrating, and even disagreeable. Their successful accomplishment is favored when the best uses of various recreational lands are clearly defined, with both lands and uses properly correlated in a master plan. The management approaches will vary with BOR class of land and the policy objectives of the agencies or owner controlling the land.

A number of tools are useful in varied adminstrative and management tasks. These include zoning and related controls of land and activities, development, environmental manipulation and rehabilitation, rules and regulations, public relations, interpretation, and research. Such activities minimize the impact of use upon environment by channeling various pursuits onto lands best able to accommodate them. When public understanding is improved through education and interpretation, visitors may assume better responsibility for the care of recreational lands. Also perhaps managers may learn from visitors in a two-way education process.

We have used the medium of the Bureau of Outdoor Recreation (BOR) recreation land classes to explain some of the differences in agency-owner management policies and use of tools of management. This approach was also used in Chapter 14 on planning. It is, of course, but one approach, and certainly will change over time. However, if it serves to show the reader some of the complexity of planning and the modern management process and to raise some questions, its use is justified.

Selected References

1. Argow, Keith A., and John Fedkiw: Recreation User Fee Income—How Far Does It Go Toward Meeting Costs? *Journal of Forestry*, vol. 61, no. 10, October, 1963.
2. Babbitt, H. E.: "Sewage and Sewage Treatment," Wiley, New York, 1947.
3. Bryant, Harold C., and Wallace W. Atwood: "Research and Education in the National Parks," U.S. Government Printing Office, Washington, 1936.
4. Burch, William R., Jr.: Two Concepts for Guiding Recreation Management Decisions, *Journal of Forestry*, vol. 62, no. 10, October, 1964.
5. Campbell, Fred L., John C. Hendee, and Roger Clark: Law and Order in Public Parks, *Parks and Recreation*, vol. 3, no. 12, December, 1968.
6. Davis, C.: Legal Problems and Liability in Outdoor Recreation, *Park Maintenance*, vol. 19, no. 12, December, 1966.
7. Doell, Charles E.: "Elements of Park and Recreation Administration," Burgess, Minneapolis, Minn., 1963.
8. Douglass, Robert W.: "Forest Recreation," Pergamon, New York, 1969.
9. Forbes, Reginald D., and Arthur B. Meyer (eds.): "Forestry Handbook," edited for Society of American Foresters, Ronald, New York, 1955.
10. Frissell, S. S., and Donald P. Duncan: Campsite Preference and Deterioration in the Quetico-Superior Canoe Country, *Journal of Forestry*, vol. 63, no. 4, April, 1965.
11. Gilbert, Douglas L.: "Public Relations in Natural Resource Management," Burgess, Minneapolis, Minn., 1964.
12. Good, A. H.: "Park and Recreation Structures," (part I, Administration and Basic Service Facilities; part II, Recreational and Cultural Facilities; part III, Overnight and Organized Camp Facilities), U.S. National Park Service, Washington, 1938.
13. Gould, E. M.: Forest Managers and Recreation Research, *Proceedings*, Society of American Foresters Annual Meeting, Denver, Colo., September 27-30, 1964, Washington, 1965.
14. Heath, Edward I.: "A Plan for the Development of Nature Trails in the University of Maine Forest," Maine Agricultural Experiment Station, University of Maine, Miscellaneous Publication 663, Orono, Maine, December, 1964.
15. Heinselman, M. L.: Vegetation Management in Wilderness Areas and Primitive Parks, *Journal of Forestry*, vol. 63, no. 6, June, 1965.
16. Hendee, John C.: "Appreciative vs. Consumptive Uses of Wildlife Refuges: Studies of Who Gets What and Trends in Use," paper presented at the Thirty-fourth North American Wildlife and Natural Resources Conference, March 4, 1969, Washington.
17. Hendee, John C., and William R. Catton, Jr.: Wilderness Users—What do They Think? *American Forests*, vol. 74, no. 9, September 1968.

18. Hunkins, R. B.: Criminal Jurisdiction in the National Parks, *Land and Water Review*, vol. 2, no. 1, January, 1967.

19. James, G., and T. Ripley: "Instructions for Using Traffic Counters to Establish Recreation Visits and Use," U.S. Forest Service, Southeast Forest Experiment Station Paper SE-3, Asheville, N.C., 1963.

20. Kilgore, Bruce M.: Restoring Fire to the Sequoias, *National Parks and Conservation Magazine*, vol. 44, October, 1970.

21. Klukas, Richard W., and Donald P. Duncan: Vegetational Preferences Among Itasca Park Visitors, *Journal of Forestry*, vol. 65, no. 1, January, 1967.

22. Koontz, Harold (ed.): "Toward a Unified Theory of Management," McGraw-Hill, New York, 1964.

23. LaPage, Wilbur F.: "Some Observations on Campground Trampling and Ground Cover Response," U.S. Forest Service, Northeast Forest Experiment Station Research Paper NE-68, Upper Darby, Pa., 1967.

24. Leopold, A. Starker et al.: Wildlife Management in the National Parks, Report to the Secretary of the Interior, March, 1963.

25. Litton, R. B., and Robert H. Twiss: "The Forest Landscape—Some Elements of Visual Analysis," *Proceedings*, Society of American Foresters Annual Meeting, Seattle, Wash., Sept. 12-15, 1966, Washington, D.C., 1967.

26. Lucas, Robert C.: User Concepts of Wilderness and Their Implications for Resource Management, *Western Resource Papers, 1964*, New Horizons for Resources Research: Issues and Methodology, University of Colorado Press, Boulder, Colo., 1964.

27. Lutz, H. J.: Soil Conditions of Picnic Grounds in Public Forest Parks, *Journal of Forestry*, vol. 43, no. 2, February, 1945.

28. Meinecke, E. P.: "Camp Planning and Camp Reconstruction," U.S. Forest Service, California Region, San Francisco, n.d.

29. Meinecke, E. P.: "The Effect of Excessive Tourist Travel on the California Redwood Parks," California State Printing Office, Sacramento, Calif., 1929.

30. Meinecke, E. P.: "A Campground Policy," U.S. Forest Service, Intermountain Region, Ogden, Utah, 1932.

31. McCurdy, Dwight R., and Raymond M. Mischon: "A Look at the Private Campground User," U.S. Forest Service Central States Forest Experiment Station, Research Paper CS-18, 1965.

32. McCurdy, D. R., and H. E. Echelberger: "The Outdoor Recreation Lease in Illinois," Southern Illinois University, School of Agriculture, Publication 25, Carbondale, Ill., 1967.

33. McCurdy, D. R., and L. K. Johnson: "Recommended Policies for the Development and Management of State Park Systems," Southern Illinois University, School of Agriculture, Publication 26, Carbondale, Ill., 1967.

34. McIntyre, A. C.: "Wood Chips for the Land," Soil Conservation Leaflet, no. 323, U.S. Government Printing Office, Washington, 1959.

35. Merriam, L. C., Jr.: An Application of Recreational Forestry, *Journal of Forestry*, vol. 58, no. 10, October, 1960.

36. Merriam, L. C., Jr., and R. B. Ammons: "The Wilderness User in Three Montana Areas," University of Minnesota, St. Paul, Minn., 1967.

37. Nason, George: "Architecture and Its Relationship to the Design of Parks," *1940 Yearbook, Park and Recreation Progress*, U.S. National Park Service, Washington, 1940.

38. National Conference on State Parks and National Park Service: "Park Practice Programs," Washington, v.d.

39. National Conference on State Parks and National Park Service: "Park Practice Design," Washington, v.d.

40. National Conference on State Parks and National Park Service: "Park Practice Guideline," Washington, v.d.

41. National Conference on State Parks and National Park Service: "Park Practice Grist," Washington, v.d.

42. National Recreation and Park Association: "Outdoor Recreation Space Standards," New York, 1966.

43. Nature Conservancy: "Protecting Dedicated Areas From Encroachment," Information Bulletin, no. 27, Washington, May, 1958.

44. Neff, P.: Applied Silviculture in Managing Outdoor Recreation Sites, *Proceedings*, Society of American Foresters Annual Meeting, Detroit, Oct. 24-28, 1965, Washington, 1966.

45. Ort, Don R.: Recommended Campground Sanitation Requirements, Guidelines for Developing Land for Outdoor Recreational Use, Cooperative Extension Service, Purdue University, West Lafayette, Ind., 1963.

46. Outboard Boating Club of America and Socony Mobil Oil Company, Inc.: "Outboard Marinas," Chicago, Ill., n.d.

47. Outdoor Recreation Resources Review Commission: "Paying for Recreation Facilities," ORRRC Study Report 12, U.S. Government Printing Office, Washington, 1962.

48. Outdoor Recreation Resources Review Commission: "Land Acquisition for Outdoor Recreation—Analysis of Selected Legal Problems," ORRRC Study Report 16, U.S. Government Printing Office, Washington, 1962.

49. Paine, L. A.: "Accidents Caused by Hazardous Trees in California Recreation Sites," U.S. Forest Service, Pacific Southwest Forest and Range Experiment Station, Research Note PSW-133, Berkeley, Calif., 1966.

50. Recreation Advisory Council: "Policy Governing the Water Pollution and Public Health Aspects of Outdoor Recreation," RAC Circular No. 3, U.S. Government Printing Office, Washington, 1964.

51. Ripley, Thomas H.: "Recreation Impact on Southern Appalachian Campgrounds and Picnic Sites," U.S. Forest Service, Southeastern Forest Experiment Station, Paper 153, Asheville, N.C., November, 1962.

52. Ripley, Thomas H.: "Tree and Shrub Response to Recreation Use," U.S. Forest Service, Southeastern Forest Experiment Station, Research Note, no. 171, Asheville, N.C., 1962.

53. Ripley, Thomas H.: Rehabilitation of Forest Recreation Sites, *Proceedings*, Society of American Foresters Annual Meeting, Detroit, Oct. 24-28, Washington, 1966.

54. Roewekamp, F. W.: Landscaping Recreational Areas, *Parks and Recreation*, vol. 48, no. 12, December, 1965.

55. Rubini, F. F.: Revenue Facilities and Services by Lease, *Parks and Recreation*, vol. 2, no. 1, January, 1967, and vol. 2, no. 3, March, 1967.

56. Rutherford, Wm., Jr., and Elwood L. Shafer, Jr.: Selected Cuts Increased Natural Beauty in Two Adirondack Forest Stands, *Journal of Forestry*, vol. 67, no. 6, June, 1969.

57. Smith, Huntington: Tourists Who Act Like Pigs, *Saturday Evening Post*, vol. 225, no. 48, May 30, 1953.

58. Snyder, A. P.: Wilderness Management—A Growing Challenge, *Journal of Forestry*, vol. 64, no. 7, July, 1966.

59. Sumner, Lowell: Regulation of High Country Pack Stock Use, *Proceedings*, Region IV Park Naturalist's Conference, Yosemite National Park, Apr. 14-18, 1948, National Park Service, 1948 (mimeographed).

60. Tilden, Freeman: "Interpreting Our Heritage," University of North Carolina Press, Chapel Hill, N.C., 1957.

61. Tocher, Ross., J. A. Wagar, and John D. Hunt: Sound Management Prevents Worn Out Recreation Sites, *Parks and Recreation*, vol. 48, no. 3, March, 1965.

62. Twiss, Robert H.: Research on Forest Environment Design, *Proceedings*, Society of American Foresters Annual Meeting, Seattle, Wash., Sept. 12-15, 1966, Washington, 1967.

63. U.S. Department of Agriculture, Forest Service: "Avalanche Handbook," U.S. Government Printing Office, Washington, n.d.

64. U.S. Forest Service, California Region: "Collecting User Fees on National Forest Recreation Sites," San Francisco, Calif., 1963.

65. U.S. Forest Service: "The American Outdoors, Management for Beauty and Use," USFS Misc. Pub. 1000, U.S. Government Printing Office, Washington, 1965.

66. U.S. Department of Agriculture, Forest Service: "Sign Handbook," Forest Service Handbook Title 7161.4, Washington, 1966.

67. U.S. Department of the Interior, National Park Service: "Talks," In-service Training Series, Washington, 1953.

68. U.S. Department of the Interior, National Park Service: "Conducted Trips," In-service Training Series, Washington, 1954.

69. U.S. National Park Service: "Securing Protection and Conservation Objectives Through Interpretation," Memorandum from the Director of the National Park Service to all Field Offices, Apr. 23, 1953 (mimeographed).

70. U.S. Public Health Service: "Drinking Water Standards," PHS Pub. 956, U.S. Government Printing Office, Washington, 1962.

71. U.S. Public Health Service: "Manual of Individual Water Supply Systems," PHS Pub. 24, U.S. Government Printing Office, Washington, 1962.

72. U.S. Public Health Service: "Manual of Septic Tank Practice," PHS Pub. 526, U.S. Government Printing Office, Washington, 1963.

73. U.S. Public Health Service: "Suggested Design Criteria for Refuse Storage, Collection, and Disposal," Pacific Southwest Inter Agency Committee and Columbia Basin Interagency Committee, 1963.

74. U.S. Public Health Service: "Environmental Health Practice in Recreation Areas," PHS Pub. 1195, U.S. Government Printing Office, Washington, 1965.

75. Wagar, J. Alan: How to Predict Which Vegetated Areas Will Stand Up Best Under 'Active' Recreation, *American Recreation Journal*, vol. 1, no. 7, July, 1967.

76. Wagar, J. Alan: "The Convection Stack—A Device for Ridding Pit Toilets of Bad Odor," U.S. Forest Service, Northeastern Forest Experiment Station, Research Note, no. 133, Upper Darby, Pa., 1962.

77. Wagar, J. Alan: "Campgrounds for Many Tastes," U.S. Forest Service, Intermountain Forest and Range Experiment Station, Research Paper INT-6, Ogden, Utah, 1963.

78. Wagar, J. Alan: "The Carrying Capacity of Wildlands for Recreation," Forest Science Monograph No. 7, Society of American Foresters, Washington, 1964.

79. Wagar, J. Alan: Cultural Treatment of Vegetation of Recreation Sites, *Proceedings*, Society of American Foresters Annual Meeting, Detroit, Mich., Oct. 24-28, 1965, Washington, 1967.

80. Wagar, J. Alan: "Simulated Trampling as a Technique in Recreation Research," XIV IUFRO Congress, Munich, 1967 Papers, VIII, Section 26.

81. Wagar, J. V. K.: Services and Facilities for Forest Recreation, *Journal of Forestry*, vol. 44, no. 11, November, 1946.

82. Wagener, W. W.: "Judging Hazard From Native Trees in California Recreation Areas: A Guide for Professional Foresters," U.S. Forest Service, Pacific Southwest Forest and Range Experiment Station, Research Paper PSW-PI, Berkeley, Calif., 1963.

83. Whyte, William H.: "The Last Landscape," Doubleday, New York, 1968.

chapter sixteen

RECREATIONAL LAND MANAGEMENT OPERATION

Since recreational land management is concerned with people, as users, and the environment, as well as with basic tools of management, the successful accomplishment of a manager's tasks can be exasperating as well as rewarding. Patience, diplomacy, resourcefulness, and initiative, along with varied technical skills, are required. Management of environment per se presents many difficult problems, but likely reactions to certain stimuli can often be determined by experience or research. Public reactions are not so predictable. Understanding what prompts human actions and reactions under certain circumstances in outdoor recreation requires considerably more factual knowledge, based upon acceptable research, than is presently available.

In addition to perpetuation of basic recreational interests and environmental quality by proper planning and management, as discussed in Chapters 14 and 15, operation of recreational areas includes:

1. Protection of the health, safety, and property of both visitors and employees; protection of facilities
2. Relations between management and operators of vital commercial services
3. Budget preparation and the acquisition and proper expenditure of funds
4. Personnel requirements and adequate training

Protection of Visitor Health, Safety, and Property

Whenever outdoor recreational lands are provided for public use, the administering agency has an obligation to guard patrons, as well as employees and their families, from conditions which may adversely affect their physical well-being or endanger their property. There are a number of basic reasons for precautions on wild-land recreational areas. Because of increasing urbanization, wild land is, for many people, an unfamiliar environment, and its hazards are often unrecognized or improperly understood. Also, growing public interest in recreational attractions often develops localized overcrowding, which promotes a variety of conditions disadvantageous to public health and safety. In addition, recreational areas are available without question to all people; there is no workable method of preliminary screening of visitors to assess their interest and attitude. Further, the nature of recreational interests and activities encourages visitors to be lax in the protection of personal belongings; the outdoors seems to foster a feeling of universal trust which, unfortunately, is not always justified. Thievery and actions which are contrary to accepted laws of decency and propriety are matters of growing concern, particular in areas used by large heterogeneous crowds [2,3] .

Hazards related to specific areas must also be recognized, carefully considered, and guarded against. In many recreational areas normal traffic dangers are complicated by rough mountainous terrain responsible for steep, narrow, winding roads. In addition, a variety of interests generally compete for the attention of the driver. Attractive scenic vistas, wild animals, colorful wild flowers, or interesting geological formations along the way militate against traffic safety.

The behavior of hikers also poses a variety of problems. For instance, rapid descent down a steep trail may make footing unsure and speed unsafe. Short-cutting switchbacks in unfamiliar terrain may lead hikers into dangerous situations. Special precautions are also required when trails are used by foot or mounted travelers or by mechanized trail bike riders. Rolling of rocks or debris from high places endangers the safety of those below.

Many other factors must be reckoned with in considering public health and safety, and protection of property, on wild lands. Woods and grass fires, in addition to modifying or destroying environmental and scenic interest and beauty, may endanger human life and property. The peculiarities of climate, such as fog, high winds, lightning, or extremes of temperature, can be dangerous if not properly understood. The unsuspected or changeable power of stream or ocean currents and the hidden dangers of unfamiliar waters are ever-present threats in some areas. The character of the surface over which hikers travel, such as snow, glacial ice, bogs, or rocky footing on steep, mountainous terrain, often necessitates specific precautions.

The presence of poisonous plants and dangerous animals involves potential danger. Obviously dangerous animals (grizzly bear, poisonous reptiles) are but part of the problem. There is danger also in overfamiliarity with less aggressive native animals that have lost their fear of man (American black bear). Such animals are not tame; their response to unexpected movement or misunderstood actions can often result in severe bodily injury to the uninformed person. Except under certain conditions, such as during the mating season, when females are caring for their young, or when suddenly surprised, truly wild animals are rarely dangerous. Their fear of man, coupled with man's exercise of normal precautions, minimizes the possibility of dangerous confrontations. Under conditions of complete protection, however, many wild animals lose their fear of man, yet react instinctively when startled, frightened, or bewildered. Under such circumstances even ordinarily inoffensive animals can inflict injury.

Recreational areas also include important hazards to public health. The greatest potential for these occurs in crowded areas; crowded conditions and resultant disruption of normal living patterns increase the possibility of contamination of food and water and the spread of contagious diseases.

The nature and degree of various hazards to public health and safety, and to property, vary with specific types of wild-land recreational areas; each type has particular problems which must be understood and solved by management. While it is impossible to detail necessary safeguards for all possible situations in this general text, some basic precautions can be noted. These include:

1. Competent personnel experienced in, and responsible for, various specialized duties
2. Organization and training of personnel to meet emergencies wherever and whenever they occur
3. Safe design and construction of facilities and efficient organization of services, together with regular inspection of both facilities and services
4. Development of an adequate public relations and interpretive program to enhance public understanding of the particular recreational function of an area and the nature of potential hazards in the wild-land environment
5. Fair, unbiased enforcement of adequate rules and regulations

The existence of a competent staff is taken for granted. Most employees of wild-land recreational areas either have regular duties which relate in some way to protection of public health, safety, and property, or may be called upon to assist in various ways in emergency situations. Of particular importance are employees whose regular duties involve enforcement of laws and related rules and regulations, or the construction, operation, maintenance, and inspection of facilities and services most likely to be involved in hazards to public health and safety (water supply, sanitation, food handling, fire hazard, refuse and garbage disposal). Certain areas (mountainous terrain, deserts, potentially dangerous waters) require employees capable of assuming leadership in various kinds of rescue operations and first-aid treatment. Other types of wild lands have other potential dangers. For instance, if rock and earth slides, avalanches, falling trees, tidal rips, and similar dangers are potential hazards in locations generally frequented by the public, employees should be skilled in recognizing likely signs of them.

However, despite the effectiveness of precautionary measures, emergency situations invariably arise. Emergency organization of staff, supported by regular training under simulated emergency conditions, and development of preplanned emergency procedures promote quick and effective action when real emergencies occur. Organization and training should involve all personnel. Tasks relevant to different emergency situations and suited to individual competence should be assigned to various individuals on several levels—first call, follow-up, support, and standby.

Safely constructed facilities and efficiently operated services have minimal hazard to public health and safety. Road and trail construction should conform to acceptable engineering standards which consider not only the nature and degree of use but also conditions likely to increase hazards (rain, snow and ice, earth and rock slides, avalanches). Properly located, clearly legible signs, especially directional ones, contribute to safe use of roads and trails. Water supply, sanitary facilities and sewage disposal, and methods of refuse and garbage disposal should conform to public health standards [1,5,9]. The same criteria should guide storage and serving of food in public restaurants. Regular inspection of such facilities and services by qualified personnel to ensure continuation of acceptable standards is important.

It should be recognized that public understanding is necessary in guarding against hazards in recreational use of wild lands. The proverbial ounce of prevention is worth a pound of cure. Since recreational areas are established for public benefit and enjoyment, those who use them must recognize that this privilege entails definite personal responsibility. For example, permission to ascend a challenging mountain depends upon preliminary satisfaction of official requirements for the undertaking (qualified leadership, experience, availability of necessary equipment, physical condition). Advance registration, posting of expected itinerary, and check-out upon return are wise moves in the case of extended backcountry trips. In some areas campfire permits for specific points may be required; this precaution not only emphasizes fire prevention but provides automatic advance information on expected route of travel and time involved.

Visitors should be made aware of the particular recreational function of the area in question and how it differs from that of other types of lands. Efforts toward public understanding should be reinforced by adequate, sensible rules and regulations which protect both area and visitor. Enforcement is the responsibility of management personnel equipped and trained for the task. Infractions of general laws, which involve more serious situations than those covered by rules and regulations, are handled by duly constituted officers (federal, state, county). How the authority is shared by the local recreational staff and "outside" law enforcement officers varies with different situations. Some situations are complicated and characterized by overlapping authority. Disposition of some cases requires coordination of authority and efforts of both groups. The trend toward unacceptable behavior and even more serious crimes in recreational areas [2,3] has prompted serious consideration of more effective law enforcement methods than in the past, including replacement of recreational management personnel by some sort of specifically trained and qualified police organization.

Rules and regulations vary, but they must be adapted to the requirements of specific areas. Topics normally dealt with include the nature of permissible activities, charges for services, personal behavior, consideration of rights of others, speed limits and other rules concerning travel on roads and trails, use of various types of recreational equipment, time limits on campground occupancy, locations for picnicking, disturbance or destruction of plants, animals, and related recreational interests, fire prevention and control, littering, vandalism, unnecessary noise, use of firearms, hunting and fishing, hazardous climbs, and related activities.

Relation Between Administration and Commercial Operators

A variety of specific commercial facilities and services is necessary to full enjoyment of many outdoor recreational areas. Hotel accommodations, meals, equipment and supplies, public transportation, and other necessities must be provided. Since most recreational lands are administered by various public agencies which, by law, are prohibited from engaging in commercial ventures, services of this type must necessarily be handled by companies or individuals experienced in and equipped for the business [4]. These concessionaires usually operate under a franchise or permit granted by the administrative agency.

It is important that the nature of these services be in accord with the **purpose of the area, that necessary commercial structures be designed and located to harmonize with its interests and the environment, and that the public be given maximum value at reasonable cost. It is also necessary to ensure the operator opportunity for fair profit, consistent with the quality of service provided and the investment required.**

A written agreement or contract between the administration and the operator should define the nature of the service, the quality and standard desired, costs to the public, and similar considerations. In many instances the administrative agency shares in revenues above a determined figure which, although rarely applied directly to the operating costs of the area, nevertheless aid indirectly in its support. By this means, as well as by regular inspection of facilities and financial records, the administration controls the activities of the operator and ensures proper performance of his duties. Inadequate or inappropriate concessionaire facilities and services reflect discredit upon the entire management of a recreational area.

Formerly, in agreements of this kind the operator was required to finance and construct necessary buildings. Later, some administrative agencies built and retained title to necessary commercial structures, which were leased to suitable bidders who provided required services. Since the administrative agency assumes responsibility for major capital investment, this system facilitates greater control over commercial activity.

Budgets

Estimates of receipts and expenditures for operations during a given period of time are as important to recreational management of land as to any enterprise. They provide for efficient utilization of funds provided by taxes, bond issues, grants, bequests, and similar sources, or available through other means, such as profit from operations, rents or leases, and sale of miscellaneous products. They are also vital in periodic presentation and justification of financial requirements of planned programs for official approval, usually by legislative bodies. In addition, by means of incorporation of carefully stated operational procedures, they indicate the degree of authority granted to various levels of management in the expenditure of funds for approved programs.

Budgets vary in type and complexity [4], depending upon their purpose and the specific information desired by management. They may be related to items in an accounting system (personnel, supplies and material, travel), to functions of an operation (maintenance, improvements, various facilities and services), or, if more than one area is involved, to specific recreational land units. In many cases they may incorporate all three of the foregoing aspects, properly detailed and cross-referenced, to satisfy varied requirements and to enable management to visualize the relation of expenditures of the different segments of operational procedures and to the progress of intended plans. If recreational areas or operations are supported by funds from more than one source, these must be separately budgeted so that expenditures may be confined to the stipulated purposes of each fund. If legal limitations are not involved in use of these accounts, separate budgets may be established by administrators to ensure their most efficient use.

Personnel Requirements and Training

Proper management of wild lands for recreation requires employees possessed of a wide variety of interests and abilities. Ideally the personnel of specific organizations are suited to the recreational values in areas under their jurisdiction and, as determined by the master plan, the manner in which these values are offered to the public. Recreational management of wild lands involves a great deal of hard, sometimes disagreeable, work. Many duties are deeply concerned with people as well as with the environment.

The basic desirable qualities of a staff member of a wild-land recreation area are:

1. An interest in and an understanding of people. Employees must recognize and understand the reasons for varied public recreational demands, have patience and insight into the vagaries of human nature, and be able to guide public interests and activities diplomatically in the proper use of a particular area.

2. An awareness of environmental interrelations responsible for varied recreational attractions and recognition of the fact that perpetuation of such attractions is related to understanding of ultimate effects on environment by different types of use and development. Understanding of recreational values of one's particular area and the manner in which these values are affected by public use and development are especially important.

3. An interest in, appreciation for, and understanding of the area in which one works. The feeling of an employee for an area will be reflected in his attitude toward the work, no matter how menial the task, and particularly in his relations with people who use the area.

4. Ability to recognize the relation of one's particular responsibilities to the broader recreational objectives pertinent to the area involved, its relation to other recreational lands in the region, and the importance of both recreational and other land uses.

5. Capability in the specific assigned tasks, ranging from maintenance to policy-making responsibilities.

Several park and recreation management agencies provide special training programs to improve personnel performance, increase job awareness, and orient new employees. Such approaches may be the organization's attempt to compensate for bigness and to increase communication and cooperation among all levels of employees. The National Park Service has two training centers which provide orientation training, management and professional development courses for employees, and some special courses for nonemployees. The two centers are the Horace M. Albright Training Center at Grand Canyon National Park, Arizona, and the Stephen T. Mather Training Center at Harper's Ferry, West Virginia. The latter center emphasizes work in environmental interpretation as well as administration [6].

Summary

Though highly technical skills and hard work are required of various employees in the discharge of their specific duties, technical perfection and application to the task at hand are not the only criteria for success in recreational administration and management. Since such activities deal in large measure with people, patience and diplomacy, often under trying circumstances, as well as initiative and resourcefulness are demanded. Workers at all levels of a recreational staff should recognize and be interested in their responsibility to visitors, be aware of and understand the effects of public use on recreational value of the area in which they are employed. They should understand the relation of their particular area and the specific recreational opportunities it offers to other recreational lands. Recreation staff should be willing to learn from their association with their visitor clientele.

Selected References

1. Babbitt, H. E.: "Sewage and Sewage Treatment," Wiley, New York, 1947.
2. Campbell, Fred L., John C. Hendee, and Roger Clark: Law and Order in Public Parks, *Parks and Recreation*, vol. 3, no. 12, December, 1968.
3. David, C.: Legal Problems and Liability in Outdoor Recreation, *Park Maintenance*, vol. 19, no. 12, December, 1966.
4. Doell, Charles E.: "Elements of Park and Recreation Administration," Burgess, Minneapolis, Minn., 1963.
5. Ort, Don R.: Recommended Campground Sanitation Requirements, *Guidelines for Developing Land for Outdoor Recreational Use,* Cooperative Extension Service, Purdue University, West Lafayette, Ind., 1963.
6. U.S. Department of the Interior, National Park Service: "Training Opportunities," Washington, 1969.
7. U.S. Public Health Service: "Drinking Water Standards," Publication No. 956, U.S. Government Printing Office, Washington, 1962.
8. U.S. Public Health Service: "Manual of Septic Tank Practice," Publication No. 526, U.S. Government Printing Office, Washington, 1963.
9. U.S. Public Health Service: "Suggested Design Criteria for Refuse Storage, Collection, and Disposal," Pacific Southwest Interagency Committee and Columbia Basin Interagency Committee, 1963.

chapter seventeen

MANAGEMENT OF FOREIGN NATIONAL PARKS AND RELATED AREAS

The subject of national parks and related areas throughout the world is a large one. The necessarily brief treatment in this chapter only alludes to its more fascinating aspects. For instance, the many features of national parks and related reserves in faraway places are only suggested, and multiple administrative and management concepts are only briefly outlined. However, all workers in wild-land recreation should be aware of activities of their counterparts in other countries. Thus, an attempt has been made to provide the reader with the fundamentals and scope of foreign national parks and similar reserves so that they may be compared with similar areas in the United States. Details of foreign national parks and reserves may be obtained in a number of excellent publications, some of which are included in the chapter references.[1]

Nature of Benefits [1,12,13,28]

Values inherent in the features of natural environment, as well as in varied objects of antiquity, have international importance. Public responsibility in their protection and preservation transcends national boundaries and political ideologies. Today, over 100 nations on all continents have established national parks, floral and faunal sanctuaries or reserves, recreational forests, and similar areas, or have placed sites of archaeological and historical importance under the protec-

---

[1] The most complete reference to national parks and equivalent reserves throughout the world is *United Nations List of National Parks and Equivalent Reserves*, prepared and edited by the International Commission on National Parks, International Union for the Conservation of Nature and Natural Resources (IUCN), published first in French in 1967 (English edition, 1971). The status of natural area protection in 136 countries is outlined and over 1,200 national parks and equivalent reserves are listed and briefly described [13].

tion of public agencies. Though methods of accomplishing such purposes vary, their generally similar objectives emphasize maintenance of environmental interests for varying benefits important to future as well as present generations.

International interest in the establishment of national parks and related reserves is motivated by (1) concern for the preservation of significant world interests, (2) enhancement of educational and cultural values, (3) improvement of scientific knowledge, (4) development of coordinated land-management programs, (5) stimulation of economic benefits through tourism, and (6) creation of a desirable world image of political maturity.

Preservation of Significant Interests

Man's natural concern with his surroundings, and his curiosity regarding things about him, are fundamental to the reserve concept and environmental protection. He has an inherent interest in the preservation of plant and animal species or significant ecological associations; of dramatic segments of terrain, scenic or not, which reflect the nature of past geological changes; and of archaeological remains or historic sites indicative of the nature, accomplishments, and trials and tribulations of his predecessors. Modern society has recognized the importance of guarding such areas against unnecessary encroachment. As heirlooms of our heritage they are worth their cost.

Enhancement of Educational and Cultural Values

Representative bits of natural and significant environment, lands on which man's works are conducted in harmony with scenic or environmental interests, and evidences of man's earlier existence, have recognized educational and cultural value. Similarly, archaeological and historical sites enable laymen to identify closely with significant events of the past.

High-quality reserves, representative of interests typical of various countries, are also a source of national pride. They also promote understanding of cultural differences between the world's peoples.

Improvement of Scientific Knowledge

Knowledge of nature's methods, as expressed in the characteristics of varied natural environmental associations, aid man in living in harmony with his surroundings. In particular, large natural areas are important as "bench marks," or "control plots," for necessary research on the varied effects of environmental manipulation resulting from different methods in the management and use of both renewable and nonrenewable resources.

Development of Coordinated Land-management Programs

As units of properly planned land-use programs, various types of reserves, with their cultural, educational, inspirational, scientific, and related values, provide necessary balance between man's varied needs. Though a major share of the earth's land and water area must necessarily serve man's utilitarian requirements, natural areas, as well as areas of carefully controlled use, are also important to man's existence. Systematized allocation of land on the basis of primary benefits offers the most suitable substitute to unnecessary sacrifice of important aesthetic values.

Stimulation of Economic Benefits Through Tourism

Varied interests typical of different areas of the world are magnets for increasing global travel favored by all forms of modern transportation facilities, particularly fast, dependable, relatively inexpensive jet aircraft. Maintenance and development of the important economic returns from tourism, as well as competition for such benefits, are largely dependent upon perpetuation of the varied basic attractions. Not the least of these attractions are the significant geological, biological, archaeological, and historical features contained in various types of reserves, and the scenic qualities of an attractive landscape. A number of countries have developed these concepts to a high level. In particular, a number of newly established nations have given high priority to considerations of this nature, largely because of economic returns resulting from foreign travel.

Development of an Image of Political Maturity

Various types of reserves throughout the world, including most national parks and related areas in former colonies of European nations, were largely instituted by older, established countries. When these former colonies achieved independence, it was generally assumed that their reserves might be abolished for, though vital to farsighted conservation programs, they were entwined with colonial policies not always in public favor with indigenous inhabitants. However, officials of many of the new governments, often with the assistance of dedicated former conservation officials, recognized the very practical aspects of maintaining the integrity of national parks and related reserves. Money brought in by tourists was, and is, an important economic factor. Enlightened leaders of these new states, seeking a position of equality in world affairs with older, established nations, recognized national parks and similar areas as popular symbols of a mature national philosophy.

History of International Interest in Parks and Reserves

The concept of governmental responsibility to environmental protection has been characterized by slow but accelerating growth over many years [1,3,4,8,9, 13,25,28,29]. Although natural conditions throughout much of Europe have been greatly modified by centuries of use, concern for the preservation of the environment and conservation of natural resources has long been associated with the culture of many European peoples. Conservation laws, designed primarily to prevent the extinction of certain species of fauna and flora, were adopted in various parts of Europe at an early date.

This concern for conservation accompanied the expansion of European culture to far-flung corners of the globe, and was manifested early in both North America and Africa. Initial efforts to prohibit the ruthless slaughter of African wildlife were made in 1846, in Transvaal, now part of the Republic of South Africa [25].

Modern Reserve Concept

Tangible action in establishing specific reserves was first manifested in different parts of the world during the nineteenth and early years of the twentieth century. Its growth has not been uniform. Greater progress has been made in some regions than others; in fact, unenlightened practices in the use of natural resources are still typical in many parts of the world.

Early reserves of the world varied in type and size, and had equally varying objectives. Although the establishment of Yellowstone National Park in 1872 is generally credited with being the first indication of this movement, it was not the first of the world's wild-land reserves. Yellowstone National Park was antedated by the establishment of several other reserves, including the Hot Springs Reserve in 1832; Fountainebleau, near Paris, France, in 1853; and the Yosemite Grant in 1864. However, the significance of the establishment of the Yellowstone area was that this action was responsible for the introduction of the national park concept, which crystallized interest in the establishment of similar areas in other countries. It also gave added emphasis to conservation in general.

However, according to Ann and Myron Sutton [26], Yellowstone was not established as a national park; initial legislation in 1872 merely stated that this area was "set aside as a public park." Nevertheless, even though the specific nomenclature "national park" was lacking in the initial legislation, Yellowstone represents the first land set aside for purposes of a national park. In the Yellowstone (1872) and Mackinac Island (1874) legislation Congress had not refined the term "national park" sufficiently to include it in the body of those acts. A Parliamentary document of New South Wales, Australia, establishing "The National Park," now Royal National Park, near Sydney, was the world's first legislative document to make specific reference to this term. United States legislation did not refer to "Yellowstone National Park" until 1883.

Another early example of the expansion of the national park concept occurred in Canada in 1885. In that year an area of ten square miles surrounding the hot springs at Banff, in the Province of Alberta, was designated as a health resort; two years later this area was enlarged to 250 square miles and christened Rocky Mountains, later Banff, National Park. This area was the nucleus of the extensive, present-day Canadian National Park System.

National parks were nonexistent in Europe until 1910, when the first one was established in Sweden. However, as early as 1880 a Finnish scientist proposed that certain areas in Europe be reserved in their natural state for posterity, and in 1884 James Bryce, member of the British House of Commons, introduced the Access to the Mountains Bill which sought to preserve public rights of access to certain types of "open country" which had been seriously curtailed. Bryce's bill, which applied only to Scotland, did not pass, but it was a harbinger of developments in Britain in later years.

In Africa the earliest area set aside specifically for the protection of native African fauna and flora was a small reserve established in 1889 by King Leopold of Belgium in what was then the Belgian Congo, primarily for the protection of elephants. Soon thereafter, in 1897, the Hluhluwe, Umfolozi, and Saint Lucia reserves were established in Natal, Republic of South Africa, and in 1898 the Sabie Game Reserve in Transvaal, forerunner of South Africa's famous Kruger National Park, was established.

Creation of various types of reserves in several Australian states dates from establishment of Royal National Park by New South Wales in 1879 and other land laws of the 1880s. A few areas came into being before 1900, but most Australian national parks and reserves are more recent. In New Zealand some reserves were established under authority of the Land Act of 1892; and in 1894 Tongariro National Park became the basis of New Zealand's Park System.

Though reservation of wild lands in Asia has little consistency, parts of that continent have a long history of nature conservation. It was initiated in Indonesia during the Dutch colonial period. In 1889, a section of the primeval jungle forest on the slopes of Mount Tjibodas, on the island of Java, was placed under the protection of the Botanical Institute of Buitenzorg, primarily to serve as a natural science research laboratory. In 1912, the Society for Nature Protection aided the colonial government in the establishment of the first of over 100 nature reserves. Since independence such areas have been administered by the government of the Republic of Indonesia. It is also significant that establishment of national parks in Asia was first suggested in Japan toward the end of the last century by Nagaroni Okabe,[2] member of the House of Peers, who had developed interest in Yellowstone National Park during a period of study in the United States. However, there were no national parks in Asia until 1934, when the first eight areas of the Japanese National Park System were established. This action followed adoption of Japan's initial National Park Law by both houses of the Japanese Diet; this law became effective in 1934 (revised 1950) through Imperial Edict. Adoption of the National Park Law resulted largely from public interest developed by the Japanese National Park Association, formed in 1927.

Establishment of Yellowstone National Park also prompted the initial suggestion of similar reserves in South America. This idea was voiced in Brazil in 1876 by Andre Rebouces, an engineer [1], but it did not bear fruit—and then

---

[2] Early interest in establishment of national parks in Japan is also credited to efforts of Edwin von Baeltz, about 1911 [1].

not in Brazil—until much later. The first South American national park was established by Argentina.[3]

Organization of the IUCN

Interest in the preservation of significant wild-land values on an international level began to develop early in the present century. Such interest, resulting largely from recognition of the basic similarity of conservation problems, was reflected in cooperative efforts by localized groups of nations in various parts of the world. In time, such efforts were approached on a continental and, eventually, on a worldwide basis.

Among the more noteworthy of early international conferences on natural resource conservation were the International Conference for the Protection of Fauna and Flora of Africa, held in London in 1933, and the Pan American Convention on Nature Protection and Wildlife Preservation in the Western Hemisphere, held in Washington, D.C. in 1942.

The desirability of an international approach to nature conservation was first suggested by Paul Sarasin, Swiss naturalist, who proposed the establishment of an international advisory committee before World War I. This movement, interrupted by World War I, was reactivated following the end of hostilities by P. G. Tienhoven of the Netherlands. Largely through his efforts the International Office for the Protection of Nature was founded in Brussels in 1928. This organization was active until 1940. After World War II a Provisional International Union for the Protection of Nature was organized by the Swiss League for the Protection of Nature. The Swiss League, working closely with the French Government and UNESCO, organized a conference held at Fountainebleau in 1948, at which the International Union for the Protection of Nature was officially established. Later, the name of this organization was changed to the International Union for the Conservation of Nature and Natural Resources; it is generally referred to as the IUCN.

Factors of Importance in Establishment of Parks and Reserves

National parks and equivalent reserves throughout the world, as well as systems of such areas, vary widely in type, size, conservation objectives, and philosophy of administration and management. Even their nomenclature lacks a standardization which adequately portrays the purpose of specific types of areas and their relationship to one another. The terms used often imply a similarity which does not actually exist. Conversely, the character of identical types may be hidden by dissimilar terminology. For instance, "national park" is a generic term which is interpreted differently in the light of local conditions and needs.

---

[3] National parks in Argentina are established under authority of the National Park Law of 1934 (with later modifications). However, Argentina's National Park System is considered to have originated in 1903, when Dr. Francisco P. Moreno donated approximately 15,000 acres of land for a national park. This area comprises part of Nahuel Huapi National Park.

The need for some sort of standardized nomenclature was recognized at both the International Conference for the Protection of Fauna and Flora of Africa and the Pan American Convention on Nature Protection and Wildlife Preservation in the Western Hemisphere [8,23]. In both cases definitions applicable to various types of reserves were adopted.[4] However, these definitions were related primarily to conditions typical of continents under discussion; they were not designed to be uniformly applicable to reserves throughout the world. Further, the term national park was the only one defined at both these international meetings. Though essentially similar, neither of these definitions of a national park are relevant to some areas known as national parks in densely populated countries where local conditions require controlled utilization of natural resources of such areas, and consequent departure from principles of strict preservation.

At the First World Conference on National Parks, held in Seattle, Washington, in 1962, it was noted that various types of reserves throughout the world were designated in about two dozen different ways [28]. Later, the IUCN developed standards for national parks and related reserves having natural interests [13], but areas with significant archaeological or historical values worthy of national park status were not included. More definitely, on December 1, 1969, the Tenth General Assembly of the IUCN, meeting in New Delhi, India, adopted a resolution defining the term national park which emphasized the necessity for (1) an essentially natural environment; (2) control by some national authority; and (3) specialized—inspirational, educational, cultural, recreational—public use. This resolution recommended that all governments adhere to IUCN standards in designating national parks, and requested that the term not be applied to areas lacking expressed essential characteristics [14].

It is important that factors underlying variations in type, size, objective, administrative philosophy, and nomenclature be understood and carefully considered when discussing and comparing reserves in different parts of the world. Among the most vital of these factors are (1) the primary interests of the areas concerned, (2) regional population density, (3) economic level of countries involved, (4) nature and stability of the political system of various governments, and (5) the history and cultural background of the people.

Primary Interests

These vary with such basic characteristics of various continents as topography, flora and fauna, and archaeology and history. These basic characteristics are related to global geographic positions of different continents; their climate, geology, nature of development, history; and the cultural and ethnic background

---

[4] The International Conference for the Protection of Fauna and Flora of Africa defined the terms national park, strict natural reserve, fauna and flora reserve, and reserve with prohibition of hunting and collecting. Reserve definitions adopted by the Pan American Convention on Nature Protection and Wildlife Preservation in the Western Hemisphere were those for national park, national reserve, strict wilderness reserve, and nature monument.

of their people. Thus, understanding of the world's varied reserves is predicated upon a knowledge of the many interrelating factors responsible for their principal interests, the perpetuation of which responds to different management programs as well as to varying types and degrees of use.

Population Density

Very large reserves are feasible only in regions where economic pressure for land, by reason of low population density or resource demand, is not acute. For instance, in contrast with sparsely populated, less developed nations, most European countries and Japan have relatively little land that is not required for production of utilitarian needs. In Europe and Japan a modified form of national parks and related reserves has evolved. Establishment of large, unmodified, wholly government-owned areas is impossible; Europeans and the Japanese have sought to reconcile modern man and nature to joint occupation of their reserves. Land-ownership patterns are not disturbed; private as well as public land is generally included; and private industry is not completely curtailed. The objective of such policy is to safeguard areas of exceptional interest, scenic beauty, and similar values against damage or destruction.

Economic Level

The establishment and maintenance of reserves, whatever their nature, are largely dependent upon the economic level of the nations involved. The probability of their establishment is in direct ratio to per capita income. A country must not only be able to afford designation of land for such use; it must also be able to meet the cost of adequate protection, administration, and management. Primarily for this reason national parks and related reserves are more numerous, larger, and generally better planned, protected, and administered, as well as better known, in countries typified by a more affluent society.

Nature and Stability of Government

Since establishment of reserves and related maintenance of environmental interest and beauty must be based upon long-term objectives, it follows that desired results cannot be achieved without governmental stability. Countries recognized as world leaders in this aspect of conservation are all characterized by stable governmental structure.

The nature of the political system under which a government operates is also important. In nature conservation, effects of varying political systems may be reflected in either a positive or negative manner. Certain totalitarian countries have adequate, often extensive, reserves of various types. These, largely reflections of the political objectives of governmental hierarchy, can be expected to be maintained so long as current policies are continued. Countries which operate on a system reflecting greater freedom of individual expression would seem to offer maximum opportunity for progress in nature conservation. However, under such a system, the attainment of a desired result is dependent upon a responsible citizenry, properly informed on the requirements and values of such objectives, and the nature and effects of alternate choices.

History

The extent and nature of various types of reserves throughout the world are often connected to the history of the countries involved. Since some European areas originated as private estates of the nobility, they were withdrawn from public use and maintained in an essentially natural condition. Later, when converted to public status, they remained largely unaltered. Similarly, reserves established as parts of colonial empires are continued by newly independent governments, largely for economic and political reasons.

Further, wherever government has encouraged individual initiative in land and resource acquisition, this has materially affected the location and distribution as well as the size and character of reserves.

Cultural Background

Public attitudes toward the natural scene, and toward past heritage, play a role in the establishment of reserves; cultural importance and value must warrant their formation. It was not an accident that the national park idea originated in the United States, and that this concept of land use was quickly adapted by other countries with a similar heritage. The emotional appeal of this idea is so strong that even in Europe and Japan, where virgin lands are largely nonexistent, the most satisfactory substitutes have been devised. Awareness of cultural values of reserves by leaders of emerging nations encourages their countrymen to accede, even though the aura of a colonial past is yet to be erased, and despite the fact that, historically, native fauna is viewed primarily as a source of food.

Administration and Management of Foreign Parks and Reserves

In addition to differences in administrative philosophy and degree of protection in various types of reserves, the relationship between public and private responsibility in the discharge of such matters is dissimilar. Further, where such areas are entirely under some form of governmental authority, this responsibility is organized in several ways. The nature and degree of their public use also varies. Still, in spite of such basic differences, there is similarity in the problems encountered in different areas.

Concepts of Administrative Philosophy and Use

On some reserves, established primarily as field laboratories for natural resource research, recreation activity is is limited and access is controlled. The general public is restricted to limited portions of the total area or to well-defined routes of travel, or the number of visitors is rigidly controlled—often through provision of only primitive facilities.

Other reserves are managed in an opposite manner, with emphasis placed upon public use and enjoyment. Though care is taken to see that the interest and beauty of the environment are not destroyed, nature is appropriately manipulated in a manner favorable to public use with minimum impact on environmental interests. In certain cases the truly natural character of the area may be completely modified, though it may still be attractive. Controlled resource use may be permitted and there is little, if any, interference with private land ownership. In such cases public access and use are provided for through agreement with private owners, though rights of private landowners are respected by designation of specific routes of travel and concentration.

The great majority of reserves are administered on concepts somewhere between these two extremes. Standards and means of public access range widely. Accommodations of varying types and standards may be operated by the administrative agency or by concessionaires under contract, subject to agency control. In some cases overnight accommodations are outside reserve boundaries, though in close proximity, and completely under private management. Other facilities and services necessary to public use also differ greatly, and visitor activities and movement, including speed on roads and highways, are subject to varying controls, dependent upon the area's interests. The general objective in such cases is to permit maximum, appropriate public use consistent with the perpetuation of specific interests of the area.

Since it is impractical, if not impossible and uneconomic, to provide for all types of public interest and activity on any one type of reserve, competing interests and activities are often accommodated on several distinct areas. Though sometimes contiguous they are generally separate, with coordination of specific uses related on the basis of regional needs.

Administrative Relationships

Varying objectives of different types of reserves prompt diversity in administrative relations. Areas noted for their geological, biological, or scenic interests are usually controlled by some public agency (federal, state, provincial, etc.), generally a park, forest, fish and game, or land department. In some cases, however, administration is by a semipublic organization (boards, commissions, authorities) whose members are private citizens with interest in and knowledge of the problems involved, and who are appointed for varying terms by an officer of an appropriate government agency. In some cases administrative responsibility is entrusted to the professional staff of a recognized university, museum, or related educational or scientific institution. The degree of government control exercised over the activities of such semipublic bodies varies, but they generally operate with considerable autonomy, within specific limitations subject to only minimal official supervision.

Archaeological and historical areas and sites are generally, but not always, administered by organizations similarly constituted. However, these areas and sites are distinct from those concerned with geological, biological, and related scenic interests.

Foreign Park and Reserve Examples

Examples from several foreign countries will serve to illustrate the nature of reserves and their problems.

Many African reserves which feature natural or scenic interests are of extensive size. Some, embracing areas of several thousand square miles, are larger than a number of American states. Though protection of their basic interests is generally of primary concern, administrative policies with respect to protection and visitor use are variable, being dependent upon the interests involved, the degree of land-use pressure in the region, and the importance of the reserve to the economics of the country. A few are restricted to scientific study,[5] while in others the general public is limited to small portions of the area.[6] However, in most reserves more liberal policies prevail, though permissible visitor activities are carefully controlled and regulated. This is particularly the case in wildlife areas which are often sensitive to disturbance or where the presence of certain animals embodies hazard to visitors. In some wildlife reserves roads and accommodations are primitive or nonexistent and visitors must accompany guided parties. A few are in close proximity to modern cities or are readily accessible by public transportation.[7] Many more remote areas have adequate facilities; however, overnight accommodations, including campgrounds, are available only at specific places which are often enclosed by a protective fence.[8] Visitors in such reserves are generally required to make advance reservations and remain within protected places during the night. Further, public travel is restricted to specific roads during daylight hours, speed limits are rigidly defined, only closed vehicles are permitted and, except for designated places, visitors are not permitted to leave their vehicle.

In certain regions policies of strict protection and controlled public use, including restricted hunting, are accommodated by coordination of several kinds of contiguous reserves which provide for various types and degrees of visitor

---

[5] **Example:** Monts Nimba Nature Reserve (aggregate area 81,250 acres) on border between Ivory Coast and Guinea.

[6] **Example:** Albert National Park (2,022,500 acres), Zaire.

[7] **Examples:** Nairobi National Park (28,160 acres), Kenya; Victoria Falls National Park (132,250 acres), Rhodesia.

[8] **Examples:** Tsavo National Park (5,141,760 acres), Kenya; Gorongosa National Park (988,420 acres), Mozambique; Wankie National Park (3,238,400 acres), Rhodesia; Kruger National Park (4,697,600 acres); Hluhluwe (57,000 acres) and St. Lucia (91,000 acres) Game Reserves, Republic of South Africa; Serengeti National Park (2,848,000 acres), Tanzania; Murchison Falls (962,500 acres) and Queen Elizabeth (488,960 acres) National Parks, Uganda; Kafue National Park (5,536,000 acres), Zambia.

use.[9] There are also a number of reserves and reserve complexes, composed of one or more types of protection, which straddle national boundaries.[10]

Many Asiatic countries have established national parks and related reserves, but, with the possible exception of Japan and the U.S.S.R., this concept of land use lacks adequate support. Because of economic, population, and political difficulties, in many countries in Asia, its reserves have problems related to personnel, boundary definition, and enforcement of protective measures. Asiatic reserves vary in size from a few acres to over 2,000 square miles.[11] The U.S.S.R., in Europe as well as in Asia, has an extensive system of nature preserves (*zapovedniki*)[12] where management emphasizes protection for education and research; general public use is not a major consideration [2,13] . Conversely, the National Park System in Japan[13] gives major consideration to public use [13,16] . A wide variety of recreational activities are permitted and commercial use of natural resources is not completely eliminated; however, as in Europe, care is taken to maintain environmental interests insofar as possible.

Although Australia and New Zealand have a similar cultural and political heritage, we find added to the obvious dissimilarity in physical size, differences in the size and distribution of population, climate, topography, economics and industrial activity, governmental structure, and attitudes of the people. These differences affect the character and nature of administration of reserves.

The expanse of relatively undeveloped land and the comparatively small population would seem to simplify problems of nature conservation in Australia. However, the Australian environment is delicately balanced and vulnerable to disturbance. Intensive agriculture, industry, and urban development are concentrated in the relatively small, most habitable portion of the continent, so inevitably environmental modification is also concentrated. Even pastoral activity, typical of much of the "outback," has a severe impact on that arid, even

---

[9] Bamingui Bangoran National Park (2,500,000 acres), Vassako-Bola Strict Nature Reserve (375,000 acres), and three game reserves (agg. area 2,250,000 acres), Central African Republic.

[10] National Park de "W" (825,000 acres) in Niger is contiguous with Pendjari Strict Faunal Reserve (688,750) in Dahomey and Cortiagu Partial Faunal Reserve (127,500 acres) in Upper Volta; Kalahari National Park (2,720,000 acres) in the Republic of South Africa adjoins a game reserve of 2,400,000 acres in Botswana.

[11] Kranji Reserve (49 acres), Singapore; Petchora-Ilych Nature Preserve (1,765,035 acres) in Asiatic U.S.S.R.

[12] No central administrative agency. Management is by various agencies of the Council of Ministers of the Union Republics, or the Academies of Science of either the U.S.S.R. or the Union Republics. A few nature preserves were established in the 1920s; most were set up at a later date. A national park, managed more for general public use, is contemplated for the Lake Baikal region.

[13] Includes over twenty areas (aggregate area about 4,500,000 acres) administered by the National Park Division of the Ministry of Health and Welfare. These areas are supplemented by about twenty "quasi-national parks," areas of secondary scenic quality (aggregate area over 1,000,000 acres) which absorb some of the tremendous outdoor recreation pressure in Japan. Quasi-national parks are administered by local prefectures, in coordination with the Ministry of Health and Welfare and the National Parks Deliberative Council.

more fragile region. In addition, Australian attitudes toward land use were somewhat comparable to early land-use concepts in the United States; until relatively recent years, when the effects of unwise use became evident, the need for corrective measures was little recognized. Long-term social and economic values inherent in protected reserves were seldom accorded the same level of interest as more expedient development for quicker, more immediate returns. Further, though characteristically interested in the outdoors, Australians lean more to physical activities rather than to the subjective interests usually related to nature conservation. Finally, Australia's political system is somewhat of a deterrent to well-organized conservation efforts. Each state has sovereign powers over its own land, and flora and fauna. The Commonwealth plays a minor role in conservation; its only responsibility in this field relates to its administration of the Northern and Capital Territories. Thus, there is no nationally uniform nature conservation policy, or procedure. Various parks and reserves have been established independently by different states, often by a variety of administrative acts; and the degree of progress in such matters, as well as in the administrative philosophy, standards, protection, and nature of management of such lands varies widely. These deficiencies, however, are being modified by the growing influence of a number of conservation organizations such as the Australian Wildlife Protection Society, the Australian Academy of Science, the Australian Conservation Foundation, and National Park Associations in a number of states.

Various Australian states and territories have established over 150 national parks (aggregate area between 6 and 7 million acres). There are also nearly 900 scenic, floral, and faunal reserves and sanctuaries (aggregate area about 14,000,000 acres). These areas vary widely in size, management objective, and location. Some are essentially for protection of particular interests; others are located near large urban centers and are developed for general recreation; whereas others are remote and difficult of access and largely wilderness.[14] Where possible, there are accommodations for visitors; a few embody carefully related industrial developments [13,20,21].

The superb National Park System in New Zealand (about ten areas, aggregating approximately 5,000,000 acres)[15] is administered by the New Zea-

---

[14] Noteworthy areas include Simpson Desert National Park (1,298,000 acres) and a number of national parks in, or in the vicinity of, the Great Barrier Reef, Queensland; Kosciusko (1,322,000 acres) and Blue Mountains (243,000 acres) National Parks, New South Wales; Wilson's Promontory National Park (102,379 acres) Victoria; Cradle Mt.-Lake St. Clair National Park (338,496 acres), Tasmania; Ayres Rock-Mt. Olga National Park (331,680 acres) Northern Territory; Flinders Chase National Park (135,715 acres), South Australia; Walpole-Nornalup National Park (32,229 acres), Western Australia.

[15] Included are Tongariro (161,552 acres) which, in addition to having an active volcano, is a winter sports center; Fiordland (2,422,883 acres) containing spectacular coastal fiords and wilderness country; and Mount Cook (172,979 acres) and Westland (210,000 acres), characterized by spectacular mountains with extensive glacier systems. There are also reserves and sanctuaries administered by the Lands and Survey Department, and Tronson Kauri Park (1,241 acres) is jointly administered by the New Zealand Forest Service and National Parks Authority.

land National Parks Authority and National Parks Board, under the framework of the Lands and Survey Department [13,22]. Management policies are somewhat similar to those of national parks in the United States.

In Europe establishment of large reserves primarily for exclusive protection of their interests is impractical. Still most European countries have established national parks and reserves adapted to local conditions and needs.[16] As in Japan, use of natural resources is generally permitted, but care is taken to protect the environment. Administrative responsibility for European national parks and reserves is vested in a variety of public or quasi-public agencies.

Great Britain has a variety of protected areas having different functions. By authority of the National Parks and Access to the Countryside Act of 1949, ten national parks have been established in England and Wales; these, essentially "landscape control zones," have an aggregate area of over 3 million acres [9]. They are augmented by twenty-one "Areas of Outstanding Scenic Beauty" (aggregate area about 2,500,000 acres; first one designated 1956) and six "Long Distance Footpaths and Bridleways" (total of 1,273 miles; first one designated 1951). These areas are administered by local planning authorities, subject to supervision of the National Parks Commission, Ministry of Housing and Local Government. There are also ten National Forest Parks (aggregate area nearly 500,000 acres) in England, Scotland, Wales, and North Ireland, administered by the Forestry Commission.

The New Forest, established in 1087 by William I (see page 32), is under the administration of Special Acts of Parliament. Timber production, protection of wildlife and commoners' animals, and safeguarding of public amenity and recreation are major management concerns. Its management illustrates the importance of tradition in Britain and in the continuity of ancient laws and rights as well as the resistance to change.

In addition, the National Trust owns areas of historic as well as of natural interest. Great Britain also has a system of about 100 National Nature Reserves (aggregate area about 400,000 acres) where greater restriction is placed on general public use; these areas are administered by the Nature Conservancy, established in 1949.

In Switzerland multiple-use forest management is common in the alpine

---

[16] France has a number of reserves of varying size; some, like Fontainebleau, date from early days. After passage of its National Park Act in 1960, France established Vanoise National Park (147,000 acres) in the Alps; it adjoins Gran Paridiso National Park (140,000 acres), one of the larger Italian national parks [13]. Bialowiesa National Park (12,682 acres), one of Poland's areas, is noteworthy as a habitat for the remaining European bison [10,13]. Sweden's National Park System [13,27] includes areas of diverse types; included are Dalby Soderskog (89 acres), a typical early-day Swedish farm, and Sarek (470,490 acres), the largest wild area in Europe. West Germany has numerous nature parks [13] (e.g., Lüneberger Heide, 49,420 acres) and smaller nature reserves. Natural resources are utilized, consistent with environmental protection; use of motorized vehicles is also greatly restricted.

forest region, yet the Swiss also have restricted access areas in the Alps where vegetation is preserved for scientific investigation. The Swiss National Park near Zernez, in the Engadine Alps, is such a preserve. Although administered by a federal commission and not the forestry agency, the park is almost one-third forested and has been subject to intensive ecological study by the Swiss Forest Research Institute. Created in 1914, the 41,670-acre park provides complete protection for all plant and animal life; no timber or other resource production is allowed (although the area was logged and mined for iron ore in the Middle Ages). The only visitor developments are closely restricted trails and a few information signs, yet many walk the trails, respecting the scientific controls.

North America's national parks and reserves range from those in extensive systems in Canada and the United States to small areas in a number of Central American countries. Canada's National Park System[17] is augmented by provincial reserves [13], a situation similar to that which exists between national and state parks in the United States. Mexico has about fifty national parks, ranging in area from less than 100 acres to more than 600,000 acres (aggregate area over 2,500,000 acres);[18] for various reasons many have been excluded from the IUCN list. They are not well known, even by many Mexicans, being overshadowed by interest in Mexico's fabulous archeological areas which are under separate administration. In Central America a number of countries have national parks and reserves, but their establishment and management is complicated by economic and political conditions and indifferent public attitude.

South America has great potential for significant national parks and reserves. However, in most countries on this continent this concept of land use is of fairly recent origin and, as yet, has not been adequately fulfilled. In the establishment and management of such areas efforts are made to adhere to policies adopted at the Pan American Convention on Nature Protection and Wildlife Preservation in the Western Hemisphere, but certain departures from these standards often typify actual practice. Establishment and adequate management is often complicated by difficulties of boundary determination, land-ownership patterns, lack of personnel, and public attitude toward the use of natural resources.

Although national parks and reserves exist in Bolivia, Colombia, Chile, Ecuador, Guyana, and Peru, most noteworthy systems in South America [13]

---

[17] Nineteen natural scenic parks (aggregate area nearly 18,000,000 acres), a similar number of national historic parks (aggregate area 14,000 acres), and several hundred historic sites. They are administered by the National and Historic Parks Branch of the Department of Indian Affairs and Northern Development.

[18] Administered by the Department of National Parks, Division of Forestry and Game, Office of the Secretary of Agriculture and Animal Husbandry. Better known areas include Iztaccihuatl-Popocatepetl (64,198 acres) and Pico de Orizaba (49,375 acres), national parks which include Mexico's most important mountains.

are found in Argentina,[19] Brazil,[20] and Venezuela.[21] Argentina's best known national parks are Nahuel Huapi (1,900,000 acres) in the Lake District east of the Andes and Iguazú (139,000 acres) on the Argentine-Brazilian border. The latter includes part of Iguazú Falls, one of the great cataracts of the world, as well as diverse flora and fauna. It adjoins Iguacú National Park (445,000 acres) in Brazil, forming an international park about the great cataract. Venezuela's national park system includes Canaima National Park (nearly 2,500,000 acres) in the remote Guiana Highlands; it embraces Angel Falls (2,648 feet high), highest free-leaping waterfall in the world.

Similarity of Problems

Despite dissimilarity in area characteristics, and differences in the sociological, economic, and political factors responsible for their existence, the problems concerned with reserve management often are quite similar. Basically, these problems concern perpetuation of the resource or environment, and the people who use these resources. These fundamental concerns apply whether an area is located in Africa or North America, whether it is maintained as a natural field laboratory with public access strictly limited or as a modified environment with controlled resource uses primarily for enjoyment of large numbers of people. Nevertheless, man's presence in an area, however controlled or limited, has a degree of impact. Even without intrusion of man geological and biological dynamics exert slow but inevitable change in the appearance and characteristics of an area. When viewed in long-term perspective, it is impossible to "freeze" any biological association at a given stage of time. Even the concept of the "everlasting hills" is a myth.

The examples presented here of parks and reserves in other countries, while perhaps confusing to the reader, illustrate the broad range of policies and variations in management in different parts of the world. Examples indicate differences with very large populations on limited land (Japan and Switzerland); the role of tradition and historical precedent (Great Britain); the impact of tourism (Africa); and a casual approach to land use (Australia). None of the examples is quite like the United States, but they serve to show the spectrum from older to newer societies. As population rises with respect to available land, restrictions on land use increase. To protect wildlife, vegetation, and natural features, public use is restricted. The need for well-defined policy and coordinated planning becomes evident.

---

[19] Eleven national parks and one natural monument (aggregate area about 6,500,000 acres). They are administered by the National Parks Administration, Ministry of Agriculture.

[20] About eleven national parks and two biological reserves (aggregate area over 5,000,000 acres). Brazilian national parks and reserves are administered by the Division of Research and Nature Conservation, Forest Service, Ministry of Agriculture.

[21] Seven national parks and three natural monuments (aggregate area about 3,500,000 acres). They are administered by the National Parks Section, Division of Renewable Resources, Ministry of Agriculture and Animal Husbandry.

Superintendents, naturalists, and rangers in American national parks and their contemporaries elsewhere in the world find great uniformity in mutual problems, though they may deal with different plant and animal species; varying intensities of public use; or dissimilar degrees of social, economic and political pressures. For this reason each profits from the experience of others, a factor largely responsible for the establishment of the IUCN.

Summary

National parks and related reserves exist today in over 100 nations throughout the world. Various reasons have motivated international interest in the reservation of such lands, ranging from concern for the preservation of significant interests to stimulation of economy through tourism and the development of an adequate world image of political maturity.

Although there were earlier reserves in various parts of the world, the establishment of Yellowstone National Park is generally credited as initiating the modern reserve concept. Yellowstone, the first area in the world specifically designated as a national park, prompted the establishment of similar reserves in other countries, beginning in the latter part of the nineteenth and early portion of the twentieth centuries. Such activity was favored by gradually expanding international interest which began to develop tangible form in the 1930s and culminated in 1948 with the organization of the International Union for the Conservation of Nature and Natural Resources (IUCN).

However, growth in this form of conservation has not been uniform; greater progress has been made in some countries than in others. Even the nomenclature of various types of areas lacks standardization which adequately portrays their character and their relationship with one another. Often terms used imply a similarity of purpose that does not actually exist; for instance, national park is a generic term interpreted differently by some countries in the light of local conditions. In addition, national parks and related reserves throughout the world vary widely in type, size, objective, and the philosophy of their administration and management. Such differences, in addition to variations in primary interests of various continents, are the result of variations in population density, economics, the nature and stability of government, and the history and cultural background of people.

Some reserves have been established primarily as a means of protecting rare or endangered interests, or as field laboratories for scientific research; these are not readily accessible to the general public, and activities which adversely affect basic values are not tolerated. In other reserves public use is emphasized, or their management is coordinated with other public needs; in some of these there is little interference with private land ownership, though resource use is carefully controlled. The great majority of reserves are administered on concepts between these two extremes, with a general objective of permitting maximum, appropriate public use consistent with perpetuation of primary interests. In addition, the nature of the administrative authority ranges from government agencies to semipublic bodies which operate with considerable autonomy.

However, despite differences in the world's national parks and related reserves there is considerable uniformity in the problems of recreational use of wild lands in the United States and in other countries. Careful planning and well-defined management policy become increasingly important as populations rise and area visitation increases.

Selected References

1. American Committee for International Wildlife Protection: "National Parks—A World Need," (Victor H. Cahalane, ed.) Special Publication No. 14, New York, 1962.

2. Bannikov, A. G.: "Nature Reserves of the USSR," (Trans. from Russian by IPST Staff, D. Greenberg, ed.) Published for the U.S. Department of the Interior and National Science Foundation, Washington, D.C., by the Israel Program for Scientific Translations, Jerusalem, 1969.

3. Buitenzorg Scientific Centre: "Buitenzorg Scientific Centre," Archipel Drukkerjii en 't Boekhuis, Buitenzorg, Java, 1948.

4. Coolidge, Harold J.: The Birth of a Union: Fountainebleau, October, 1948, *National Parks Magazine*, vol. 23, no. 97, April-June, 1949.

5. Curry-Lindahl, Kai and Jean-Paul Harroy: "National Parks of the World," (2 vols.) Golden Press, New York, 1972.

6. Encyclopedia Americana, Americana Corporation, New York, 1957.

7. Encyclopaedia Brittanica, Encyclopaedia Brittanica, Inc., Chicago, 1947.

8. Great Britain, Parliament, House of Commons: "International Convention for the Protection of Fauna and Flora, with protocol, Treaty Series No. 27 (1936), London, November 8, 1933," His Majesty's Stationery Office, London, 1936.

9. Great Britain, Ministry of Town and Country Planning and Central Office of Information: "National Parks and Access to the Countryside," His Majesty's Stationery Office, London, n.d.

10. Gut, Stephen: "National Parks in Poland," State Council for Conservation of Nature, Warsaw, 1960.

11. Hays, G. D.: How Independence Saved an African Reserve, *Oryx*, vol. 8, no. 6, December, 1966.

12. IUCN: "International Commission on National Parks," Washington, n.d.

13. IUCN: International Commission on National Parks, "United Nations List of National Parks and Equivalent Reserves," Hayez, Brussels, 1971.

14. IUCN: Resolutions Adopted by the Tenth General Assembly of IUCN, *IUCN Bulletin*, vol. 2, no. 14, January-March, 1970.

15. Japan, National Parks Association: "Chronological History of the National Parks of Japan," Welfare Ministry, Tokyo, August, 1952.

16. Japan, National Parks Association: "The National Parks Portfolio of Japan," Tokyo, 1954.

17. Kalliola, Reino: Protection of Nature, Soumi: A General Handbook on the Geography of Finland, Fennia Series, vol. 72, no. 17, pp. 274-284, Geographic Society of Finland, Helsinki, 1952.

18. Menzi, W., and D. Feuerstein: "Kleiner Fahrer durch den Schweizerischen National-parks," 2d ed., Verkehrverein fur Graubunden, Chur, Switzerland, 1948.

19. Merriam, Lawrence C., Jr.: European Forest Recreation Policies and Possible United States Implications, *Journal of Forestry*, vol. 67, no. 12, December, 1969.

20. Morcombe, Michael: "Australia's National Parks," Landsdowne Press Pty Ltd., Melbourne, 1969.

21. Mosley, J. G.: "National Parks and Equivalent Reserves in Australia: Guide to Legislation, Administration, and Areas," Australian Conservation Foundation Special Publication No. 2, Australian Conservation Foundation, Canberra, Australia, 1968.

22. New Zealand, National Parks Authority: "National Parks of New Zealand," Government Printer, Wellington, 1965.

23. Pan American Union: "Nature Protection and Wildlife Preservation in the Western Hemisphere," Convention between the United States of America and Other American Republics, Washington, 1940, Treaty Series No. 981, U.S. Government Printing Office, Washington, 1943.

24. Pop, Emil, and N. Salageanu: "Nature Reserves in Romania," Meridiane Publishing House, Bucharest, 1965.

25. South Africa, National Parks Board of Trustees: "60 Years Kruger Park," (Comp. by R. J. Labusschagne), Pretoria, S.A., 1958.

26. Sutton, Ann, and Myron Sutton: "Yellowstone: A Century of the Wilderness Idea," Macmillan, New York, 1972.

27. Sweden, Forest Service: "Swedish National Parks," National Board of Crown Forests and Lands, Stockholm, n.d.

28. U.S. Department of the Interior, National Park Service: "First World Conference on National Parks, Seattle, Washington, June 30-July 7, 1962" *Proceedings*, (Alexander B. Adams, ed.), U.S. Government Printing Office, Washington, 1964.

29. Van Der Merwe, Nico J.: "The Position of Nature Conservation in South Africa," South African National Parks Board, Pretoria, S.A., 1962.

30. Williams, John G.: "National Parks of East Africa," Collins, London, 1967.

31. World Almanac Division: "The 1970 World Almanac and Book of Facts," (Luman H. Long, ed.) Newspaper Enterprise Association, Inc., New York, 1969.

INDEX